SAINTS

AND THEIR MIRACLES

IN LATE ANTIQUE GAUL

SAINTS

AND THEIR MIRACLES

IN LATE ANTIQUE GAUL

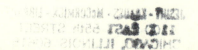 *Raymond Van Dam*

PRINCETON UNIVERSITY PRESS

PRINCETON, NEW JERSEY

Library of Congress Cataloging-in-Publication Data

Van Dam, Raymond
Saints and their miracles in late antique Gaul / Raymond Van Dam.
p.   cm.
Includes English translations of selections from Fortunatus and Gregory of Tours.
Includes bibliographical references and index.
ISBN 0-691-03233-5 (alk. paper) — ISBN 0-691-02112-0 (pbk.)
1. Christian saints—Cult—France—History.   2. Christian pilgrims and pilgrimages—
France—Tours—History.   I. Fortunatus, Venantius Honorius Clementianus, Bishop of
Poitiers, ca. 530-ca. 609. Selections. English. 1993.   II. Gregory, Saint, Bishop of Tours,
538-594. Selections. English. 1993.   III. Title.
BX4659.F8V36   1993
235′.2′094409021—dc20   92-40285 CIP

This book has been composed in Sabon Typeface

Princeton University Press books are printed on acid-free paper and meet the guidelines for
permanence and durability of the Committee on Production Guidelines for Book Longevity
of the Council on Library Resources

Printed in the United States of America

10 9 8 7 6 5 4 3 2 1

10 9 8 7 6 5 4 3 2 1
(Pbk.)

For My Father and Mother

CONTENTS

MARTIN OF TOURS required a historian to mold and publicize his subsequent prominence; Gregory of Tours needed a patron saint to bolster his ecclesiastical career and inspire his writings. In the solitude of their studies modern historians can perhaps imagine their relationship with their subject matter in a similar interactive fashion: they shape it, and it animates them. But the process of scholarly research and writing has become so complex and demanding that it moreover requires proper resources and reassuring criticism. At the University of Michigan the Rackham School of Graduate Studies awarded me a Faculty Fellowship for summer support, and the College of Literature, Science, and the Arts subsidized some of the production expenses with a grant from the Faculty Assistance Fund. Joanna Hitchcock, Lauren Osborne, and Lauren Lepow have been wonderful editors at the Press; Sabrina Meyers drew the map. I am also grateful to Mel, Andy, and John Heath for an invitation to speak about illness and healing, and to Jody Maxmin. As Gregory discovered upon becoming a writer, to interpret the lives of others demands contemplation of one's own life, and to record the assistance of patron saints is also to recall the love of friends and parents.

ACW	*Ancient Christian Writers* (Westminster).
Budé	Collection des Universités de France publiée sous le patronage de l'Association Guillaume Budé (Paris).
CChr.lat.	*Corpus Christianorum*, series latina (Turnhout).
ChLA	*Chartae Latinae Antiquiores: Facsimile Edition of the Latin Charters Prior to the Ninth Century*, ed. A. Bruckner and R. Marichal. Vol. 13, *France I*, ed. H. Atsma and J. Vezin (Zurich, 1981).
CSEL	*Corpus Scriptorum Ecclesiasticorum Latinorum* (Vienna).
FC	*Fathers of the Church* (Washington, D.C.).
LCL	Loeb Classical Library (Cambridge, Mass., and London).
MGH	*Monumenta Germaniae Historica* (Berlin, Hannover, and Leipzig).
AA	Auctores antiquissimi
Epp.	Epistolae
SRM	Scriptores rerum Merovingicarum
NPNF	A Select Library of Nicene and Post-Nicene Fathers of the Christian Church, 2d series (reprinted Grand Rapids).
PL	*Patrologia latina* (Paris); and Supplementa, ed. A. Hamman (Paris, 1958–1974).
PLRE	*The Prosopography of the Later Roman Empire*. Vol. 1, ed. A.H.M. Jones, J. R. Martindale, and J. Morris (Cambridge, 1971). Vol. 2, ed. J. R. Martindale (Cambridge, 1980).
RICG	*Recueil des inscriptions chrétiennes de la Gaule antérieures à la Renaissance carolingienne* (Paris).
SChr.	*Sources chrétiennes* (Paris).
TTH	Translated Texts for Historians (Liverpool).

De cursu, GC, GM, Hist., MA, VJ, VM, VP: references to the writings of Gregory of Tours omit his name; for details, see the list of editions and translations.

SAINTS

AND THEIR MIRACLES

IN LATE ANTIQUE GAUL

INTRODUCTION

THE FIFTH CENTURY marked an important period of transition for late antique Gaul. During the later fourth century the Roman frontier along the Rhine and upper Danube rivers had still protected Gaul successfully enough that even rumors of barbarian incursions never disturbed Bishop Martin of Tours until he visited the imperial court at Trier.[1] But during the fifth century Franks and other barbarians repeatedly sacked Trier, and at the beginning of the sixth century King Clovis of the Franks visited the church of St. Martin at Tours in order to assume some of the trappings of an emperor. Several consequential trends had obviously overlapped. One was the gradual demise of Roman administration as imperial magistrates and troops retreated to southeastern Gaul. A second involved the migrations of various barbarian groups. Although many peoples settled or passed through Gaul, eventually the Visigoths became dominant in southwestern and central Gaul, the Burgundians in eastern Gaul, and the Franks in northern Gaul. Once an imperial court and its magistrates vanished even in Italy during the 470s, at the level of administration a barbarian Gaul had replaced a Roman Gaul. A third important trend included the widening spread and growing influence of Christianity and the development of its theology, ethics, and liturgy into a comprehensive worldview for aristocrats and ordinary people in Gaul, as well as for the new barbarians in their midst. The three defining characteristics of subsequent medieval society would thus be its memories and occasional revivals of the Roman Empire, the impact of the barbarians, and the ascendancy of Christianity.[2]

The Christianity that developed stressed certain distinctive features, however. Bishops considerably enhanced their influence, in part because cities, their sees, now assumed vital administrative functions, in part too because local aristocrats began to view clerical offices as a means of maintaining or enhancing their traditional local standing. Another characteristic feature was the increasing prominence of relics and saints' cults.

---

[1] Sulpicius Severus, *Vita Martini* 18.1–2.

[2] Recent good surveys of the early Franks include James (1982) and (1988), and Geary (1988). Older but still perceptive surveys include Dill (1926), Dalton (1927), and Wallace-Hadrill (1962). Griffe (1964–1966) discusses Christianity in Gaul through the fifth century; Wallace-Hadrill (1983) covers the Frankish period.

Sulpicius Severus set the tone for much subsequent hagiography by composing a *Vita* of Martin of Tours already before the bishop's death in 397; during the fifth century various bishops of Tours contributed both to the saint's cult and to the enhancement of their own see by constructing many churches and shrines; and as the Merovingian dynasty of the Franks consolidated its control over Gaul, its kings granted privileges to the church of St. Martin at Tours. The development of the cult of St. Martin at Tours thus provides a general paradigm of the development of saints' cults throughout late antique Gaul: more hagiography, more churches and shrines, and a wider impact.

The study of late Roman and early medieval saints' cults has expanded considerably during the past two decades, and the leading impresario of this revived interest has been Professor Peter Brown, whose articles on holy men and book *The Cult of the Saints* have been deservedly and widely influential. A brief summary can only hint at the many important insights in his book about saints' cults in the Latin Christian world. After criticizing the common tendency to attribute the emergence of beliefs in the efficacy of relics to the influence of the vulgar superstitions of ordinary people, Brown emphasized instead the decisive role of elites in propagating these beliefs.[3] But because both great aristocrats and ecclesiastical leaders, such as bishops in particular, promoted these cults, their rival patronage generated an inherent structural tension between private and communal interests, between the elevation of particular individuals or their families and the development of a community cult in which ordinary believers could readily participate. Brown then discussed two important aspects of saints' cults. One was the psychological connection between beliefs in saints and personal identities, as a result of which "the patron saint still has the ancient quality almost of an unconscious layer of the self."[4] Intimacy with a patron saint hence became one powerfully effective means of coping with conversion and its consequent reorientation of social identity, or with deep anxieties about sin and guilt. The second was the connection between cults and communities, as a result of which the beliefs surrounding saints and relics could mitigate divisions by promoting an ideal concord and could reaffirm the exercise of beneficial authority by retelling the saints' victories over unjust powers. The ceremony of exorcism provided Brown with an extended example of a public ritual that involved confessions, judgments, and reintegration.

---

[3] Brown (1981) 121, "a slow but sure pressure from on top." For a similar emphasis on the role of ecclesiastical elites, see L. Pietri (1983) 485, and Wallace-Hadrill (1983) 78. This interpretation is nevertheless as misleadingly one-sided as the emphasis on the influence of "popular" superstitions; for criticism, see Fontaine (1982) 24, 37–40, Murray (1983) 201, Van Dam (1988) 16–18, Graus (1989) 101, and Rousselle (1990) 218–24.

[4] Brown (1981) 56.

In his book Brown concentrated primarily on the late fourth and early
fifth centuries and used the writings of such important contemporaries as
Augustine of Hippo, who died in 430, and Paulinus of Nola, who died in
431.[5] Augustine had, somewhat incongruously, ended his *City of God*, his
massive examination of God's providence in history, with an account of the
miracles of St. Stephen; Paulinus had composed a series of poems in honor
of St. Felix and his shrine at Nola. But the best-documented cult in the late
antique West is that of St. Martin at Tours, in part because of the writings of
Sulpicius Severus, but primarily because in the later sixth century Bishop
Gregory of Tours collected hundreds of miracle stories about the saint and
his cult. Gregory also collected many miracle stories about the cult of St.
Julian, centered at Brioude in the Auvergne, and his friend Fortunatus
collected more stories about the cult of St. Hilary at Poitiers. Despite the
intrinsic importance of their anthologies there are no complete translations
into English; and one of the goals of this book is to make these miracle
stories finally available in accurate translations. This volume in addition
includes translations of some related texts: an anonymous account of the
martyrdom of St. Julian, an anonymous sermon about St. Martin, and the
inscriptions about St. Martin from various buildings at Marmoutier and
Tours.

A second goal of this book is to provide some orientation to the usefulness and implications of Gregory's and Fortunatus's miracle stories; in the
process, it also supplements and modifies some of Brown's (and others')
interpretations.[6]
—Not only did Brown anachronistically use material from the writings of
Gregory of Tours in his discussion of earlier centuries,[7] but he also failed to
differentiate sharply the distinctive development and the diverse functions
of different cults. Chapter 1 of this book investigates the unpredictable
ways in which cults could develop in late antique Gaul. Although the cult of
St. Martin did not expand at Tours until decades after his death, eventually
it became so dominant that even Frankish kings avoided visiting the city. At

---

[5] The subtitle of Brown's book on the cult of the saints is *Its rise and function in Latin
Christianity*. Since most of his discussion emphasized "function," some reviewers have criticized his inadequate explanation of "its rise": see, e.g., Van Uytfanghe (1989), a fine survey of
the difficulties early Christians had in finding biblical and theological justification for the
veneration of saints.

[6] Two earlier discussions of Merovingian hagiography deserve special recognition, Marignan (1899), for a thorough and systematic collation of the literary texts, and Graus (1965), for
a finely differentiated analysis of the literary characteristics of hagiographical legends.

[7] Also peculiar was his use of evidence from the Greek East, not least because of his own
contrast between Western and Eastern attitudes toward saints and holiness: see Brown (1982)
166–95. Boesch Gajano, in her review of Brown's book in Desideri et al. (1984) 961, emphasizes the importance of respecting geographical diversity and chronological change; Head
(1990) stresses the usefulness of regional studies of saints' cults.

Poitiers, however, the residence of a former Frankish queen posed a potentially crippling threat to the cult of St. Hilary. The cult of St. Julian meanwhile remained largely a rural cult associated with a particular aristocratic family in the Auvergne.

—Brown also stressed the psychological benefits of personal identification with a patron saint. Because Gregory of Tours provides one fine example of such a relationship, chapter 2 is an attempt to re-create the impact of saintly patronage on his life. But in the process of advancing himself and his ecclesiastical career Gregory not only relied upon his various patron saints, he also promoted their cults. Both bishop and saints benefited from this relationship.

—In his discussion of saints and communities Brown likewise stressed the psychological and emotional implications of beliefs in saints' cults;[8] in his view, the ceremony of exorcism was a "psychodrama" of authority and reintegration.[9] Chapter 3, in contrast, stresses the social, political, and theological implications of the rituals of illness and healing. Because illnesses usually presupposed the violation of shared norms and healings often involved readmission into the community, Gregory's stories about miraculous healings were fundamentally meditations on the dynamics of early medieval towns. Because therapeutic techniques, whether pagan, heretical, or orthodox Christian, consistently created relationships of dependence, saints and their representative bishops challenged the authority of kings and their counts, who were unable to perform miracles of healing. And because the process of illness and healing presupposed particular ideas about people's own bodies as well as about the social body, it was also linked to theological doctrines about death, resurrection, and final judgment.

—At the end of his book Brown discussed the "socialization" of the countryside in terms of a contrast between saints' cults that commemorated holy people and pagan shrines that had venerated natural phenomena. People often journeyed to these new Christian shrines, and chapter 4 discusses pilgrims and their vows. But although the cult of St. Martin at Tours certainly attracted many pilgrims during the later sixth century, the geographical origins of these pilgrims and the restricted diffusion of shrines to St. Martin also indicate the limits on his cult's impact in late antique Gaul.

A third goal of this book is the conservative application of comparative

---

[8] Brown (1981) 85, "the extraordinary emotional feat." Note, though, that Brown (1978) 10–11 had argued against interpretations of religious change that relied on emotional and subjective qualities.

[9] Brown (1981) 82, "the public reading of the [martyr's] *passio* was . . . a *psychodrame*"; 111, "Possession and exorcism was . . . a *psychodrame*"; 118, "*psychodrame* of dependence and authority." But note that Brown (1982) 188 had suggested that there were no *psychodrames* at the tomb of St. Martin.

studies in interpreting these miracle stories. Because its scholars come from
so many different backgrounds, the study of late antiquity still gropes for
an autonomous identity. Medievalists have long been in the vanguard of
those committed to comparative studies; ancient historians and classicists
have become less resistant; but patristics scholars have no strong tradition
of interdisciplinary studies. Yet saints' cults, relics, and miracles are the
sorts of subjects that demand the use of the most up-to-date methodologies, and scholars who continue to be suspicious of what they call
"trendy non-religious explanations"[10] only resemble the thirteenth-
century monk who in an attempt to promote his own sainthood "threw
stones with all his might at anyone who jokingly talked to him of marriage."[11] Because so many of its issues are problems common to historical
analysis in general, the interpretation of hagiography and saints' cults
cannot be a self-contained field.[12] The study of miracle stories in particular, and of late antiquity in general, will only benefit from marriages with
other disciplines and other methodologies.

The writings of Gregory of Tours are certainly the most extensive literary
sources for our understanding of early Merovingian Gaul; but it is also
apparent that his experiences and his perspectives were not necessarily
representative even of other bishops. The canons of the contemporary
Gallic councils did not display the same fixation on saints' cults, and other
bishops privileged other strategies for defining themselves and their
roles.[13] The goals of this book about late Roman and early Merovingian
Gaul are therefore deliberately modest: an emphasis on new interpretive
perspectives, such as the differences between particular cults, the sociology
of small communities, the cognitive aspects of beliefs in saints' cults, and
the implications of pilgrimage; the deployment of comparative material
from other periods and other disciplines; and translations of neglected
texts. Yet there is no doubt too that saints' cults were influential not only in
defining early Christian spirituality, but also in shaping culture and politics
throughout the early medieval world. So although focused on sixth-
century Gaul, perhaps this book will also be a stimulus for the writing of
the up-to-date and comprehensive survey of the meanings and functions of
saints' cults that would be so helpful for our understanding of both the
Latin West and the Byzantine East during the early medieval period.[14]

---

[10] H. Chadwick (1981) 12.

[11] Munitiz (1981) 166.

[12] Emphasized by Lotter (1979) 300.

[13] Cf. Beck (1950) 309, on Caesarius of Arles: "Nowhere . . . does he refer at all to the
relics of saints."

[14] The widespread veneration of relics might even allow us to interpret medieval Christen-
dom as an example of "a world-system . . . in which political and economic forces were
largely subordinated to a symbolic order": see Woolf (1990) 54.

PART I

CHAPTER ONE

Different Saints, Different Cults

D IVERSITY has long been a distinguishing feature of France. Perhaps the most consequential example has been the distinction between north and south France that still marks a contrast between modern French dialects. This particular distinction was already important in Roman and early medieval Gaul too. By being incorporated comparatively early into the Roman empire southeastern Gaul was closely linked to Italy, and its cities and local aristocrats quickly absorbed the lifestyle and classical culture characteristic of the Mediterranean world. Northern and central Gaul, in contrast, were among the last components of the empire and always retained their connections with and orientation toward Britain and Germany. Classical culture and its corresponding lifestyle were slow to spread; so in northern regions in which beer remained a common beverage, wine from the Mediterranean became the equivalent of the "firewater" that would later assist Europeans in their conquest of the New World, an addictive commodity that allowed the civilized conquerors from the south to exploit the natives in Gaul and Germany.[1] Within these larger divisions more localized diversity was also readily apparent, because each region, each city, even each village often retained its own patois, dress, and customs.

Christianity in Gaul spread at first primarily into cities near the Mediterranean or along the Rhone River and long retained its contacts with the Greek East. Eventually Christianity extended its influence into central and northern Gaul, but only from the later fourth century, precisely the period during which the Roman administration was beginning to retreat to the south. Despite its claim to represent a singular orthodoxy Christianity was no more successful at overcoming local diversity than Roman magistrates had been at imposing an effective centralized administration. The bishops who met at Gallic councils may have scolded peculiar local customs, but they were unable to impose uniform practices and beliefs even on fellow bishops who preferred to preserve their own autonomy. Tours offers a telling example of the persistence of these local variations, in part because

---

[1] See Tchernia (1983) and (1986) 74–94, for the impact of Italian wine on pre-Roman Gaul, and Van Dam (1992), for the contrast between northern and southern Gaul.

the Loire River is often taken as an approximate boundary between northern and southern Gaul,[2] in part too because as a metropolitan see its ecclesiastical province included cities in Brittany, a region that had always been marginal to Roman Gaul. In the early sixth century Bishop Licinius of Tours and two of his suffragan bishops warned priests in Brittany against the use of women as "fellow hosts" during the celebration of mass. Although these bishops attributed this challenge to "ecclesiastical unity" to the influence of a Greek heresy, in fact the ministry of these women perhaps indicated the survival of an ancient Celtic practice.[3] Local diversity remained common in Gallic Christianity at the end of the century. Councils may have occasionally tried to promote liturgical uniformity, if only within ecclesiastical provinces, but Gregory of Tours offhandedly acknowledged that various cities celebrated the liturgy differently.[4]

The rise of saints' cults coincided with the general expansion of Christianity in late Roman Gaul. Because the local affiliations of these cults became so dominant, it is predictable that their development would reflect the particularism generally characteristic of Gallic society. The distinctiveness of three saints' cults in central Gaul is particularly well documented. Julian was thought to have been a martyr during one of the last general persecutions of Christianity; Hilary served as bishop of Poitiers until his death in 367; and Martin served as bishop of Tours until his death in 397. Tours eventually became the center of the cult of St. Martin. Not only did his cult become the most illustrious in late antique Gaul, it is also the best documented for modern historians, primarily because in the later sixth century Bishop Gregory of Tours compiled a large anthology of miracle stories about the saint. Gregory and his friend Fortunatus also compiled collections of miracle stories about the cults of St. Julian at Brioude and St. Hilary at Poitiers respectively. Although these two cults were not as popular as the cult of St. Martin, their particular characteristics emphasize firmly that the cult of St. Martin was not necessarily representative of saints' cults in late antique Gaul. The following sections of this chapter will discuss how the cult of St. Martin eventually overcame the slowness of its development at Tours to become so dominant that Merovingian kings hesitated to visit; how the presence of a former Merovingian queen overshadowed the cult of St. Hilary at Poitiers; and how the rural cult of St. Julian had little impact at Clermont, the episcopal seat of the diocese. A candid acknowledgment of these distinguishing characteristics allows

[2] Braudel (1989) 209: "For the two complementary halves of France, the south and the north, come together at the Loire."

[3] Letter in *PL* Suppl. 3.1256–57. N. Chadwick (1965) 274 suggests Celtic influence; for the relationship between Tours and Brittany, see L. Pietri (1983) 188–92, and below, chapter 4, section 1.

[4] *VM* 3.38.

modern historians to avoid two weaknesses common to many studies of late antique saints' cults. One is conflation of the evidence, the tendency to use information about different saints' cults indiscriminately to create a virtually generic "cult of the saints"; the other is chronological compression, the failure to recognize that particular cults went through phases of prominence and obscurity. Even though Gregory may have insisted that "a single Lord works through the powers of many saints,"[5] cults differed and cults changed over time. The diversity and particularism characteristic of Gallic society therefore combined with historical circumstances to generate three quite different cults of St. Martin, St. Hilary, and St. Julian.

1. The Cult of St. Martin

The cult of St. Martin first appeared within his lifetime. During his travels people pulled threads from his clothes and gathered the straw on which he had slept as relics that later protected them from illnesses; one man placed a letter of Martin on his feverish daughter, who then recovered; and even non-Christians knew about his reputation.[6] People also began to collect stories about Martin's life and miracles. After hearing some of these stories a young Gallic aristocrat named Sulpicius Severus decided to compose a *Vita* of Martin.[7] When he visited Tours, Martin's magnetism and insight so impressed him that he completed his *Vita* before the bishop's death; in fact, in a dream he once saw Martin smiling as he held a copy of the book.[8] By the time of its hero's death Sulpicius's *Vita* had already transformed Bishop Martin into St. Martin, someone "worthy of imitation" whose example would "stimulate readers to true wisdom."[9]

Immediately after Martin's death in 397 the saint's body became an object of rivalry between the two cities that had a special claim to his patronage, Poitiers and Tours. According to a tradition that Gregory later recorded, upon hearing that Martin had become ill at Candes both cities had sent delegations to hover in anticipation at his deathbed. The citizens of Poitiers noted that Martin had once lived as a monk at Ligugé in the Poitou and claimed that they should have his body because Tours had enjoyed his blessing during his episcopacy. The citizens of Tours argued that because Martin had revived two dead men before becoming bishop but only one afterward, they should keep his body so that he could com-

---

[5] *VM* 4.12; cf. *VP* praef.

[6] Sulpicius Severus, *Vita Martini* 18.4–5, 19.1, *Dial.* 2.4.4, 8.8–9.

[7] Sulpicius Severus, *Vita Martini* 25.1, 6.

[8] The news of Martin's death woke Sulpicius from this dream: see Sulpicius Severus, *Ep.* 2.3. Sulpicius had already sent a copy of the *Vita* to Paulinus of Nola, who praised it in a letter written in 397: see Paulinus of Nola, *Ep.* 11.11.

[9] Sulpicius Severus, *Vita Martini* 1.6.

plete what was unfinished during his lifetime. That night the citizens from Tours spirited the saint's body away through a window of his cell. At Tours an enormous funeral procession accompanied the body to its tomb.[10]

Since this tradition explained how his episcopal see rather than his first Gallic monastery had acquired his body, it seems to suggest that after his death the image of St. Martin as bishop took precedence over the image of the saint as monk. In fact, however, the image of the saint as a model bishop did not become dominant, even at Tours, until a generation later. Bishops had been among Martin's earliest critics, and already at his consecration some had objected that his unkempt appearance made him unworthy of the episcopacy of Tours.[11] After his death bishops and clerics in Gaul still refused to honor St. Martin for fear that his merits would highlight their own inadequacies.[12] Instead communities of ascetic aristocrats or of monks were responsible for the earliest development of the saint's cult, although here too each community supported different ideals.

While continuing to collect additional stories about St. Martin and to publish them in his *Dialogues*, Sulpicius also founded a secluded fellowship on his family's estate in southern Gaul, for which he built two new churches. Between the churches he constructed a baptistery, in which he featured a portrait of St. Martin. This icon was now to represent "the paradigm of the perfect life" for the newly baptized, whose faith the saint protected with his "deeds and courageous words."[13] But although Sulpicius may certainly have admired Martin and wanted to perpetuate his memory for this community, in the process he modified the saint's image in accordance with his own aristocratic outlook. Although Martin had come to Gaul as a soldier from Pannonia and was not a local aristocrat, Sulpicius's conception of the saint as "the rule of righteousness and the compendium of virtues" corresponded closely with the values of the aristocratic life-style in which he himself had been trained.[14] His ascetic community too mimicked the life of rural retirement that Gallic aristocrats had enjoyed for centuries. Furthermore, at his settlement Sulpicius also commemorated the tomb of Clarus, a priest who had established his own small monastic community near Martin's monastery at Marmoutier and who had died shortly before Martin's death.[15] Although Sulpicius and his friend Paulinus of Nola virtually equated the two in their admiration of

[10] *Hist.* 1.48, Sulpicius Severus, *Ep.* 3.18–21, with Carrias (1972).

[11] Sulpicius Severus, *Vita Martini* 9.3.

[12] Sulpicius Severus, *Dial.* 1.26.4–6.

[13] Paulinus of Nola, *Ep.* 32.3, in verses Paulinus composed to accompany the portrait.

[14] Paulinus of Nola, *Ep.* 32.4. See Fontaine (1972) 580–87, and (1979), on aristocratic asceticism; Van Dam (1985) 119–40, on the assimilation of the "outsider" Martin into Gallic society; and von der Nahmer (1987), on Sulpicius's reluctance to present Martin as a monk.

[15] Sulpicius Severus, *Vita Martini* 23, *Ep.* 2.5, with Fontaine (1967–1969) 3:989–1014.

"the example of St. Martin and St. Clarus,"[16] it is not obvious how Clarus had earned this comparable respect, since it had been Martin who had powerfully influenced Sulpicius's decision to reject secular honors and who had once healed Paulinus.[17] But for Sulpicius and Paulinus perhaps Clarus's most attractive feature was that, like them (and in contrast to Martin), he had been a "most distinguished young man" before committing himself to an ascetic life.[18] The traditional values of the Gallic aristocracy certainly died hard. In the early fifth century Sulpicius dedicated one of his new churches with Clarus's tomb, and Paulinus composed verses to describe Clarus's achievements; so both gave more homage to the tomb of this aristocratic disciple of Martin than to the tomb of St. Martin at Tours.[19]

Another version of St. Martin appeared at Marmoutier, the monastery Martin had founded outside Tours across the Loire River. During his lifetime some monks had doubted his claims to have had visions of Christian saints and pagan gods.[20] But after his death the monks had a series of verse inscriptions engraved near the saint's cell. These four inscriptions conveyed a strong sense of longing for a lost leader who may now have become their patron before God in heaven, but who would never again appear in person: "The warrior sleeps, a man who must be missed."[21] So although Marmoutier remained a functioning monastery, it seems to have lost much of its wider influence after Martin's death. In a passage written before Martin's death Sulpicius had claimed that all cities wanted monks from Martin's monastery as their bishops.[22] In fact, few did become bishops, and Marmoutier became increasingly important simply as a shrine to St. Martin. All four inscriptions leave the impression of being placards describing

[16] Paulinus of Nola, *Ep.* 23.3; cf. 27.3. See Rousselle (1990) 187–208, for the influence of Sulpicius and Paulinus on the development of relic cults.

[17] Sulpicius Severus, *Vita Martini* 19.3–5. Paulinus had once met Martin at Vienne: see Paulinus of Nola, *Ep.* 18.9.

[18] Sulpicius Severus, *Vita Martini* 23.1, "adulescens nobilissimus."

[19] Paulinus of Nola, *Ep.* 32.6. In *Ep.* 17.4 Paulinus mentioned Sulpicius's frequent trips to Tours; Fabre (1948) 24–27, dates this letter to late summer 398 or 399. But since Paulinus linked the trips with visits to Martin, Sulpicius probably discontinued them soon after Martin's death in 397: see Fontaine (1967–1969) 1:36–37, 48. Later authors ignored St. Clarus. Paulinus of Périgueux, *De vita S. Martini* 3.260–362, and Fortunatus, *Vita S. Martini* 2.222–77, only elaborated what they had read in Sulpicius's *Vita*; Gregory of Tours never mentioned him.

[20] Sulpicius Severus, *Dial.* 2.13.7.

[21] Le Blant (1856–1865) 1, no. 166, with L. Pietri (1983) 816–17, for discussion and dating of the inscriptions, and below, Appendix 3, for translations; Gilardi (1983) 11 suggests instead that Bishop Perpetuus commissioned these inscriptions at Marmoutier. Stancliffe (1983) 160–73 investigates the possibility of a "Marmoutier tradition" about Martin.

[22] Sulpicius Severus, *Vita Martini* 10.8–9. But with the exception of Brictio it is difficult to identify any monks from Marmoutier who became bishops: see L. Pietri (1983) 67n.206.

various sites and objects for visitors, such as the saint's cell, his stool, his
bed, and the spot where he had prayed. Other monks hence made pilgrimages to Marmoutier to visit these sites and remember the monastic life
of Martin.[23] In addition, by the middle of the fifth century the liturgical
celebrations at Tours included a trip to Marmoutier during Lent, during
which crowds of people visited these "stations" commemorating the
saint's monastic career: "the people licked and kissed and moistened with
their tears each spot where the blessed man had sat or prayed or where he
had eaten food or laid his body to rest after his many tasks."[24] At the end of
the fifth century Bishop Volusianus of Tours expanded the settlement at
Marmoutier by constructing a church dedicated to St. John.[25] So although
Martin may have founded this monastery in order to escape the bustle of
Tours by re-creating the "solitude of the desert,"[26] eventually Marmoutier
lost some of its isolation by becoming primarily a memorial shrine that
attracted the congregation of Tours, pilgrims, and perhaps mere tourists
too.

At Tours itself the incipient cult of St. Martin had meanwhile fallen into
apparent disfavor. His successor in 397 was Brictio, who had lived at
Marmoutier before becoming a cleric. Brictio had once confronted his
bishop and claimed that he himself was "more holy" because decades
earlier Martin had defiled himself with his service in the Roman army, and
because Martin had anyway now become senile. At the time Martin had
tolerated these invectives by concluding that demons were influencing Brictio.[27] According to a tradition that Gregory recorded, Martin had furthermore not only foreseen Brictio's accession to the episcopacy, he had also
warned him to anticipate many misfortunes. Both predictions were accurate. Lazarus, who later became bishop of Aix but may have been a monk
at Tours at the time, eventually made some unspecified "diabolical accusations" against Brictio, although other Gallic bishops, as well as Pope
Zosimus of Rome, then defended him.[28] But by 430 the citizens of Tours
were no longer willing to tolerate their bishop's arrogance and accused him
of adultery. Brictio first attempted to demonstrate his innocence before the
tomb of St. Martin and then traveled to Rome to appeal for the assistance
of Pope Xystus. In his absence two other men served as bishops of Tours,
until Brictio finally regained his see in 437.[29]

[23] VM 2.39.
[24] VM 1.3.
[25] Hist. 10.31.
[26] Sulpicius Severus, Vita Martini 10.4.
[27] Sulpicius Severus, Dial. 3.15.
[28] Zosimus, Ep. 3.3 (PL 20.656–57) = Collectio Avellana 46.4–7, ed. O. Guenther, CSEL
35.1 (1895) 103–5, and Ep. 4.2 (PL 20.662–63) = Epistolae Arelatenses 2, both dated to
417; with Mathisen (1989) 20–21, on the possible wider ecclesiastical feuds.
[29] Hist. 2.1.

The accession of Brictio seems to indicate the ascendancy at Tours of a faction that had been opposed to Bishop Martin, and his subsequent disgrace perhaps suggests a revival of support for the cult of St. Martin. The monks at Marmoutier and ascetics elsewhere may have been venerating the memory of St. Martin for decades already, but at Tours the cult of St. Martin finally developed comparatively late, and then primarily as a device to resolve lingering feuds over the meaning of Bishop Martin's career. In 430 Brictio had appealed for the saint's assistance at his tomb, and after his return from Rome he constructed over the saint's tomb a "small church" that he apparently dedicated to St. Peter and St. Paul, the illustrious apostles of Rome whose bishops had supported him during his conflicts.[30] So not until almost the middle of the fifth century did the cult of St. Martin finally acquire two consequential associations at Tours, one with the citizens that allowed the cult to serve as a unifying rather than a divisive force in the city, and the other with the bishops, who now usually staked their reputations on the cult's prominence. Thereafter people began to visit the saint's tomb to be healed; and Brictio and most subsequent bishops of Tours were now also buried in the church over the saint's tomb.[31]

The influence of St. Martin subsequently became more widespread, both at Tours and throughout Gaul. Brictio's successor was Eustochius, who constructed a church dedicated to St. Gervasius and St. Protasius inside the walls of Tours. By the middle of the fifth century Tours was on the edge of the settlement of the Visigoths in Aquitaine, who were Arian Christians. Eustochius may well have decided to honor these two Italian martyrs because of their connection with Bishop Ambrose of Milan, a contemporary of St. Martin whose discovery of these martyrs' relics had been part of his campaign against Arianism. Yet according to the tradition that Gregory recorded generations later, St. Martin had himself acquired these relics.[32] Because this tradition therefore interpreted Eustochius's new church as an indication of his homage for some saints whom St. Martin had once honored, people could instead consider St. Martin himself as a champion of Catholic Christianity against the Visigoths and their Arianism. In 458 the Visigoths besieged the Roman general Aegidius in Arles, who was rescued after appealing for St. Martin's assistance. And when Gregory later argued with Arian Visigoths from Spain, he classified St. Martin with heroes from

[30] When Bishop Perpetuus later built a new church over the tomb, he decided that the ceiling of the old church was too elegant to be discarded; so he reused it in a new church dedicated to St. Peter and St. Paul (*Hist.* 2.15, 10.31, *VM* 4.35). Perhaps he also transferred the original dedication of the old church over the tomb of St. Martin: see Ewig (1976–1979) 2:343, and Vieillard-Troiekouroff (1976) 324–25.

[31] *Hist.* 10.31, *VM* 1.2.

[32] *Hist.* 10.31, *GM* 46, with Courcelle (1964) 286–91, who argues that Martin had acquired these relics during a visit to Vienne.

the Old Testament as witnesses to the correctness of Catholic Christian-ity.[33] In comparison with some of his contemporaries, such as his mentor Bishop Hilary of Poitiers, Bishop Martin had been remarkably aloof from current arguments over Arianism; but by the middle of the fifth century his cult nevertheless came to represent Gallic opposition to Visigothic Arianism.

At about the same time the saint's cult was expanded again at Tours, this time by Perpetuus, who became bishop in 458 or 459. His promotion of the cult had several components. One was the construction of a new church over the saint's tomb. Once Perpetuus decided that the original small church was "unworthy of the miracles" that St. Martin performed at his tomb, he constructed a larger church. Both locals and others helped; the citizens of Tours transported the columns, and the bishop of Autun sent marble for the cover over the saint's tomb. Perpetuus also commissioned a series of murals for the walls of the church and a set of accompanying inscriptions that were engraved on the walls and that described and inter-preted some of the murals.[34] At least two of the more illustrious poets of later fifth-century Gaul contributed. Paulinus of Périgueux composed a poem for the nave of the church, and Sidonius, later bishop of Clermont, one for the apse. Upon the completion of the church Perpetuus convened neighboring bishops, abbots, and clerics to the festival of St. Martin on July 4 that commemorated the saint's consecration as bishop; and as a result of Perpetuus's revitalization of the cult, thereafter this festival also celebrated both the dedication of this new church and the transfer of the saint's sarcophagus to its apse.[35]

Transfer to this new church effectively consolidated a new image for St. Martin. During the dedication of Perpetuus's church, people became dis-couraged because of their difficulty in lifting the saint's sarcophagus. Ac-cording to a tradition that Gregory later recorded, finally an angel ap-peared in the guise of an old abbot and helped them move the sarcophagus to the new church. Previously ascetics and monastic communities had promoted the saint as a monk. Now, even though St. Martin would remain an important patron for monastic establishments, this angelic abbot had helped effectively to bury the image of St. Martin the monk in favor of a revised image of St. Martin the bishop. So during the sixth century one man

[33] VM 1.2, Aegidius; Hist. 5.43, Spain.

[34] Hist. 2.14–15, VM 1.2. For discussion and translation of these inscriptions, see below, Appendix 3.

[35] VM 1.6. Although L. Pietri (1983) 374, and Gilardi (1983) 17, suggest that Perpetuus dedicated his new church in 471 on the centennial of Martin's consecration as bishop, the dating of this construction project is uncertain: see Van Dam (1986) 571. Perpetuus also apparently honored St. Gervasius and St. Protasius, the two Italian saints whose relics Martin was thought to have acquired: see Le Blant (1856–1865) 1, no. 182.

visualized the saint "clothed in a bishop's robe"; and when St. Martin appeared to another man in a vision, he introduced himself as "Martin, bishop of Tours."[36] Because of the reforms of Perpetuus, the bishops of Tours and not the monks of Marmoutier now became the major guardians of the cult of St. Martin the bishop.

Perpetuus also revamped the schedule of the liturgical festivals at Tours by drawing up precise timetables of fasts and vigils for the entire year.[37] St. Martin was one of the few saints in Gaul to have two annual festivals, on July 4 and November 11 (the latter marking his death), and his festivals were certainly prominent in these timetables. So was his new church. Perpetuus's schedule of vigils mentioned both universal Christian festivals and the festivals of local Gallic saints. The cathedral within the walls of Tours was the setting for the vigils of some of the universal festivals such as Christmas, Epiphany, and Easter; other churches or shrines dedicated to other saints provided the settings for the vigils before their festivals; but the church of St. Martin was the setting not only for the vigils before his two festivals but also for the vigils before some of the universal festivals, such as Ascension Day and Pentecost, and before the festivals of other Gallic saints and other bishops of Tours. With Perpetuus' revision the new church of St. Martin in the suburbs had effectively replaced the cathedral as the focal point of most of the liturgical calendar at Tours.

A final component of Perpetuus's promotion of the cult of St. Martin involved written accounts. Just as Sulpicius Severus had once come from outside Tours to compose a *Vita* of Martin, so Paulinus of Périgueux had already begun independently to versify Sulpicius's *Vita*, perhaps because St. Martin had relieved his eye ailment. Paulinus's initiative therefore hints at the existence of veneration for the saint's shrine even among laymen outside Tours. Perpetuus was impressed enough by Paulinus's poem that he sent him Sulpicius's *Dialogues* and invited him to versify it too. Paulinus sent his completed versification back to the bishop, along with a cover letter in which he complimented Perpetuus extravagantly while bemoaning his own literary inabilities equally extravagantly. Perpetuus had meanwhile been compiling a collection of stories about the saint's posthumous miracles, and eventually he invited Paulinus to versify that anthology as the final book of his long ballad about St. Martin.[38]

Perpetuus's promotion of the saint's cult was a self-conscious revision and updating of the past. His new church replaced a smaller church; the murals and inscriptions memorialized various deeds of Bishop Martin; in the process of rewriting Sulpicius's books Paulinus of Périgueux had also

[36] *VM* 1.6, 2.40, 3.23.
[37] *Hist.* 10.31.
[38] For detailed discussion see Van Dam (1986).

made them more relevant to his times; and Perpetuus had effectively written a sequel to Sulpicius's books by collecting the saint's posthumous miracles. Because buildings, murals, and books were all means of communicating messages about the saint's power that were comprehensible to both literates and illiterates, Perpetuus had effectively "popularized" the cult, not in the sense of aiming it simply at ordinary people, but rather in the sense of making it more accessible both to educated elites throughout Gaul who might read Paulinus's verses, and to ordinary people who could visit the church, view its murals, participate in the festivals, and listen to readings about the saint. Subsequent revitalization of the cult, and presumably of other saints' cults elsewhere too, followed the same pattern. A century later when Gregory again promoted St. Martin's cult at Tours, he too reconstructed churches, repaired the murals in the church of St. Martin and added more in the cathedral, reiterated the importance of the writings of Sulpicius and Paulinus of Périgueux, and collected more posthumous miracles as a sequel to Perpetuus's collection. The past shaped the present, and the present repeated the past; the apparent timelessness of the miracle stories that Sulpicius, Perpetuus, and eventually Gregory recorded is itself a telling indication of the continuing vitality of the saint and his cult over these two centuries.

Perpetuus's activities transformed Tours into "the city of Martin."[39] Yet although Perpetuus was obviously a pivotal figure in the development of St. Martin's cult, it is important to put his actions into a wider context. Perpetuus was not the only bishop who now promoted a local saint's cult. During the second half of the fifth century the construction of churches and the expansion or initiation of saints' cults were common throughout Gaul.[40] The cult of St. Martin was therefore one among many, and the mere availability of more evidence should not necessarily imply that it was already in the later fifth century the most prominent cult in late Roman Gaul. Other unforeseen historical circumstances influenced its further development.

Under the Roman Empire Tours had been distant from any hostile activity on the frontier along the Rhine. Although during the mid-third century that frontier had nearly collapsed, by the end of the century the activities of a series of usurping "Gallic emperors" and then of the Roman emperors had again restored control, and during the fourth century an emperor and his court were usually resident in northern Gaul at Trier. But in the early fifth century even the pretense of an effective frontier had disappeared as many barbarian tribes migrated into Gaul. Among them had been the Visigoths, who in 418 settled in Aquitaine. Initially the Visigoths assisted

---

[39] Paulinus of Périgueux, *De vita S. Martini* 5.295, "Martini . . . in urbe."
[40] Van Dam (1985) 167–72.

Roman troops as allied federates, but by the middle of the century as Roman administration became increasingly a memory they began to expand their own kingdom into eastern and central Gaul. Occasionally emperors or their commanders sent assistance to various Gallic cities.[41] But without an effective Roman administration in northern and central Gaul to provide the semblance of a central authority, local Gallic aristocrats and Roman generals joined barbarian chieftains in asserting their own influence. In north-central Gaul, for instance, the Roman general Aegidius established a renegade principality centered at Soissons, and some of the Franks who had been settled in northern Gaul since the early fourth century even accepted him as their own "king"; his son Syagrius succeeded him with the wonderfully hybrid title of "king of the Romans."[42] In contrast to its isolated location in Roman Gaul, Tours was now caught in the middle between Visigothic, Frankish, and Roman kingdoms.

The bishops of Tours therefore had to make political choices about which of these competing kingdoms to support. Unlike other Gallic aristocrats and bishops, they tended to look north to Soissons rather than south to the Visigothic capital of Toulouse, and the traditions that Gregory later recorded claimed that the Visigoths had deposed some of Perpetuus's successors for disloyalty. These bishops of Tours probably preferred to oppose the Visigoths in part because of their uneasiness about the Visigoths's Arianism, in part too because St. Martin had already once before assisted Aegidius.[43] But when Syagrius, Aegidius's son, faced defeat by the Frankish king Clovis, he fled to the Visigoths at Toulouse.[44] Syagrius hence abandoned more than his kingdom at Soissons, because by fleeing south he had also disavowed his family's association with the cult of St. Martin and its opposition to Arianism. So by assuming control over Soissons, Clovis also in a sense inherited this connection with the cult of St. Martin and its promotion of Catholic Christianity against the Arian Visigoths.

Clovis's campaigns marked the further expansion of the Franks from their earlier settlements in northern Gaul, as well as the consolidation of his own rule over other Frankish groups. But he and his dynastic successors were always somewhat uneasy about the effectiveness of their royal authority, because not only were they attempting to control their Frankish supporters, they also had to cope with great Gallo-Roman aristocrats who retained much local influence. Gallic aristocrats had already survived the

[41] Note Sidonius, *Carm.* 5.210–11, for Majorian's defense of Tours, with Wightman (1985) 303.

[42] *Hist.* 2.12, 27.

[43] *Hist.* 2.26, 10.31. The exile of these bishops of Tours was apparently an exception to the generally harmonious relationship between Arian kings and Catholic subjects: see Wood (1985) 257–58. For Gauls supporting Visigothic kings, see Heather (1992) 89–93.

[44] *Hist.* 2.27.

imposition of a Roman administration centuries earlier. Some had acquired the distinguished ranks and high offices that were indications of imperial patronage; a few had even attempted to become emperors themselves; most had retained control over or ownership of the land, always the surest source of influence and wealth in the ancient world, and had been content to function as brokers between imperial administrators and the native population. With the dissolution of the imperial administration during the fifth century their descendants had cultivated new means for maintaining their local reputations and influence. One was promotion into the ecclesiastical hierarchy; another related method was association with saints' cults. At Tours Bishops Eustochius, Perpetuus, and Volusianus had all been members of a wealthy Gallic family that claimed senatorial rank, and their activities in constructing new churches and patronizing the cult of St. Martin certainly also promoted their own and their family's reputations.[45] Other families came to dominate other sees and other cults. So by the time the Franks began to expand beyond northern Gaul during the later fifth century, many of these saints' cults were already linked closely with particular cities, their bishops, and some of the leading families.

In order to facilitate his acceptance among Romans, Clovis had to demonstrate his support for these established saints' cults. Although he also fought in eastern Gaul with or against the Burgundians and the Alamans, eventually he prepared a campaign against the Visigoths in 507. According to Gregory's later account, in preparation for this battle Clovis ordered his troops not to pillage the territory of Tours, sent gifts to the church of St. Martin at Tours, and received the assistance of St. Hilary at Poitiers. After his victory he returned to the church of St. Martin at Tours in 508, assumed some of the trappings of a Roman emperor, and distributed largess to the citizens.[46]

It is most important, however, not to overestimate Clovis's support for the church of St. Martin. In a final attempt to mediate between the Franks and the Visigoths, King Theoderic of the Ostrogoths did not mention any religious disputes;[47] and although Gregory had stressed Clovis's respect for St. Martin, in fact the king did not mention the saint in his instructions to his army before the battle with the Visigoths.[48] During the sixth century the cult of St. Martin certainly did not become any sort of "royal cult" for

---

[45] *Hist.* 10.31.

[46] *Hist.* 2.37–38; Fortunatus, *Vita Hilarii* 20–23. Clovis may also have already once visited the church of St. Martin: see *Epistolae Austrasicae* 8, in which in the mid-sixth century Bishop Nicetius of Trier cited Clovis's behavior as a paradigm for a Lombard king: "he went humbly to the threshold of lord Martin and promised that he would be baptized immediately."

[47] Cassiodorus, *Variae* 3.1, 4, with Wood (1985).

[48] As subsequently reported to the bishops of Gaul: see *Epistola ad episcopos*, a.507/511, ed. A. Boretius, *MGH*, Leges 2 = Capitularia regum Francorum 1 (1883) 1–2.

the Frankish kings; Clovis, for instance, soon went to Paris and never returned to Tours. His departure from Tours neatly symbolized the uneasiness that these new kings felt in trying to accommodate themselves and their royal authority to a dominant cult. Although he and his Merovingian successors realized that they had to come to terms with the cult of St. Martin, just as they had to accommodate influential bishops, great Roman aristocrats, and their own Frankish supporters, acknowledging dependence upon St. Martin was not an easy concession to make. According to a later, probably apocryphal, story, after Clovis had had to pay twice what he intended in order to retrieve his horse from the church of St. Martin, he admitted that the saint drove a hard bargain for his assistance.[49] Subsequent kings usually respected the power of St. Martin, in particular by granting immunity from taxation to the citizens of Tours. They also released a captive who called on the assistance of St. Martin, threatened to execute men who robbed the saint's church, and sealed their treaties by citing the saint as one of the "judges and avengers" who guaranteed compliance.[50] But most would probably have tacitly agreed that the price of deference for St. Martin's support was too high. During the sixth century only Chlothar ever again visited Tours during his reign to pray at the tomb of St. Martin, in part perhaps because he was still upset over his wife Radegund's departure, in part too because he needed forgiveness for having been responsible for the death of his son Chramn.[51] Renegade sons of the royal family might come to Tours to seek sanctuary at the church of St. Martin, and dowager queens such as Clotild, Clovis's widow, might serve at the saint's church and even influence the selection of bishops at Tours,[52] but the ruling kings (and queens) kept their distance, never even bringing their ill sons to the saint's tomb.[53] Even when a king wanted to consult with St. Martin, he did not go in person. King Chilperic instead sent a letter that was placed on the saint's tomb, along with a blank sheet of paper for the saint's response; but St. Martin did not reply.[54] Only King Childebert may have built a church dedicated to St. Martin, but then in such an

---

[49] *Liber historiae Francorum* 17, "vere beatus Martinus bonus est in auxilio et carus in negotio."

[50] *Hist.* 4.2, 9.30, immunity; *Hist.* 6.10, 7.6, *VM* 1.23.

[51] Gregory mentioned two visits, one sometime before 559 (*Hist.* 6.9), the other in the year before the king's death in December 561 (*Hist.* 4.20–21). Baudonivia, *Vita Radegundis* 6–7, probably also referred to this latter visit in noting that Chlothar, while on his way to Poitiers to see Radegund, took his son Sigibert and went to Tours "as if to pray" at the church of St. Martin.

[52] *Hist.* 2.43, 3.28, 10.31. Later traditions also credited Clotild with having founded a monastery dedicated to St. Peter in the suburbs of Tours: see *Vita Chrothildis* 11.

[53] Even desperation was not enough incentive to visit Tours. In 590 when the queen regent Fredegund faced the loss of her influence because her sole surviving son, Chlothar II, was gravely ill, she only promised much wealth to the church of St. Martin (*Hist.* 10.11).

[54] *Hist.* 5.14.

obscure spot in northern Gaul that modern scholars cannot identify it with certainty.[55] During the sixth century the cult of St. Martin was not closely associated with the Merovingian kings.[56]

Instead, Clovis and his royal successors preferred to promote new cults for new saints. His father Childeric had once granted the requests of Genovefa (Geneviève), an ascetic at Paris; after her death in ca. 502, Clovis and his queen Clotild constructed a church near her tomb.[57] By the time Clovis was buried in this church in 511, it was dedicated to the Holy Apostles, perhaps in imitation of the church that the emperor Constantine had similarly dedicated in his new capital city of Constantinople and in which he had been buried; and by the time Clotild, a daughter, and two grandsons were buried in this church, it had also been dedicated to St. Peter, a patron saint of Rome. So in the process of adopting the new cult of a recent Gallic saint, Clovis had furthermore expanded his pretensions by linking himself and his dynasty with the greatest cities of the Roman Empire and their imperial associations.[58]

During the sixth century his successors promoted other new cults in Paris, Soissons, and Chalon-sur-Saône. These cities were three important early centers of Merovingian influence in north-central Gaul and Burgundy; they were also, significantly, not metropolitan sees. At Paris King Childebert constructed a church dedicated to St. Vincentius, a Spanish martyr whose relics he had apparently acquired after invading Spain in 541; by the end of the century he, his nephew king Chilperic, two of Chilperic's sons, and Chilperic's wife Queen Fredegund had been buried in this church.[59] Bishop Medard of Noyon once consecrated Radegund, formerly a wife of King Chlothar, as a deaconess;[60] after Medard's death, Chlothar and his son Sigibert constructed a church in his honor at Soissons, in which both were eventually buried.[61] King Chilperic, another son of Chlothar, also venerated St. Medard by composing a poem in his

[55] So Vieillard-Troiekouroff (1976) 122–23, based on *Hist.* 9.12. But the subject of *construxit* is ambiguous; perhaps Ursio, who owned the nearby villa (*Hist.* 9.9), had built the church.

[56] It is therefore misleading for Ewig (1976–1979) 2:376–84 to include the sixth century in his discussion of "Martin als merowingischer Reichspatron," and for Prinz (1965) 32–33 to describe St. Martin as the "merowingischer Reichsheiliger" immediately after Clovis's reign.

[57] *GC* 89, *Vita Genovefae* 26, 56, with Heinzelmann and Poulin (1986) 97–106.

[58] *Hist.* 2.43; 3.10, 18; 4.1, *GC* 89, with Krüger (1971) 40–54, on Sainte-Geneviève, 469–71, on imperial precedent. Traditions at Rome noted that Clovis once sent a diadem studded with precious jewels to St. Peter, but dated the gift to the papacy of Hormisdas from 514 to 523: see *Liber Pontificalis* 54.

[59] *Hist.* 3.29, 4.20, 6.46, 8.10, *Liber historiae Francorum* 37, with Krüger (1971) 103–24, and Vieillard-Troiekouroff (1976) 211–14, on Saint-Germain des Près.

[60] Fortunatus, *Vita Radegundis* 26–28.

[61] *Hist.* 4.19, 21, 51, *GC* 93; Fortunatus, *Carm.* 2.16.161–64, a request that St. Medard assist Sigibert for having helped construct the saint's church; and [Fortunatus,] *Vita Medardi*

honor, by granting some villas to the saint's church, and by hoping to find a cure for an ill son at the church.[62] At Chalon-sur-Saône King Guntramn promoted the cult of St. Marcellus, an obscure local martyr about whom even Gregory knew very little. The king built, or rebuilt, the saint's church, founded a monastery there, and richly endowed both. He celebrated the saint's festival in this church, and both an assassin and a refugee knew they might find him there. His wife Austrigild and their two sons were probably buried in this church of St. Marcellus, and upon his own death in 592 he was buried there too.[63] The cults of St. Genovefa, St. Vincentius, St. Medard, and St. Marcellus were therefore associated with Frankish kings from their inceptions, and the eventual spread of these saints' influence might be an indication of the acceptance of royal influence too. Leontius of Bordeaux, for instance, may have once pretentiously introduced himself to a king as the bishop of an "apostolic see," but he also had the sense to construct a church dedicated to St. Vincentius.[64] Bishop Germanus of Paris likewise had a reputation for occasionally confronting Frankish kings, and he maintained a close association with the cult of St. Symphorianus, in whose monastery at Autun he had once served as abbot; but upon his death in 576 he was nevertheless buried in the church of St. Vincentius at Paris.[65] Relics of St. Vincentius were also found in villages near Poitiers and Tours, and Bishop Eufronius, Gregory's predecessor, had constructed a church in his honor at Tours.[66] Eufronius was also probably responsible for placing relics of St. Medard in a church in another village in the Touraine, and Gregory himself owned the saint's staff and once visited his tomb at Soissons.[67]

The Merovingian dynasty thus gradually acquired its own patron saints, whom even bishops considered important enough to honor. The dynasty also eventually developed a closer relationship with the cult of St. Martin,

---

37, another appeal to remember Sigibert, who was now dead. This *Vita Medardi* was written before the death of King Theudebert II in 612, but probably not by Fortunatus. See Krüger (1971) 125–33, on Saint-Médard, and Gerberding (1987) 150–59, for the importance of Soissons to the Merovingians.

[62] *Hist.* 5.3, 34; *Ymnus in solemnitate S. Medardi*, ed. K. Strecker, *MGH*, Poetae 4.2 (1914) 455–57 = *PL* Suppl. 4.1464–65.

[63] *Hist.* 5.17, 35; 9.3, 27, GM 52, Fredegar, *Chron.* 4.1, 14; with Krüger (1971) 138–48, Vieillard-Troiekouroff (1976) 264–65, and Beaujard et al. (1986) 71–72, on Saint-Marcel. For the epitaphs of Austrigild and the two sons, see Le Blant (1856–1865) 1, no. 218–20, and R. Peiper (ed.), *MGH*, AA 6.2 (1883) 191–92.

[64] *Hist.* 4.26, Fortunatus, *Carm.* 1.8–9.

[65] *Hist.* 4.26, 51; 5.8, 8.33, GC 88; Fortunatus, *Vita Germani* 9; also 20, 26, 28, 34, 83–85, 93, 172, for other contacts with the cult; GC 79, for Germanus's visiting the church of St. Symphorianus at Bourges.

[66] *Hist.* 10.31, GM 89.

[67] VP 19.2, with Vieillard-Troiekouroff (1976) 119–20, and L. Pietri (1983) 496–97; GC 93, saint's staff.

although still often by avoiding direct contact with Tours. First, some
Merovingian queens and princesses took the lead by following Clotild's
example and demonstrating their own devotion for the cult. The Merovingian princess Bertha, for instance, even after marrying King Æthelberht
of Kent continued to worship in a church dedicated to St. Martin outside
Canterbury.[68] In 588 Fortunatus visited Metz and the court of King Childebert, who had three years earlier regained Tours for his kingdom. There
Fortunatus celebrated the summer festival of St. Martin by reciting a poem
in the presence of the king and his mother Brunhild in which he claimed
that "kingdoms" honored the saint as their patron.[69] Brunhild seems to
have noted the hint, because during her subsequent period of ascendancy
she promoted the saint's cult, in particular by joining with Bishop Syagrius
of Autun in the construction of a church dedicated to St. Martin in the city's
suburbs.[70] Second, although Merovingian kings still did not visit Tours,
some continued to honor the saint's cult. King Dagobert I donated royal
taxes to the church of St. Martin at Tours and also provided the funds to
have the saint's tomb decorated with gold and jewels.[71] In the middle of the
seventh century his son King Sigibert III perhaps rebuilt a church dedicated
to St. Martin in his capital city of Metz, in which he was then buried.[72] And
finally, the Merovingian kings eventually also acquired a special relic of St.
Martin. In his versification of the writings of Sulpicius, Fortunatus had
retold the story about Martin cutting his military cloak in half to share it
with a beggar at Amiens: "this soldier's white cloak is more valuable than
an emperor's purple cloak."[73] He had reiterated his praise for the saint's
cloak in his laudatory poem before Childebert and Brunhild.[74] As relics
from their visits to Tours most pilgrims had had to settle for dust from the
saint's tomb, slivers of wood from the railing, or wax from the candles in
the church; but by the later seventh century at the latest the Merovingian
dynasty had acquired the cloak of St. Martin.[75] This cloak was now probably the only major relic of St. Martin outside the Touraine, and its acquisi-

[68] Bede, *HE* 1.25–26, 2.5; Wallace-Hadrill (1988) 36–37, and Rollason (1989) 69, suggest that this was a fifth-century dedication. Bertha was a daughter of King Charibert (*Hist.*
4.26, 9.26).

[69] Fortunatus, *Carm.* 10.7.31.

[70] Gregory I, *Registrum* 13.5, 11. Brunhild was perhaps buried in this church: see Beaujard
et al. (1986) 44, and Krüger (1971) 161.

[71] *Vita Eligii* 1.32.

[72] The evidence is either late or unreliable: see Krüger (1971) 149–55, and Gauthier
(1986) 52.

[73] Fortunatus, *Vita S. Martini* 1.66, based on Sulpicius Severus, *Vita Martini* 3. Note that
an oratory at Amiens commemorated the miracle but apparently had no relics (*VM* 1.17).

[74] Fortunatus, *Carm.* 10.7.57.

[75] Pardessus (1843–1849) 2:185, no. 394 = Pertz (1872) 45, no. 49 = *ChLA* 13, no. 567,
a *placitum* from King Theuderic III in 679, with van den Bosch (1959) 25, and Ewig (1976–
1979) 2:379; Leclercq (1948) is still the best survey. For a discussion of the politics of the

tion is a telling indication of how, in order to feel comfortable in acquiring the saint's patronage, the Merovingian kings had had to abstract a part of him from his stronghold at Tours. Although kings had patronized the church of St. Martin at Tours and some dowager queens had even visited, the Merovingians seem to have preferred to support both his and other saints' cults elsewhere than at Tours.

The acquisition of St. Martin's cloak indicated in part an attempt by the Merovingians to maintain their authority in the face of challenges from great aristocrats, in part too an attempt to bolster specifically the prominence of the Neustrian subkingdom in northwest Gaul. Another indication of Neustria's prominence during most of the seventh century was the increasing importance of the cult of St. Dionysius (St. Denis), who was thought to have been the first bishop of Paris and a martyr during the third century. Genovefa had once promoted the construction of a church dedicated to St. Dionysius at Paris.[76] Although King Clovis had honored the cult of St. Genovefa, during the sixth century St. Dionysius did not immediately become a distinctively royal saint.[77] King Chilperic may have been an early patron. In 574 soldiers from the army of his brother King Sigibert tried to loot the saint's church at Paris; aristocrats allied with Chilperic swore oaths in the church; and in 580 one of his sons was buried there.[78] In the early seventh century his grandson King Dagobert I certainly began to patronize the church, and soon the saint's church and monastery became a principal site for Merovingian, and eventually some Carolingian, royal tombs.[79] So by promoting their own saints' cults at Paris, Soisson, and Chalon-sur-Saône the Merovingians had effectively created a buffer along the Seine and Saône rivers between their primary interests in northern and eastern Gaul and St. Martin's shrine at Tours.[80]

The cult of St. Martin had developed slowly during the first part of the fifth century, in part because Martin had been a distinctly unconventional

---

670s, see Gerberding (1987) 67–91. Eventually an oath "in our palace over the cloak of lord Martin" became a formulaic component of royal judgments: see Marculf, *Formulae* 1.38.

[76] *Vita Genovefae* 17–22, with Heinzelmann and Poulin (1986) 94–96.

[77] In fact, the bishops of Bordeaux, who were notorious for their independence from the kings, had constructed another early shrine to St. Dionysius: Fortunatus, *Carm.* 1.11.

[78] *Hist.* 5.32, 34, *GM* 71.

[79] See Krüger (1971) 171–89, and Vieillard-Troiekouroff (1976) 252–53, for the church; Wallace-Hadrill (1983) 126–33, 140–41, and Semmler (1989), for royal patronage for the abbey of Saint-Denis. Note in particular Fredegar, *Chron.* 4.79, for King Dagobert's burial in 639 in the church of St. Dionysius that he had already enriched. His son King Clovis II later committed sacrilege by cutting off St. Dionysius's arm: see *Liber historiae Francorum* 44.

[80] Note the correspondence between this frontier of shrines and other political and economic distinctions within the Merovingian realm; J. Werner (1961) 327–29, for instance, takes the Seine as the division between economic zones in early Merovingian Gaul with contrasting attitudes toward the use of coins.

bishop whose confrontational behavior and controversial claims had led to dissension even at his episcopal see of Tours. The "domestication" of Bishop Martin into St. Martin at Tours was hence perhaps a more difficult process than the spread of Christianity into the countryside of the Touraine. But once a more pragmatic mythology of St. Martin had modified the historical memories of Bishop Martin, both the bishops of Tours and their congregation could accept the saint's cult as a means for harmony rather than disintegration in their community. The prominence of the cult of St. Martin made Tours an important city in late antique Gaul. Various ascetics and other pilgrims began to visit.[81] Eventually King Clovis also visited; but after his departure most of the Merovingian kings kept their distance from Tours during the sixth and seventh centuries. The power and the influence of the saint's cult that other pilgrims found attractive was disconcerting to these kings, who had enough problems trying to establish their authority. They instead decided to promote other saints' cults, new cults for which their patronage was decisive at their inceptions. In fact, the pedigrees of some of the saints they now supported also made them more attractive to these kings, since Medard certainly and Genovefa perhaps too had had Frankish ancestors.[82] As the Franks settled into Roman Gaul, their kings preferred to patronize these semi-Frankish saints, or at least to promote the cults of recent saints. The success of the bishops of Tours in expanding the cult of St. Martin had therefore not only limited interference by the Frankish kings at Tours; it also kept most of them from visiting at all. So even though King Clovis, soon after his victory over the Visigoths, had once worn the cloak of a Roman general and paraded like a Roman emperor at Tours, not until more than a century and a half later did the Merovingian kings finally dare to acquire the cloak of St. Martin.

2. The Cult of St. Hilary

Although the cult of St. Hilary was less prominent than the cult of St. Martin, its early development was somewhat similar. Like Martin, Hilary was thought to have revived some dead people; unlike Martin, he had made his reputation as an opponent of Arianism already during his episcopacy at Poitiers.[83] At least by the later fifth century a church that contained his tomb had been constructed in the suburbs of Poitiers. People thereafter venerated his shrine as a place to obtain healings, and him as a champion of

---

[81] *Vita Genovefae* 45–47; *Vita Lupicini* 8.

[82] [Fortunatus,] *Vita Medardi* 4: Medard had a Frankish father and a Roman mother. On Genovefa's ancestry, see Heinzelmann and Poulin (1986) 81–86.

[83] *Hist.* 1.38–39. Fortunatus, *Vita Hilarii* 42–45, described his revival of a baby boy, supposedly after the mother challenged him to match the accomplishment of St. Martin.

Catholic Christianity, the "blessed defender of an indivisible Trinity."[84] Perhaps because Hilary had once been Martin's mentor, perhaps too because of the proximity of Tours and Poitiers, their cults in these "twin cities" were often linked.[85] Bishop Perpetuus included the festival of St. Hilary in his schedule of the vigils that were celebrated at Tours; Abbot Aredius of Limoges named both saints as his heirs; and kings cited both saints as the guarantors of a treaty.[86]

But as with the cult of St. Martin, the early Merovingian kings had little direct contact with the cult of St. Hilary. In 507 when Clovis was preparing his campaign against the Visigoths, he sent envoys to the church of St. Martin, and later a fiery beacon from the church of St. Hilary guided him to battle. In 580 when Gregory objected to Chilperic's idiosyncratic theological pronouncements by citing the teaching of St. Hilary, the king had the sense to realize that this saint would be a powerful opponent.[87] Merovingian kings also continued to influence the selection of bishops at Poitiers, as at Tours and other cities. But Gregory never mentioned a single instance of royal patronage or financial support for the church of St. Hilary at Poitiers or for the saint's cult anywhere else in Gaul.[88] Neither did Fortunatus, who also never mentioned St. Hilary in any of his verse panegyrics for the Merovingians. Even though kings acknowledged the influence of St. Martin and St. Hilary, they preferred to keep their distance from both.

In fact, although Bishop Germanus of Paris visited and some pilgrims came from Cahors and perhaps Bourges,[89] most who went to the saint's church were apparently locals. The most prominent supporters were the bishops of Poitiers. As successor to Bishop Pientius King Charibert promoted Pascentius, the abbot of the church of St. Hilary.[90] Pascentius soon commissioned both a *Vita* of St. Hilary and a collection of miracle stories. The Italian poet Fortunatus had arrived in Poitiers by 567, and although he knew little about St. Hilary, he soon learned, probably from the bishop himself, since in the dedication of his *Vita* Fortunatus described Pascentius

---

[84] *Hist.* 3 praef., GC 2.

[85] Fortunatus, *Carm.* 10.14.10, "geminas urbes."

[86] *Hist.* 7.6; 10.29, 31.

[87] *Hist.* 2.37, 5.44; Fortunatus, *VH* 20–21. In 577 the powerful aristocrat Guntramn Boso had left his daughters for safekeeping in the church of St. Hilary (*Hist.* 5.24).

[88] Although later traditions claimed that Clovis had "enriched the churches of St. Martin and St. Hilary with many gifts" after his victory over the Visigoths: see Fredegar, *Chron.* 3.24.

[89] Fortunatus, *VH* 6–14, *Vita Germani* 125.

[90] *Hist.* 4.18. The exact year of Pientius's death and Pascentius's elevation is uncertain. Neither shows up in the extant lists of subscribers at the sixth-century councils; King Charibert took control of Poitiers after the death of King Chlothar in 561, and himself died late in 567 (*Hist.* 4.26). On secular abbots see the note to *VM* 4.11.

as the saint's "special favorite."[91] The cult of St. Hilary at Poitiers again
resembled the cult of St. Martin at Tours. Bishops of Tours also developed
special relationships with the patron saint of their see, and the cult of St.
Martin, although more influential than the cult of St. Hilary, was still
predominantly a regional cult.

But in the middle of the sixth century both the cult of St. Hilary and the
bishops of Poitiers suddenly faced a novel challenge when Queen Radegund left her husband, King Chlothar, and decided to adopt an ascetic life.
After Bishop Medard of Noyon consecrated her as a deaconess, she endowed the shrines of various saints before visiting the church of St. Martin
at Tours and the shrine commemorating his death at Candes. Then she
went to a villa in the Poitou where, "like a new Martha," she began caring
for the ill and destitute.[92] Despite her connections with the royal court,
important bishops, and various saints' cults, Radegund's presence was not
necessarily a threat to the bishops of Poitiers. Other royal women, usually
upon being widowed, had retired to other cities and had patronized cults.
Radegund also decided to found a convent within Poitiers that King Chlothar then endowed.[93] Again, her convent and its royal patronage were not
necessarily threats. At Tours, for instance, she had already founded a
monastery;[94] and Ingytrud, who was probably an aunt of King Guntramn,
founded a convent in a courtyard of the church of St. Martin in which a
daughter of King Charibert temporarily resided.[95]

Bishop Pientius hence helped Radegund in the construction of her convent. Duke Austrapius also assisted, and King Chlothar then began groom-
ing him as Pientius's successor.[96] So even though Bishop Germanus of Paris
had served as the liaison between Radegund and King Chlothar,[97] initially
the bishop of Poitiers and his apparent successor intended to cooperate
with Radegund and her convent. But after Chlothar's death in 561 King
Charibert inherited control of Poitiers; and upon the death of Bishop Pientius, Charibert supported as his successor Pascentius, who had close ties
with the cult and church of St. Hilary. Pascentius and his successor Maroveus were not closely involved in the subsequent expansion of Radegund's
convent. Several bishops eventually wrote to commend Radegund upon

---

[91] Fortunatus, *Vita Hilarii* 2, "quasi peculiarem vernulam."

[92] Fortunatus, *Vita Radegundis* 42.

[93] *Hist.* 3.7, 9.42.

[94] Baudonivia, *Vita Radegundis* 16.

[95] *Hist.* 9.33. Ingytrud was the mother of Bishop Bertramn of Bordeaux, who was related to
Guntramn through the king's mother Ingund (*Hist.* 4.3, 8.2); so Ingytrud and Ingund were
probably sisters: see Ewig (1974) 52–56

[96] *Hist.* 4.18; Baudonivia, *Vita Radegundis* 5, mentioning both Pientius and Austrapius.
L. Pietri (1983) 230n.237, dates the beginning of Radegund's residence in her convent to late
560 or early 561.

[97] Baudonivia, *Vita Radegundis* 7; also Fortunatus, *Vita Germani* 125, for Germanus's
visiting the church of St. Hilary at Poitiers.

the foundation of her convent, including the metropolitan bishop Eufronius of Tours, four of his suffragan bishops, the metropolitan bishop of Rouen, and Bishop Germanus of Paris.[98] Significantly, neither the bishop of Poitiers nor his metropolitan, the bishop of Bordeaux, signed this letter. In this letter the bishops noted that Radegund was following the example of St. Martin; but they did not mention St. Hilary at all. They also noted that the women joining Radegund's convent were coming from their episcopal dioceses;[99] but they did not mention the Poitou as a recruitment area. Agnes became the first abbess of this convent, and although Radegund claimed that the bishop of Poitiers had consented to her selection, Bishop Germanus of Paris consecrated her.[100] Radegund and Agnes later exchanged greetings and gifts with Bishops Ragnemod of Paris, Avitus of Clermont, and Gregory of Tours, and with Abbot Aredius of Limoges.[101] When Radegund once invoked the patron saints of her convent, she mentioned St. Hilary with St. Martin but listed both after the True Cross and the Virgin Mary. And when in a vision she instructed a man to construct an oratory, she also told him to dedicate it with relics of St. Martin.[102] So although Gregory later insisted that she and her convent had always been subject to bishops,[103] Radegund's clear reliance upon bishops and saints from elsewhere in the foundation of her convent certainly posed a challenge to the authority of the bishops of Poitiers and the cult of St. Hilary.

Bishop Maroveus had reason to be apprehensive, all the more so because Radegund also started to collect relics. Once she sent an envoy directly to the patriarch of Jerusalem to fetch relics of an Eastern saint.[104] Soon after Maroveus assumed the episcopacy of Poitiers, Radegund wrote to King Sigibert, who then controlled Poitiers, and asked his permission to request a relic of the True Cross from the emperor Justin II in Constantinople.[105] In

---

[98] *Hist.* 9.39. The date of this letter is debatable. Meyer (1901) 93, 97–98, and Krusch (1920) 342, suggest that since the bishops who signed this letter all attended a council convened by King Charibert at Tours in November 567, they perhaps also wrote the letter then; L. Pietri (1983) 232n.247, 234n.253, dates it after the problems with Maroveus in 569 and argues that it was a response to Radegund's letter cited in *Hist.* 9.42.

[99] Cf. *GM* 5, Fortunatus, *Vita Germani* 101, for girls from Le Mans and Tours who joined Radegund's convent.

[100] *Hist.* 9.42.

[101] Fortunatus, *Carm.* 3.21.11–12, 22a.13–14 (Avitus); 5.19.11–12 (Aredius); 9.7.77–78 (Gregory); 9.10.9–14 (Ragnemod's gift of marble and jewels).

[102] *Hist.* 9.42, saints; Fortunatus, *Vita Radegundis* 87–90, oratory.

[103] *Hist.* 9.40.

[104] Baudonivia, *Vita Radegundis* 14, a finger of St. Mammes.

[105] Baudonivia, *Vita Radegundis* 16, also mentioning Queen Brunhild. Gregory explicitly noted that Radegund received Sigibert's reply after Maroveus became bishop (*Hist.* 9.40). For the sending of the envoys in 568 and their return in 569, see Cameron (1976). Although Sigibert had acquired control over Poitiers only in 567 after the death of Charibert, his brother Chilperic had tried to usurp control by force (*Hist.* 4.45); so Sigibert's support for Radegund was perhaps also an attempt to solidify his authority at Poitiers.

568 she sent envoys to the imperial court, who returned the next year with a Gospel Book decorated with gold and jewels, many relics of Eastern saints, and, of course, a piece of the wood of the True Cross, also decorated with gold and jewels. Fortunatus then composed a laudatory poem in honor of Justin and his wife Sophia for presentation at the Byzantine court. In this panegyric Fortunatus stressed no fewer than three times that Radegund had requested these relics; but he did not mention Bishop Maroveus.[106] Presumably Maroveus had not supported this overture to the imperial court, and upon the arrival of these relics at Poitiers he made his displeasure apparent. When Radegund asked him to celebrate the transfer of these relics to her convent, Maroveus "rejected her request, mounted his horse, and rode to his villa." Radegund then appealed to King Sigibert, and at his intervention Bishop Eufronius and his clergy came from Tours to transfer the relics to the convent: "the bishop of Poitiers was absent."[107] Once this prize relic of the True Cross was in place in the oratory, ill and possessed people were healed "through the power of the holy Cross" at this shrine.[108] The animosity between bishop and queen lingered, however, and after Maroveus turned down Radegund's repeated requests for his support, she adopted the monastic Rule for nuns once composed by Bishop Caesarius of Arles that insisted upon the autonomy of a convent from episcopal interference.[109] The nuns also put themselves under the protection of whichever king controlled Poitiers, because "they were unable to find any concern for their protection from the man who should have been their shepherd."[110]

In his account Gregory was careful to blame neither Radegund nor Maroveus. Radegund was obviously well connected throughout Gaul, and her support had assisted him in acquiring the episcopacy of Tours in 573; Maroveus was simply defending both his prerogatives as bishop and the influence of the patron saint of the city. But by describing Maroveus as "a deservedly praiseworthy disciple of the most blessed Hilary,"[111] Gregory

---

[106] Fortunatus, *Carm.* Appendix 2.57–58, 87–90, 96.

[107] *Hist.* 9.40. Baudonivia, *Vita Radegundis* 16, was more circumspect in noting that although the bishop and the people wished to accept these relics, some objected: "it is not appropriate for me to discuss this."

[108] Baudonivia, *Vita Radegundis* 16; cf. *Hist.* 6.29, *GM* 5.

[109] Gregory thought that Radegund and Agnes now actually traveled to Arles to acquire the Rule of Caesarius (*Hist.* 9.40). But in an earlier letter to local bishops Radegund stated that she had imposed the Rule apparently soon after the foundation of her convent and before the selection of Agnes as first abbess (*Hist.* 9.42); and Caesaria the Younger, the abbess at Arles since ca. 524, had already sent a copy of the Rule to Radegund: see *Epistolae aevi Merowingici collectae* 11, with Meyer (1901) 97–98, 101–2, and Gäbe (1989) 11n.63, 14n.90. For a fine discussion of the tension between episcopal control and the convent at Arles, see Klingshirn (1990).

[110] *Hist.* 9.40.

[111] *VM* 2.44.

acknowledged that the bishop's authority depended upon the saint's reputation. Even St. Hilary, however, could not compete with a relic of the True
Cross. St. Hilary was only one among the many "confessors," believers
who had missed the opportunity to become martyrs for the faith and so
had to compensate by "persecuting" themselves: "they mortified their
bodies so as to live for Christ alone."[112] Jesus Christ, in contrast, had not
only been, in a sense, the first martyr,[113] but his death and resurrection
were paradigmatic examples of the struggle and reward that all believers
were to anticipate. Gregory was obviously fascinated by the relics of Jesus
Christ's death and resurrection, among them the nails from his crucifixion,
his crown of thorns, his tunic, and the clay from his tomb;[114] he was also
remarkably hesitant in acknowledging their power. During one trip to
Poitiers Gregory first went to the tomb of St. Hilary and then visited
Radegund in her convent. During their conversation he criticized Agnes for
not replacing a lamp that was dripping oil. When Agnes replied that the
lamp was not cracked and that the power of the True Cross was making the
oil overflow, Gregory was surprised: "I was silent, and finally I proclaimed
the power of the venerable cross." At another time a man brought Gregory
a tattered silk robe that he claimed had once been wrapped around the
Lord's cross at Jerusalem. Gregory was hesitant, even after the man explained how he had acquired the robe. But he finally accepted the robe as a
genuine relic after it healed some ill people. So although Gregory eventually conceded the wondrous power of these relics, he also realized that they
required special handling and more stringent verification.[115]

   During his episcopacy Gregory was hence careful in acquiring and locating such relics. In an oratory in the cathedral residence he kept a robe in
which the True Cross had been wrapped and some white silk curtains
embroidered with crosses. But he preferred to emphasize the other saints
whose relics were also in the oratory, among them his two special patron
saints, St. Martin and St. Julian.[116] A relic of the True Cross was located in
an oratory in a courtyard of the church of St. Martin, although when he
mentioned this shrine, Gregory again preferred to emphasize the power of
St. Martin and St. John the Baptist, whose relics he had himself placed
there.[117] Gregory also honored relics of the Virgin Mary, another saint
whom Radegund promoted. He once visited an oratory dedicated with the

[112] *VP* 2 praef.
[113] *GM* 3.
[114] *GM* 5–7.
[115] *GM* 5.
[116] *GC* 20, Fortunatus, *Carm.* 2.3, with the interpretation of L. Pietri (1983) 500–501.
[117] *GM* 14. Vieillard-Troiekouroff (1976) 309, suggests that this oratory should perhaps
be identified with the baptistery in which Gregory mentioned that he had deposited relics of
St. John and St. Sergius (*Hist.* 10.31, *GM* 96). L. Pietri (1983) 402–3, prefers to associate this
oratory with the convent of Ingytrud and speculates that Radegund had donated the relic.

Virgin's relics on an estate in the Auvergne, and he eventually wore a
reliquary that contained relics of both the Virgin Mary and St. Martin.[118]
But by associating these potent relics with the relics of other saints and by
locating them in less prominent shrines and even in a personal reliquary,
Gregory was remarkably successful in minimizing the potentially disruptive impact of the cults of the True Cross and the Virgin Mary at Tours.

At Poitiers Maroveus had not been as successful; there a shrine with a
piece of the actual wood from the True Cross was now inside the city's walls
next to the cathedral in a convent he did not control, not out in the suburbs
with the church of St. Hilary. "Who can describe," wrote a nun in the
convent, "how impressive a gift the blessed Radegund bestowed upon this
city?"[119] Nor was this the end of Radegund's benefactions to the city. Just
outside the city's walls she had also constructed a church dedicated to the
Virgin Mary that was intended for her own tomb.[120] And she herself was
given credit for performing miracles when people invoked "the power of
mistress Radegund."[121] For all her humility and asceticism Radegund had
become an influential patron at Poitiers and more widely throughout Gaul;
like a bishop, even like a king, at her convent she presided from a throne.[122]
So in 580 when a disgraced count who had taken refuge in Poitiers began to
dishonor the church of St. Hilary with his scandalous behavior, Radegund
(and not Maroveus) ordered him to be ejected from the church.[123] She also
could intimidate kings, in part because none of them could match her
international contacts with both Constantinople and Jerusalem. She sent
letters to various kings and their magistrates requesting that they not make
war on each other; in 584 when king Chilperic wished to retrieve a daughter whom he had stashed at Radegund's convent in order to marry her to a
son of the Visigothic king in Spain, Radegund vetoed the scheme; and in
585 the pretender Gundovald requested her arbitration in his war with
King Guntramn.[124] At her funeral Gregory was so impressed that he com-

---

[118] GM 8, 10. Eventually the church of St. Martin at Tours owned this estate: see Vieillard-
Troiekouroff (1976) 158. Weidemann (1982) 1:206, 233, 2:109, suggests that the church
owned the estate already in the sixth century; Wood (1983) 40–41, raises the possibility that
Gregory's family owned the estate.

[119] Baudonivia, Vita Radegundis 16.

[120] Hist. 9.42.

[121] Baudonivia, Vita Radegundis 11–12, 15, 17, "per virtutem ipsius dominae Radegundis"; Fortunatus, Vita Radegundis 64–90.

[122] Hist. 3.7, for her reputation; Baudonivia, Vita Radegundis 12, "in cathedra beatae
reginae." Cf. Hist. 5.17, for the cathedra of King Guntramn.

[123] Hist. 5.49, mentioning only "the queen," who was presumably Radegund.

[124] Hist. 6.34, 7.36; Baudonivia, Vita Radegundis 10. Radegund was also one of the few to
befriend both Brunhild and Fredegund: see below, chapter 2, section 1, for Radegund and
Brunhild's supporting Gregory as bishop of Tours, and Fortunatus, Carm. 9.1.128, for the
connection between Radegund and Fredegund.

pared Radegund to "the blessed mother of the Lord."[125] In a culture in which the costliness and the magnificence of people's tombs were meant to be lasting indications of their previous status, Radegund's casket was twice normal size.[126]

For twenty years Maroveus had to tolerate the presence of this influential nun and a cult that overshadowed him and the cult of St. Hilary. Once a nun had escaped from the convent, taken refuge in the church of St. Hilary, and made some accusations against Radegund, before repenting and returning to the convent.[127] But such public misgivings were rare, and many at Poitiers supported Radegund. One man contributed one hundred gold coins to the construction of her church dedicated to the Virgin Mary.[128] The poet Fortunatus had once composed a *Vita* of St. Hilary and a collection of the saint's miracle stories for Bishop Pascentius, and he had continued to live in Poitiers thereafter. But although Fortunatus wrote poems in honor of many bishops throughout Gaul, in his extant works he never once mentioned Bishop Maroveus. Instead, he had become associated with Radegund and Agnes, for whom he wrote many poems and with whom he exchanged affectionate gifts. As a clear indication of his revised allegiances, after her death Fortunatus wrote a *Vita* of Radegund in which he mentioned, as some of the models for her asceticism and miracles, the stories in the Gospels and the deeds of St. Martin and St. Germanus, a bishop of Auxerre during the early fifth century; but he never mentioned St. Hilary.[129]

Radegund died in August 587, and Gregory immediately went to Poitiers for her funeral. There he found Agnes and about two hundred other nuns mourning their loss; but he did not find Bishop Maroveus, who had been detained while visiting his parishes.[130] Since Gregory was able to arrive in time from Tours, he has obviously here suggested a face-saving excuse for Maroveus, who apparently insisted on remaining churlish to the end in his dispute with Radegund. At the request of the leading men and the citizens of Poitiers, Gregory substituted in conducting much of the funeral service, although he was careful to leave Maroveus with the honor of celebrating the final mass and covering Radegund's tomb. With the death

---

[125] Baudonivia, *Vita Radegundis* 23.

[126] *GC* 104. See *GC* 41, for tombs and status, and Young (1986), for the oversize tombs associated with the burials of "chieftains."

[127] *Hist.* 9.40.

[128] The *vir inluster* Leo, who had already placed his daughters in Radegund's convent: see Baudonivia, *Vita Radegundis* 15.

[129] Fortunatus, *Vita Radegundis* 37, 40, 84. For the friendship between Fortunatus and Radegund, see Koebner (1915) 45–66. Gäbe (1989) distinguishes contrasting images of Radegund in the *Vitae* by Fortunatus and Baudonivia by analyzing their attitudes toward episcopal control, monasticism, and royalty.

[130] *Hist.* 9.2, death; *GC* 104, funeral.

of its "mother" the convent was in a much more precarious position. Agnes once more requested the support of Maroveus, and although he was at first inclined to refuse again, he eventually agreed to defend the nuns as their "father."[131] Radegund had once written to convince the neighboring bishops to protect the rights of her convent after her death, and in particular had warned against the bishop of Poitiers's acquiring any new concessions. But now, perhaps as a condition of offering his protection to the nuns, Maroveus solicited from King Childebert an edict that granted him control over this convent, "just as over his other parishes."[132] Upon the death of Radegund, Maroveus was finally able to assert his episcopal authority, and the convent now accepted his paternal authority in place of Radegund's independent maternal guidance.

His problems with this convent were not over, however. For despite the challenges the presence of this convent posed, Radegund and Abbess Agnes had at least been able to control its members; in fact, Radegund had once refused to allow a hooting owl to disturb her nocturnal tranquillity![133] But Agnes too soon died and was replaced by Leubovera; and early in 589 about forty nuns revolted against their new abbess. Their leaders were Chrodechild, daughter of King Charibert, and Basina, daughter of King Chilperic. Since Chrodechild complained that in the convent they had been treated like the offspring of servants and not like the daughters of kings, and since one of her schemes was to replace Leubovera with herself, perhaps she was upset that royalty had not been a factor in the selection of a new abbess. So she planned to appeal her case directly to the Merovingian kings. First, though, she and the other dissident nuns walked to Tours in late winter. Gregory tried to reason with them by suggesting that they return to the convent and that he consult with Bishop Maroveus; when Chrodechild and the other nuns rejected his "episcopal advice" and furthermore accused Maroveus of deceit and lingering resentment against the convent, Gregory explained that they were flirting with excommunication. In the summer Chrodechild alone went to King Guntramn, who agreed to appoint a tribunal of bishops to investigate their complaints with Abbess Leubovera. During her absence some of the other rebellious nuns married (and thereby provided perhaps a truer indication of their motivations). After Chrodechild and the remaining nuns returned to Poitiers, they took refuge in, of all places, the church of St. Hilary. There they began to hire a gang of armed men.[134]

Gundegisil, metropolitan bishop of Bordeaux, then arrived in Poitiers.

[131] *Hist.* 9.39: bishops noted that nuns had replaced their mothers with Radegund; 40, Maroveus as *pater earum*.

[132] *Hist.* 9.40, convent and parishes; 42, Radegund's letter.

[133] Baudonivia, *Vita Radegundis* 19.

[134] *Hist.* 9.39–40, 10.22.

Accompanied by three of his suffragan bishops, including Maroveus, he confronted the nuns at the church of St. Hilary and excommunicated them. They responded by unleashing their armed retainers, and Chrodechild began to seize the convent's properties. But by resorting to violence the nuns lost much sympathy. King Childebert ordered his count in Poitiers to smother the riot; Abbess Leubovera circulated to neighboring bishops (among them apparently Gregory) an earlier letter in which Radegund had pleaded that even after her death the kings and bishops were to preserve the convent's original prerogatives; Gundegisil repeated the ban of excommunication on the nuns; and he and his suffragan bishops wrote to the bishops who were meeting with King Guntramn. These other bishops replied by supporting Gundegisil's actions.[135] But their letter significantly did not include Maroveus in its salutation. For after hearing the nuns' accusations against himself, Maroveus had suggested that he restore communion with them and then appear for a hearing before his metropolitan Gundegisil and the other suffragan bishops. Gundegisil refused; and although King Childebert was so annoyed by all the partisanship that he tried to negotiate a compromise, he too failed.[136]

This revolt of 589 brought to the surface several basic tensions characteristic not just of the situation at Poitiers but also of early Merovingian society in general.[137] First, various kings had long fought over control of the city; like Tours, Poitiers had the misfortune of ending up consistently on the edges of various kingdoms. Although Sigibert had inherited the city after the death of Charibert, his brother Chilperic always had designs. After the assassination of Sigibert in 575, Chilperic had finally ousted Childebert, Sigibert's son; and after the assassination of Chilperic in 584, Guntramn had prevented the citizens of Poitiers from reasserting their loyalty to Childebert. In 585 Bishop Maroveus had led the opposition to Guntramn and was accused of treason before the king. Although later in 585 Guntramn had finally conceded Poitiers to Childebert, and in 587 the two kings concluded a treaty verifying the division of cities, Guntramn probably carried a lingering grudge against the bishop.[138] Because the leaders of these dissident nuns included two of his nieces, Guntramn again had an opportunity to meddle in the affairs of Poitiers.

Second, a metropolitan and some of his suffragan bishops also at-

[135] *Hist.* 9.41–42. These bishops also postponed further action until they could all meet at a council King Guntramn intended to convene on November 1; but this council was eventually canceled (*Hist.* 9.32, 41).

[136] *Hist.* 9.43.

[137] Scheibelreiter (1979) is an excellent discussion of other underlying tensions, among them the relationships between kings and bishops, kings and their kin, and bishops and lay patrons of monasteries, as well as of the symbiosis of Christian values with an aristocratic lifestyle.

[138] *Hist.* 5.24; 7.12–13, 24, 33; 9.20.

tempted to interfere in the affairs of another suffragan bishop. The bishops of Bordeaux were notoriously high-handed, even to the point of asserting their autonomy from kings; so in 585 Bishop Bertramn had supported the pretender Gundovald against King Guntramn. But like other metropolitan bishops, the bishops of Bordeaux were not always successful in influencing their suffragan sees, especially when control over the cities in their ecclesiastical province was divided among different kings. Gundegisil had become bishop of Bordeaux in 585 with the support of Guntramn, who had ignored Bertramn's own choice, and his intervention now not only again advanced the king's wish to meddle at Poitiers but also presumably indicated his own intention to deflate the standing of a suffragan bishop.[139]

Finally, as if antagonistic kings and zealous bishops were not enough, Maroveus himself was now caught in the middle at Poitiers. After the death of Radegund he had agreed to support the convent and then presumably also Leubovera, its new abbess whose selection he perhaps engineered. Yet the dissident nuns, even though they criticized him, were also implicitly critical of Radegund and her behavior (as became particularly apparent in the next year), and they had taken refuge in the church of St. Hilary. The irony in the situation verged on black comedy, because Maroveus was now the patron of a convent he had never appreciated, while some of its nuns were appealing for the protection of a saint whom the foundation of the convent and the promotion of its own relics had previously overshadowed. And if trying to negotiate his way at Poitiers had not been difficult enough, Maroveus had also been involved in arbitrating a dispute over an inheritance between other nuns with royal connections. At Tours Ingytrud had been trying for years to persuade her daughter Berthegund to join her convent. After the death of her brother, Bishop Bertramn of Bordeaux, in 585, Berthegund moved to Poitiers, despite her mother's objections. They also started arguing over the family inheritance, and both appealed to King Childebert, who finally asked Bishops Maroveus and Gregory to arbitrate. In 589 they were almost successful, until Ingytrud again appealed to Childebert.[140]

Maroveus, and Kings Guntramn and Childebert too, were probably at their wits' end trying to deal with disaffected nuns who had royal connections. The next year brought no relief. Even Ingytrud's death in March 590 did not end the feud with her daughter, because Berthegund again appealed to King Childebert, who awarded her all her family's property. So after stripping bare the walls of her mother's convent, she returned to

---

[139] *Hist.* 7.31, 8.22. Note though that the tribunal of bishops in 590 insisted that Gundegisil and his suffragan bishops had gone to Poitiers "at the kings' command" *(Hist.* 10.16).
[140] *Hist.* 9.33.

Poitiers.[141] During the same year the dissident nuns at Poitiers caused more trouble. A week before Easter Chrodechild sent her armed retainers to invade the convent. After Abbess Leubovera hid in the oratory that contained the relic of the True Cross, these men instead seized Justina, the convent's prioress who was also Gregory of Tours's niece. Upon realizing their mistake they released her, seized Leubovera, and took her to Basina's headquarters in the church of St. Hilary. Although Maroveus threatened Chrodechild and Basina, and although Leubovera was eventually rescued, the looting and the violence were out of control. King Childebert suggested that he and King Guntramn appoint a tribunal of bishops, and he ordered the count of Poitiers to end the riot; so the count and his men simply slaughtered Chrodechild's retainers. Chrodechild herself took refuge in the oratory of the convent and, in another ironic twist, tried to protect herself by holding up the relic of the True Cross.[142]

The tribunal consisted of Bishop Gundegisil, his suffragan bishops including Maroveus, the bishop of Cologne, and Gregory of Tours. The bishops first heard the accusations of Chrodechild and Basina against Abbess Leubovera and then Leubovera's rebuttals. After they dismissed the accusations against Leubovera as "trivial," they turned to the "more significant crimes" of the rebellious nuns. In this examination they were most concerned, predictably, with the authority of bishops and kings; in their opinion, these nuns had failed to respect the advice of Maroveus, had attacked Gundegisil and his suffragan bishops, had rejected the kings' attempt at mediation, and had forcibly resisted the count. So the tribunal restored Abbess Leubovera, excommunicated the dissident nuns, and recommended that the kings restore the convent's property.[143]

Since this tribunal apparently did not consider the nuns' complaints against Maroveus, he had presumably emerged with his authority enhanced. The cult of St. Hilary also subsequently revived. Radegund's prominence had reflected the singular combination of her personal influence with her possession of a relic of the True Cross. After her death, because Radegund herself had once insisted upon stringent sanctions against nuns who left the convent for any reason, they lost direct contact with their patroness who was buried outside the convent. Already during her funeral the nuns could only crowd the walls of the convent and watch the procession from a distance; they would rejoin Radegund only upon their deaths when they too would be buried in the church of the Virgin

---

[141] *Hist.* 10.12.

[142] *Hist.* 10.15.

[143] *Hist.* 10.16. In November 590 King Childebert convened a council at Metz, at which he pardoned Chrodechild and Basina. Chrodechild was exiled to a villa in the Poitou, and Basina was returned to the convent in Poitiers (*Hist.* 10.20).

Mary.[144] Conversely, although people were healed at her tomb,[145] Radegund had lost her contact with the relic of the True Cross, which remained
in the convent. The reputations of both Radegund and this shrine of the
True Cross therefore declined; and at the beginning of the seventh century
when Baudonivia, a nun in the convent, wanted to emphasize the power of
the church in which Radegund was buried, she compared it with the power
of the church of St. Hilary.[146] The shrine of St. Hilary now again set the
standard as the site of the most influential cult in the city.

The cult of St. Hilary and the bishop of Poitiers also revived their prestige
because St. Martin helped both. Gregory thought that the power of St.
Martin had been responsible for the release of the captives in Poitiers
during Easter 590.[147] In 591 Plato, Gregory's archdeacon at Tours, succeeded Maroveus as bishop. Gregory himself escorted Plato to Poitiers;
Fortunatus clearly identified Plato as a "foster son" of St. Martin who now
intended to honor St. Hilary; and Plato still wore a reliquary containing
dust from the tomb of St. Martin that was immediately effective in stopping
a fire that threatened his new cathedral residence at Poitiers.[148] Given the
success of St. Martin in dominating the cult of the True Cross at Tours,
perhaps these miracles were indications of the saint's again boosting his
onetime patron, St. Hilary, in the face of his competition at Poitiers. Plato's
successor as bishop of Poitiers was Fortunatus, who was an ideal compromise choice because of his connections with the cults of St. Hilary and St.
Martin and with the convent. Yet although Fortunatus had once been a
close confidant of both Radegund and Agnes, later generations remembered him primarily for his devotion to the cult of St. Martin, his episcopacy at Poitiers, and his skill as a poet.[149] The convent, its nuns, and its
once-powerful cult had been neutralized.

But the foundation of the convent, the prominence of Radegund, and
then this uprising in 589–590 had clearly demonstrated that a new cult
and its patrons could challenge, even if only temporarily, both the local
bishops and an established cult such as that of St. Hilary. The cult of the
True Cross was, admittedly, uniquely powerful, and the wonder is that in
Gaul during the sixth century it was left primarily to the patronage of nuns
with royal connections such as Radegund, perhaps Ingytrud at Tours, and

[144] *Hist.* 9.39, sanctions; *GC* 104, funeral; Baudonivia, *Vita Radegundis* 23, graves of
other nuns, 24, funeral procession.
[145] Baudonivia, *Vita Radegundis* 25–27, with Krüger (1971) 219–30, on Sainte-Croix
and Sainte-Radegonde.
[146] Baudonivia, *Vita Radegundis* 27, with Gäbe (1989) 20.
[147] *VM* 4.16.
[148] *VM* 4.32; Fortunatus, *Carm.* 10.14.
[149] Carolingian epitaphs to Fortunatus include Paul the Deacon, *HL* 2.13; and Alcuin,
Carm. 99.17, ed. E. Duemmler, *MGH*, Poetae 1 (1881) 326.

finally Chrodechild and Basina, who even had the effrontery to bring the relic of the True Cross to their public hearing before the tribunal of bishops.[150] Unlike the Byzantine emperors the Merovingian kings did not directly patronize the cult;[151] nor did any of the Merovingian queens such as Brunhild or Fredegund who remained active in royal politics after the deaths of their husbands; nor did most bishops, who were usually more interested in promoting cults of local saints. Radegund was an example of how competitive a patron of the cult of the True Cross could be both with kings and with a bishop and his local patron saint; and when Maroveus finally acquired jurisdiction over her convent and the bishops and the kings disciplined these rebellious nuns, perhaps they were implicitly also trying to control the disrupting challenge of this potentially threatening cult.

3. The Cult of St. Julian

Tours and Poitiers each had an obvious choice to become its local patron saint; in contrast, Clermont had no clearly dominant patron saint, even though one of its saints had been a contemporary of St. Hilary and St. Martin. Illidius had been bishop of Clermont during the later fourth century. Like Martin, he had once visited the court of the emperor Maximus at Trier where he had exorcised a demon from a girl; and as with the tombs of both St. Martin and St. Hilary, eventually a church in the city's suburbs contained his tomb, where Gregory himself was once healed when a young boy.[152] But at Clermont the cult of St. Illidius did not become very prominent. Gregory noted that some people thought that Illidius had not performed enough miracles to be considered a saint, and he conceded that any miracles performed before his own boyhood in Clermont had been forgotten.[153] The general expansion of saints' cults in Gaul during the fifth century seems not to have affected the cult of St. Illidius at Clermont.

---

[150] *Hist.* 10.16.

[151] *GM* 5, emperors. Note that the church of St. Vincentius at Paris was also known as the "church of the blessed Cross": see Fortunatus, *Vita Germani* 116, with Vieillard-Troiekouroff (1976) 211–14. Perhaps Bishop Germanus of Paris, through his connections with Radegund, had acquired a relic of the True Cross for this church; a later tradition claimed that King Childebert had brought a "gold cross set with precious jewels" back from Spain: see Gislemar, *Vita Droctovei* 12. But the Merovingians, even though some were buried in the church, did not emphasize the association.

[152] *Hist.* 1.45, *VP* 2.1, Maximus's court; *VP* 2.2, with Vieillard-Troiekouroff (1976) 90–93, on the saint's church. Gregory later repaid the favor by importing the saint's relics to an oratory at Tours (*VP* 2.3).

[153] *VP* 2.2. Note, though, that Gregory also included a story about the miraculous healing of a baby boy "who was thought to be an *abnepos* of the blessed Illidius" (*VP* 2.4). If this boy really was Illidius's great-great-grandson and not simply a distant descendant, then he was healed perhaps about the middle of the fifth century.

One cult in the Auvergne that did expand during the mid- and later fifth century was that of St. Julian, whose principal shrine was located not in Clermont but about forty miles south in the village of Brioude. The origins of his cult are obscure. Julian was thought to have become a martyr during the later third or early fourth century. One tradition recorded in the saint's *Passio* mentioned that he had been a Christian at Vienne before fleeing to the Auvergne, while another tradition that Gregory recorded added that he had been martyred at Brioude; hence, as after the death of St. Martin, two sites could lay claim to him. In this case both acquired major relics, since his head was buried at Vienne in the tomb of St. Ferreolus and his body at Brioude. According to another tradition, a man whom the emperor Maximus had sentenced to death was freed after his wife prayed at the saint's tomb at Brioude.[154] This is the earliest miracle that both the *Passio* and Gregory recorded about the saint, and veracity aside, it neatly associated St. Julian with the same emperor whom Martin and Illidius had visited. Already during the later fifth century when the *Passio* was composed as well as a century later when Gregory was writing, the traditions about the expansion of Christianity in Gaul pointed to the importance of the later fourth century.

Although this woman fulfilled her promise to construct a stone shrine over the saint's tomb, until the later fifth century the cult of St. Julian remained relatively insignificant. A cult dedicated to the classical pagan gods Mars and Mercury was more prominent at Brioude, and its sanctuary, statue, and festival overshadowed the saint's small shrine. Bishop Germanus of Auxerre was given credit for finally helping the locals discover the proper date for the saint's festival. Probably at about the same time someone at Clermont composed a *Passio* that included a short account of St. Julian's martyrdom, burial, and miracles.[155] In 456 Avitus, an aristocrat from the Auvergne who had served briefly as emperor at Rome, was on his way to Brioude when he died; so he was buried next to the tomb of St. Julian. At Vienne Bishop Mamertus constructed a new church to which he transferred the tomb of St. Ferreolus that also contained the head of St. Julian. At Brioude the locals constructed a larger church over the saint's tomb for which Victorius, who governed the region as duke on behalf of King Euric of the Visigoths during the 470s, contributed the columns.[156] When a band of Burgundians attacked Brioude in the later fifth century, a Gallic aristocrat from Le Velay and his supporters defended the shrine.[157]

---

[154] *VJ* 1, 4; *Passio* 2–4.

[155] *VJ* 5–6, pagan cult; 29, Germanus; and below, Appendix 1.

[156] *Hist.* 2.11, Avitus; *VJ* 2, Mamertus; *VJ* 9, *Passio* 6, church; *Hist.* 2.20, Victorius. Fredegar, *Chron.* 3.13, distorted this last tradition by giving credit for the construction of this new church of St. Julian to King Euric himself.

[157] *VJ* 7–8.

Whatever the historical value of these meager traditions, two implications are significant. The first is that the development of the cult of St. Julian was, again, not unique, because its timing coincided with the development of many other saints' cults in Gaul and, like Perpetuus's promotion of the cult of St. Martin, its expansion included a new church and a new written account. The second implication, however, is that unlike many other saints' cults, the cult of St. Julian at Brioude expanded apparently without local episcopal patronage.

After about 470 the bishop of Clermont was Sidonius, a son-in-law of the Avitus who had been buried at Brioude. Sidonius once mentioned the shrine of St. Julian at Brioude, but only, literally, in passing, since it was on the route that his volume of collected poems was about to take.[158] He also complimented Mamertus for promoting the cults of St. Ferreolus and St. Julian at Vienne, but primarily because he hoped for the bishop's assistance for Clermont against the Visigoths.[159] So although Sidonius composed a poem that Bishop Perpetuus had inscribed in the apse of his new church for St. Martin, hoped to write poems about martyrs, and promised to write a *Vita* of Bishop Anianus of Orléans, he was not a noted patron of the cult of St. Julian in his own diocese.[160] His successor Aprunculus, formerly bishop of Langres, had fled to Clermont when the Burgundians suspected him of treason and threatened to kill him. Because at least one Burgundian king respected St. Julian, Aprunculus might have been expected to patronize the saint's cult as a demonstration of his own loyalty; but Gregory did not associate him with any saints' cults.[161] The next bishop of Clermont was Eufrasius, about whom Gregory knew virtually nothing. Upon his death Apollinaris became bishop for a few months. Apollinaris had a rather checkered relationship with Clermont. Although he was the son of Bishop Sidonius, in about 479 he had had to flee to Italy with Duke Victorius, probably as a consequence of feuds among Gallic aristocrats, and in 507 he had led a contingent from Clermont in support of the Visigoths in their losing battle against Clovis. In 515 his sister and his wife nevertheless schemed for him to become bishop, and probably during his brief episcopacy they began to construct at Clermont a church in honor of another martyr, St. Antolianus.[162] His successor was Quintianus, who had

---

[158] Sidonius, *Carm.* 24.16–19. Sidonius published his collected poems in 469: see Loyen (1960–1970) 1:xxx–xxxv. Sidonius, *Ep.* 4.6.2, refers to people's traveling apparently to the shrine of a martyr who might be St. Julian; but many martyrs had shrines in the Auvergne.

[159] Sidonius, *Ep.* 7.1, partially cited in *VJ* 2.

[160] Sidonius, *Ep.* 8.15, 9.16.3, lines 57–84, with Van Dam (1985) 157–76, on Sidonius's attitudes toward relic cults.

[161] *Hist.* 2.23, *VJ* 8.

[162] *Hist.* 2.20, 37; 3.2, *GM* 44, *VP* 4.1, with *PLRE* 2:114; and *GM* 64, church of St. Antolianus.

previously been a bishop at Rodez. Before the Visigoths threatened him for supporting the Franks and forced him to leave his first see, he had enlarged the church of St. Amantius. At Clermont he faced challenges from disaffected clergy and a rival count, and he successfully opposed an invasion by King Theuderic in 524. Even though during this invasion the shrine of St. Julian at Brioude offered a refuge to many people, Gregory did not associate Quintianus with the saint's cult.[163]

So up to the death of Quintianus in 525 none of the bishops of Clermont had directly promoted or even associated himself with the cult of St. Julian. Yet during this period they and various royal magistrates had promoted other cults in or near Clermont. In the middle of the fifth century Bishop Namatius had constructed a new cathedral in which he placed relics of St. Agricola and St. Vitalis, two Italian martyrs. His wife had constructed in the city's suburbs a church dedicated to St. Stephen, in which Bishop Quintianus was eventually buried.[164] Bishop Sidonius composed an epitaph for the tomb of the abbot Abraham in the church of St. Cyricus.[165] Duke Victorius financed Abraham's funeral; he also constructed a church dedicated to St. Laurentius and St. Germanus at Saint-Germain-Lembron, and once prayed at the tomb of St. Amabilis in Clermont.[166] In fact, in the early sixth century Clermont had so many churches and so many cults that King Theuderic called off his siege when one of his generals described the city's powerful fortifications: "I am talking about the saints whose churches surround the city's walls."[167]

Not only was St. Julian not one of those defenders, however, but his cult was not even attuned to urban affairs at all. In the early sixth century Bishop Tetradius of Bourges left an estate to the saint's church at Brioude, which also owned other fields that it let to tenants.[168] The church also owned many flocks that grazed in the neighboring mountains, and as dedicatory offerings it received cattle, horses, pigs, and bulls.[169] Unlike the cults of St. Martin and St. Hilary, the cult of St. Julian at Brioude was primarily concerned with rural affairs. Respect for St. Martin prevented the Merovingian kings from levying a "public tax" on the citizens of Tours; St. Julian was concerned only about the imposition of a "pasture tax" on his flocks.[170] At Tours and Poitiers fires gutted the cathedral, churches, or houses; at Brioude a fire in a haystack killed sheep and horses.[171] Gregory's

---

[163] *Hist.* 2.36, *VP* 4.1; and note to *VJ* 13, for Theuderic's invasion.
[164] *Hist.* 2.16, *GM* 43, cathedral; *Hist.* 2.17, *VP* 4.5, church of St. Stephen.
[165] *Hist.* 2.21, *VP* 3.1; Sidonius, *Ep.* 7.17.
[166] *Hist.* 2.20, *GC* 32.
[167] *VP* 4.2.
[168] *Hist.* 3.16, *VJ* 14–15.
[169] *VJ* 17, 31.
[170] *Hist.* 9.30, *VJ* 17.
[171] *VJ* 27.

stories about the saint's shrine leave the impression that it catered primarily to peasants and shepherds who came on horseback;[172] he did not mention any visits from the bishops of Clermont.

But when bishops were unwilling or unable to encourage particular cults, local aristocratic families stepped forward, and the family that patronized the cult of St. Julian was that of Gregory's father. Not only was this a wealthy family that owned estates in the southern Auvergne, but at the end of the fifth century Georgius, Gregory's paternal grandfather, was still claiming "senatorial" rank.[173] One of his sons was Gallus, who decided to become a monk at a monastery in Cournon, a few miles from Clermont. When Theuderic threatened the Auvergne in the early sixth century, Gallus walked barefoot to the shrine of St. Julian at Brioude in order to find sanctuary.[174] Florentius, Gregory's father and Gallus's brother, furthermore took his entire family on pilgrimages to Brioude to celebrate St. Julian's festival on August 28.[175] Since none of the bishops of Clermont had established any firm links between Clermont and the cult of St. Julian, the journeys of both Gallus and Florentius therefore indicated their own and their family's private preferences for a local shrine. The family also maintained some standing at Clermont itself, because when Gallus succeeded Quintianus as bishop of the city, one of his uncles was already serving there as a priest. In 543 an outbreak of the plague endangered the entire region. Gallus responded by instituting some penitential rogations during the middle of Lent that included a pilgrimage on foot to the church of St. Julian at Brioude. Through the celebration of this pilgrimage the people of Clermont were spared from the plague.[176]

In reaction to this threat Gallus had therefore introduced into the liturgical calendar of Clermont a pilgrimage to a shrine that his family had previously patronized for at least a generation. Yet the behavior of Gregory's mother neatly indicates that the cult of St. Julian, even in the context of the urban liturgy of Clermont, was still associated more closely with a particular family than with the city at large. Armentaria probably participated in the pilgrimage to Brioude, but she received more reassurance from a vision of St. Benignus, a martyr whose cult her grandfather had invented at Dijon;[177] at a moment of uncertainty her own family's patron saint still took priority over her husband's family's patron saint. So if Gallus had not become bishop and then seized the opportunity to promote a specifically family cult, the shrine of St. Julian might well have remained a backwater,

---

[172] *VJ* 18, 21, with G. Fournier (1962) 85–99, on settlements in the Auvergne, 160–69, on the development of Brioude.

[173] Below, chapter 2, section 1.

[174] *VJ* 23, *VP* 6.1.

[175] *VJ* 24–25.

[176] *VP* 6.6.

[177] *GM* 50.

important certainly to Gregory and his father's family but neither a significant component of the liturgical practices of Clermont nor an object of episcopal patronage.

Once Gallus established a connection between Clermont and the shrine of St. Julian at Brioude, however, subsequent bishops apparently maintained it. Cautinus, Gallus's successor, participated in the pilgrimages to Brioude both during Lent and before the saint's festival, and his successor Avitus allowed one of his priests to acquire relics of St. Julian.[178] Yet these successor bishops also promoted other cults that presumably had more personal significance. Before becoming bishop Cautinus had served as a deacon in the village of Issoire at the tomb of St. Stremonius, who was thought to have been the first bishop of Clermont. After he remodeled the shrine, people began to pray there and request the saint's assistance.[179] Since Cautinus faced a powerful contender for the episcopal succession in 551, the support of the city's first bishop would have been a convincing argument in favor of his promotion. After his accession to the episcopacy in 571 Avitus promoted several cults at Clermont. He rebuilt the crypt for the tomb of St. Illidius; he demolished and rebuilt the church for St. Antolianus that had been built during the episcopacy of Apollinaris; and he built a church over the tomb of St. Genesius at Thiers.[180] In most of these cases Gallus's successors preferred to promote cults somehow associated with their episcopal predecessors rather than a rural shrine associated with a family whose influence at Clermont was fading.

So people other than the bishops of Clermont again promoted the cult of St. Julian. A monk, himself named Julian, healed fevers at the saint's church at Brioude. One man constructed a church at Rheims for which he acquired, apparently on his own initiative, relics of the saint. Near Saintes an aristocratic woman constructed a church in the saint's honor on her own estate. Abbot Aredius of Limoges built a church near his monastery at Saint-Yrieix, and he and his mother sometimes visited the saint's church at Brioude. At a village in the Touraine a man built a church in which Gregory placed relics of the saint.[181] And in fact, Gregory himself was the most conspicuous patron of the cult of St. Julian during the later sixth century. Since Gregory always considered himself a "foster son" of the saint, he often traveled to the saint's church; in 571, for instance, when the plague again threatened Gaul, Gregory went to Brioude for protection (even though Bishop Cautinus of Clermont significantly did not). Two years later Gregory first went to Brioude for the saint's festival before going on to

---

[178] *Hist.* 4.13, 10.8, *VJ* 48.

[179] *GC* 29.

[180] *GM* 64, 66, *VP* 2.4.

[181] *Hist.* 4.32, monk Julian; *VJ* 32, Rheims, 47, Saintes, 50, Touraine; *Hist.* 10.29, *VJ* 41, Aredius.

assume his new episcopacy at Tours. And as bishop Gregory imported relics of the saint to various shrines in the Touraine.[182] So through the sixth century the cult of St. Julian remained largely a family cult, and as that family's influence shifted from Clermont to Tours, so did the cult. In the later sixth century the cult of St. Julian was hence perhaps better represented and more popular in the Touraine than in the Auvergne.

Gregory also promoted the cult of St. Julian by compiling *The Suffering and Miracles of the Martyr St. Julian (VJ)*, a collection of miracle stories about the saint. Several considerations motivated him to write this book. One was to present St. Julian as a proper model for others to imitate. Gregory began the *VJ* with a discussion of the "path of righteousness" that had led biblical heroes to the kingdom of heaven; as a martyr St. Julian had traveled on the same journey.[183] A second goal was to link St. Julian with St. Martin. Since St. Julian had not made much impact even at Clermont whereas St. Martin had a reputation throughout much of Gaul, they would seem to form an odd couple. The common denominator, however, was now Gregory, whose attachment to the cult of St. Julian, his family's patron saint, had once bolstered his standing at Tours with the cult of St. Martin, his new episcopal patron saint. By collecting stories about the miracles of St. Julian Gregory was repaying the favor, and in the *VJ* he concluded that St. Julian shared the gift of healing with St. Martin and that the two saints were now allies.[184] A final purpose for writing the *VJ* was simply Gregory's own deep emotional attachment to the saint. As he began to write, he characteristically apologized for his literary inadequacies: "But what am I to do? My love for my patron [saint] compels me." As he concluded the book, he also characteristically requested that St. Julian act as his advocate before God.[185]

Gregory's relationship with St. Julian was therefore strongly personal, a legacy of his family's connections in the Auvergne. For a few decades the ascendancy of his family at Clermont ensured the wider prominence of the family's cult in the Auvergne; but in the long run the cult remained relatively insignificant. Unlike St. Martin at Tours and St. Hilary at Poitiers, St. Julian did not become the distinctive patron saint for the Auvergne. In fact, Clermont never seems to have settled on a single dominant patron saint. In the later seventh century, for instance, Praeiectus, a native of the Auvergne, may have once appealed for St. Julian's assistance during his youth; but after he became a cleric and then bishop of Clermont, he promoted other saints.[186] By the early tenth century there were more than fifty churches at

---

[182] Below, chapter 2.
[183] *VJ* 1.
[184] *VJ* 35, 47, 50.
[185] *VJ* 4, 50.
[186] *Passio Praeiecti* 4, St. Julian; 9, 11, 17, other saints.

Clermont, in which the number of shrines dedicated to St. Julian ranked third behind those dedicated to the Virgin Mary and St. Peter. But these churches also contained shrines dedicated to over ninety more saints, not to mention "the other saints whose names God knows."[187]

The fifth century, and especially the later fifth century, marked a period of reorganization and transition in Gallic society. In particular, the rise of Christianity and the expansion of barbarian kingdoms opened new opportunities, even as the disappearance of the imperial administration removed others. As we have noted, Gallic aristocrats adopted different strategies for the preservation of their traditional perquisites. Apollinaris, for instance, was a native of Lyon who had served as prefect of the Gauls in the early fifth century; as a younger contemporary of Bishop Martin he had also been the first member of his family to reject paganism and accept Christian baptism.[188] In the middle of the century his son had served as prefect of the Gauls representing the imperial court in Italy; and toward the end of the century when the Visigoths were expanding their kingdom in central Gaul, his grandson Sidonius became bishop of Clermont. But Sidonius always retained a strong nostalgia for the Roman Empire, and some of his friends too now reasserted their connections with great men in earlier Roman history. Sidonius compared the writings of one of his correspondents with the orations of Cicero, Pliny the Younger, and Fronto, and even described Fronto as another man's ancestor; he noted that another Gallic aristocrat had the walls of his villa decorated with murals of an ancient Roman campaign; and he looked forward to reading another friend's laudatory declamation about Julius Caesar.[189] In the face of the Roman administration's retreat Gallic aristocrats emphasized all the more firmly their place in Roman history.

The barbarians who settled in Gaul during the fifth century also had to come to terms with Roman history. Eventually folklore and then learned accounts elaborated various traditions that the Franks were descendants of the Trojans and their kings were direct descendants of King Priam of Troy.[190] One implication of these new Frankish traditions is particularly striking. Since unlike contemporary Gallic aristocrats the Franks could not fit themselves directly into Roman history, they adopted a "pre-Roman"

[187] List of churches and shrines in *Libellus de ecclesiis Claromontanis*; quotation from *Libellus* 3.

[188] Sidonius, *Ep.* 3.12.5, lines 13–16, with Matthews (1975) 333–34, 339, and Heinzelmann (1982) 556.

[189] Sidonius, *Carm.* 22.158–68, *Ep.* 8.3.3, 10.3; 9.14.7.

[190] Gerberding (1987) 11–30, is a particularly clear discussion of these traditions.

heritage that made them the peers of the Romans, whose Trojan ancestry had become part of their foundation myths too. If Romans and Franks shared a common ancestry, then ideological and cultural symbiosis became more feasible; the absence of any restrictions on intermarriage furthermore helped Franks to assimilate with the Romans much more readily than did barbarians in other kingdoms.

The Franks faced a similar problem in ingratiating themselves with established saints' cults, because already under the later Roman Empire Gallic cities and aristocratic families had appropriated many of these saints as their special patrons.[191] Merovingian kings were prepared, even if sometimes reluctantly, to concede the importance of these saints and their cults. But in the same way that they had bypassed the difficulties of their integration into Roman history through the development of parallel traditions, so these kings neatly sidestepped the dominance of the established cults by promoting new saints' cults. During the sixth century their links with the cults of St. Martin, St. Hilary, and St. Julian remained comparatively minimal. The early Franks therefore certainly influenced the development of saints' cults in late antique Gaul, in part because of their patronage for new cults, but in part too because of their aloofness from established cults.

[191] Although eventually, in an ironic twist, the Carolingian kings would congratulate themselves for honoring the saints whom "Romans" had martyred: see *Lex Salica* (D, E), prologus 3.

CHAPTER TWO

Gregory of Tours and His Patron Saints

T O MODERN READERS Gregory of Tours is most familiar for his *Histories*, often known in translations as the "History of the Franks." Yet the *Histories* constituted less than half of his writings. His other works included a commentary on the Psalms,[1] a book about the liturgical offices of the church,[2] a preface for a collection of liturgical masses,[3] a translation of an account of some legendary martyrs at Ephesus known as the Seven Sleepers,[4] and probably a book about the miracles of St. Andrew.[5] The most important of his other writings was the *Miracles*, an anthology of eight books of miracle stories.[6] This enormous collection included a book about martyrs and the miracles at their shrines, a book about confessors and the miracles at their shrines, and a book of short biographies of illustrious men and women of the church. The remaining books collected the miracles of two of Gregory's own patron saints, St. Julian and St. Martin. Gregory's extensive writings therefore provide the most important evidence for our evaluation of early Merovingian Gaul.

Yet Gregory was also surprisingly reticent about himself, and even when he wrote short biographies of other members of his family or of his mentors and acquaintances, he often mentioned his own relationships or involvement with them only in passing. Modern historians must hence reconstruct Gregory's life from suggestive allusions and oblique inferences; so far their reconstructions have been content primarily to sort into chronological

---

[1] Of which only an introduction, a partial table of contents, and a few fragments survive: ed. B. Krusch, *MGH, SRM* 1.2 (1885) 874–77; introduction and fragments also in *PL* 71.1097–98.

[2] Gregory's own title was somewhat misleading, since the first part of this book described the great man-made and natural wonders of the world, and the second part calculated the correspondence between the movement of the stars and the liturgical hours during the night. The book is usually cited now with the title given it in an eighth-century manuscript, *De cursu stellarum ratio*, "Calculation concerning the movement of the stars."

[3] *Hist.* 2.22.

[4] Ed. B. Krusch, *MGH, SRM* 1.2 (1885) 848–53, and again in *SRM* 7 (1920) 761–69; trans. McDermott, in Peters (1975) 199–206.

[5] Below, section 2.

[6] Cf. *GC* praef.

order the scattered references to events in his early life and subsequent episcopal career.[7] In the process these reconstructions have failed to note subtle but still consequential transitions within Gregory's life. Admittedly, Gregory was not as reflective and self-analytical as any of the great church fathers such as Augustine of Hippo, and his writings were certainly not as revealing of his inner self as the *Confessions* or even a collection of personal letters. Yet the immediacy and the unpretentious candor of his writings do allow glimpses into his personality, and especially so in his collection of the miracle stories of St. Martin. Not only did he record most of these stories in chronological order during the two decades of his episcopacy, but Gregory increasingly defined his behavior and even his own identity in terms of St. Martin. Although he and his family provide an important example of the survival of the late Roman aristocracy in Merovingian Gaul, the only explicit "genealogy" that Gregory mentioned for himself was, significantly, a list of the previous bishops of Tours in which his most distinguished "ancestor" had been St. Martin.[8]

This chapter stresses the transitions in Gregory's life and career. Although the available literary evidence provides the basic foundation, like any other ambitious historical analysis this interpretation also relies upon some creative intuition in order to discover patterns and changes in a lengthy process of growth and accommodation. Gregory was part of an extended network that included family members, friends, and supporters as well as rivals and opponents, and all influenced his development and outlook. In the making of Gregory events involving his immediate family were especially important in determining the shape of his ecclesiastical career: the early loss of his father, the support of older relatives, the unwavering encouragement of his mother. After he finally became a bishop he faced the additional challenges of establishing and maintaining his authority at Tours in the face of opposition from other powerful men, in particular the Frankish kings and their counts. The expansion of his authority during the twenty years of his episcopacy was a gradual, and sometimes even dangerous, process. Dominating these changes throughout his life were his relationships with various patron saints; but here again, not only did the nature of these relationships shift, so did the identity of the saints. St. Martin emerged as Gregory's primary patron saint only comparatively late in his life.

---

[7] Useful introductions to Gregory's career and family include Krusch (1951), Buchner (1955), Weidemann (1982) 1:205–20, and L. Pietri (1983) 247–64. Vinay (1940) 42–52 discusses his personality; Vollmann (1983) is a fine survey of recent research; de Nie (1987) analyzes the coherence and significance of Gregory's imagery.

[8] *Hist.* 10.31, with the comments of Brown (1983), on saints and personal identity.

1. Becoming a Bishop

Gregory grew up essentially without his father. Florentius was a member of a distinguished "senatorial" family from Clermont[9] and seems to have been a generation older than his wife, Armentaria.[10] They were married in 533, and Gregory was born a few years later, probably in 538.[11] Gregory had few memories of his father. When he was still a young boy just learning the alphabet, he had twice had visions that showed him a cure for his father's gout. His father had also once told him about one of his own boyhood encounters with an old abbot near Clermont. Florentius apparently died when Gregory was still quite young, however, for although during the sixth century it was common for aristocratic boys to be educated at home, by the age of eight Gregory was learning to read with his great-uncle Nicetius at Lyon.[12]

Relatives now assumed much of the direct responsibility for teaching Gregory. He and his family still sometimes stayed on an estate that probably belonged to his father's family in the Limagne, a plain in the southern Auvergne whose haunting beauty Gregory always admired, and he and his mother once celebrated the festival of St. Polycarp in Riom, a village north of Clermont.[13] When he became gravely ill, Gallus, his father's brother and bishop of Clermont since 525, demonstrated his "singular affection" by

[9] Gregory associated senatorial rank with several of his ancestors, including his paternal grandparents Georgius and Leocadia (*VP* 6.1, 14.3) and his maternal great-grandfathers Gregorius (*VP* 7.1) and Florentinus (*VP* 8.1). These ancestors had apparently acquired senatorial rank in regions controlled by the Visigoths and Burgundians before the expansion of the Franks: see Stroheker (1948) 112–13, and Brennan (1985b).

[10] Indirect evidence implies a substantial difference in age. Florentius's older brother Gallus was born in 486/487, and their father Georgius died in 507 (note to *VJ* 23); Florentius died probably in the mid-540s; but Armentaria was still alive in 588 (*VM* 3.60). Gregory's parents had hence followed a typical "Mediterranean" pattern of late male–early female marriage: see Saller (1987), and Shaw (1987), for the pattern in the western Roman Empire. Only more systematic analysis can determine whether this was the common pattern among Gallic aristocrats. But since with this marriage pattern wives would often outlive their husbands, it is striking that the adult child–surviving parent relationship Gregory commonly mentioned involved men and their mothers, such as Nicetius of Lyon and Artemia, Abbot (later Bishop) Salvius of Albi and his mother (*Hist.* 7.1), and Aredius of Limoges and Pelagia (note to *VJ* 28). Fortunatus, *Vita Paterni* 9, mentioned another bishop's mother who had been a widow for almost sixty years; Armentaria would have been a widow for more than forty years.

[11] *GM* 83: Florentius was "recently married" when Theudebert took hostages at Clermont upon hearing that his father King Theuderic was dying late in 533 (*Hist.* 3.23). For the date of Gregory's birth, see the notes to *VM* 1.35, 3.10.

[12] *GC* 39, gout; *VP* 14.3, abbot; *VP* 8.2, Nicetius. For education at home, see Riché (1962) 241, 252–54.

[13] *Hist.* 3.9, *GM* 83, Limagne; *GM* 85, Riom.

visiting his young nephew.[14] But Gregory, along with his mother, his brother, and his sister, seems to have left the Auvergne soon. Nicetius, his mother's maternal uncle, was from a family that was prominent in the region of Burgundy around Geneva and Lyon.[15] After becoming a priest in 543 he had started a "choir school," apparently at Lyon, in which young boys, such as now Gregory, learned to read and recite the Psalms. Nicetius quickly became more than a teacher for his great-nephew, however, because years later Gregory still had a vivid memory of how Nicetius had embraced him "with the sweetness of a father's love."[16] So Gregory apparently found substitutes for his father first in Gallus and then in Nicetius.

Living near the cities associated with both his father's and then his mother's families meant that Gregory also developed relationships with an extended "family" of saints. As a young boy at Clermont he had once been healed at the church of St. Illidius, a former bishop of the city.[17] More important, the specific preferences and allegiances of his father's family also directly influenced his own devotion to particular saints' cults. When in 533 King Theudebert had taken hostages from among the sons of aristocratic families at Clermont, Florentius had filled a gold medallion with the ashes of unknown saints. Although hostages were sometimes not returned to their families and instead became slaves,[18] Florentius insisted that these relics had saved him from both bandits and natural disasters. Eventually Gregory inherited and wore his father's reliquary when he was still a young man.[19] Florentius and his brother Gallus had also promoted the cult of St. Julian. In his youth Gallus had once found sanctuary by limping all the way to the shrine of St. Julian at Brioude. Florentius seems to have taken his entire family on annual pilgrimages to Brioude to celebrate the festival of St. Julian on August 28. During one of these pilgrimages Gregory's older brother Peter was cured by dust from the saint's tomb; the next year Gregory himself was cured of a headache at the nearby shrine of St. Ferreolus.[20] In 543 when the plague threatened Clermont, Bishop Gallus instituted

[14] *VP* 2.2. Since Gregory mentioned only the grief of his mother, his father was probably already deceased; and although he was old enough to make a vow about his future, he described himself as a *parvulus* and *in adolescentia degens*. Gregory was about thirteen when Gallus died in 551.

[15] Note that Florentius's mother, Leocadia, had also claimed descent from the family of a distinguished martyr of Lyon (*VP* 6.1). So his own marriage to Armentaria represented the second generation of his family's alliance with families from Lyon.

[16] *VP* 8.2, "paternae dilectionis dulcedine."

[17] *VP* 2.2.

[18] Cf. *Hist.* 3.15, a particularly apposite story since it involved a nephew of Gregorius of Langres, one of Gregory's great-grandfathers.

[19] *GM* 83.

[20] *VJ* 23–25.

rogations that were celebrated during Lent and that included another pilgrimage to the church of St. Julian at Brioude.[21] Florentius and Gallus had
therefore ensured, and publicized, the close relationship between their
family and the cult of St. Julian, and as bishop Gallus had incorporated the
saint's cult into the annual liturgy of Clermont. As a consequence, even as
Gregory always retained an association with Clermont and the Auvergne,
he also favored their local saints. He visited other local shrines and celebrated some festivals there, and he may have stayed there again at some
time.[22] In particular he always remained self-consciously proud of his close
relationship with St. Julian, the "martyr of Clermont," and he un-
abashedly called him his "own special patron." And by describing himself
as the saint's *alumnus*, "foster son," Gregory also seems to have imagined
himself as an abandoned child whom St. Julian had nurtured not because
of the demands of blood or law, but strictly because of his selfless
kindness.[23]

Through his father's family Gregory therefore developed durable relationships with various saints of the Auvergne, in particular with St. Julian.
Until his death in 551 his uncle Gallus was a constant reminder of the
family's special relationship with the latter's cult, not least because he
would proudly display the scar of the wound on his foot that St. Julian had
once healed as evidence of the saint's lasting power.[24] If Gregory's father
had lived longer, or if Gregory had grown up primarily in Clermont, then
saints associated with the Auvergne would have remained his primary
patron saints. But after his father's death Gregory moved to Lyon to live
with his great-uncle Nicetius, who equally proudly displayed a scar of his
own as proof of another saint's power. When as a young boy Nicetius had
suffered from a festering sore on his face, his mother Artemia had prayed to
many saints, and in particular to her special patron, St. Martin. Upon his
recovery Nicetius had conceded that St. Martin had restored his health.
Although Nicetius had become a cleric after the death of his own father, he
had also continued to live with his mother, to whom "he was as obedient as

---

[21] *Hist.* 4.5, *VP* 6.6; cf. *GM* 50. Since Gregory insisted that the Lord had promised that no
one from Clermont would die of this plague during the remaining eight years of Gallus's life,
presumably his own father was not a victim. For another, undated visit by Gregory to Brioude,
see *Hist.* 4.32.

[22] *GM* 8, 86, *GC* 5. Although Weidemann (1982) 1:206 concludes that Gregory made
these visits while he was a cleric but before he became bishop of Tours, in fact Gregory did not
say that he presided at these services, only that he attended them. See *GC* 1, for a possible later
stay.

[23] *Hist.* 2.11, *VJ* praef., 1–2, 50. For the quasi-familial relationship implied by the term
alumnus in a Roman and then in a Christian context, see Rawson (1986) 173–86, and
Boswell (1988) 116–21.

[24] *VJ* 23.

if he were one of her slaves."[25] For the young Gregory, Nicetius therefore became not just another substitute father and his teacher, but also a model for his subsequent relationships both with his mother and with St. Martin. After being healed at the church of St. Illidius, Gregory too had vowed to become a cleric, and he also continued to respect and visit his mother, even after she had returned to her family's lands in Burgundy.[26] In 563 he confirmed his own relationship with St. Martin. When he suffered from a debilitating fever, Gregory first invoked the name of St. Martin and then made a difficult pilgrimage to the saint's tomb at Tours where he recovered his health. Gregory immediately concluded that St. Martin had become his patron to whom he could petition on behalf of one of his ill servants, and he began to use the saint's relics to protect one of his own estates, to frighten off bandits, and to heal his brother-in-law.[27] He also became a deacon and served under Nicetius, who had become bishop of Lyon a decade earlier.[28] Through Nicetius Gregory therefore acquired some of his early education, initial promotion in the ecclesiastical hierarchy, and, most significant, an introduction to the cult of St. Martin.

The marriage between Florentius and Armentaria had hence represented not only a dynastic merger between two prominent families in central and eastern Gaul, but also an alliance of allegiances to different saints. Gregory certainly benefited both from his family's connections and from his own familiar relationships with all these saints. His paternal connection with the saints of the Auvergne remained as a source of confidence and security at times of stress, in particular before he became bishop at Tours. Once while traveling to meet Bishop Nicetius at Lyon, Gregory detoured to Vienne in order to pray at the tomb of St. Ferreolus, simply because he considered himself also to be the "foster son" of the saint who had been St. Julian's companion.[29] In 571 the plague again threatened several cities in central Gaul, among them Clermont and Lyon. Almost thirty years earlier in similar circumstances Gregory's father and uncle had invoked the assistance of St. Julian; now Gregory went again immediately to Brioude, "so that I who could not be protected by my own merits might be shielded by the protection of the blessed martyr Julian."[30] And a few years later the patronage of St. Julian helped Gregory consolidate his new episcopacy at Tours, the center of the cult of St. Martin.

Assuming the episcopacy at Tours was somewhat surprising, however,

[25] VP 8.1–2.
[26] GM 83, VM 1.36, 3.60, VP 2.2.
[27] VM 1.32–33, 36; 2.2.
[28] VM 1.35, VP 8.3.
[29] VJ 2.
[30] VJ 46a.

because even though Gregory had once made a pilgrimage to the church of
St. Martin there, any future advancement in the ecclesiastical hierarchy
would seem to lie elsewhere. Armentaria's father's family had become
prominent in the region around Autun and Langres. Gregorius, Gregory's
great-grandfather, had been count of Autun before serving as bishop of
Langres (and Dijon) during the early sixth century. His son Tetricus had
succeeded him as bishop, and even after his death in 572/573 the tradition
of family service at Langres continued. One possible successor as bishop
was another relative, and Gregory's brother Peter also served there as a
deacon. In fact, it is possible to guess that, just as Gregory had been placed
with his great-uncle Nicetius after his father's death, so Peter had been
entrusted to the guardianship of another great-uncle, Tetricus, at Langres.

Peter was therefore perhaps being groomed to become bishop for what
Fortunatus now called the "family see" of Langres.[31] After Gregorius had
become bishop of Langres in ca. 506/507, one means he used to consolidate his position was association with saint's cults. Often he would recite
Psalms during the night in a baptistery that contained the relics of saints.
He also founded a cult of his own by refurbishing the crypt of the martyr
Benignus and then constructing a church in the saint's honor.[32] After his
accession in 539/540 Tetricus consolidated his own position as new bishop
of Langres in a similar fashion by enlarging a church at Dijon, although
with the significant innovation that the cult he promoted there was one
dedicated to his father. During the dedication of this church the lid on
Gregorius's sarcophagus slipped aside, so that everyone could again see his
smiling face, still undecayed; thereafter people were healed before the tomb
in which St. Gregorius was now thought to be "sleeping."[33]

Gregorius's granddaughter Armentaria maintained this devotion to the
patron saints of her father's family at Langres. She herself had been named
after Gregorius's wife, and she had once been cured of a fever by sleeping in
Gregorius's bed. Even after her marriage and her move to Clermont, although her husband and his brother appealed for the assistance of St.
Julian when the plague appeared in 543, she was reassured instead by a
vision of St. Benignus.[34] Her sons inherited these relationships with both
her father's family and its saints. Gregory's full name was Georgius Florentius Gregorius; the first two names came from his paternal grandfather and
father respectively, but he himself may have added the third (by which he is

---

[31] Fortunatus, *Carm.* 4.3.2, "patriae sedes," in an epitaph for Tetricus. The episcopal
dynasty may have gone back even further if Gregorius's wife, Armentaria, was a daughter of
Armentarius, bishop of Langres from ca. 479 to ca. 506/507: see Heinzelmann (1976) 213–
14, and (1982) 560.

[32] *GM* 50, *VP* 7.2, *GC* 42.

[33] *VP* 7.4–5.

[34] *VP* 7.1–2, *GM* 50.

now known) after Bishop Gregorius, the one acknowledged "saint" in the family.[35] Gregory also once used ointment blessed by St. Benignus to heal an eye inflammation.[36] His brother Peter served as a deacon with Bishop Tetricus at Langres and acquired a reputation for assisting the poor. Ecclesiastical intrigues, however, finally led to his death. In his old age Bishop Tetricus suffered a stroke. An adjunct bishop was designated to serve as archpriest and eventually to succeed Tetricus, but he soon had to flee after being caught up in the rivalries among the Frankish kings. Peter then proposed a relative named Silvester as his replacement. Silvester had been ordained a priest by the time Tetricus died in 572/573, but he in turn died of an epileptic fit before being consecrated as bishop. This time Peter took the blame. Silvester's son joined with Lampadius, a deacon whom Tetricus had once dismissed for mismanagement of funds for the poor and who still had a grudge because Peter had supported his dismissal. Both now accused Peter of having murdered Silvester "through magical practices"; and Bishop Felix of Nantes would later even taunt Gregory by claiming that Peter had done so because he wanted to become bishop himself. At a hearing in Lyon before his great-uncle Bishop Nicetius, other bishops, and important laymen, Peter swore he was innocent. But two years later, still at the instigation of Lampadius, Silvester's son met Peter on the road and stabbed him to death.[37]

As a deacon at Lyon Gregory would have known about these intrigues; he would also have realized that the reputation of his mother's father's family was now tainted at Langres because various members were openly squabbling over the see. He was hence perhaps more concerned about the vindication of his immediate family's interests there than about himself competing for the episcopacy. When Silvester's son was killed a few years later in an unrelated blood feud, Gregory nevertheless commented that his death was an indication of God's judgment for having killed his "innocent relative." Tetricus's successor finally turned out to be Pappolus, an archdeacon from Autun, who apparently did not respect his predecessors, because Gregory later insisted that he was such a terrible bishop that Tetricus eventually threatened him in a dream and warned him to leave the see. Pappolus's successor in 579/581 was Mummolus, formerly an abbot at Tonnerre, a village near Langres.[38] Mummolus had acquired the sobriquet

---

[35] For his full name, see *GM* praef., *VM* 1 praef., *VP* praef., and the *Explanatio* to his *Commentarius in psalterii tractatum*. Fortunatus referred to him simply as Gregorius. For the suggestion that Gregory himself added his third name, see Krusch (1951) IX, based on the variant manuscript readings; L. Pietri (1983) 252 suggests that he did so when he became bishop.

[36] *GM* 50.

[37] *Hist.* 5.5.

[38] Jonas of Bobbio, *Vita Iohannis* 19.

"the Good"; and among his many virtues Gregory mentioned specifically his love of justice, which he may have thought Mummolus had demonstrated primarily because he finally reduced Lampadius to poverty by confiscating the church properties that he had stolen.[39] So although Gregory's family temporarily lost some of its influence at Langres during the episcopacy of Pappolus, in the end it had its revenge on both Silvester's son and Lampadius and recovered some of its prominence. Peter had even been buried with St. Gregorius at Dijon, and in 585 King Guntramn would admit to Gregory that Bishop Tetricus still haunted him in his dreams.[40]

If Langres had been first intended for Peter and then put off limits by his actions, the two obvious cities in which Gregory might still have anticipated becoming bishop were Clermont and Lyon. In 551 Gregory's uncle Gallus had died at Clermont. The priest Cato received the support of the people, other clerics, and other bishops, but the archdeacon Cautinus acquired the support of King Theudebald and his advisers at Metz and was consecrated there as the new bishop. Because the church at Clermont was now openly split into factions, Bishop Cautinus attempted to consolidate his position in conventional ways. Like other bishops he looked for the support of an established saint by participating in the pilgrimage to the shrine of St. Julian during Lent, and he promoted the relatively new cult of St. Stremonius, who was supposed to have been the first bishop of Clermont. He also attempted to rid himself of his rival by recommending that Cato become bishop of Tours in 556, although Cato instead decided that he might yet obtain the episcopacy at Clermont through his friendship with Chramn, whom his father King Chlothar had placed in charge of the city; and eventually Cato even appealed directly to Chlothar to replace Cautinus with himself.[41]

Although no longer living in Clermont, Gregory had little respect for either faction. He admired Cato for assisting people during the plague but criticized his arrogance. He also criticized Cato's ally Chramn for his vindictive administration in Clermont and for listening to an adviser who thought that St. Martin had left nothing of value to the royal treasury. Gregory's great-uncle Bishop Tetricus shared this low opinion of Chramn, because in 556 he refused him entry into Dijon. But Gregory was particularly critical of Bishop Cautinus and accused him of public drunkenness, a lack of education, dependence on the flattery of Jews, and greediness so

[39] *Hist.* 5.5.

[40] *Hist.* 8.5. A century later it was claimed that King Guntramn had willed a villa to the church of St. Benignus at Dijon: see the *placitum* issued by King Chlothar III in 663, in Pardessus (1843–1849) 2:132, no. 349 = Pertz (1872) 38–39, no. 41.

[41] *Hist.* 4.7, factions; 4.13, 10.8, St. Julian; *GC* 29, St. Stremonius; *Hist.* 4.11, 15, Chramn and Cato.

excessive that he even tried to confiscate one man's property by burying him alive.[42]

For Gregory's father's family seems to have lost much of its ecclesiastical influence in Clermont during these years.[43] Since Bishop Gallus had once refused to marry before he became a cleric, and since his nephews Peter and Gregory had gone to live elsewhere after their father's death, no younger members of the immediate family were now available to serve the church there. After Gallus's death in 551 the cult of St. Julian also seems to have lost some of its prestige. Bishop Cautinus may have participated in some of the pilgrimages to the saint's shrine, but he also promoted his own new cult of St. Stremonius, and in 571 when the plague again approached the Auvergne, he did not go to Brioude before finally dying in Clermont.[44]

Gregory in contrast did go to the shrine of St. Julian for assistance in 571; but although he was therefore probably in the Auvergne when Cautinus died, after his long absence in Lyon he no longer had the local support at Clermont to be included among the many candidates for the vacant see. One leading candidate was the priest Eufrasius, a member of a powerful family at Clermont where his grandfather, father, and brother had already served as counts. Although Eufrasius received financial backing from Jews, he acquired little support elsewhere, perhaps because his family had once been cursed by Quintianus, bishop of Clermont from 516 to 525, who had predicted that no one from this family would ever become a bishop. Quintianus had also been an early mentor to Gallus, and on the assumption that old animosities lingered, Gregory was probably not now Eufrasius's ally.[45] Another leading candidate was the archdeacon Avitus, who was perhaps a member of another distinguished family that had produced several previous bishops at Clermont. Since the two became close friends, Gregory probably supported him strongly now. Although Firminus, the count of Clermont, opposed his selection, Avitus nevertheless received the support of the people, the clergy, and, most important, King Sigibert, who even had him consecrated at his court in Metz.[46]

Even though Gregory would not have been a viable candidate for the episcopacy of Clermont in 571, with the deepening of his friendship with

---

[42] *Hist.* 4.32, Cato; 4.13, 16, *GM* 65, Chramn; *Hist.* 4.16, Tetricus; 4.12, Cautinus.

[43] But the family may have gained some secular influence, if Georgius, a citizen of Velay who served as count of Clermont perhaps in the middle of the sixth century (*GC* 34), was a relative: see Stroheker (1948) no. 176, and Selle-Hosbach (1974) 100. Nicetius, the husband of Gregory's niece, may also have served as count and duke of Clermont: see below, n. 125.

[44] *Hist.* 4.31.

[45] *Hist.* 4.35, Jews; *VP* 4.3, Quintianus's curse; 6.2, Gallus.

[46] *Hist.* 4.35. For the suggestion that Avitus was a member of the same family as Bishops Eparchius, Sidonius, and Apollinaris (*Hist.* 2.21–23, 37; 3.2, *GM* 44, 64), see Wood (1983) 37–39.

Avitus he could again resume a closer connection with the city. He noted Avitus's many virtues as bishop and occasionally visited him.[47] He was especially indebted in that Avitus now encouraged his further study of ecclesiastical writings, in particular the Psalms and the New Testament.[48] He also praised some of Avitus's attempts to restore harmony at Clermont and consolidate his new episcopacy. In 576 Avitus took advantage of the recent accession of the young King Childebert to take his revenge on the Jews who had supported his rival Eufrasius five years earlier by condoning the destruction of their synagogue and driving from the city those who refused baptism.[49] In conventional fashion he also repaired a church at Clermont dedicated to St. Antolianus and constructed another in honor of St. Genesius.[50] And he revived some cults that had long-standing connections with Gregory and his family by enlarging the crypt containing the sarcophagus of St. Illidius and by distributing relics of St. Julian.[51] So after 571 Gregory again had two influential supporters in the Auvergne, the bishop of Clermont and St. Julian.

This support was all the more important because Gregory's position in Lyon became suddenly tenuous after Bishop Nicetius died in April 573. Until then Lyon had looked to be another "family see," since Nicetius had become bishop in succession to his uncle Sacerdos, who died probably in

[47] *Hist.* 4.35, 10.6, virtues; *VP* 11.3, Gregory and Avitus together visited Caluppa, a monk at Méallet in the Auvergne, who died in 576 (*Hist.* 5.9); *VM* 3.60, dated to 587/588; *GC* 40, undated; *VP* 12.3, Avitus as the source for a story.

[48] *VP* 2 praef. Since Avitus was still alive when Gregory ceased writing the *Histories*, and since Gregory was in his mid-fifties when he died in 594, Avitus could not have been much, if at all, older than Gregory. It is therefore not obvious when the two studied together. Although Riché (1962) 235, and L. Pietri (1983) 258, suggest that Avitus was one of Gregory's boyhood teachers, most of their contact seems to have occurred after Avitus became a bishop: Gregory explained that he learned by listening to him preach, he consistently described Avitus as a bishop, and he mentioned virtually nothing about Avitus's life before he became a bishop. Avitus was therefore most likely not one of Gregory's boyhood teachers; perhaps he instead replaced Nicetius of Lyon, who died in 573, as Gregory's intellectual mentor. In fact, since Gregory began writing (his extant works, at least) only after he became a bishop himself, it might be possible to guess that Avitus's guidance also influenced Gregory to become a writer; in particular, Avitus might have encouraged Gregory to write his commentary on the Psalms. Fortunatus, *Carm.* 5.5.145, described Gregory in 576 as Avitus's *alumnus*, by which he probably meant "friend" or "protégé," but which is also the same term Gregory used to describe his relationship as a "foster son" of various saints.

[49] *Hist.* 5.11; Gregory also sent a description of this incident to Fortunatus, who versified it as *Carm.* 5.5. Since Jews sometimes provided financial backing for Frankish kings (cf. *Hist.* 6.5), Avitus had to wait for the succession of a weak king. Brennan (1985a), and Goffart (1985), emphasize the place of Jews in Merovingian society but overlook the immediate circumstances of royal instability and Avitus's revenge.

[50] *GM* 64, 66.

[51] *VJ* 48, *VP* 2.4.

552.[52] Nicetius had then had the support of King Childebert, and Gregory of course subsequently praised his virtues as a bishop. But even Gregory also had to concede that Nicetius had a quick temper and readily antagonized others.[53] Nicetius once peremptorily warned Armentarius, the count of Lyon, not to interfere in a judicial case; he became annoyed at the priest who honestly reported back the count's angry reply; and he then criticized people for causing dissension in the city, even though his own sharp tongue was perhaps the primary culprit.[54] Immediately after his funeral people began to censure him openly. One priest claimed that many people had always thought that their bishop had been insensitive; true to form, Nicetius appeared to this priest in a dream and punched him in the throat. Another deacon whom the bishop had once flogged for adultery was only too ready to strip the roof from the cathedral residence where the "most wicked Nicetius" had lived.[55]

Because of this underlying hostility Gregory probably never had a chance to succeed Nicetius, even though his great-uncle may well have preferred him as his successor.[56] Deacons who had served with Nicetius anyway did not have a good record as bishops; at one recent council two had been accused of murder and adultery.[57] So Gregory's participation in the bishop's funeral cortege may have been one of his last public appearances at Lyon.[58] Initially the people at Lyon preferred Aetherius, who later at least promoted the memory of Nicetius; but King Guntramn selected one of his stewards named Priscus, who had long opposed Nicetius and who now set out to dishonor his predecessor. Bishop Priscus gave

[52] *Hist.* 4.36, *VP* 8.3. Coville (1928) 321–22, 331–32, argues that Sacerdos died in September 552; Krusch and Levison (1937–1951) 168nn.5, 9, suggest that Nicetius was not consecrated until January 553; Heinzelmann (1976) 130, discusses the problems over the date.

[53] *Hist.* 4.36. Note also *Vita Nicetii* 5: some thought that Nicetius was *sensu tepidus*, "aloof."

[54] *VP* 8.3. Since both Gregory's mother and her grandmother were named Armentaria, this Count Armentarius may have been a relative as well; if so, this is another example of the sort of family squabbling that was now also apparent at Langres. Nicetius's epitaph claimed, rather amazingly, that he had avoided "petty feuds and the clatter of judicial cases"; it furthermore listed gentleness, patience, and calmness among his virtues: see Le Blant (1856–1865) 1, no. 25.

[55] *Hist.* 4.36, *VP* 8.5.

[56] Note *Vita Nicetii* 17, "qui [= Nicetius] illum [= Aetherium] sibi successorem esse secundo loco praedixit." Nicetius's prediction that Aetherius would be his second successor (or, perhaps, that Aetherius was his second choice as successor) perhaps implies that he hoped Gregory would be his immediate successor.

[57] *Hist.* 5.20, Salonius of Embrun and Sagittarius of Gap, who were eventually defrocked in 579 (*Hist.* 5.27).

[58] Cf. *GC* 60, for the deacons in Nicetius's funeral procession.

Nicetius's cloak to a deacon, who used it as a bedspread and made slippers from its hood. He persecuted and, according to Gregory, even killed many of Nicetius's friends.[59] Gregory survived and in the end had the last laugh on Nicetius's opponents. For once he even spoke candidly of vengeance,[60] and he was only too pleased to record their grim fates: the one deacon fell from the roof, the other burned his feet, Priscus's wife went mad, and Priscus himself suffered from fevers. Gregory also emphasized that, in contrast, miracles of healing were being performed at Nicetius's tomb, where crowds bustled "like happy bees around their hive."[61] But after April 573 his own prominence at Lyon had collapsed, and by the time Bishop Aetherius, the successor to Priscus, finally again revived the cult of St. Nicetius by restoring his bed and by commissioning a new *Vita*,[62] Gregory was long gone.

In the early 570s Clermont, Langres, and Lyon had all acquired new bishops. Because of his family connections and his devotion to local saints' cults Gregory might have anticipated being a candidate for each vacancy. But his extended absence and a decline in the influence of St. Julian's cult had eliminated his opportunity at Clermont, the city of his father's family. Family rivalries and the charges against his brother Peter had ruined his own chances at Langres, the city of his maternal grandfather's family. And the abrasive personality of his mentor Nicetius had prevented him from succeeding at Lyon, the city of his maternal grandmother's family. By the middle of 573 not only was Gregory presumably in disrespect at Lyon, but his prospects for becoming a bishop anywhere were quite bleak. Much of his earlier influence seemed to have dissipated, and his principal remaining supporters were now his mother Armentaria, his new friend Bishop Avitus of Clermont, and his boyhood patron saint, St. Julian. Directly or indirectly, each now helped him become bishop of Tours.

At this point St. Martin too reemerged in Gregory's life and career. During his pilgrimage to Tours in 563 he had certainly met Eufronius, who had been a priest at Tours before becoming bishop in 556. Gregory mentioned only a few anecdotes about his episcopacy. Eufronius had once interceded on behalf of a man taken captive by King Chlothar; he had also had the good sense not to participate in a scheme proposed by Bishop Leontius of Bordeaux against the authority of King Charibert, who later repaid the favor by canceling the public tax at Tours out of respect for St.

---

[59] *Hist.* 4.36, VP 8.5. See Le Blant (1856–1865) 1, no. 26, for Priscus's epitaph that described him as a *regis domesticus*; and *Vita Nicetii* 17, for the politics.

[60] VP 8.5.

[61] VP 8.6, GC 60.

[62] VP 8.8; *Vita Nicetii* 17. This *Vita* was written before King Guntramn died in 592 and was known to Gregory and others (*VP* 8 praef., 12). Priscus was still bishop in 585 (*Hist.* 8.20); Aetherius had replaced him by 589 (*Hist.* 9.41): see Coville (1928) 338–52.

Martin.[63] Outside Tours Eufronius sanctioned the foundation of Radegund's convent at Poitiers and later presided at the arrival of relics of the
True Cross there in 569. And like other bishops he supported various
saints' cults. He repaired two churches after a fire in Tours in 558, built a
new church in honor of St. Vincentius in the city's suburbs, and constructed other churches in various villages throughout the Touraine.[64] He
also had ample opportunity to demonstrate his support for St. Martin,
because in 559 the church of St. Martin in the suburbs was itself burned.
With the financial assistance of King Chlothar, Eufronius had a new tin
roof installed on this church.[65]

To Gregory, however, Eufronius was more than simply the current
guardian of the cult of St. Martin at Tours. In 556 King Chlothar had
preferred to select Cato, the priest from Clermont, as bishop of Tours.
When Cato declined, a delegation from Tours suggested Eufronius instead.
Chlothar agreed when he heard that Eufronius was a grandson of Gre-
gorius of Langres: "this is one of the foremost distinguished families in the
land," he was supposed to have said. Eufronius was therefore a cousin of
Gregory's mother, and his pedigree certainly seemed influential at Tours;
Gregory would later claim that all but five of his episcopal predecessors at
Tours had been related to his family.[66]

Just when Gregory's career at Lyon and his influence at Langres were in
tatters during the summer of 573, Eufronius died. Despite his limited
previous contact with Tours, Gregory now, surprisingly, became the new
bishop there. The astonishment was not simply that Gregory was not very
well known at Tours. Because this was an illustrious metropolitan see,
others had designs on becoming its bishop; a few years later a man would
be elated at the prospect of becoming bishop of Tours after misunderstanding a prophecy about his future. So in 573 the archdeacon Riculf seems to
have expected promotion to the episcopacy and may even have acquired the
support of some of Tours's suffragan bishops.[67] Gregory, however, acquired
the support of King Sigibert and his wife Brunhild, of Radegund, the
former queen now living in her convent in Poitiers, and of Bishop Egidius of
Rheims.[68] Upon the death of King Charibert in 567 his three surviving

[63] *Hist.* 4.26, 9.30, *VM* 1.23. Charibert may have begrudged the cancellation of taxes,
because he once tried to confiscate an estate that belonged to the church of St. Martin (*VM*
1.29).

[64] *Hist.* 9.39–40, 10.31; cf. *GM* 89, *VP* 15.1, *GC* 18.

[65] *Hist.* 4.20, 10.31.

[66] *Hist.* 4.15, 5.49. Other than Eufronius, who certainly was related, and Martin, who
certainly was not, the relationships of Gregory's other episcopal predecessors to his family are
conjectural: see Mathisen (1984).

[67] *Hist.* 5.14, prophecy; 49, Riculf.

[68] The only explicit reference to Gregory's supporters is in Fortunatus, *Carm.* 5.3.13–16, a
poem addressed to the citizens of Tours: "[This is the man] whom the blessed hand of father

brothers, Kings Guntramn, Sigibert, and Chilperic, had agreed upon the division of his kingdom, but they soon began scheming against each other. Tours unfortunately was on the edges of all their kingdoms. Although it had been agreed that Sigibert would inherit Tours, he had first had to expel a son of Chilperic and acquire the support of both St. Martin and Bishop Eufronius.[69] He then tried to stake his claim over his other newly acquired cities and villages by controlling the selection of their bishops. Rheims was the capital city of Sigibert's kingdom, and its Bishop Egidius consecrated a new bishop for Châteaudun, a town north of Tours that Sigibert had also inherited from the former kingdom of Charibert. But Châteaudun was located in the territory of Chartres, a city controlled by Guntramn, and both he and its Bishop Pappolus quickly complained about this challenge to their respective royal and ecclesiastical prerogatives.[70] The consecration of Gregory as bishop of Tours may have been another component of Sigibert's plan to ensure his control over various cities. For by now, even though councils had repeatedly insisted that the people and the local clergy should select new bishops, royal patronage was usually decisive. Gallus had become bishop of Clermont in 525 by being the first to the court of King Theuderic; Cautinus had gone directly to the court of King Theudebald in 551; and Avitus had gone to the court of King Sigibert in 571. In fact, in 573 Avitus may have been the one who advised Gregory to go likewise to the court of Sigibert.[71]

Gregory's consecration in Rheims was another indication of the irregularity of his appointment. At least one Gallic council had already specified that new bishops were to be consecrated in the cities they were to govern, or at least within their own ecclesiastical provinces.[72] Although Gregory never directly mentioned his own consecration, he was certainly aware of this canonical regulation. In 571 Sigibert had insisted that Avitus be consecrated in Metz; Gregory later explicitly noted that this consecration was quite contrary to canonical regulation, although he also argued that it was nevertheless an indication of the king's respect and favor.[73]

Even though Gregory may therefore have thought the same about his

---

Egidius has consecrated to the Lord so that he might revive the people, [and] whom Radegund would love. The triumphant Sigibert as well as Brunhild promotes him for this honor, and by the king's decision this noble and prominent man is here." Note that Fortunatus had close ties with Sigibert's court and with Bishop Egidius, who had once been his host: see Fortunatus, *Carm.* 3.15.29–32, with Meyer (1901) 10–15. Another supporter of Gregory in 573 may have been the royal secretary Siggo (note to *VM* 3.17).

[69] *Hist.* 4.45, *VM* 1.29.
[70] *Hist.* 4.22, 9.20; *Epistola* of Bishop Pappolus, *apud* Council of Paris a.573.
[71] *VP* 6.3, Gallus, with Claude (1963) 31–38, on royal patronage.
[72] Council of Orléans a.541, Can.5.
[73] *Hist.* 4.35.

own consecration, the circumstances of his appointment made his position at Tours uncertain. Gregory himself was apparently not very confident about assuming the episcopacy at Tours, because after his consecration in August he did not go directly to his new see. Instead he first went to the Auvergne to celebrate the festival of St. Julian on August 28; while at Brioude, he pulled some threads from the shroud over the saint's tomb. Then he went to Tours, where he arrived by September, "the second month after my consecration." Immediately he became ill, and was finally cured by drinking a potion mixed with dust from St. Martin's tomb.[74] Even though this miracle clearly demonstrated that St. Martin was now supporting the new bishop, his congregation was more hesitant in accepting him. Shortly after he was healed, Gregory felt compelled to reprove people who had mocked a priest for reading the liturgy in an uncouth manner; indirectly these people may have been criticizing their new bishop, who never failed to acknowledge the awkwardness of his own speech and writing.[75] Gregory also did not attend the council that met at Paris in mid-September to decide the dispute between Kings Sigibert and Guntramn over Châteaudun,[76] perhaps because he was still ill, perhaps too because his own position was too compromised. And to make matters worse, soon after this council Chilperic sent his son Theudebert to devastate the Touraine, which led to more civil wars among all three kings over control of Tours.[77]

Gregory's position at Tours was therefore initially tenuous, and his only open support came, predictably, from his mother, who stayed for a few months "because she loved me"; during her visit she too was healed by St. Martin.[78] Although Gregory was now struggling to reassert his and his family's connection with Tours, he was probably not fully accepted in the community until the next spring. Significantly, monks and St. Martin took the lead in endorsing the new bishop. Sometime after his arrival Gregory had received a visit from Senoch, the head of a small monastic community that included an oratory in which St. Martin was said to have once prayed; Senoch came simply to greet the new bishop with a kiss.[79] In April 574 when some monks asked Gregory to dedicate a church outside the city with his relics of St. Julian, he first secretly brought his reliquary to the

---

[74] VJ 34, VM 2.1.

[75] VM 2.1, 3.

[76] The bishops at this council decided to depose Promotus, the new bishop of Châteaudun, and wrote to both King Sigibert and Bishop Egidius about their decision: see the *Epistolae synodi, apud* Council of Paris a.573. Promotus was finally deposed only after the death of King Chilperic when Guntramn apparently acquired control of Châteaudun (*Hist.* 7.17).

[77] *Hist.* 4.47, 49.

[78] VM 3.10.

[79] VP 15.1–2. Since Gregory later reprimanded Senoch for allowing his holiness to become arrogance, perhaps he also had to assert his control over local monastic discipline. Senoch died in 576 (*Hist.* 5.7).

church of St. Martin, where another man then reported seeing a brilliant
flash of light enter the church. Gregory concluded that this flash represented the power of St. Julian, and he placed his relics on the altar in the
church. The next day he took the relics and led a procession to the new
church; upon his arrival, a possessed man began to shout that St. Martin
had invited St. Julian to this region. The implication of this man's proclamation is clear: if St. Martin had invited St. Julian to Tours, then the
congregation should accept as their bishop this "foster son" of St. Julian.[80]
Lest the people forget, St. Julian continued to display his power by performing other miracles at this church. Gregory also mentioned how during
the night before the dedication of this new church the power of St. Julian
had produced wine out of season without grapes; in a similar fashion
Gregory, who had come to Tours alone but for the patronage of St. Julian,
would now blossom as bishop of Tours with the support of St. Martin.[81]

During the early years of his episcopacy Gregory continued to face numerous problems, among them the ceaseless feuds among the Frankish
kings, the imposition of an unfriendly count, and the lingering hostility of
Riculf that finally led to a plot to remove Gregory from his see. But during
these same years Gregory worked at consolidating his authority at Tours,
in particular by promoting saints' cults. His support specifically for the cult
of St. Martin is too obvious to require further elaboration at this point,
although it is worth emphasizing that he soon began work on the first book
of *The Miracles of the Bishop St. Martin* (VM) that concluded, certainly
deliberately, by demonstrating how the saint had been his patron already
before he became bishop. He also founded other new cults and shrines at
Tours. During the first year of his episcopacy he dedicated an oratory in the
cathedral residence and placed in its altar relics of St. Martin, St. Saturninus, St. Julian, and St. Illidius. Since relics of St. Saturninus, a martyr at
Toulouse, were also found in a shrine near Brioude, this oratory therefore
contained relics of saints of both the Touraine and the Auvergne, and
during the ceremony of dedication at which Gregory presided, both clerics
and distinguished citizens rallied around their new bishop.[82] Gregory was
probably also responsible for the deposit of relics of St. Julian in a village in
the Touraine, and he began to write the *VJ*, which he perhaps originally
intended to climax with stories about how the saint had assisted him in
becoming bishop at Tours. As a result of his activities the cult of St. Julian
became so common at Tours that Gregory could claim that St. Julian and

---

[80] *VJ* 34–35. Cf. Fortunatus, *Carm.* 5.3.11–12: "Julian sends his own foster son to Martin, and he offers to his brother the man who was dear to himself."

[81] *VJ* 36–39.

[82] *VJ* 30, St. Saturninus; *VP* 2.3, *GC* 20, oratory. This oratory also contained relics of St.
Stephen (*GM* 33), perhaps the relics of other saints, and relics connected with the True Cross:
see above, chapter 1, section 1.

St. Martin were now allies.[83] By implication, Gregory and St. Martin were also allies.

Other new cults represented the interests of his own and his family's connections with Lyon and Langres. At Artannes Gregory repaired the roof of an oratory that contained the relics of, among others, St. Martin and St. Julian again, as well as of his great-uncle St. Nicetius of Lyon.[84] In churches at Pernay and elsewhere he placed more relics of St. Nicetius, sometimes in combination with those of St. Julian. In a baptistery at Tours he deposited relics of St. Benignus, the martyr whose cult had been discovered at Dijon years earlier by his great-grandfather and namesake, Bishop Gregorius of Langres.[85] So although as bishop Gregory had become the guardian of the cult of St. Martin, he probably introduced more new saints to the Touraine than had any of his predecessors, and many of those saints were already connected to his family.[86] The success of these new cults' importation can perhaps be measured by reciprocal pilgrimages, since some of Gregory's clerics later visited Nicetius's tomb at Lyon.[87]

Clermont, Langres, Lyon, Tours, and their respective saints' cults: it is important to distinguish these various strands in Gregory's life and ecclesiastical career, if only to stress again how unlikely it had been for him to end up as bishop at Tours. When Artemia, mother of Nicetius of Lyon, had been pregnant, she had known already that her son would be a bishop; Gregory too may have been raised to become a bishop, but it is quite misleading to suggest that he was "predestined" precisely for Tours.[88] And his subsequent promotion of the cult of St. Martin cannot be allowed to obscure either the limitations on his early contact with Tours and St. Martin or his lasting relationships with other saints elsewhere.

Among Gallic aristocrats in general, alliances with various saints' cults now molded marriages and careers, and any analysis of aristocratic and ecclesiastical factions in late Roman and early Merovingian Gaul should include a prosopography of saints and their cults. But as we have seen in the

[83] *VJ* 40, 47.

[84] Fortunatus, *Carm.* 10.5, 10.

[85] *VJ* 50, *VP* 8.8, St. Nicetius; *Hist.* 10.31, St. Benignus.

[86] Despite lingering skepticism, Zelzer (1977), and Prieur (1989) 1:8–12, 119, now argue again that Gregory was the author of the *MA*, a collection of miracle stories about St. Andrew. In this book Gregory mentioned that because he had been born on St. Andrew's festival day on November 30, he considered himself an *alumnus* of the saint (*MA* 38). Relics of St. Andrew had already been placed in a church at Neuvy-le-Roi (*GM* 30), perhaps during the episcopacy of Eufronius: see Vieillard-Troiekouroff (1976) 193, and L. Pietri (1983) 495–96. Although Gregory himself did not mention it, this translation of the relics of St. Andrew from Burgundy to the Touraine neatly previewed his own transfer from his family connections in Burgundy to the episcopacy of Tours.

[87] *VP* 8.6.

[88] As does L. Pietri (1983) 247. See *VP* 8.1, for Artemia's prediction.

case of Gregory, these cults also offered aristocrats, both secular and ecclesiastical, a means to resolve some of their conflicting ambitions; for if saints
were prepared to accept each other, then their supporters should do likewise. Even as loyalties to saints' cults reinforced divisive alliances within
the Gallic aristocracy, so the beliefs and rituals associated with those cults
also offered a means of harmony and cooperation. As far as Gregory was
concerned, his episcopacy should have produced a consensus at Tours that
mimicked the rhythmic harmony among his various patron saints who
were, as he put it, dancing together in heaven. In addition to resolving these
feuds between aristocratic peers, allegiances to saints' cults allowed
bishops to establish links with their clergy and their congregations. As
another preacher noted, each festival of St. Martin was a "day on which the
holy Catholic church . . . dances in manifold joy as it celebrates the festival
of someone whom it knows . . . to be a partner among the citizens of
heaven."[89] Dancing with saints: Gregory may initially have been suspect as
bishop at Tours, but eventually the public ceremonies associated with the
cult of St. Martin permitted him and the local population to celebrate
together on festival days.

2. Being a Bishop

Once Gregory became bishop at Tours, the cult of St. Martin became the
focus of his life and his career; the support of St. Julian and other saints may
have assisted his initial acceptance at Tours, but as bishop he soon began to
identify himself with the city's patron saint. His collection of stories about
the miracles of St. Martin is therefore also an implicit chronicle of his own
standing at Tours and more widely in Gaul, and any discussion of his
episcopacy must also consider the reputation of the cult of St. Martin.

During the first years of his episcopacy Gregory faced stiff challenges to
his authority. One challenge came from the Frankish kings. Shortly after
Gregory had become bishop, King Chilperic again seized control of Tours;
Sigibert finally regained control and held the city until his assassination in
late 575; Sigibert's son Childebert was then proclaimed king, but since he
was a young boy, his uncle Chilperic yet again seized Tours.[90] A second
challenge came from some powerful men who took sanctuary in the church
of St. Martin. In 575 Guntramn Boso, a duke of King Sigibert, had taken
refuge in the church of St. Martin after he killed one of King Chilperic's
sons. Merovech soon joined him because his marriage to Brunhild, his
uncle Sigibert's widow, made his father Chilperic suspicious. "The Touraine therefore suffered great disasters," Gregory wrote, and although

---

[89] *VJ* 50, "in caelo trepudiat"; *Sermo* 1.
[90] *Hist.* 4.47, 49, 51; 5.4, 48, *VM* 2.27.

much of this distress was due to the armies that King Chilperic sent to capture both Guntramn Boso and Merovech, the two refugees were not above scheming against each other either before they left together in 577. Gregory seemed to be helpless, because Chilperic and these other men not only threatened him and his diocese, they also plundered the possessions of St. Martin.[91]

Eventually Gregory rose to the occasion. In 577 he attended a council at Paris that King Chilperic convened to hear an accusation of disloyalty against Praetextatus, the bishop of Rouen who had married Merovech and Brunhild. While the other bishops remained timidly silent, Gregory spoke out. As a historian he could draw upon his research about late Roman Gaul to remind them of Abbot Avitus, who had once warned an earlier Frankish king against taking revenge; and as the guardian of the cult of St. Martin he drew upon his familiarity with the writings of Sulpicius Severus to tell these other bishops about the emperor Magnus Maximus, who had once suffered misfortune after bullying Martin. When Chilperic then threatened to mobilize the people of Tours against their bishop, Gregory replied that the city was more likely to demonstrate against the king and pointedly reminded him of the impending judgment of God. And when Chilperic finally passed judgment on Praetextatus, Gregory insisted that the king strictly follow canonical regulations.[92] Gregory's boldness at this council seems to have enhanced both his own standing and his patron saint's reputation with the king and with other bishops. Although Chilperic barricaded the church of St. Martin against Merovech one last time, tried to penalize the dependents of the cathedral and the church of St. Martin for not serving in his army in 578, and tried to raise taxes in 579, he sent no more soldiers to the Touraine.[93] Gregory meanwhile recorded more miracles than usual at shrines of St. Martin for 577; in the same year the bishop of Avranches requested relics of St. Martin; and soon the bishop of Poitiers attended a festival of St. Martin. During 577 Gregory seems to have come into his own and the cult of St. Martin expanded its influence; appropriately enough, the year even ended with a booming roll of thunder.[94]

Gregory needed this additional support because the most immediate challenge to his authority during these early years of his episcopacy came from Leudast, who served as count of Tours first under King Charibert, then briefly under King Chilperic shortly after Gregory became bishop, and finally again under King Chilperic from 576. Gregory loathed the man, for several reasons. Their backgrounds and earlier careers contrasted markedly. Gregory had distinguished aristocratic connections and had

[91] *Hist.* 4.48, 50; 5.2–4, 13–14, *VM* 2.17, 27; quotation from *Hist.* 5.14.
[92] *Hist.* 5.18; cf. *Hist.* 3.6, *GC* 97, for Abbot Avitus.
[93] *Hist.* 5.18, 26, 28, 34.
[94] *Hist.* 5.23, thunder; *VM* 2.36, 44.

pursued a career in the church, while Leudast had worked his way up through the royal household; Gregory prided himself on having become the *alumnus*, the "foster son" of various saints, while Leudast had shamelessly advanced his early career by becoming the *alumnus* (by which Gregory here perhaps meant "lackey") merely of King Charibert's wife.[95] Leudast's behavior also disturbed Gregory. As count he may have repeatedly sworn his respect for the bishop, but he still ignored the sanctuary of the church of St. Martin by trying to kill Merovech, he once intimidated Gregory by wearing armor and carrying weapons in the cathedral residence, and he abused both citizens and clerics.[96] Late in 579 Chilperic finally replaced him as count. Gregory and his congregation were so relieved that large crowds attended the festival of St. Martin in November. The healings of a crippled man and a blind man during this festival were public affirmations that the saint's power had finally been effective after all.[97]

But Leudast's dismissal in fact initiated a most trying year for Gregory. For Leudast had apparently already been plotting against Gregory with two clerics at Tours, a priest named Riculf who had been archdeacon under Bishop Eufronius, and a subdeacon also named Riculf. As subsequently revealed by the subdeacon Riculf under torture, their scheme had many objectives: Fredegund, Chilperic's queen, was to be exiled, her sons and Chilperic were to be killed, Chlodovech was to inherit his father Chilperic's kingdom, Leudast was to become a duke, the priest Riculf was to become bishop of Tours, and the subdeacon Riculf was to become archdeacon. Upon his dismissal Leudast therefore immediately accused Gregory of wanting to transfer Tours to the control of King Childebert, son of Sigibert, and of criticizing Fredegund for committing adultery with Bishop Bertramn of Bordeaux; if true, these accusations might have compelled Chilperic to exile both Gregory and Fredegund. At first the king simply imprisoned Leudast, who then identified the subdeacon Riculf as the source for Gregory's remarks. Now the plot became more hostile. The priest Riculf was arrogant enough to curse Gregory on Good Friday, and on Easter Saturday Leudast had Gregory's friend Galienus and his archdeacon Plato arrested as material witnesses. Soon Duke Berulf and the new count Eunomius spread a rumor that King Guntramn intended to seize Tours, which allowed them to post guards in the city and effectively put Gregory under arrest; they also advised the bishop to flee to Clermont. Gregory was now facing such a major threat to his episcopal authority that even a besotted relic-monger who happened to wander into Tours during

---

[95] *Hist.* 5.48.
[96] *Hist.* 5.14, 48, VM 2.58.
[97] *Hist.* 5.47, VM 2.49–50, and note to 2.58.

that spring of 580 could threaten him with the vengeance of King Chilperic.[98]

In late summer or early autumn[99] Chilperic convened a council of bishops to his estate at Berny near Soissons. Gregory had meanwhile not been inactive. Already in late spring he had visited Paris where he celebrated a service in a church dedicated to St. Julian, met with Bishop Ragnemod, who had been a close supporter of Chilperic in 577, and dined with other bishops.[100] So by the time of this hearing before Chilperic, Gregory was confident enough to deny the accusation about Fredegund directly to Bishop Bertramn. His earlier lobbying had been successful. During the hearing people demonstrated in his favor; one of Chilperic's daughters fasted on his behalf; the other bishops turned against Leudast; and the subdeacon Riculf was tortured and condemned to death, until Gregory acquired a pardon for him.[101] During this hearing Gregory's friend Fortunatus also delivered a verse panegyric in honor of the king. Although most of his panegyric praised Chilperic's military victories and literary abilities, Fortunatus also mentioned the king's moderation in exercising justice; in this context, his comment was perhaps less a recognition of the king's past accomplishments than a reminder of how the king ought to behave now.[102] Gregory's troubles were not quite over, however, because upon his return to Tours he discovered that the priest Riculf was already acting like the bishop and had even contemptuously moved into the cathedral residence. But by now Gregory also had much support at Tours. All the citizens came to greet him upon his arrival, and with the approval of his suffragan bishops he banished the priest Riculf to a monastery.[103]

During the first years of his episcopacy Gregory had not been firmly established or respected at Tours. Other powerful men, including kings, had bullied him, and at least some of his subordinate clerics at Tours continued to resent him as an interloper from Clermont; when, for instance, Riculf had attempted to usurp the episcopacy, he also claimed that he had "cleansed" the city of this family from the Auvergne.[104] It is therefore most important that modern historians not overestimate the epis-

---

[98] *Hist.* 9.6.

[99] Twenty days after this council two of Chilperic's sons died of dysentery (*Hist.* 5.50). This plague first appeared in August (*Hist.* 5.34); after his sons' deaths Chilperic went to another estate in October (*Hist.* 5.39).

[100] *Hist.* 5.18, 9.6.

[101] Gregory also successfully interceded with Fredegund on behalf of a former magistrate (*Hist.* 5.39).

[102] Fortunatus, *Carm.* 9.1.85–90, with the interpretation of George (1989).

[103] *Hist.* 5.49.

[104] *Hist.* 5.49.

copal authority of Gregory at Tours (or of other bishops elsewhere in Gaul), and that they recognize the difficult and ongoing process whereby bishops first established and then constantly struggled to maintain their authority. Alliances with saints' cults had assisted Gregory in gradually consolidating his position at Tours; he now used the same strategy in improving his standing with Frankish kings. Just as after his outspokenness at the Council of Paris in 577 other bishops had wanted to be associated with the cult of his patron saint, so Gregory himself was flexible (and prudent) enough to add new saints to his own network of supporters. King Chilperic, for instance, had begun to support the new royal cult of St. Medard whose church at Soissons his father Chlothar and his brother Sigibert had constructed. So when Gregory was scheduled to appear before Chilperic in 580, he made a point of first going to observe vigils in this church at Soissons—and St. Martin made a point of performing a miracle together with St. Medard![105] As a result, not only could Gregory clear himself of the accusations at this hearing, he was also able to warn Chilperic of the stupidity of his doctrinal pronouncements about the Persons of the Trinity.[106] Eventually Gregory even acquired the staff of St. Medard, which of course gave him another prop in his uneasy relationship with Chilperic.[107]

The events of 580 had redefined Gregory's standing as bishop, both at Tours and generally in central Gaul. The priest Riculf eventually took refuge with Bishop Felix of Nantes, Leudast was on the run, and King Chilperic was too preoccupied with the deaths of two of his sons in a plague, the murder of another son, and his own interest in hunting.[108] Many of Gregory's lingering challenges at Tours had now been resolved. It was probably not a coincidence that he ended both *Hist.* 5 and *VM* 2 with the events of 580 and in particular with stories about Leudast. As he recorded the miracles of St. Martin for this pivotal but still trying year, it is also no surprise that he came down with a series of throbbing headaches. As usual, however, he was healed at the tomb of St. Martin, his patron saint who had also, Gregory pointedly now noted, once survived "secret onslaughts and public insults."[109]

[105] *Hist.* 5.49; and above, chapter 1, section 1.

[106] *Hist.* 5.44. Their theological confrontation probably took place at this hearing. Chilperic had perhaps been influenced in formulating his new theology after talking with Agila, an envoy from the Arian king Leuvigild of Spain who also stopped in Tours and argued with Gregory over theology (*Hist.* 5.43): see below, chapter 3, section 3. Gregory mentioned that Bishop Salvius of Albi also opposed Chilperic's theology; and Salvius attended this hearing (*Hist.* 5.44, 50).

[107] *GC* 93.

[108] Note that Fredegund engineered the deaths of both Chlodovech and Leudast, in part perhaps because of their involvement in this plot (*Hist.* 5.39, 6.32).

[109] *VM* 2.60, and note to 2.58.

Even though Gregory had perhaps been one of those impressed by Chilperic's "wisdom and restraint" during the hearing of 580,[110] his subsequent relationship with the king remained uncomfortable. Initially they were more cordial. Since Chilperic still retained control over Tours, Gregory soon visited him at his estate at Nogent, outside Paris, where the king proudly displayed the gold coins he had received from the Byzantine emperor. After the king and the bishop together argued in support of Christian doctrines against a Jewish financier, Gregory even offered Chilperic a blessing. Later in 581 Gregory was able to use his new influence with Chilperic when thieves who had robbed the church of St. Martin were brought before the king. In conscious imitation of St. Martin, who had occasionally appealed to emperors, Gregory petitioned Chilperic by letter and acquired a pardon for the thieves. Gregory and Chilperic now seem to have begrudgingly realized that both would retain influence at Tours.[111]

But Gregory was now also caught up in further diplomatic intrigues over which he had no control. The young King Childebert had gradually come under the influence of advisers who included Bishop Egidius of Rheims. Egidius led the delegations of notables who represented Childebert in concluding an alliance with Chilperic in 581 and in renewing it in 583. Gregory could have been pleased with this alliance, since it united the king who controlled Tours with the son of the king who had promoted him as bishop. Gregory was furthermore indebted to Egidius, who had consecrated him as bishop; and the duke who staked Childebert's claim to Marseille was Gundulf, another of Gregory's great-uncles.[112] But the foe of this alliance was to be King Guntramn, who already in 577 had wanted to adopt his nephew Childebert and who also had ties with Gregory's family, in particular at Lyon. Gregory, and Tours, were now caught in the middle. In their campaigns against Guntramn the dukes of Chilperic also devastated parts of the Touraine. When Gregory went to Rheims to visit Egidius, he was suspicious and uneasy enough to make a point of carrying relics of St. Martin. The alliance between Chilperic and Childebert finally collapsed in 583 when Childebert's soldiers rioted and claimed that Egidius was "selling" the kingdom.[113] Gregory may well have approved; he had already noted how the bishop of Périgueux had once complained

---

[110] *Hist.* 5.49.

[111] *Hist.* 6.3–5, 10. Buchner (1955) XI, and Reydellet (1977) 187–88, prefer to date the expansion of Gregory's political role from Chilperic's death in 584, but only by ignoring Gregory's earlier influence with the king after 580.

[112] *Hist.* 6.3, 31, delegations; 6.11, 26, Gundulf. Gundulf's family seems to have remained influential into the Carolingian period in the Frankish kingdom of Austrasia, in particular around Metz: see K. F. Werner (1978) 153–55.

[113] *Hist.* 6.12, 31; *VM* 3.17, visit to Rheims.

that having control over his city transferred from Guntramn to Chilperic was equivalent to falling from Paradise into Hell. In 584 Childebert replaced his infernal alliance with his uncle Chilperic by making peace with his uncle Guntramn.[114]

One of Gregory's most insistent complaints about the Frankish kings was their endless civil wars, and he seems to have held Chilperic responsible for most of them. Upon Chilperic's assassination later in 584 he was exceptionally harsh in his assessment of the king for "singing like Nero" as he burned the countryside. Gregory also resented Chilperic for mocking various bishops as silly, stupid, or arrogant;[115] even though he certainly knew bishops who fit those descriptions, with his standing now as a leading bishop in central Gaul he preferred to defend the honor of the church against a king who had showed no respect. King Guntramn, in contrast, enhanced his reputation with Gregory by demonstrating more respect for the church. After his brother's death Guntramn could dominate his two nephews, the teenage Childebert and the infant Chlothar II, son of Chilperic and Fredegund. Although the people of Tours wished to belong again to the kingdom of Childebert, Guntramn nevertheless initially forced the city to submit to himself. Gregory was perhaps not displeased, because Guntramn had shared his dislike for Chilperic; in fact, Guntramn had once had a vision in which he had seen Chilperic being boiled alive![116] At first, however, their relationship too was tentative. One problem was caused, again, by the advisers of King Childebert, among them still Bishop Egidius of Rheims; at one negotiating session Guntramn accused Egidius of deceit and had all the envoys showered with horse manure. Later in 585 when Guntramn reasserted his adoption of Childebert and restored Tours to his control, he also warned his nephew against accepting the advice of Egidius.[117] A second problem was caused by other fugitives at Tours. After Fredegund announced that the chamberlain Eberulf had been responsible for the death of her husband Chilperic, he fled to the church of St. Martin. Gregory now felt compelled to protect him, even though Eberulf showed no regard for the church and its clergy and, more important, even though Guntramn wanted to take revenge on him for his brother's death. Early in 585 when Gregory was out of town, the man whom Guntramn sent to apprehend Eberulf caused a brawl by killing him within the courtyard of the church. More fugitives replaced him when in the spring several supporters of the pretender Gundovald sought refuge at the church of St. Martin to escape Guntramn's vengeance.[118]

[114] *Hist.* 6.22, 33, 41.
[115] *Hist.* 6.46.
[116] *Hist.* 7.12, 8.6.
[117] *Hist.* 7.14, 33.
[118] *Hist.* 7.21–22, 29, 37–39, 43; 8.6.

Gregory's initial relationship with Guntramn seemed to be poisoned by the same sort of uncontrollable intrigues and royal feuds that had weakened his relationship with Chilperic. But Gregory was now in a much stronger position, not least because the kings seemed to respect the cult of St. Martin. Guntramn had at least warned his envoy not to outrage the church of St. Martin while seizing Eberulf. In early July 585 Gregory visited and dined with Guntramn at Orléans. The next morning Guntramn paid a courtesy call at Gregory's lodgings, where he received bread consecrated to St. Martin. Gregory also felt bold enough to intercede on behalf of two men who had supported Gundovald against Guntramn, and he could even smile when he identified the *dominus*, the lord who had sponsored him on this appeal, as St. Martin.[119] The influence of St. Martin, in combination with Gregory's seniority as bishop and his extensive contacts, now allowed him to maneuver among the various kings. Shortly after this visit he sent relics of St. Martin to Soissons, the capital city of Chilperic's old kingdom; and later in 585 he visited King Childebert at Coblenz, where he even acted as the king's spokesman in responding to envoys from Guntramn. When the relics of St. Martin that Gregory was carrying prevented an overcrowded boat from sinking, it was obvious that the power of his patron saint also traveled with him.[120] At some point Childebert may even have constructed a church dedicated to St. Martin in northeastern Gaul.[121]

In November 587 Guntramn and Childebert ratified the allocation of various disputed cities, and early in 588 Gregory again went to visit Childebert at Metz.[122] On this journey he stopped at Rheims, perhaps for a courtesy call on his former patron, Bishop Egidius, who was about to face an accusation of treason. Egidius's intrigues were now finally catching up with him. Although this time Childebert forgave him, two years later the king convened a council of bishops to hear additional charges of treason. When Egidius this time finally confessed that he had been plotting against

---

[119] *Hist.* 8.1–6.

[120] *Hist.* 8.13–14, *VM* 3.47. Elsewhere Gregory mentioned that he carried a gold cross containing relics of the Virgin Mary, St. Martin, and other saints (*GM* 10). Gregory did not attend the council at Mâcon convened by Guntramn in October 585 (*Hist.* 8.20), nor probably Childebert's simultaneous consultation with the notables of his kingdom (*Hist.* 8.21): see Weidemann (1982) 1:216.

[121] See above, chapter 1, section 1.

[122] Gregory did not attend the negotiations between Childebert and Guntramn at Andelot in 587 (*Hist.* 9.11, 20). Meyer (1901) 22, 45–46, Koebner (1915) 108–9, and Brennan (1985) 75–76, suggest that Fortunatus accompanied Gregory to Metz in 588. Fortunatus stayed for a boat trip on the Moselle and Rhine (note to *VM* 4.29), and then celebrated the festival of St. Martin with Childebert and Brunhild: see Fortunatus, *Carm.* 10.7. Gregory was apparently back in Tours on July 4 (*VM* 4.4).

the king, the council defrocked him and sent him into exile.[123] Gregory, however, had fortunately been able gradually to disentangle himself from Egidius's schemes, probably because first Chilperic's and then Guntramn's control over Tours had kept him on the fringes of Childebert's court. So in 588, not only did Gregory perhaps help his former patron acquire a pardon, he now also seems to have replaced him as one of Childebert's chief episcopal advisers, since the king immediately sent Gregory as an envoy to Guntramn. And in 590 Gregory was one of the bishops selected by Childebert to meet with bishops selected by Guntramn and resolve the scandal in Radegund's convent at Poitiers.[124]

Gregory had finally emerged as a respected influence in royal and ecclesiastical politics. Previously the central location of Tours had led to destruction and looting because of the endless intrigues among the kings over its control; but after the death of King Chilperic its bishop became an excellent choice as mediator between Childebert, who claimed Tours and whose father Sigibert and mother Brunhild had promoted Gregory as bishop, and Guntramn, who was now the dominant king and whose kingdom included various cities such as Lyon, Chalon-sur-Saône, and Langres with which Gregory's family had long-standing connections.[125] In fact, on the embassy in 588 Gregory had met Guntramn at Chalon-sur-Saône, where his elderly mother was (most likely) now living on her family's lands.[126] Gregory also seems to have become virtually a chaplain for some of the women associated with the Merovingian dynasty; in 587, for instance, he presided at the funeral of Radegund, and in 589 Ingoberg, the elderly widow of King Charibert, summoned him to help put her affairs in order before her death.[127] In contrast, Gregory remained relatively isolated from the court and supporters of Chlothar II, the young son of Fredegund and Chilperic.[128] Fredegund was the one Merovingian queen whom he always distrusted; and although in 590 in a panic over her son's illness she

[123] *Hist.* 9.13–14, 19, and note to *VM* 4.22.

[124] *Hist.* 9.20, 10.15.

[125] Note that Nicetius, the husband of Gregory's niece (*Hist.* 5.14, *VM* 4.36), may have served both Childebert and Guntramn, if he is to be identified with the Nicetius who in 585 participated in one of Guntramn's campaigns, and whom Childebert appointed as count of Clermont, duke of Clermont, Rodez, and Uzès, and finally in 587 governor of Marseille and other cities in Provence (*Hist.* 8.18, 30, 43; 9.22): see Buchner (1933) 95–96, Selle-Hosbach (1974) 138–40, and Weidemann (1982) 1:52.

[126] *VM* 3.60.

[127] *GC* 104, Radegund; *Hist.* 9.26, Ingoberg.

[128] In 591 King Guntramn went with some bishops from his kingdom to a village outside Paris to celebrate the baptism of Chlothar II. One of those bishops was Syagrius of Autun (*Hist.* 10.28); and since Gregory mentioned that Syagrius had "recently" told him a story "in the presence of King Guntramn" (*VP* 8.10), perhaps Krusch (1951) XVI, is correct in suggesting that Gregory also attended this baptism; Weidemann (1982) 1:219 is more skeptical.

may have promised gifts to the church of St. Martin, during the same year a
former magistrate of Chilperic raided the Touraine in search of plunder.[129]
But because both Guntramn and Childebert increasingly encroached on
Chilperic's former possessions, and because Gregory had ready access to
both of their courts, he was now remarkably well-informed about events
throughout much of Frankish Gaul. Gregory furthermore began to expand
his contacts outside Gaul and even sent one of his deacons to Rome to
collect relics of its local saints.[130] For modern historians Gregory's enhanced personal influence throughout Merovingian Gaul and even beyond
during this period has significant implications, because fully 40 percent of
his *Histories*, which began with Adam and Eve in Paradise, was in fact
devoted to the decade after 584. Although in the first part of his *Histories*
Gregory had been most familiar with the regions and cities specifically
associated with his family's influence, for this last decade he could also rely
on his connections at royal courts and with royal magistrates to provide
more extensive coverage.

In his own city too his position was considerably stronger. After 585
there were no more attempts to steal any of the possessions of St. Martin;[131] Gregory likewise faced few challengers at Tours. During the early
years of his episcopacy Count Leudast had intimidated him; now Gregory
worked with, and sometimes dominated, the counts of Tours and other
royal magistrates. In 585 a bloody feud terrorized the city. After a hearing
before local citizens was unsuccessful in stopping it, Gregory and the count
together tried to mediate.[132] In the next year Pelagius, the supervisor of the
royal herds, began to seize the possessions of various churches and churchmen. At first Gregory excommunicated him for stealing some sea urchins,
but then readmitted him after Pelagius swore his innocence in a church

---

[129] *Hist.* 10.5, 11.

[130] *VP* 8.6, a story about "my deacon" Agiulf, who was returning from Rome where he
claimed he had gone because of "the devotion of my bishop" (i.e., Gregory), in order to "visit
the tombs of Eastern martyrs" (a telling Gallic perspective on the saints of Rome, by the way).
Agiulf is probably to be identified with "my deacon" who brought back to Gregory relics that
Pope Pelagius had given him (*GM* 82). He is probably also to be identified with "my deacon"
who received relics from the future pope Gregory I and then remained in Rome for his
consecration (*Hist.* 10.1). Since Pelagius died in early February 590 and Gregory I was not
consecrated until early September, Agiulf probably left Tours in 589 and did not return until
late in 590. O. Chadwick (1948) argues that Gregory's deacon was instead in Rome earlier
during the 580s; but see Krusch (1951) xxn.3, and Buchner (1955) xxvn.1.

[131] Cf. *Hist.* 7.21.

[132] *Hist.* 7.47. If Guntramn still controlled Tours, then this count was perhaps Willachar,
the count of Orléans whom Guntramn appointed also as count of Tours after Chilperic's
assassination (*Hist.* 7.13). If the mediation took place after Guntramn transferred Tours to
Childebert in 585, then this count was perhaps Gregory's friend Galienus (notes to *VM* 4.6,
35). Three years later when these same families were feuding again, King Childebert and
Queen Brunhild intervened directly (*Hist.* 9.19).

dedicated to the Virgin Mary. When Pelagius next attempted to seize a meadow belonging to a convent, he died from a fever. Gregory had been vindicated: the Virgin Mary had exposed the man's perjury, St. Martin had rejected the sarcophagus that Pelagius had prepared for himself and that was now found broken in pieces, and Gregory even had his culinary delicacies returned.[133] In 589 when King Childebert sent Florentianus, the mayor of the royal household, and Romulf, count of the palace, to reassess taxes at Tours, Gregory first lectured them on the immunities previously granted to the city and then sent envoys to the king, who again exempted Tours.[134] By then the count of Tours was Galienus, his friend who had been arrested as Gregory's supporter in 580. Two years later Gregory was able to intercede successfully with the count on behalf of an innocent prisoner.[135] Gregory's authority and confidence at Tours had certainly increased considerably. Years earlier in 580 even a drunken relic-monger had threatened him with the wrath of King Chilperic; now an itinerant charlatan no longer posed a threat. In 587 a impostor named Desiderius wandered into Tours, described himself as the equal of the apostles Peter and Paul, and claimed to heal people with his painfully tortuous techniques. He was temporarily popular, but only because Gregory was absent; upon his return, Gregory had him thrown out of the city.[136]

During the 580s Gregory also compiled, or completed, his large books of miracle stories about the martyrs and confessors of Gaul, the smaller anthology of miracle stories about St. Julian, and some of the *Vitae* eventually included in his collection of biographies.[137] Although he had certainly been hearing about and collecting these stories over the previous years, now he finally had the time and incentive to write these works. And since all of these books included personal recollections as well as stories about relatives and friends, perhaps too only now did Gregory feel confident enough to record his memories and publicize the wide-ranging influence of his family and acquaintances. His political and ecclesiastical prominence, although earned only gradually, therefore had an immediate impact on his own literary plans and their fulfillment.

His collection of miracle stories about St. Martin, however, seems to

---

[133] *Hist.* 8.40.

[134] *Hist.* 9.30, VM 4.6.

[135] VM 4.35.

[136] *Hist.* 9.6.

[137] Although Gregory often revised his works, he composed much of the VJ during the early 580s, the GM between 585 and 588, and much of the GC during the winter and spring of 587–588 : see Monod (1872) 43–45, and James (1991) XII, for the VP; Van Dam (1988a) 4–5, and (1988b) 4–5, for the GM and GC; and the introductions to the translations of the VJ and VM, below.

have been an ongoing project throughout his episcopacy, and it is most important always to recognize that Gregory's influence now, as from the beginning of his episcopacy, was directly correlated to the prominence, and the resources, of the cult of St. Martin. Each supported the other.[138] The assets of the cathedral had allowed Gregory to resolve the feud at Tours by using its wealth to pay the composition fees; St. Martin had not allowed Pelagius to be buried in his church at Candes; and Childebert's magistrates had been impressed by the saint's miracles at Tours, and the king himself had demonstrated due respect for the saint. In return, Gregory protected St. Martin's reputation and enhanced his cult. In the most telling example, when the imposter Desiderius had tried to establish his reputation at Tours by claiming that he was more powerful than St. Martin, Gregory had him classified as a magician and expelled. Gregory also repaired the walls of the church of St. Martin, and by 589/590 he finished rebuilding the cathedral that had been burned some thirty years earlier. As Fortunatus neatly put it, the rededication of the cathedral promoted both the cult of St. Martin and Gregory's own reputation.[139]

Outside Tours too, as we have seen, Gregory had extended his influence during this period, and his many stories about the miracles of St. Martin in various cities were therefore also indications of the extent of his own prominence. At Rheims, for instance, the demolition of a prison by the saint's power in 591 was another sign that Gregory's influence too had survived there, as well as at the court of King Childebert, even after the disgrace of Bishop Egidius.[140] Often as Gregory traveled he asked his hosts whether St. Martin had demonstrated his power in their regions; indirectly he was also inquiring about his own standing in these cities. Just as St. Martin's reputation was spread throughout Gaul, so too now was Gregory's.[141] In 592 they demonstrated their influence in tandem again. After the death of King Guntramn, Gregory went to Orléans to meet King Childebert; and while he was there, his relics of St. Martin healed two court attendants.[142]

After Guntramn's death Queen Brunhild dominated Merovingian politics for the next two decades; but Gregory's own death mercifully spared him

---

[138] The suggestion of Brown (1982) 240 that the "secure holiness" of relics supported the "fragile holiness" of bishops is therefore misleading, since the popularity of saints' cults was equally fragile.

[139] *Hist.* 10.31; Fortunatus, *Carm.* 10.6.12, "et rediit priscus cultus honorque suus."

[140] *VM* 4.26.

[141] *Hist.* 8.16, *VM* 3.51, 4.30–31, requests; 3.38, reputation.

[142] *VM* 4.37.

from becoming involved in her schemes.[143] Largely because of these intrigues of Brunhild as well as those of Fredegund that Gregory himself had
described, formidable royal mothers have always been favorite subjects for
modern historians of Frankish Gaul. The mothers of Gallic churchmen
deserve equal emphasis. Gregory mentioned several influential mothers,
among them some in his own family, such as Artemia, mother of Nicetius of
Lyon. Another was his own mother Armentaria, whom Fortunatus even
compared to the mother of the Maccabees.[144] Armentaria was still alive
when her son was about fifty, and Gregory remained uncommonly devoted
to her; he always remembered, for instance, how she had worried about her
"sweet son" when as a young boy he had become ill.[145] His mother also
helped him make the transition to his episcopacy by staying with him at
Tours during the first months, and then by encouraging him to overcome
his own misgivings about his literary abilities in order to record the miracles of St. Martin.[146] In one of these miracle stories he described how an
infant, after being healed at a shrine dedicated to St. Martin, had then been
able again to drink his mother's milk.[147] This connection between the
saint's compassion for his dependents and a mother's love for her child
provided a paradigm for Gregory's relationship too, since his devotion to
St. Martin was always associated with the loving encouragement of his
mother. Because his mother's side of his family had introduced him to St.
Martin, Gregory was similar to a later canon at Tours who had "imbibed a
warm and lasting love [for St. Martin] with his mother's milk."[148]

For Gregory St. Martin was therefore more than simply a powerful
patron saint who supported his authority at Tours and helped him to
survive the intrigues of kings and great aristocrats. Their bonding involved
the sort of genuine affection that had characterized the relationship between Jesus Christ and his "special disciple" John, "whom he loved more
than the other apostles."[149] This relationship provided Gregory with a

---

[143] The latest dated event Gregory mentioned occurred in July 593 (VM 4.45). Although he
also provided a precise date for the completion of the Histories (Hist. 10.31), he unfortunately
referred to four years that do not synchronize: the twenty-first year after his consecration as
bishop, i.e., 593–594; the fifth year of the episcopacy of Pope Gregory I, i.e., 594–595; the
thirty-first year of the reign of Guntramn, i.e., 591–592; and the nineteenth year of the reign of
Childebert, i.e., 593–594. Krusch (1885) 453 suggested that Gregory died in November 593;
Monod (1872) 38, Krusch (1951) XVIII–XIX, and Weidemann (1982) 1:220, argue that he
died in 594. See Nelson (1978), on Brunhild's intrigues, and Stafford (1983), on early medieval queens.
[144] Fortunatus, Carm. 10.15.10: Gregory was "her glory, her reward, and her honor."
[145] VP 2.2.
[146] VM 1 praef.
[147] VM 3.51.
[148] Sitwell (1958) 85.
[149] GM 29.

model for his ties with members of his own congregation and with the pilgrims who visited Tours. So another "special foster son" of St. Martin, Gregory's friend Abbot Aredius of Limoges, was so noted for his kindness, humility, and love that when he stroked a paralyzed woman, he had felt "the hand of the blessed Martin."[150] Kings and aristocrats were often fierce and uncompromising with their dependents, but saints provided churchmen with an alternative model of familial compassion and tenderness.

Many of Gregory's miracle stories involved parents and their ill children who were healed at the shrine of St. Martin. Their anguish and then their joy transcend the centuries, and Gregory himself was most candid in expressing his own emotions when he thought of these ill children. He wept as he recorded the symptoms of a plague that had killed children; but he was overjoyed when some children once stopped him after mass to describe their own cures at the church of St. Martin.[151] Gregory too was often ill, and he in fact began and ended each of the books about the miracles that St. Martin performed during his episcopacy with stories about himself; he too had once felt the hand of St. Martin as it cleared his sore throat.[152] These healings were of course demonstrations of the saint's lasting support for his bishop; they were also indications of his lasting love. Gregory always remembered how, after his father's early death, his uncle Gallus and his great-uncle Nicetius had openly demonstrated their affection for him when he had been ill; now, even though a bishop, in the helplessness of his illnesses he could still rely with confidence upon the love of St. Martin, in whom he had found another, but this time also the final, substitute for his father.

---

[150] *VM* 3.24, 4.6.
[151] *Hist.* 5.34, *VM* 4.18.
[152] *VM* 3.1.

CHAPTER THREE

Bodily Miracles

ANCIENT SOCIETY was unrelentingly brutal and precarious, and the world of Gregory of Tours was no exception. As in modern underdeveloped countries most people had to cope with squalor, misery, and grinding poverty. Senseless violence and cruelty were common; one man, for instance, kept his oath not to separate two of his servants who had fallen in love by having them buried alive together.[1] Intemperate weather could easily disrupt agrarian production. An enormous swarm of locusts, a late frost, a heavy hailstorm, an extended drought—any of these catastrophes readily caused local famines that demoted people to the level of animals, forced to eat stalks and grass.[2] Harsh living conditions, inadequate nutrition, and the consequent sicknesses and disabilities also reduced people to a subhuman existence. One mute man could only imitate "the lowing of an animal"; another who communicated by clicking boards together was hired as a scarecrow.[3]

Most of these problems were beyond solution. The poor had always had to rely upon the generosity of the wealthy, and beggars were a common sight, some of whom were shrewd enough to display deformed children to play on others' sympathies.[4] Churchmen of course recommended that Christians demonstrate their faith through their generosity, and they themselves sometimes used the endowments of their churches or shrines to establish a *matricula*, a register of poor people who received support. In the Touraine there were at least three such registers, two in Tours associated with the church of St. Martin and the monastic church of St. Julian and one in the village of Candes.[5] But as laudable as these almshouses were, they could not cope with the many hungry and indigent. In 567 a regional council at Tours encouraged cities to care for their own poor and thereby prevent them from drifting elsewhere;[6] because the resources of the church

---

[1] *Hist.* 5.3.

[2] *Hist.* 6.44, 7.45.

[3] GC 28, VM 2.26; cf. 2.30.

[4] VM 2.24, 3.58.

[5] *Hist.* 7.29, VM 1.31, 3.14, church of St. Martin; *VJ* 38, church of St. Julian; VM 2.22–23, 3.23, Candes; with L. Pietri (1983) 714–24.

[6] Council of Tours a.567, Can.5.

of St. Martin were so attractive, churchmen at Tours were perhaps especially concerned about the burden of these vagrants.

Violence too resisted solution, primarily because it was embedded in,
and even defined, a fundamental value system and a corresponding hierarchy of authority. The image of military success was so vital to the preservation of royal authority that even a Merovingian queen once tried to "arm
herself like a man"; great aristocrats not only fought to enhance their own
standing and influence but sometimes settled legal disputes by offhandedly
murdering their rivals; and the demands of blood feuds compelled many
men to demonstrate that they were not "weak women" by avenging their
relatives.[7] As one of the Frankish kings insisted, "If I do not avenge my
brother's death this year, I should not be considered a man"—and this was
a brother with whom he had fought in the past![8] In the face of this powerful
undertow of mayhem bystanders had few options. One was to respond in
kind. Gregory may have been too intimidated to react when a count wore
his armor into the cathedral residence, but other bishops outright "armed
themselves like laymen" and fought in battles. And when armed thugs
invaded the precincts of the church of St. Martin to assassinate a refugee,
the beggars gathered there turned on this "band of gladiators" with stones
and clubs.[9] Another response was reliance upon the power of saints. St.
Martin had the perfect pedigree to become attractive to warriors, since he
had himself once served in the Roman army and King Clovis had once
appealed for his assistance in a campaign against the Visigoths. Yet during
the sixth century not only did St. Martin consistently punish armed men
who violated his shrines, he also projected a more pacific image. Sulpicius
Severus had long ago minimized the saint's military career in his *Vita*, and
during the sixth century a preacher reiterated how already as a soldier
Martin had substituted the sign of the cross for his shield and helmet.[10] For
Gregory St. Martin was now primarily a civilian saint, at most a "soldier of
Christ"; so when a demon once appeared in the guise of a soldier and
claimed to be the saint, he was promptly rejected.[11] But in a period during
which kings and great aristocrats continued to contest each other's authority in Gaul even as they promoted expansion into Germany and other
campaigns in Italy and Spain, Gregory's and others' attempts to reduce the
use of armed force were but pale previews of the peace movements that
finally appeared only centuries later.

In contrast, Gregory's world did seem to have solutions for many physical afflictions, since at saints' shrines people were healed of all sorts of

[7] *Hist.* 6.4, 8.32, 9.19.
[8] *Hist.* 8.5.
[9] *Hist.* 5.48, Gregory and Count Leudast; 4.42, 5.20, 7.37, warrior bishops; 7.29, beggars.
[10] *Sermo* 3, with Fontaine (1963).
[11] *VM* 2.18, 4.26.

sicknesses and disabilities. In the middle of the sixth century Bishop Nicetius of Trier once suggested that the king of the Lombards would convert to Catholic Christianity if he were to visit the shrine of St. Martin at Tours, "where at the present time we see the blind receive their sight, the deaf their hearing, and the mute their health."[12] These miraculous healings raise significant questions for our understanding of Merovingian society, because miracles, as events that by definition defy the normal boundaries of human existence and the natural order, seem to challenge a genuinely historical analysis.[13] Modern historians have adopted various strategies for dealing with miraculous cures. One is to suggest that the disabilities and ailments were the consequences of psychological rather than physical causes; hence, in an "anxiety-ridden atmosphere" people developed "psychogenic disorders" that were then susceptible to "faith healing."[14] Another common strategy is to concentrate exclusively on the biomedical aspects of the ailments and explain their alleviation in terms of faulty diagnosis, mistaken prognosis, spontaneous cure, or natural remission.

Both strategies reflect a modern clinical emphasis on the malfunctionings of the psychological and biological processes of the body; but for a historical analysis both are also inadequate and reductionist. With its emphasis on anxiety and its alleviation, the psychological approach depreciates people's own experiences, as if they were consistently unable to cope with their times or their lives; with its corresponding emphasis on misunderstanding and bewilderment, the biological approach depreciates the social and cultural context, as if diseases and their cures involved only a corpus of physiological data of which people in late antique Gaul were unfortunately ignorant. In contrast, an anthropological approach to health care systems has stressed a distinction between "diseases," which are due to biological or psychological malfunctionings, and "illnesses," which include the social experiences and symbolic meanings attached to various ailments. The "cures" associated with diseases might well represent mere remissions, but the "healings" associated with illnesses include symbols and rituals that redefine notions of community, others, and self. Consideration of the process of illness and healing hence provides a more rewarding interpretive perspective by recognizing that, like kinship, religion, and language, medicine too lends itself to symbolic analysis because it defined another cultural system. As such, this process was both descrip-

---

[12] *Epistolae Austrasicae* 8.

[13] See Ward (1982), for an overview; Van Uytfanghe (1981) discusses Gregory within the context of the long-standing uneasiness about miracles among biblical and patristic writers.

[14] So Stancliffe (1983) 250–51, in a discussion of Martin's healing miracles. Rousselle (1990), an expanded restatement of Rousselle (1976), is a more sophisticated but still speculative discussion of "la situation psychologique des Gallo-Romains au IVᵉ siècle" (p. 52).

tive and prescriptive; it reinforced existing relationships and community norms by validating them in terms of experiences of illness and healing, and it simultaneously produced a model for subsequent behavior and even for the reformulation of current norms by instructing people in how they should act and think.[15] Rather than indicating an inability to cope with stress and fear, the process of illness and healing enabled people to manage their circumstances; and rather than demonstrating simple ignorance of biological data, this process presupposed a complex system of ideas that enabled people to think and talk about themselves and their relationships with others. For our historical understanding of the role of saints' cults in this process of illness and healing, considerations of psychological anxiety and biomedical ignorance are of less importance than the social and personal meanings that people expressed through these rituals and symbols.

The analysis in this chapter will discuss three aspects of the process of illness and healing. Since both the experience of illness and the therapy of healing presupposed interaction between individual responsibility and shared sanctions, the first topic is the interplay between body and community. The second topic involves the proper location and distribution of power in society. Because transactions between healers and patients established relationships of authority and influence between superiors and dependents, "doctors" such as saints and their guardian bishops posed challenges to both Merovingian kings and the counts they appointed as their representatives in cities. The final topic is the theological significance of illness and healing. Because both communities and individuals articulated their deepest concerns in terms of illnesses, and because illnesses were closely linked with guilt for sins, saints and bishops were as much concerned about forgiveness as healing. "Thinking about biological misfortune always implies thinking about the world and society, and in ages when God was the great principle of everything, illness was bound to fall within its purview."[16] Churchmen such as Gregory consistently linked ordinary illnesses and healings with larger theological concerns about the incarnation of Christ and the bodily resurrection of the dead. All three topics discussed in this chapter are different aspects of the same process of illness and healing, and interpretations that use the insights of social anthropology are hence complements to, and not necessarily replacements for, other

[15] Kleinman (1980) 24–45 (medicine as cultural system), 71–80 (disease and illness). Note also Herzfeld (1986) 108: "What is recognized as illness . . . is a model of the disorder rather than the disorder itself. Thus, the illness is above all an *interpretation* and as such constitutes a *text . . . upon* which the cure—a *reading* of the text and, as such, a further interpretation—is performed."

[16] Herzlich and Pierret (1987) 104, in a fine discussion of the making of modern attitudes toward sickness.

interpretations that still emphasize clinical techniques and psychological disorders.[17]

1. Body and Community

Discussion of the personal and social aspects of illness requires an initial candid statement of certain distinguishing features. The first is that this analysis is obviously based almost entirely on those miracles of healing performed by St. Martin that Gregory recorded during his episcopacy at Tours. Although it is reasonable to assume that similar rituals and meanings were associated with other saints' cults throughout Gaul, adequate evidence is available at this time only for this city. A second caution is that, because these miracle stories cover over two decades, their evidence is not similar to the essentially synchronic observations of anthropologists who sample a community or a society for a year or two. In order to approximate the thickness of anthropological observations the discussion in this section conflates the available information and ignores most transitions over time. Unlike the discussion in chapter 2 that tried to distinguish subtle developments during Gregory's episcopacy, this analysis is essentially static within his episcopacy. A final assumption concerns the fundamental accuracy of Gregory's accounts. Although Gregory once insisted that he tried to discourage skepticism by collecting his stories either directly from the participants or from the custodians of the church,[18] some modern critics have still suspected the employment of literary stylization or typological formulas in his (and others') collections of miracle stories. In the absence of alternative accounts of the same miracles no certain evaluation is possible. But the subsequent discussion assumes that any apparent stylization was characteristic of people's actual behavior and not necessarily of Gregory's account of it; by making possible more generalized interpretations of people's behavior this assumption is useful because it allows us to attempt a historical and not merely a literary analysis.

In Gregory's miracle stories the most common ailments were blindness and forms of paralysis and lameness. Occasionally he noted the causes for these afflictions, or at least what the ill people themselves diagnosed as the causes for their misfortunes; one woman, for instance, had lost the use of her foot because of "fear," and one man had become blind because of an inflammation, the spread of cataracts, and a blow to his head.[19] Gregory's indifference to the physiological etiology of various ailments was not neces-

---

[17] So Kleinman (1980) 373, in the conclusion to a penetrating study: "Cultural healing is a special dimension of the healing process that anthropology forces us to consider."

[18] *VM* 3.45.

[19] *VM* 2.11, 41.

sarily due to his lack of interest in or knowledge about current medical doctrine, because he was somewhat familiar with medical terminology, techniques, and symptoms. He knew that epilepsy was the proper expert description for what countryfolk called the "falling sickness"; he carefully described the blisters that accompanied a plague; he was apparently acquainted with some of the procedures and implements of surgeons; and he may even have read some of the medical manuals then in circulation.[20]

Gregory was instead more intent on placing these ailments in a moral and religious context. Most commonly, physical afflictions were the consequences of people's sins. When, for instance, Gregory mentioned a cleric whose hands had been disabled from birth, he also conceded that he could not decide whether this infirmity was due to this man's or his parents' sins; and when Gregory himself once requested St. Martin's healing assistance, he characterized himself, not as an invalid, but as a sinner.[21] Other ill people apparently shared Gregory's evaluation and accepted personal responsibility for their physical afflictions. One woman admitted that she had been "blinded by her sins"; one man thought that his hands were paralyzed because of some misdeed he had committed; another woman decided that her sins were the obstacles that prevented her disabled hands from being healed.[22]

Since Gregory and his informants usually did not mention the precise sins, presumably many people simply considered their ailments in general as the physical manifestations of their internalized sense of guilt. Sometimes people did indicate the exact sins that had caused their afflictions. Most commonly, they had infringed upon the constraints of organized Christianity, and more specifically upon the expectations of saints' shrines. Some of them had insulted saints or harmed specific shrines. Others had disregarded the liturgical calendar by failing to observe Sundays or saints' festivals and instead performing some activity "that was inappropriate to the day." Repairing a fence during Lent or on a Sunday, baking on the night before a Sunday, working in the fields during a saint's festival, and gathering hay on a Sunday were some of the offenses for which people were blinded or crippled.[23] One of Gregory's stories about a woman who had conceived a child during the night before a Sunday provided a reminder for his entire congregation about the consequences of ill-timed behavior: "if [sexual intercourse] takes place, then children are born who are crippled or

---

[20] VM 2.18–19, 3.34. See Riché (1962) 248–49, and Bonnet (1890) 218–20, for his use of some Greek medical terms, and Rousselle (1990) 83–96, for the importance of Greek in the learned medical tradition.

[21] VM 2.26, 60, "mihi peccatori."

[22] VM 2.28, 40, 56.

[23] VM 3.55, "huic diei . . . incongruum"; 2.13, 57; 3.29, 56; 4.45.

suffer from epilepsy or leprosy. Let this be the proof, so that a sin that is committed on one night might not be endured for the space of many years."[24]

This linkage between illnesses and infractions was so habitual that often the physical ailments closely corresponded to the nature of the misdeeds. A man who reneged on a promise found that "a fingertip of the hand that had made this oath began to throb painfully"; a woman who tried to hoe her field on a festival day felt that her hands were on fire; a man who tried in two consecutive years to grind grain on another festival day discovered both times that his hand became so stiff that he could not release the lever; a man who tried to make a key on a Sunday found that his own hands were locked into fists.[25] Even in an instance in which there was no apparent linkage between sin and illness, Gregory still stressed the connection with a simile: a man who had threatened to burn down the church of St. Martin slowly died from dropsy, "just like a wax candle that drop by drop wastes away at the sight of a flame."[26] Since the eyes were often associated with lust and greed, blindness was an appropriate penalty for thieves; and since strong hands and legs were required for any physical labor, paralysis and lameness were appropriate penalties for people who worked at the wrong times. Gregory neatly summarized the physical consequences of extortion when he described the fate of a man who had tried to seize a field that belonged to a saint: "his tongue that had suggested that the field be taken was bound, his eyes that had coveted were closed, and his hands that had seized the field were contracted."[27] Because these ailments were also means of publicizing people's guilt, their sins were no longer a matter simply of their private consciences. Their dependence upon guides and others' assistance meant that people could not conceal their lameness, paralysis, blindness, deafness, or muteness. Skin rashes or lesions on their faces were particularly embarrassing, and people so afflicted might well be considered "lepers" and treated as outcasts.[28] The fate of a woman who suffered from blisters on her face after working during a saint's festival highlighted this connection between private misdeeds and public shame: "this wretched woman burned no less from the anguish of embarrassment than from the pain in her body, because she had unwillingly exposed what she had done in secret." Sinful misbehavior caused physical blemishes that were comparable to "the horrible ulcers of ghastly leprosy."[29]

---

[24] *VM* 2.24, with Van Dam (1985) 286–87, for other examples of these conflicts with liturgical time; and below, chapter 4, section 1.

[25] *GC* 67, *VM* 2.57; 3.3, 7.

[26] *VM* 2.27.

[27] *GC* 78.

[28] *VM* 2.58. It is therefore not always clear whether the "hospitals" that bishops constructed (cf. *GC* 85) were infirmaries for sick people or asylums for outcasts.

[29] *VM* 2.57, embarrassment; 4 praef., leprosy.

Illnesses therefore presupposed a strong sense of personal guilt. Occasionally Gregory mentioned people who were attacked by demons. One man went mad because a "lunatic demon" made him think that he was being assaulted by a swarm of frogs; and a little boy became crippled "because of an attack by a clever demon, as he himself always claimed."[30] Although the healing of a few people therefore also involved the expulsion of demons, the process of healing must not be confused with exorcism, which Gregory in fact rarely mentioned. Rather than attributing their ailments and misfortunes to the influence of external demonic agents, people usually conceded that they were personally responsible for both their sins and their illnesses.

In the world of Gregory illnesses were the public manifestations of hidden or private sins for which people were now liable. Their healing therefore required, not particularly cures, but rather confession, judgment, forgiveness, and reconciliation. The reintegration of ill people took place on several levels that, even if intertwined in practice, should be distinguished. Three types of healing were common: of the community, as ill people moved from isolation to sociability; of relationships, as ill people exchanged one rank or status for another; and of people's selves, as they were forgiven and made whole.

By the later sixth century Christianity provided the dominant ideology within Gallic cities. Urban communities were now largely Christian communities too; particular saints functioned as urban patrons; and bishops were often notable leaders in cities. People who sinned therefore transgressed not just religious standards but also the norms of communities, and as ill people they themselves became afflictions within the social body. Because they could not participate in or contribute to the life of a community, ill people became, literally, burdens; often, for instance, others had to carry them about in their arms.[31] Since the misdeeds of individuals affected the entire community, the process of healing had to include both the ill people and the "healthy" members; and since the illnesses became public, the process of healing was typically a public ritual.

This ritual of public healing involved both specific places and specific times. At Tours, ill people usually went directly to the church of St. Martin. There they would kneel, weep, perhaps kiss the saint's tomb, perhaps touch the shroud over it, and certainly pray. People commonly thought that saints were "sleeping" in their tombs, no longer alive but not quite dead either. In these tombs saints' bodies were preserved intact, without decay or putrefaction; in fact, their bodies were more "healthy" than those of the ill people who visited their tombs. Bishop Gregorius of Langres, for instance,

---

[30] VM 2.18, frogs; 3.27, demon; with de Nie (1987) 230–37, and (1991).
[31] VM 2.5.

whose face was still as red as roses and whose corpse was as white as lilies, remained the picture of good health even after his death.[32] As ill people appealed to these saints, they sometimes themselves slipped temporarily into a similar state of "suspended animation" by falling asleep at the tombs. In their sleep they shared in the health of the saint. St. Martin, for instance, might appear to people in dreams and sometimes even speak with them about their illnesses or their sins; so one man dreamed that he was able to stretch his lame foot.[33] Upon awakening, these ill people would often be healed and would even come to resemble the "healthy" saint in his tomb. Putrefied and withered limbs became moist and supple, and pale, emaciated flesh regained its color: "a red flush was restored to his cheeks."[34] The focal point of the entire process of healing was therefore, somewhat incongruously, the saint's tomb. Upon their arrival, some ill people were thought to be almost dead, but at the tomb they recovered their health: there "a man on the verge of death might have life."[35]

The process of healing could certainly be effective at almost any time, and some people in fact had waited for years. Often, though, the precise moment of healing corresponded with the celebration of the liturgy. Many of the miracles of healing that Gregory recorded occurred during one of the two annual festivals of St. Martin. Some even happened precisely during the reading of selections from the saint's *Vita*: "the lector took the book and began to read the *Vita* of the holy confessor, and immediately this man's arm was cured." Just as the tomb marked a place where ill people who fell asleep could converse with St. Martin who was himself only dozing in his sarcophagus, so the reading of his *Vita* marked a moment when St. Martin might reenact the miracles of healing that as bishop he had once performed during his lifetime. Past and present coincided: "while the miracle stories were being read from the *Vita* of St. Martin, a flash similar to a lightning bolt flared over the blind men."[36] This correspondence between healing and the celebration of liturgy furthermore guaranteed the presence of a large audience. Ill people were healed "as the people watched": "the entire congregation of people witnessed these great deeds of God." And as ill people were healed of their physical ailments, so they were also reconciled with the larger community: "during the recitation of the Lord's Prayer this mute woman too opened her mouth and began to chant the holy prayer with the other people."[37] In place of the immobility of paralysis people now danced together during the celebration of the

32 VP 7.3.
33 VM 2.4.
34 VM 3.59.
35 VM 2.52.
36 VM 2.29, lightning bolt; 2.49, lector.
37 VM 2.55, congregation; 2.30, mute woman.

liturgy;[38] and in place of the isolation of blindness people now watched together as the bishop celebrated mass. After the process of healing, ill people were no longer an encumbrance on the community. Blind people whom guides had led to the church of St. Martin left without anyone's assistance; even the paralyzed man whom others had carried to the saint's tomb walked away after being healed.[39]

In the language of Christianity, healed people were reborn and now "flourished like a fresh flower."[40] These metaphors indicate the impact of the process of healing on people's sense of themselves and their identities. Modern discussions of personality and self in the ancient world have emphasized primarily notions of sexuality, and sometimes also attitudes toward food and eating. Notions of illness and healing provided another powerful idiom with which people could think about and describe their own identities.[41] Since illnesses usually accompanied the important transitions in his life, Gregory was his own best example. His entrance into and then his promotion up the ecclesiastical hierarchy neatly corresponded to a sequence of illnesses. As a young boy at Clermont he had suffered from a stomachache and fever; after being healed at the church of St. Illidius, he promised to become a cleric. In 563 he had suffered from an infection and a fever; after a successful pilgrimage to the church of St. Martin at Tours, he became a deacon.[42] The timing of the illnesses was not coincidental, since in each case the recovery of his health accompanied a change in his ecclesiastical rank. So upon his promotion to an episcopal see he again, predictably, became ill.

Shortly after his arrival at Tours as the new bishop Gregory suffered from such painful dysentery and high fever that he began to plan his own funeral. Although he thought he would die from this "sharp pain that penetrated my entire stomach and went down to my intestines," he was healed after drinking a potion that included dust from the saint's tomb.[43] This was a timely illness and recovery, and not simply because it clearly demonstrated St. Martin's acceptance of the city's new bishop. Because the irregularity of his consecration in 573, as described in chapter 2, had left Gregory vulnerable at Tours, he certainly needed the support of St. Martin to strengthen his position. But in a more potent symbolic sense, in overcoming the anticipation of impending death with a remedy acquired at the saint's tomb Gregory, the deacon from Lyon, had now died and been reborn as the bishop of Tours. The ache in his stomach and his intestines

[38] *Sermo* 1.
[39] VM 2.5, 11; 3.19.
[40] VM 3.27.
[41] Some hints in Rousselle (1990) 255–56, and Bynum (1991).
[42] VP 2.2, Clermont; VM 1.32–33, Tours.
[43] VM 2.1.

had signified the "birth pains" of a new bishop that only a doctor such as
St. Martin could alleviate. Significantly too, when his mother Armentaria
visited him at Tours soon after his consecration, the pain in her leg, as sharp
as "a piercing nail," that she had experienced since Gregory's birth was
finally healed.[44] The suggestive symbolic meanings of both mother's and
son's illnesses overlapped. Artemia, an ancestor, had once announced that
she was "pregnant with a bishop";[45] her prophecy came true when her son
Nicetius became bishop of Lyon. With this sort of expectation as part of the
family legacy Armentaria may have anticipated the same of her sons, and
so with Gregory's episcopal consecration the pains of her pregnancy with
him were finally over. Gregory now also went through a process of "rebirth" as he became the virtual reincarnation of Martin as bishop of
Tours.[46] And finally, since both Gregory's and Armentaria's illnesses can
be linked with Gregory's struggle to establish himself as bishop, their
healings collectively symbolized that the congregation at Tours was also to
be healed of its hostility to the new bishop. With the final completion of his
mother's extended "birth pains" and with his own "rebirth" Gregory had
effectively exchanged one family for another; and since St. Martin had now
accepted him as bishop, his new "mother church" should also.[47]

Gregory's subsequent illnesses and healings continued to validate this
identification with his new mother church and its patron saint. Although
"divine providence" may have conveniently allowed him to begin and end
each of his books about the miracles that St. Martin performed during his
episcopal tenure with miracles performed on his behalf, Gregory considered them as manifest proofs of the saint's continuing support: "I call God
as my witness that I am not deprived of [Martin's] compassion."[48] His
repeated infirmities and healings were hence the equivalent of the scars that
some of his older relatives had had as permanent evidence of the healing
power of their patron saints. Gregory's illnesses were also ongoing reminders to himself of his subordination to the will and identity of St.
Martin, and he often followed the same ritual as others who requested
remedies: "I approached the tomb, knelt on the pavement, wept and cried

[44] *VM* 3.10.

[45] *VP* 8.1.

[46] Note that the doctor who was unable to heal Gregory's dysentery and fever was named
Armentarius. Since his name was common in Gregory's family, perhaps he was a relative. If so,
the ineffectiveness of his assistance was all the more telling; only St. Martin, and not a member
of Gregory's natural family, could act as the "doctor" for the birth of Gregory's new
episcopacy.

[47] Gregory once claimed that Noah's ark was a symbol of the "mother church" that
protected people with her "tender embrace" (*Hist.* 1.4); he also stressed the uncontested
leadership of Bishop Avitus at Clermont precisely when Christians and Jews were reconciled
"in the bosom of the mother church" (*Hist.* 5.11).

[48] *VM* 3 praef.; 2.60, providence.

at length, and requested the confessor's assistance."[49] But as bishop of Tours, St. Martin's current representative, Gregory himself also became a source for remedies. During his journeys throughout Gaul Gregory often carried relics of St. Martin, in particular dust from his tomb, that he could then mix into potions that triggered healings.[50] By offering these relics of his patron saint, Gregory had closely fused his identity with that of St. Martin; and by consistently referring to St. Martin simply as "the bishop of Tours," Gregory was also being neatly ambiguous about the identity of the current occupant of the see.

The ritual of healing therefore involved a process of reconciliation on several intersecting levels as disrupted communities and shattered selves were mended. Although this particular therapy was now dominant, other rituals of social exclusion and reintegration were also available. One alternative involved the use of ecclesiastical sacraments. Exclusion from the celebration of the liturgy and in particular from participation in mass was one possible sanction against misbehavior. Gregory, for instance, once suspended a man who stole some of the possessions of St. Martin from participation in the celebration of the Eucharist; and Bishop Nicetius of Trier refused to celebrate mass with King Theudebert until the king's retainers who were accused of murder and adultery had been expelled.[51] A second alternative involved the use of judicial institutions. Both ill and healthy people sometimes affirmed their innocence by taking oaths, often in the presence of relics; the man whom Gregory excommunicated, for instance, temporarily cleared himself with an oath in the church of the Virgin Mary. But when this man then attempted to seize a meadow belonging to a convent, he died from a fever. So during the sixth century the ritual of illness and healing frequently coincided both with the celebration of the liturgy, since illnesses prevented people from attending and healing allowed them to participate, and with the ceremony of making an oath. Eventually, however, the intermediate ritual of healing would become superfluous, and an internal awareness of their guilt would alone prevent people from participating at masses or motivate them to take oaths. As part of a general process of structural differentiation liturgical and judicial institutions were eventually distinguished from the process of illness and healing.

As another aspect of this historical transition the notions of sin and reconciliation became more private and interiorized. With the development of a system of penitentials people sinned in private, confessed to their priests in private, and often even performed their prescribed penances in

[49] VM 3.1.

[50] VM 3.60. Fortunatus once thanked "doctor Gregory" for his assistance: see Carm. 8.11.1.

[51] Hist. 8.40, VP 17.2.

private. In the process of illness and healing that Gregory described, bodily suffering had been a public manifestation of sins that then required public healing; in contrast, in the process of confession and penance, forgiveness involved private suffering and deprivation as people deliberately tortured their bodies to heal their souls. Physical pain was no longer a manifestation of illnesses, but rather an aspect of the healings, even the "medicine" itself: "The penitentials intended that the soul of the sinner be influenced by means of the suffering inflicted on his body."[52] As a council in the middle of the seventh century put it, the penance that sinners performed was a "remedy for the soul."[53] So as a solution for misdeeds private individual suffering would eventually come to replace public community healing.

2. Body and Power

In early Merovingian Gaul the process of illness and healing also helped to define the allocation of authority and influence. Because illnesses marked conditions of weakness and dependence while healings represented both the bestowal and the acceptance of assistance, in combination they affirmed or created relationships of domination and subordination. Gregory often complained about other healers, not necessarily because their remedies were less effective, but because they were rivals to the one true "doctor," St. Martin. Gregory's insistence upon the efficacy of the relics of St. Martin was therefore also an argument supporting the authority of the saint. But as a powerful healer St. Martin then posed a challenge to other powerful men, in particular to the Frankish kings who were anyway struggling to assert their own royal authority throughout the sixth century. Counts, who were often called judges because of their legal functions, were additional rivals, especially since Gregory frequently imagined illnesses and healings in terms of crimes and judgments and viewed St. Martin as both "advocate" and "judge." And once the ritual of healing took on these quasi-judicial overtones, it could also provide legal sanctions for people who were otherwise often powerless before the law, such as women and people treated as slaves. This section is hence a discussion of how metaphors transferred not only meanings but also functions and roles; for even if St. Martin may have assumed secular functions "by analogy," his challenge to kings, counts, and other rivals was certainly intimidating.

As in most traditional societies, so in sixth-century Gaul different types

---

[52] Gurevich (1988) 29; Jonas of Bobbio, *Vita Columbani* 5, "penitentiae medicamenta." Cf. McNeill and Gamer (1938) 6, and Beck (1950) 187–222, for the transition from public procedures to private rites, and Riché (1981) 66–71, for the influence of Irish monasticism on Merovingian spirituality during the seventh century.

[53] Council of Chalon-sur-Saône a.647/653, Can.8, "medilla animae."

of healers were available. Some were professional physicians who offered the most sophisticated techniques and remedies and may even have studied surgery at Constantinople. Others were folk healers, "soothsayers" who relied upon traditional medicinal recipes and customized concoctions in prescribing amulets, herbal potions, or incantations. Of these folk healers, some were also accepted as Christian holy men and holy women who nevertheless similarly employed oil, saliva, wine, herbs, incantations, and massages in their therapies.[54] Still other healers were saints. Not only did Gregory pointedly describe them too as "doctors," he also insisted that they were the only true doctors and that their medicines, regardless of how unlikely they may now appear to us, were the only effective remedies.[55] Perhaps the most common medicine that St. Martin prescribed was dust from his tomb. Gregory himself drank it in potions, carried some with him on his journeys, recommended it to others, and was impressed enough to claim that it combined the powers of many therapeutic herbs: "like scammony it purges the stomach, and like hyssop, the lungs; and like pyrethrum it cleanses even the head."[56]

Since surgeons and folk healers offered techniques and remedies that were alternatives to reliance upon the cult of saints, occasionally Gregory railed against both: "a bit of dust from the church of St. Martin is more powerful than those men with their foolish medicines."[57] But Gregory was most annoyed at the healers who, while ostensibly using relics and professing Christian beliefs, in his judgment in fact promoted themselves and their own influence at the expense of saints and their respective guardians, the local bishops. Firsthand experience only confirmed his indignation. After Gregory ignored a relic-monger who visited Tours in 580, the man went on to Paris, collected a crowd of supporters, and began to celebrate an alternative rogations. So Bishop Ragnemod had the man imprisoned and his relics inspected, which turned out to include herbal roots, moles' teeth, mouse bones, and bear claws. In 587 another man appeared at Tours and claimed to be more powerful than St. Martin and the equal of the apostles Peter and Paul. Once a crowd gathered, this "apostle" tried to heal the lame by stretching their limbs to the breaking point. Eventually Gregory had him run out of town. And in 591 when the plague again spread through Gaul, a man dressed himself in skins like a monk and at Javols collected a large following that included some clerics. Not only did this man heal people, he also identified himself as Christ, addressed one of the women in his entou-

---

[54] *Hist.* 10.15, VM 2.19, physicians; *Hist.* 5.34, VM 4.36, folk healers; VP 15.3, 16.3, 19.3, 20.3, GC 24, Christian healers.
[55] VM 2.52.
[56] VM 3.60.
[57] VM 1.27.

rage as Mary, and threatened to unleash his "army" against bishops who refused to worship him. The bishop of Le Velay, however, was so unimpressed that he sent thugs who killed this "Christ" and tortured "Mary."[58]

Although he thought that surgeons and folk healers were often simply ineffective, Gregory denigrated these men who used Christian symbols much more harshly as false prophets who, despite appearances, had resorted to "black magic" and not "holiness" to attract supporters. Yet the fundamental issue at stake in his animosity to surgeons, folk healers, and false prophets alike was not particularly a dispute over proper procedures or remedies, but rather a rivalry over authority and influence. Because such a pluralism of health regimens was available, ill people always had to make choices about which healer to approach and which therapy to try.[59] Even Gregory himself, despite his evident devotion to St. Martin, sometimes considered alternative therapies. When he arrived as the new bishop of Tours in 573, he apparently brought along his own doctor. Sometimes he considered the possibility of bloodletting, once when he suffered from a throbbing headache, again when he suffered from a swollen tongue and a sore lip. Yet Gregory finally decided that none of these remedies was effective: "I confess, often I took baths and bound hot pads over these pains in my stomach, but nothing could relieve this ailment." In the end, he always decided to use the remedies offered by St. Martin.[60] He obviously thought that others should do likewise. Saints may have been the true "doctors," but it is most significant that bishops consistently took the initiative in protecting the prerogatives of their shrines by opposing rival healers. In communities that were now primarily Christian the process of miraculous healing was one means of acknowledging the authority of saints and their representative bishops. By extension, because the process of healing defined influence and dependence, it also raised a challenge to other powerful men in Gaul who did not pose as healers, such as the Frankish kings and their counts.

Despite their patronage for new saints' cults the assimilation of Frankish kings into Gallic society was still not an easy process. If kings were wary about the cult of St. Martin at Tours, they were also ambivalent about Catholic Christianity in general. Arian Christianity at least offered special

---

[58] *Hist.* 9.6, relic-monger and "apostle"; 10.25, "Christ."

[59] The suggestion in Brown (1981) 115 that the medical treatise by Marcellus, a contemporary of Martin of Tours, was an attempt to avoid the creation of dependence by allowing autarchic self-healing is mistaken: see Van Dam (1985) 129–30. Marcellus may have allowed sick people to participate in their healing therapy, but he still recommended the use of trained doctors: see Rousselle (1990) 85–96, 101–2, for a fine discussion of Marcellus's treatise.

[60] *VM* 2.1, doctor; 2.60, headache; 4.1, stomachache; 4.2, swollen tongue.

status to rulers,[61] but Catholic Christianity expected kings to behave like other laymen and respect the clergy. Baptism was perhaps the most grating aspect of their new religion, and Clovis's baptism had set two annoying precedents.[62] During this ceremony Bishop Remigius of Rheims had suggested that Clovis was now to be "meek," even though in fact any king who wanted to retain his throne had to demonstrate that he was "overpowering," especially in combat. But thereafter Gregory would constantly remind these kings that what they valued most highly, success in wars, was in fact most disruptive in Gallic society, and that they became "good kings" only when they demonstrated their charity and kindness.[63] Like Clovis during his baptism, subsequent kings should replace their armor with the "helmet of salvation."[64] Bishop Remigius also set another precedent by equating Clovis's baptism with a healing: the water of baptism had washed away Clovis's "leprosy." The particular malady is significant. Clovis was not "blind" or "mad" like other unbelievers; instead, in a Gaul that was still Roman and now also Christian, it was his image that was "horrible and repulsive," as Gregory once described a woman who had such abrasions on her skin that people considered her a leper.[65] So Clovis submitted to the cleansing of a "secular baptism" at Tours and a liturgical baptism at Rheims. "Healing in this sense is comparable to a conversion experience. Through the construction of adaptive models and the use of powerful cultural symbols religious healing is often able to transform what might otherwise be defined as deviant or pathological behavior into socially acceptable or even highly valued behavior."[66] Just as after his victory over the Visigoths Clovis would look like a Roman magistrate by donning a general's cloak in the church of St. Martin and then progressing like an emperor,[67] so he would look like a Catholic Christian once Bishop Remigius had healed his blemishes.

But because these transformations implied homage to long-standing traditions, subsequent kings had difficulties with the implications of both baptisms, "Roman" and Catholic. Even though descendants of the imperial forces once stationed in Gaul continued to wear Roman uniforms

[61] Note *Hist.* 3.31, for royalty using a separate chalice during the celebration of an Arian mass. For the political implications of Arianism, see Williams (1951).

[62] *Hist.* 2.31; Gregory probably based his account on a *Vita* of Remigius.

[63] *Hist.* 7.8, "robustus"; 5 praef., disruption; 3.25.

[64] Avitus of Vienne, *Ep.* 36.

[65] *VM* 1.8.

[66] Danforth (1989) 57. Gregory also associated the conversion of the Sueves with their acceptance of Catholic Christianity, their baptism, and the disappearance of an outbreak of leprosy (*VM* 1.11).

[67] *Hist.* 2.38. McCormick (1989) is an interesting discussion of Clovis's imitation of the ceremonies associated with Byzantine generals.

when they fought in Frankish armies during the sixth century, subsequent Merovingian kings did not imitate Clovis in explicitly assuming the attire or prerogatives of Roman emperors or generals; if anything, the archaeology of graves and cemeteries indicates the spread of Frankish clothing and weapons among the Roman population.[68] Frankish kings instead considered themselves the peers of the emperors in Constantinople, and one contemporary Greek historian was annoyed to learn that these kings stamped images of themselves, and not of the Eastern emperors, on their gold coins.[69] Frankish kings could likewise not easily subordinate themselves to the Christian God. Although kings did usually have their sons undergo baptism, as a ritual of protection it was not always successful, and as a ritual of obedience it was sometimes irksome.[70] Deference clearly did not come easy to Frankish kings, and some of them certainly resented, and sometimes tacitly ignored, the expectations of Catholic bishops and their warnings against becoming "ill." At least two kings, Chlothar and Chilperic, sometimes seemed to think of the King of Heaven as merely another of their royal rivals. The visit of an envoy from the Arian Visigoths once apparently influenced Chilperic to consider himself an amateur theologian, since he soon suggested abolishing the distinction of Persons in the Trinity; significantly, however, he relented precisely when Gregory pointedly reminded him of his baptismal confession that perhaps had included the same recognition of the Persons of the Trinity that Clovis was thought to have once defended against heretics.[71] As Gregory noted elsewhere, a man had to observe his baptismal confession faithfully in order to avoid any blemishes,[72] which seems to be a warning about both moral stains and corporeal ulcers; so in his admonition to Chilperic Gregory was tacitly cautioning the king about avoiding the "leprosy" that had afflicted Clovis before his baptism. King Chlothar had initially been upset when his wife Radegund abandoned him, not so much because she became an ascetic, as because her preference for "the embraces of the King of Heaven" damaged his own manly reputation; two generations earlier, for instance, his own grandmother (another Thuringian queen, no less) had abandoned her husband (Radegund's grandfather, no less) in favor of another king, the Frank

---

[68] Procopius, *De bello Gothico* 5.12.17–19, with James (1979) 64: "The political and social dominance of the Franks not only persuaded Gallo-Romans to adopt Frankish burial customs but also Frankish fashions of dress." The Greek historian Agathias thought that Franks differed from Byzantines only by retaining their barbarian attire and language: see Agathias, *Hist.* 1.2.4, with Cameron (1968).

[69] Procopius, *De bello Gothico* 7.33.5.

[70] Cf. *Hist.* 6.27, 34–35.

[71] *Hist.* 5.44, Chilperic; 3 praef., Clovis. Cf. *Hist.* 2.34: the Burgundian king Gundobad was never baptized because he was unable to confess "in public" the equality of the Persons of the Trinity.

[72] *VJ* 50.

Childeric whom she admired for his "virility."[73] And although he may have been one of the few kings to pray at the tomb of St. Martin, on his deathbed Chlothar was still miffed at the King of Heaven for failing to show any professional courtesy by allowing other great kings such as himself to die in pain![74]

But whatever pretensions these kings may have entertained about heavenly King and Byzantine emperors, their most immediate rivals were saints and bishops; and although kings had armies, bishops had other advantages. Some ostensibly appropriated royal prerogatives and effectively "reigned" in their cities.[75] Frankish kings did not fail to note this challenge to their authority, and King Chilperic once moaned that as churches accumulated wealth, "only bishops exercised royal rule."[76] Bishops furthermore were careful to insist that miraculous healing was a monopoly reserved for the power of the saints and their representatives, such as the bishops themselves. Chlothar, for instance, was one of the few Frankish kings during the sixth century to allow himself to be healed by a bishop; after he kissed the cloak of Bishop Germanus of Paris and confessed his misdeeds, he recovered from a fever.[77] Since healings created relationships of dependency, kings would probably have preferred to be the doctors rather than the patients. Although eventually people did attribute the power of miraculous healing to French kings, during the sixth century only King Guntramn became a healer (once) when threads from his royal cloak cured a feverish boy; and even then Gregory rather neatly minimized the significance of the episode by noting that Guntramn was merely acting "like a good bishop."[78]

Healing, baptism, and Catholic Christianity in general hence all posed stiff challenges to the consolidation of Merovingian kings' authority. The counts these kings assigned to cities also faced competition, in part because saints and bishops sometimes usurped some of their secular functions too. Because illnesses were so closely identified with sins, the process of healing was closely linked with notions of judgment and forgiveness. Gregory's metaphorical language (and ours too, for that matter) readily associated physical ailments with seizure, confinement, and imprisonment, and he sometimes explicitly classified captivity and incarceration as illnesses and considered ransom and release as further examples of the healing that St. Martin performed. One sightless man, for instance, had been bound by

---

[73] *Hist.* 2.12, Childeric; Baudonivia, *Vita Radegundis* 4.

[74] *Hist.* 4.21.

[75] *GM* 33, on Bertramn of Bordeaux: "episcopatu urbem regebat." Since Bertramn was related to the Merovingian dynasty (*Hist.* 9.33), perhaps he was a special case.

[76] *Hist.* 6.46.

[77] Fortunatus, *Vita Germani* 68–70.

[78] *Hist.* 9.21.

"the chain of blindness"; a madman who suffered from seizures was bound in chains; a boy kidnapped by Count Leudast also immediately suffered from fevers and blisters; a deaf and mute man requested, not a cure, but liberation: "Lord Martin, free me!" Healing was therefore a form of release and acquittal. When St. Martin freed the boy from Leudast's chains, he also healed him; and when a crippled man was healed, "suddenly the bonds that held his knees tight were loosened."[79] Gregory's accounts of the miracles of St. Martin consistently stressed these "judicial" aspects of the saint's remedies. At the saint's tomb people were expecting not only remedies for their ailments, but also a pardon for their guilt.[80]

This homologous association between healing and adjudication meant that saints, as well as their representative bishops, might also be expected to judge secular cases. Since one of the primary duties of a count was the application of justice for his city, his jurisdiction coincided, but also some-times conflicted, with that of the local bishop.[81] Sometimes bishops and counts joined together to oppose the general lawlessness of the times, in particular when great aristocrats took the law into their own hands. One man was lynched "without proper judicial process"; another man, al-though innocent, was hauled off to Tours by "evil men" to be imprisoned; but in both cases either an abbot or a bishop worked with the count to free the prisoners.[82] Sometimes bishops and abbots confronted, or at least opposed, counts. Abbot Eparchius of Angoulême once saved a man from the gallows and then charmed the count into pardoning him; Bishop Bad-egysil of Le Mans was accustomed to arguing secular cases with counts (even if only in order to ensure that he could take his own revenge on his opponents!); during a banquet Bishop Germanus of Paris once discussed compassion and mercy with a count.[83] At Tours St. Martin often released imprisoned men who then took refuge in the cathedral or the saint's church and received a pardon from the count.[84] In a period during which even the agents of justice sometimes resorted to excessive cruelty, the healing power of saints provided an alternative model, and an alternative reality, of lenient correction.

By being considered the functional equivalent of a judicial procedure the process of healing itself acquired quasi-judicial sanctions, especially for

[79] VM 2.26, 47, 53, 58; 4.20, "caecitatis . . . catena."

[80] VM 3 praef.

[81] See Claude (1964) 4–11, 38–45, and Weidemann (1982) 1:264–70, on counts and their jurisdiction.

[82] VM 3.53, 4.35.

[83] Hist. 6.8, GC 99, with Van Dam (1988b) 102n, on the discrepancies between the two accounts of Eparchius; Hist. 8.39, Badegysil; Fortunatus, Vita Germani 86.

[84] VM 4.16, 39, 41.

those who otherwise had little legal recourse, such as women and people treated as slaves. In ancient and medieval society, as in many traditional societies, marriages were vital to the interests of families in producing heirs and confirming alliances with other families; a man was expected to marry in order to "produce the seed that would benefit his family in subsequent generations."[85] A woman usually had little say in choosing a husband, defining the nature of the marriage, or initiating its dissolution. Some women in Frankish Gaul did try to control their own marriages; one woman even had her lover kill her new husband and his brother who had arranged the marriage.[86] More often women were little more than pawns in the political and personal intrigues of their male relatives. Bishop Felix of Nantes, for instance, had once tried to prevent the marriage of his niece by forcing her to become a nun; but upon his death her fiancé rescued and married her. Although her relatives continued to disapprove, perhaps they no longer minded, since her new husband now had royal support.[87] Once married, a woman was also expected to remain chaste, since any suspicion of adultery tainted the reputation of her family. At Paris an accusation of adultery led to a feud between a woman's husband's family and her father's family; when the woman was summoned to a hearing, she strangled herself. Other women accused of adultery were weighted with stones and tossed into rivers or burned alive; one husband simply killed his wife and the abbot he found in her bed.[88]

Although men could abandon their wives and remarry,[89] women had few ways to leave their husbands. At Chartres Monegund had married "because of her parents' wishes," but after the deaths of her daughters she abandoned her husband to live as an ascetic. When she later took up residence near the church of St. Martin at Tours, her husband came with friends and neighbors and brought her back. But after Monegund returned to Tours and established a small convent, her husband no longer bothered her. When Berthegund wished to join the convent founded by her mother Ingytrud at Tours, her husband protested to Gregory, who threatened to excommunicate Berthegund. A few years later when she again left her husband, she appealed for the protection of her brother, Bishop Bertramn of Bordeaux; this time her husband complained directly to King Guntramn. Her husband seems finally to have given up on her once she vowed to perform penance as a nun at the church of St. Martin at Tours. So both Monegund and Berthegund were finally able to complete the unilateral

[85] *VP* 20.1.
[86] *Hist.* 6.13, 7.3.
[87] *Hist.* 6.16.
[88] *Hist.* 5.32, suicide; 6.36, burning; 8.19, murder; *GM* 68–69, drowning.
[89] *Hist.* 9.13, 10.8.

dissolution of their marriages, but only through the sanction of St. Martin.[90]

The saint's power also assisted other women by associating the dissolution of their marriages with the process of illness and healing. One blind woman, upon being healed at the church of St. Martin, abandoned her husband and children to become a nun; another blind woman refused to leave after being healed at Candes.[91] Since this latter shrine commemorated St. Martin's bed in his monastery, this example of healing also neatly indicates the implicit sexual tension involved. Like King Chlothar, these husbands were losing their wives to another "bridegroom."[92] The process of illness and healing hence provided a quasi-judicial mechanism that allowed some women to dissolve their marriages, even against their husbands' objections. Even though conciliar canons continued to prohibit unilateral repudiation as well as divorce by mutual consent, this acknowledgment of the consequences of miraculous healing nevertheless allowed ecclesiastical authorities to accommodate themselves to social (and legal) realities by permitting the dissolution of some marriages. Not until the Carolingian period did ecclesiastical and secular laws regarding marriage finally begin to coincide.[93]

The process of illness and healing was also relevant in another legal context. Because kings failed to impose an effective central authority, while great local notables maneuvered to improve their influence, some free people became or were treated as slaves. To guarantee their treaties Frankish kings might hold hostages, some of whom were eventually sold as slaves. One such hostage was Attalus, a grandson of Bishop Gregorius of Langres and therefore a cousin of Gregory's mother. When a treaty between two kings collapsed, Attalus had to serve a Frankish master in "public slavery" at Trier. After his new master refused to accept Gregorius's offer of ransom, Attalus finally fled, and his escapades in avoiding his pursuers subsequently became some of the family's prize traditions.[94] Incessant wars also led to the seizure of many captives who were sold as slaves. Other people were simply unable to cope with unexpected hardships. In 585, for instance, famine was so severe throughout Gaul that poor people sold themselves into slavery. Although they forfeited their liberty, at least they had acquired masters who would presumably protect and feed

---

[90] VP 19.1–2, Monegund; Hist. 9.33, Berthegund.

[91] VM 2.9, 3.22.

[92] Cf. Hist. 6.29. Strict secular attitudes spilled over to affect religious attitudes. In their letter sanctioning the foundation of Radegund's convent, bishops insisted that if a nun left to marry, both she and her new husband were committing adultery (Hist. 9.39).

[93] McNamara and Wemple (1976) is a fine survey.

[94] Hist. 3.15.

them.[95] Not all masters were so charitable, however. One woman who had earned her freedom was sold again by her former master's sons; a girl whose parents had been freed was enslaved again by their former master's sons.[96]

In response, many bishops acquired reputations for ransoming captives and slaves.[97] St. Martin acquired a similar reputation, although with an added dimension because healings commonly accompanied his "ransoms." The woman unjustly sold into slavery became crippled, until at the church of St. Martin she recovered both her health and her freedom. A slave woman from Poitiers was also healed at Tours but relapsed when her masters tried to enslave her again. After she returned to Tours, her masters accepted a ransom from the wealth of St. Martin; so this woman too was healed and freed. One master promised to free his crippled slave if St. Martin healed him. Gregory was duly impressed by the healing that followed: "Who ever spent a thousand talents for a ransom just as this powerful benefactor did on behalf of our misdeeds?"[98] In a society in which for many the distinction between freedom and slavery was blurred and in which there were few effective legal means or even incentives for restoring freedom to people who had slipped into slavery, the process of illness and healing again served as a makeshift mechanism, almost a judicial process in its own right. St. Martin now became the new master for these liberated people; upon being healed the crippled slave, for instance, "was tonsured, received his freedom, and now serves the needs of the blessed lord Martin." As a continuous reaffirmation of freedom, healings and the support of saints were perhaps even more effective than any legal instruments. So some former captives "remained with perpetual freedom, even though without the security of any written document."[99]

In a world characterized by violence and infirmity, justice and health were typically the prerogatives of the powerful, and recognition of those prerogatives established relationships of dependency and submission. But as people realized that justice and health were now also available at the tomb of St. Martin, the saint became another powerful patron who could compete with and overshadow his competitors. Because he was a doctor prescribing effective remedies, people became his patients; because he was an advocate and judge dispensing justice, people became his clients. Acknowledgment of St. Martin's miraculous healings therefore presented

---

[95] *Hist.* 7.45. Whittaker (1987) is an excellent survey of "all the varied and tacit bargains that were struck locally between the powerful and the weak as they fought to survive" (p. 114).

[96] *VM* 2.59, 3.41.

[97] Klingshirn (1985).

[98] *VM* 3.46, slave woman; 2.4, ransom.

[99] *GC* 67.

challenges for other holders of power, such as kings and counts, as well as opportunities for people who otherwise had little judicial recourse, such as women and those on the edge of slavery. Gregory's descriptions of people's devotion to the saint's tomb are again most revealing of their attempts to accommodate this new authority within existing protocols. In the later sixth century canon law had once tried to define the relative status of churchmen and secular magistrates by carefully outlining the appropriate gestures of deference: "If a secular magistrate meets a cleric of even the lowest rank, he is to bow his head to him respectfully . . . ; if both the magistrate and the cleric are riding horses, the magistrate is to tip his hat and offer a warm greeting; if the cleric is on foot and the magistrate is on horseback, he is to dismount immediately and show the appropriate respect of sincere devotion for the cleric."[100] People also now had to incorporate saints into this hierarchy of power and status. Kneeling at the feet of powerful men was a common indication of submission and a common means of petition; so when Radegund once requested the support of bishops, she claimed to be bowing at their feet. Because people approached saints in the same way, Gregory often mentioned that people came to Tours in order to kneel "at the feet of the most beloved lord Martin."[101]

In return, another gesture often accompanied healings and assistance. One debtor was fettered in chains because "there was no one to extend him a compassionate hand"; a blind man begging for alms at the church of St. Martin asked only that someone extend "a hand of compassionate consideration."[102] St. Martin obviously listened to these pleas. A crippled nun was healed after dreaming that the saint had gently stroked her limbs; another woman was healed when in a dream she saw the saint take her hand and straighten her twisted fingers; a mute man recovered his speech when the saint appeared in a vision, touched him, and made the sign of the cross on his forehead.[103] Perhaps it is possible to assume that these visions of St. Martin extending his hand corresponded to one of the representations of the saint that people could see in the murals on the walls of his church. When a storm threatened men who were crossing the Loire River, one of them reassured the others by pointing out "that the holy man's right hand has been readied to offer assistance especially when needed." Inside the church of St. Martin over the north door facing the Loire River was a fresco of Jesus walking on the water; as an accompanying inscription described the scene, "the Lord extended his hand to St. Peter who was sinking, and that man was saved from danger." Since in retelling another story about how St. Martin had rescued some people on the Loire Gregory

---

[100] Council of Mâcon a.585, Can.15.
[101] *Hist.* 9.42, Radegund; *VM* 2.4.
[102] *VM* 2.8, 3.47.
[103] *VM* 2.31, 56; 3.23; with de Nie (1987) 247–49, on St. Martin's "touch."

specifically added a comparison to Jesus rescuing Peter, apparently others too now visualized the saint's assistance in terms of him, like Jesus, offering his hand.[104]

This gesture with the hand had a judicial and an emotional impact.[105] Powerful patrons would protect their dependents in legal proceedings by shielding them with their hands, or simply by gesturing to the presiding judge. So the Lord favored one abbot by demonstrating the power of saints "through his hands"; one saint sat up from his tomb in order to embrace a thief and protect him from any legal penalty; and St. Martin once saved a condemned man from the gallows by extending "his compassionate right hand."[106] Likewise in his concern over his fate at the Final Judgment before the King of Heaven Gregory once hoped that St. Martin would promote his cause with "his sacred right hand."[107] But with this gesture St. Martin not only protected, judged, and healed these people, he also indicated his love for them. Joining hands and touching lips were two common ways of sealing durable and supportive relationships. A couple celebrated their engagement with a kiss; married couples, even those committed to chastity, joined hands; eventually in later medieval society lords and their vassals joined hands and exchanged kisses in order to guarantee their mutual feudal obligations.[108] Transposed to the relationships between saints and their dependents, the gestures appropriate to the rigid protocol of a Gallic society stratified by rank and power acquired a deeper emotional intimacy and civility. During the later sixth century ill people kissed the tomb or the threshold of the church of St. Martin and then knelt at the saint's feet;[109] in return their patron touched them with his hand.

3. Body and Theology

The community dynamics and the wider politics of the rituals of illness and healing were not necessarily Gregory's own primary concerns. As a foster son of St. Martin he was confident that the saint would continue to demonstrate his healing power; as a pastor he hoped that members of his congregation would acknowledge their sins and seek forgiveness; as a compassionate man he wanted people to be relieved of their pains and afflictions. As a prominent bishop, however, Gregory was fundamentally concerned

---

[104] *VM* 1.2, comparison; 2.17, St. Martin's hand; and below, Appendix 3, for the fresco.

[105] It also had liturgical overtones, in particular by suggesting baptism. Note the epitaph for a girl buried at Vienne after being "baptized by the right hand of the noble Martin": ed. Le Blant (1856–1865) 2, no. 412, and *RICG* 15 = Descombes (1985) 268–73, no. 39.

[106] *Hist.* 10.29, abbot; *GC* 61, embrace; *VM* 3.53.

[107] *VM* 2.60.

[108] *VP* 20.1, kiss; *Hist.* 1.47, hands; and Ganshof (1964) 72–79.

[109] *VM* 2.49, 4.14.

with correct doctrines and their acceptance: "many burned with their faith in Christ, but some were lukewarm."[110] Although his extant works certainly do not present him as a distinguished theological thinker or writer, he did include in his *Histories* detailed discussions of certain doctrines such as the incarnation of Christ and the resurrection of the dead. The choice of issues is significant. Gregory and other bishops in central and northern Gaul had apparently little interest in or even familiarity with the contemporary arguments over grace, free will, and predestination that still smoldered in southeastern Gaul, or with the Christological controversies that were splintering the Eastern church.[111] Instead, these particular discussions of incarnation and resurrection had clear implications for people's thinking about their own bodies and the bodies of the saints buried in their tombs, and it is therefore important to recognize that Gregory's (and presumably others') interest in saints' cults and the ritual of healing overlapped with these larger theological concerns. Gregory's theological discussions provide an additional context for our understanding of the many stories of miraculous healing that he collected. Typically, Gregory did not discuss these doctrines in any abstract, or even polite, manner; instead he portrayed himself in debate, and his arguments usually took the form of polemical confrontations during which he relentlessly overwhelmed his opponents. In the middle of one argument, for instance, his opponent turned "insane with rage" after having to listen to Gregory's platitudes; Gregory concluded that this man was simply stupid.[112] Much of Gregory's theology was reactionary, in the sense that he was distinguishing himself from other theological positions; and the alternatives about which he apparently worried most were Arianism and Judaism.

Gregory participated in three debates about the correct relationship between the Father and the Son in the Trinity and the significance of Christ's incarnation. In 580 Agila, an envoy sent by King Leuvigild of the Visigoths to King Chilperic, stopped at Tours. There he irritated Gregory by citing Jesus' admission in the Gospel of John that the Father was greater to support his conclusion that the Son was therefore inferior to the Father in age and in power. Agila also concluded that the Son's obedience to the will of the Father was an indication of his inferiority, and that because Jesus was called the Son of God only after he had become man, "there was a time

---

[110] *Hist.*, praef., with Vinay (1940) 21–32, on Gregory's theology.

[111] Gregory did not mention Augustine; Fortunatus, *Carm.* 5.1.7, conceded his unfamiliarity with Augustine's writings; neither mentioned Pelagius. The kings of Austrasia may have exchanged envoys with the Byzantine court at Constantinople, but the bishops of northeastern Gaul were not well informed about imperial preferences for theological positions: see *Epistolae Austrasicae* 7, a rambling letter to the emperor Justinian from Bishop Nicetius of Trier.

[112] *Hist.* 5.43.

when he was not." Agila's arguments corresponded closely to the standard objections that Arians had been posing for centuries to Nicene Christianity, and Gregory now defended Catholicism by rehearsing equally traditional arguments. In particular, Gregory attributed Jesus' concession of inferiority to the "humility of the flesh that he had assumed"; but he also insisted upon the necessity of the Son's becoming "truly man" as a guarantee for the redemption of mankind. When Agila then further questioned the equality of the Holy Spirit within the Trinity, Gregory ignored his criticism and replied instead that the descent of the Spirit had been contingent upon the success of the Son's redemption.[113]

Because Agila was more sophisticated and more skillful in their debate, in the end Gregory simply misrepresented his arguments by casting him as a supporter of paganism as well as of heresies. For the doctrines of the incarnation and the assumption of a human body had always posed major challenges to the Catholic insistence on the equality of the Father and the Son, and in support of his *fides*, his confession that the members of the Trinity were indivisible, Gregory finally had to cite the activities of St. Martin, "our patron who is now present." In Gregory's perspective, by questioning the equality of the Son with the Father Arians had also denied the possibility that God's power was still accessible through miracles. Hence, the miracles performed by St. Martin and other saints were additional proofs for his Catholic position; and in fact, in his collections of miracle stories Arians were consistently unable to perform or even benefit from miracles. An Arian bishop who intended to heal a man who was feigning blindness instead left him sightless; after a Catholic deacon retrieved a ring from a pot of boiling water without being harmed, an Arian priest who tried the same found that "his flesh was melted down to the very joints of his bones."[114] So Gregory typically equated doctrinal disagreement with illness; not only was Agila stupid, he was also "poisoned" and needed to be "cleansed" by Gregory's blessing. Although at the time Agila refused, eventually Gregory could feel vindicated, because after Agila returned to Spain, he did finally convert to Catholicism when he was "weakened by an infirmity." Miracles, Catholic miracles, could heal both heretical stupidity and bodily illnesses.

In 581 Gregory participated in a second debate over the relationship between the Father and the Son, this time with a Jew named Priscus who served in the household of King Chilperic. Unlike Agila who had at least acknowledged the existence of both a Son and a Holy Spirit and some roles for them, Priscus preferred to think of a God who "does not need a mar-

---

[113] *Hist.* 5.43. Note also *Hist.* 1 praef., for Gregory's own creed and reaffirmation of Nicene Catholicism.
[114] *Hist.* 2.3, GC 13, blindness; GM 80, boiling water.

riage and is not blessed with a Son." Even if he conceded that God had conceived the Son "from a spiritual womb," he questioned whether God could become a man or be born from a woman. Gregory replied that the Son had had to become man in order to release mankind from its sins and that only Christ's death could compensate for the expulsion from Paradise. He also, again but this time more explicitly, linked redemption with healing: "Your prophet Isaiah said that Christ would come to heal our sicknesses." In Gregory's miracle stories contrition often preceded a healing; in this case, because Priscus was unconvinced and therefore showed no remorse, he refused to convert. Eventually Priscus paid the price for his failure to be "healed" through conversion. During the next year when King Chilperic ordered many Jews to be baptized, Priscus was still so obstinate that the king had him imprisoned. Upon his release another Jew who had already converted to Christianity killed him.[115]

Gregory's third debate about the Trinity was with Oppila, another envoy from King Leuvigild to King Chilperic who in 584 stopped at Tours. Although Oppila claimed to be a Catholic, Gregory was surprised when he refused to participate during the celebration of the Eucharist. Oppila explained that he objected to a phrase in the Catholic doxology that attributed glory to the Father, Son, and Holy Spirit; he instead thought that since the Son was an agent of the Father, glory was to be given to the Father through the Son. Gregory responded that glory was to be given to God, but "in accordance with the distinction of his Persons"; hence the Son, who was also God, was glorious with the Father. Not only did Gregory insist that Oppila had fundamentally misunderstood the passages in the New Testament that he had cited, but he also, typically, described Oppila's ignorance as an "illness" and suggested that he needed a salve for his inflamed eyes. Since this debate was apparently part of the conversation during a banquet that Gregory hosted for Oppila, it was not as confrontational as the other disputes; in fact, Gregory even made a polite pun by concluding that Oppila could not hear the truth because his ears were "oppilated," obstructed.[116]

On several levels these arguments certainly resonated beyond their immediate theological implications. One was diplomatic and political. Both Agila and Oppila represented the king of the Visigoths in Spain, who were still Arians. Generations earlier King Clovis had driven the Arian Visigoths from most of Gaul and had become a champion of Catholic Christianity. Gregory's arguments now against Arianism were hence reminders to the current Frankish kings of the commitment associated with their dynasty. King Chilperic was one king who apparently needed such reminders. Soon

[115] *Hist.* 6.5, 17.
[116] *Hist.* 6.40.

after Agila visited his court he issued a royal charter that denied the existence of the three Persons and identified the Trinity simply as God; but he eventually changed his mind when Gregory threatened him with the wrath of God and the saints.[117] By 581 Chilperic was actually helping Gregory in his arguments against the Jew Priscus.

Another level of resonance involved people's thinking about the human body and its illnesses. The celebration of Christmas provided people with an annual opportunity to consider how "the Father had joined the Word to flesh." The Son was God; by assuming flesh the Son had sanctified the human body; so other people's bodies were also sacred, to be kept "without blemish" by avoiding sins.[118] In a roundabout way the Catholic doctrine of Christ's incarnation reaffirmed the causal links between sins and illnesses and between correct behavior and good health that were so influential in shaping private and public conduct, even as it extended the implications of that nexus of associations. Not only did people want to remain healthy in order to ensure their standing in their communities, but they also had to think about the future by assuming the responsibility of preparing their bodies, and not simply their souls, for eventual residence in Paradise.[119]

Gregory too linked his debates over the nature of the Trinity with a belief in the resurrection of the body. He had cautioned Agila against belittling the Holy Spirit, "if you have any hope of a resurrection"; he had hinted that Oppila denied the resurrection; and his debate with Oppila had taken place on Easter. Gregory also recorded a debate in 590 with one of his own priests who denied the possibility of any future resurrection. Although Gregory claimed to rely upon apostolic tradition and biblical teachings, the priest was equally well versed, and their debate started as a duel of competing biblical citations. The priest began by citing God's harsh verdict upon a disobedient Adam: "You are dust, and you will return to dust." Gregory replied that souls in fact live on after their departure from bodies and eagerly await the resurrection to come; that people "asleep in death" would be resurrected from their graves; and that through his own resurrection the Lord had re-created life for the dead. The priest then conceded the resurrection of the Lord but still could not acknowledge that other dead people too would rise again. Gregory's response to this hesitation changed the direction of the debate. Not only did he insist that the Son of God had assumed flesh and died in order to save mankind from "eternal death"; he also claimed that the Lord had released the "souls of the just" from the "infernal prison" in which they had been confined and tortured. After this

---

[117] *Hist.* 5.44.

[118] *VM* 3.16, the Word; *GM* praef., the Son; *VP* 7 praef., "corpus sine macula."

[119] Cf. *VP* 7.4: "Magnificent is that soundness of body and heart that displays its beauty in this present age and bestows eternal life in the future."

argument the priest no longer objected to the principle of universal resurrection. Instead he was concerned specifically about the fate of the bodies
with which those souls would be again united, and about the Final Judgment. As also in the debates over the Trinity and the incarnation, what had
started as an argument about resurrection now became a discussion about
bodies and sin.

The priest then asked some pointed questions about people's bodies.
Could bones burned to ashes be resurrected? Could flesh that had been
devoured by beasts or swallowed by fish and then excreted as waste to rot
on the ground or in the water be resurrected? Gregory insisted in reply not
only that God who had once created from nothing could easily "repair"
these bodies at the moment of resurrection, but also that he did so for a
specific purpose, "so that the body that once existed in this world might
receive the penalty or the reward that it deserves." In response to questions
about this Final Judgment, Gregory stressed that even an unbeliever had to
be resurrected in the body, so that "he might suffer his punishment in the
body in which he had sinned." Until then, saints were in heaven and sinners
in the infernal prison; but without a resurrection of the dead, none could
receive his final judgment. Prior sins, resurrection, Final Judgment, rewards or punishments: all presupposed the importance of people's bodies.
Properly humbled (and probably duly chastised), the priest then left.[120]

Gregory's arguments were again not all that impressive intellectually,
and he himself perhaps did not fully understand their subtleties. Some of
his assertions seem inconsistent. At one point he claimed that the Son of
God had died in order to free the souls of the just from an infernal prison;
later he stated that only sinners awaited their resurrection and the Final
Judgment in this infernal prison because saints were already residing in
heaven. In order to preserve both claims Gregory apparently stressed Jesus
Christ's own death and resurrection as a transition point; thereafter only
sinners waited in this prison. Gregory also initially emphasized the separa-
tion of the soul (*anima*) from the body at the moment of death and their
eventual reunification at the moment of resurrection. Later he mentioned
the departure of the spirit (*spiritus*) from a dead body, but without indicating whether he now identified soul and spirit.[121]

Although Gregory's collages of biblical citations can sometimes seem a
bit scatterbrained, these were nonetheless genuine theological concerns.

[120] *Hist.* 10.19. These questions about the fragmentation and reassembly of people's
bodies lingered through the medieval period: see Bynum (1991) 239–97, who links them
with fundamental concerns about identity.

[121] Probably he did not. For Gregory, *anima* "was immortal but had no share in the divine
nature" (*Hist.* 1 praef.). *Spiritus* usually signified the "breath of life" whose departure marked
a person's death; note GC 74, for a corpse regaining its *spiritus* in order to make some final
comments.

Gregory claimed that the priest had been "infected by the poison of the Sadducees"; and since most of the citations that the priest used to support his objections were from the Old Testament while Gregory relied primarily (but not exclusively) upon the New Testament, this particular argument is indicative perhaps of a wider contemporary debate between Christians and Jews over the possibility of a bodily resurrection, perhaps too of a Jewish community at Tours that posed a specific challenge to the Christian community, its doctrines, and its bishop. In fact, precisely in 590 Gregory went out of his way to ensure that he celebrated Easter one week after the Jewish Passover.[122] It is also important, however, to underscore the relevance and application of these doctrines to the life of Christian communities. Theology was more than an intellectual exercise that offered an excuse for a formal debate, and modern handbooks of early Christian theology that treat it as primarily a collection of abstruse doctrines and ideas are fundamentally misleading. Both specific behavior within communities and more abstract philosophical formulations were equally powerful ways of conceptualizing and articulating correct theological doctrines. As his language makes clear, Gregory barely distinguished the two. In particular, during this debate Gregory emphasized that the belief in a bodily resurrection in the future was associated with notions of illness and healing and of captivity and release; and with those associations his theology of a bodily resurrection merged directly with the healings performed by St. Martin and their social implications.[123]

One argument Gregory cited to support his theological position was Ezekiel's vision of the revitalization of the "dry bones": "when Ezekiel mentions that man was re-created after his dry bones were covered with flesh, strengthened with sinews, moistened with blood, and animated with the breath of the spirit, he is most certainly indicating the future resurrection." Gregory, and apparently others too, conceptualized illnesses and healings in similar terms. The ill were "dead" people, deprived of the "breath of their spirit." They had become hot, dry, stiff, tight, withered: "the bones in his legs were twisted like ropes."[124] Their healings hence often included a loosening, straightening, flowing, cooling, dampening; after the healing of one boy's withered hand, Gregory commented that "you might think that a sponge that had been long dry had been immersed in water and was thirstily soaking up the liquid."[125] The analogies used in another set of miracles neatly illustrated the contrast between the fiery

---

[122] *Hist.* 10.23.

[123] Note Bynum (1991) 77: "the same basic assumptions underlie theological discussion of resurrection and pious veneration of somatic miracle"; see also Gager (1982) and C. Pietri (1984), who links veneration for cults with theological debates.

[124] *VM* 3.6.

[125] *VM* 2.55.

retribution due to misdeeds and the cool assistance associated with healings. A man who assaulted the clerics at the shrine of St. Julian was struck
with a lightning bolt and "burned like a flaming funeral pyre"; but ill
people who requested the saint's patronage were healed: "the burning of
fevers is quenched as quickly as if you were to see waves tossed on a huge
funeral pyre and all its flames extinguished."[126] Illnesses and healings were
thus not simply analogies of death and resurrection, they were also reaffir-
mations of the validity of correct Christian doctrines and reminders that
present behavior had significant implications for future well-being.

Future consequences reiterated the importance of sins and forgiveness.
Gregory sometimes worried about the Final Judgment before God. At that
moment he prayed that St. Martin would serve as his personal advocate:
"This is the man for whom Martin petitions."[127] Gregory's theological
arguments suggest that he thought this Final Judgment was sometime off in
the future, when people's bodies and souls would be reunited "at the
moment of the resurrection of all flesh."[128] At least two people, however,
had received their final verdicts immediately, and in both cases the decision
effectively focused on the fate of their bodies: Jesus had ascended to heaven
with his body; and after Mary's death he had retrieved her body from her
tomb and reunited it with her soul in Paradise.[129] But Gregory also sometimes implied that other people too were judged promptly after their
deaths, and that the condition of their bodies at the moment of death was a
preview of that divine verdict. The bodies of saints, for instance, not only
did not decay but actually became more healthy after they died. So in a neat
reversal the worms that had infested the body of an ascetic at Nice disappeared after his death; and the intact corpse of one bishop demonstrated
that it was "already prepared for the glory of the future resurrection."[130]
Saints' tombs were fertile, and in contrast to the bleakness of most grave-
yards they hinted already at the fragrance of the garden of Paradise. At one
saint's tomb a withered lily blossomed annually as a sign that the saint
"flourishes in heaven like a palm tree."[131] In contrast, sinners often died
miserably. A man who mistreated the bishop of Angoulême literally
burned up from his fever: "his lifeless body was so black that you might

[126] VJ 15, flaming pyre; 3, waves.
[127] VM 2.60.
[128] VM 3.60.
[129] Hist. 1.24, GM 3, ascension; and GM 4, apparently the first formulation of the doctrine
of the bodily Assumption of the Virgin in Western orthodox theology: see van Esbroek (1981).
Brown (1988) 444–46 has some sensitive comments about the cult of the Virgin Mary.
[130] Hist. 6.6, VP 7.3.
[131] GC 50. Note also GC 51: tombs buried beneath a pavement "sprouted" and worked
their way to the surface as a demonstration of the purity of the bodies within. Even Frankish
aristocrats shared this conceit: see Epistolae Austrasicae 22, for the roses blooming at an
abbot's tomb in Metz.

think it had been placed on coals and burned"; a man who stole from the possessions of St. Julian became so overheated from a fever that "smoke poured from his body as if from a furnace."[132]

In his theological arguments Gregory had stressed that, after the final resurrection, some people would suffer bodily for their bodily sins. In fact, Gregory's vision of these torments in Hell was an elaboration of his description of people's illnesses, especially their burning fevers. Because in Hell people suffered from "eternal flames," an appropriate symbol of those "infernal fires" was a sulfurous volcano in Sicily.[133] Conversely, his vision of life in the garden of heaven was a reflection of the cool relief and health that people found at saints' tombs.[134] People therefore wanted to live healthy now in order to die healthy and be resurrected healthy in the future. Since, as we have seen, illnesses were the results of sins, healings represented not only forgiveness for those sins now but also guarantees of favorable verdicts in the future at the Final Judgment. So in 567 Bishop Eufronius of Tours and some of his suffragan bishops had warned their congregations to avoid sexual immoralities lest "a soul be snatched from this world while still impure."[135] Illnesses led to constriction, bondage, and darkness, much like being confined in a prison: "the door to this prison was locked, its bar strengthened by iron and its bolt shut with a key."[136] But when St. Martin appeared at this prison, he introduced himself as *absolutor vester*, "your liberator" or "your redeemer"; and his healings resembled the liberation and redemption that the Lord had offered through his own death and resurrection. Each ritual of healing was a reenactment of the original Easter, and the Easter festivals that Gregory and his congregation celebrated often included both healings and releases from captivity. Gregory had debated with his priest about the possibility of resurrection probably during the Lenten season of 590.[137] An appropriate miracle then occurred during the celebration of precisely that Easter. As a prisoner was being transported across the Loire, he was released by the

---

[132] *Hist.* 5.36, coals; *VJ* 17, smoke.

[133] *VM* 4.1, flames; *De cursu* 9, 13, volcano.

[134] Cf. *Hist.* 6.29, for a nun's vision of the garden of heaven.

[135] *Epistola, apud* Council of Tours, a.567. Although Gregory once described the "river of fire" that awaited abbots who failed to enforce discipline (*Hist.* 4.33), he was unfamiliar with the notion of a Purgatory in which people could cleanse themselves of their own sins: see Le Goff (1984) 96–127. He did concede the possibility that others might offer requiem masses on behalf of the souls of the deceased (*GM* 74, *GC* 64). For the shift already in the early medieval period from a concern for the collective fate of mankind at the end of time to an appraisal of the personal fate of each individual immediately after death, see Gurevich (1988) 111–23, 138–39.

[136] *VM* 4.26.

[137] In the chapter before this debate Gregory had mentioned Ingytrud's funeral on March 9; he later celebrated Easter on April 2 (*Hist.* 10.12, 23).

power of St. Martin: "the chains that held the man captive were broken, and the ropes were loosened and fell from his hands."[138] Bodily miracles therefore confirmed and conformed to Catholic doctrines about the body. Liberation, healing, forgiveness: current miracles were validations of the Lord's bodily resurrection long ago, guarantees of others' bodily resurrection in the future, and previews of people's ultimate verdicts at the Final Judgment.

The ritual of healing presupposed an apparent paradox, that health and a new life were available only at the tomb of a dead saint; as Gregory summarized one of his own treatments, "I received my health from the tomb."[139] Acceptance of this paradox became a mark of membership in the Christian community, and non-Christians certainly found it baffling. At Bordeaux a Jew bluntly insisted that St. Martin could not help an ill man because, having been buried in his tomb, the saint had decayed into dust: "the dirt pressing down [on him in his tomb] has made him into dirt. In vain do you go to his shrine; a dead man will not be able to provide medicine for the living." Because of his disbelief, this Jew himself became ill.[140] For the church of St. Martin at Tours, like other saints' shrines elsewhere, created a therapeutic milieu whose rituals and symbols encouraged people to accept certain Christian explanations about the etiology of illnesses, the proper treatments for them, and the efficacy of those treatments. Healing implied a new way of thinking that resolved not only the paradox about the availability of health at the tombs of saints, but also the larger paradox about the meaning of the death of Jesus Christ that was central to Christianity's message of salvation. Some of the prize relics from the Holy Land were tokens made of clay from Jesus' tomb. At the tomb of St. Martin too people collected dust, which they then mixed with water and swallowed as a "powerful antidote": "O heavenly purgative!"[141] Such a triumphant exclamation about the healing power of dirt presupposed both an emotional commitment and a way of thinking.

Because modern historians no longer share either that commitment or that thinking, stories about miraculous healings seem to require special explanations. The interpretations in this chapter too are not immune from attempting to relieve our uneasiness by accounting for ancient healings in

[138] VM 4.16; also 1.21, where Gregory compared a rescue from the gallows to the resurrection of a dead man. Note the explicit comparison in Fortunatus, Vita Albini 46: men freed from a prison "emerged alive, as if from a tomb."
[139] VM 2.1.
[140] VM 3.50.
[141] GM 6, Holy Land; VM 2.1, antidote; 3.50, purgative.

terms of comparative anthropology, theological doctrines, and social conventions. Gregory and his contemporaries would probably have cared little for these discussions about community values, personal identities, definitions of power, and doctrinal analogues; for them, these were simply stories about their lives. Suffering and misery were not temporary deprivations from which they had to be rescued and returned to a normal existence; instead, because pain and hardship were routine components of their ordinary lives, miracles represented special moments, flickering opportunities for the realization of hopes and dreams in an otherwise bitter life. Lords and masters may have demanded subservience and hard work, but saints expected only devotion. In return, saints demonstrated their own love and concern, and their healings emphasized caring over curing. Diseases required cures, for which Merovingian medical techniques were no more adept than those of their classical predecessors; but the beliefs and rituals associated with saints' shrines were very successful at providing the care required for healing ill people and ill communities.

CHAPTER FOUR

Pilgrimages and Miracle Stories

I N THE ANCIENT WORLD traveling was always arduous and slow. In late antique Gaul some people hitched rides on the boats that moved commodities on the extensive network of rivers;[1] some rode horses or jostled along in wagons; but most walked. Delays and accidents were common as people struggled against the tyranny of distance. Highwaymen threatened the travelers, and inclement weather threatened the roads, as stiff winds blew up clouds of blinding dust and heavy rains turned roadways into tracks of mud and potholes; so it is not surprising that the first concern of the bishops who met at one council was to request quick decisions, "lest a winter storm keep us from our own sees."[2] Gregory himself once fell off his horse during a storm.[3] In comparison with modern France and its various forms of high-speed transportation, late antique Gaul seemed enormous. Even comparatively simple journeys from Tours to Poitiers, Orléans, or Paris, 70 to 120 miles, required days or even weeks for Gregory to complete. Weariness was everyone's constant companion; in the early fifth century one Gallic preacher had pointed out to his congregation that only the relics of saints could travel without suffering any fatigue.[4]

But relics had it easy, because others transported them; and by the later sixth century most saints were securely buried at shrines, blissfully sleeping in their tombs while people struggled to visit them. In early Merovingian Gaul, as elsewhere around the Mediterranean world, pilgrimages to various shrines were common; the tomb of St. Martin made Tours a particularly attractive destination. Many of these pilgrims contemplated these journeys precisely while they were already ill or bereft; yet with their decisions they also committed themselves to enduring additional physical pain and emotional dislocation. Modern accounts of ancient pilgrimages tend to overlook the sheer effort involved, as well as the burning commitment that made that effort possible. Every pilgrimage represented a voluntary vow that demanded fulfillment, and failure to honor that vow was

[1] Cf. VM 4.29.
[2] Council of Mâcon a.585, praef.; VM 1.36, bandits; Hist. 9.19, 39, GC 18, mud.
[3] GM 83.
[4] Victricius of Rouen, De laude sanctorum 9, "sine peregrinationis fastidio."

perhaps more ignominious than not receiving a healing or a blessing at the shrine. Once people left their communities and families, the constraints of ordinary timetables became insignificant. Journeys were long; many people stayed at Tours for months, even years; most lived on charity, no longer participants in the social conventions of their communities or the ecological rhythms that dominated agrarian societies. Instead, because people visited shrines that commemorated specific saints, pilgrimages entailed direct involvement in or even reenactment of particular historical or mythological events. Pilgrimages were not simply trips from somewhere to Tours, they were also journeys from the present into the past in order to fulfill vows about the future. Subsequent sections of this chapter will discuss pilgrims' geographical origins and their vows, their destination of Tours and the church of St. Martin, the diffusion of relics of St. Martin, and Gregory's stories about those pilgrimages and relics; the emphasis throughout is on these aspects of effort, commitment, and reenactment. Each pilgrimage was a lengthy process, and as such it could symbolize, in a wonderfully resonant way, a long journey, an extended project of construction or writing, or even a rededication of one's life.

1. Pilgrimages to Tours

As he collected the miracles of St. Martin, Gregory once claimed that "innumerable people" came "from remote regions" to request the saint's assistance at Tours.[5] Since he was by then the guardian of the shrine, his enthusiasm is understandable; but because Gregory recorded so many stories, it is possible to examine, and challenge, his own claims. Gregory provided information about almost 300 pilgrims who came to Tours. Not all came to visit the shrines associated with St. Martin. Some visited other shrines and tombs in the Touraine, such as a church at Pernay dedicated with relics of St. Julian and St. Nicetius; others went to other shrines in Tours itself, such as a church dedicated to St. Julian. In fact, one blind woman who came to pray at the tomb of St. Martin was told in a vision to go instead to the church of St. Julian.[6] But most pilgrims to Tours had St. Martin on their minds.

Gregory mentioned more than 250 pilgrims who came to the shrines of St. Martin at Tours primarily during Eufronius's and his own episcopacies; and he furthermore provided information about the geographical origins of about 160 of them. Almost three-quarters came from cities outside the Touraine: 22.5 percent of the pilgrims came from Clermont and Limoges

---

[5] VM 2.53.

[6] VJ 50, VP 7.8, Pernay; VJ 37–39, church of St. Julian; VJ 47, blind woman; other examples in L. Pietri (1983) 548n.100.

in the Massif Central and the nearby city of Bourges; 18 percent came from
cities in the old Roman province of Third Lugdunensis that by now ap-
proximated the ecclesiastical province dependent upon the metropolitan
see of Tours; 15.5 percent came from cities in northern Gaul such as
Rheims, Soissons, and Metz, or from royal courts associated with those
cities; 13 percent came from cities in Aquitaine; 11 percent came from
Paris, neighboring cities, and cities in Normandy; and most of the remaining pilgrims came from other cities in eastern Gaul.[7] On the assumption
that these pilgrims with known geographical origins formed a representative sample, these figures stress the impact of the cult in central and northern Gaul. They also hint at the limitations of the attractiveness of St.
Martin's cult. Some of the regions that supplied few or no pilgrims were
also regions peripheral to Frankish control. The far southwestern corner of
Gaul and the slopes of the Pyrenees maintained their reputations for autonomy from centralized rule that had been apparent already under Roman
domination. Of the pilgrims from Aquitaine in general, almost all came
from Poitiers, in the northern part of the region, whose city territory was
contiguous to the Touraine. The rest of southern Gaul not only had little
contact with the cult of St. Martin at Tours, it also maintained its autonomy from the control of the Merovingian kings. Although a mad recluse
from Bordeaux once visited Tours, increasingly the bishops of Bordeaux
were already beginning to challenge Frankish kings by fancying themselves
as the holders of an "apostolic see."[8] A boy from Albi once traveled to
Tours,[9] but the heartland of the old Gothic kingdom remained marginal to
Frankish control long after the Visigoths were forced to leave for Spain.
Provence and southeastern Gaul had also been late additions to Frankish
control and still retained their close links with northern Italy. So even
though the cult of St. Martin at Tours was not closely associated with the
Merovingian kings, its attractiveness seemed to coincide largely with the
primary Frankish interests in central and northern Gaul. As in both earlier
Roman and subsequent medieval periods, southern Gaul was distinguished from central and northern Gaul, not only in terms of administrative control but now also in terms of saints' cults.

Clustering the geographical origins of these pilgrims according to these
larger regions nevertheless conceals some fundamental implications about
the positions of both Tours and Bishop Gregory. First, Gregory's own
personal and family connections linked him closely with cities and regions
in eastern and central Gaul such as Clermont and the Auvergne, Lyon,

---

[7] L. Pietri (1983) 550–57 clusters the cities in these particular larger regions and calculates
these statistics about the pilgrims with known geographical origins.

[8] *Hist.* 8.34, recluse; 4.26, "apostolic see."

[9] *VM* 3.30.

Langres, and Burgundy. When Gregory became bishop at Tours, he had brought with him relics of saints from some of those cities and regions. Yet very few pilgrims came to Tours from those cities; in fact, one man came to Tours from Clermont not as a respectful pilgrim but only because he had become deaf and mute for having insulted St. Martin.[10] On the basis of the information available in Gregory's writings, he and his companions in 563 were apparently the only pilgrims to Tours from Lyon, and his mother, after her retirement to her family's lands, the only pilgrim from Burgundy (and she presumably came in part to visit her son). Since pilgrims therefore seem not to have followed either the extension of an important aristocratic family's influence or the subsequent exportation of relics of their own local saints, perhaps the diminishment of his family's influence at Clermont, Lyon, and Langres had affected the number of pilgrims from those cities. The incidence of pilgrimage reflected not only the popularity of particular cults, but also the networks of influence among various aristocratic, and later royal, families.

A second hidden implication concerns the prominence of Tours. Just over one-quarter of pilgrims with known geographical origins came from the Touraine; if the pilgrims whose origins Gregory did not identify were also locals (a plausible assumption), then more than half of the total pilgrims were from the Touraine. Even the most prominent cult in early Merovingian Gaul was largely a local, diocesan cult. Furthermore, most pilgrims from outside the Touraine came from cities within about 125 miles of Tours, such as Paris, Limoges, Bourges, Angers, and Poitiers (and the latter three cities were also all contiguous to the Touraine). So even though pilgrims certainly traveled farther than these direct distances, and even though some pilgrims came to Tours from more remote cities, in particular from the royal courts in Soissons and Metz, the wider attraction of St. Martin's cult outside the Touraine was still regional, restricted primarily to central Gaul.[11] Merovingian kings were apparently not alone in deciding to patronize other cults. Although Abbot Aredius of Limoges often visited Tours, he also carefully maintained his links with the shrine of St. Julian at Brioude, named both St. Martin and St. Hilary as his heirs, and at his deathbed was attended in addition by several other saints; and one blind man, after being healed in the church of St. Hilary at Poitiers, never completed his pilgrimage to Tours.[12] Even Gregory made only a single pilgrimage to Tours before becoming bishop in 573. Nor was the reputation of St. Martin as widespread as Gregory claimed. He himself once

[10] *Hist.* 4.16.

[11] So Lelong (1960), against the overstatement of L. Pietri (1983) 556–57. For similar restrictions on the impact of cults of Aquitanian saints, see Higounet (1953) 160.

[12] *Hist.* 10.29, *VJ* 28, 41, 45, Aredius; Fortunatus, *VH* 17–19, blind man.

talked with a man who admitted that as a boy he had not known the location of the saint's tomb.[13] Despite all the information that Gregory collected about pilgrims to Tours, it is essential not to overstate the prominence of the cult of St. Martin in early Merovingian Gaul.

A third implication concerns the standing of both Tours as metropolitan see and Gregory as metropolitan bishop. Gregory's personal and family connections pointed south and east of Tours to the Auvergne, Lyon, Langres, and Burgundy; his political connections linked him in addition with cities and courts north and northeast of Tours; and his historical writings about events in Gaul mirrored all those geographical interests. Yet his ecclesiastical province, which included the suffragan sees of Angers, Le Mans, Nantes, and Rennes, as well as, in Brittany, Vannes and other cities, faced west toward the Atlantic Ocean. Although pilgrims did come to Tours from some of his suffragan cities or from Brittany in general, both Gregory and his episcopal predecessors seem to have had little impact in or control over their ecclesiastical province.[14] In the far west Brittany had already been marginal to the Roman Empire, and Bretons still retained a distinctive ethnic hairstyle and costume. In the sixth century Brittany was under the control of four counts who each ruled a small "kingdom" that was only nominally responsible to Frankish authority, and who repeatedly attacked neighboring cities such as Nantes and Rennes. Frankish kings occasionally conducted campaigns against the Bretons but were generally unsuccessful with their threats; in fact, Brittany was a region in which men could safely hide from Frankish kings.[15] The Frankish kings had furthermore divided the cities in this ecclesiastical province among their various kingdoms, and the king who controlled Tours rarely also controlled many, if any, of its suffragan cities. After Charibert's death in 567 Guntramn, Sigibert, Chilperic, and the sons of the two latter kings had all wrangled over these cities and sometimes turned them against each other. When King Chilperic acquired control over Le Mans, for instance, he used its men in a campaign against Tours in 576.[16]

In a region so fragmented and so vulnerable, bishops attempted to defend their cities from these attacks, and in the process they enhanced their local influence. Tours was not the only family see in the region. In 549 Felix

[13] *Hist.* 8.15.

[14] The usurper Magnus Maximus had apparently created the province of Third Lugdunensis during the 380s: see Harries (1978) 36–38. Since Tours had therefore become a civil metropolitan capital only shortly before Roman administration began collapsing during the fifth century, perhaps few loyalties had developed between it and the other cities in the new province.

[15] *Hist.* 10.9, hairstyle; *Hist.* 4.4, Breton kingdoms; *Hist.* 5.31; 9.18, 24; 10.9, GM 60, attacks; *Hist.* 4.20, 5.48, asylum.

[16] *Hist.* 5.1, 4.

had succeeded his father as bishop of Nantes.[17] As bishop he tried to reconcile one of the counts of Brittany with his brother and to negotiate with the Bretons after a devastating invasion; and he had meanwhile masterminded a huge construction project for taming the Loire River.[18] Felix's own vanities increased proportionally. Upon completing a new cathedral he dedicated it, not only with relics of important (and neighboring) Gallic saints such as St. Martin and St. Hilary, which went into the side chapels, but also with relics of St. Peter and St. Paul.[19] While attending the ceremony of dedication Fortunatus was so impressed that he conferred a particularly "Italian" compliment on all these accomplishments: here in a city at the "edge of the world" Felix had conjured up a "new Rome."[20]

Gregory in contrast was simply intimidated by the achievements of this suffragan bishop, and like his episcopal predecessors at Tours he had little impact in the suffragan sees of his ecclesiastical province. Brittany had long since acquired an ecclesiastical autonomy to match its political independence, and it was perhaps predictable that at the beginning of the sixth century Bishop Licinius of Tours had complained about the unconventional liturgical practices of priests in Brittany.[21] Cities in the ecclesiastical province of Tours sometimes looked elsewhere for leadership. Monastic establishments in some of its cities, such as Le Mans and Rennes, had close connections with monasteries in other cities along the coast, such as Coutances, Bayeux, and Avranches, that were in the ecclesiastical province subordinate to Rouen.[22] Bishop Germanus of Paris once went to Angers to help Bishop Eutropius and other local bishops transfer the body of St. Albinus to a new church;[23] he also visited Nantes, where in gratitude for his healings the local merchants gave him money to distribute to the poor;[24] Bishop Dumnolus of Le Mans invited him to participate in the dedication of a new monastery and church;[25] in fact, Germanus seems to have visited these cities more often than did their own metropolitan bishop.

[17] See Fortunatus, *Carm.* 4.1, for Felix's father Eumerius, with Heinzelmann (1976) 214–15, for the family and its long-standing influence.

[18] *Hist.* 4.4, 5.31; Fortunatus, *Carm.* 3.10.

[19] Fortunatus, *Carm.* 3.7.

[20] Fortunatus, *Carm.* 3.8.3, 20, "hic nova Roma venit." Fortunatus also sometimes stayed at Felix's estate near Nantes: see *Carm.* 5.7, 11.25.7.

[21] Above, chapter 1. Since Licinius was originally from Angers (*Hist.* 10.31), perhaps he had firsthand knowledge.

[22] Fortunatus, *Vita Paterni* 33, for the monasteries Paternus founded in these five cities in Brittany.

[23] Fortunatus, *Vita Albini* 55. Albinus had still been bishop of Angers in 549, and his successor Eutropius was no longer bishop by the time of the Council of Paris that may have met in the later 550s: see Krusch (1885) 808n.3.

[24] Fortunatus, *Vita Germani* 129–34; also 158.

[25] *Actus pontificum Cenomannis in urbe degentium*, ed. Busson and Ledru, 80–81.

Bishops of Tours nevertheless still occasionally tried to impose their authority. In 567 Bishop Eufronius convened a regional council at Tours that insisted that no one could become a bishop without the consent of the metropolitan and other bishops in the ecclesiastical province.[26] Although Felix of Nantes and other suffragan bishops from Angers, Rennes, and Le Mans attended this regional council, no bishops from Brittany were present. This council represented perhaps a final moment of unanimity between the metropolitan and some of his suffragan bishops, since soon thereafter the kings divided these cities among their various kingdoms. And a suffragan bishop such as Felix was anyway himself already an imposing figure. When Eufronius and his other suffragan bishops attended the dedication of the new cathedral at Nantes, Fortunatus's description of this convocation left the impression that Felix had convened his own regional council.[27] Felix may also have been able to place one of his clerics as bishop of Rennes.[28] So this suffragan bishop, who had more seniority than his metropolitan, perhaps also had more local influence.

But at least Eufronius had been a few years older. In 573, however, Felix suddenly became the suffragan of a metropolitan young enough to be his son. His subsequent behavior made it difficult for himself and Gregory to get along. Felix was the only bishop from his ecclesiastical province to attend the council at Paris that decided rival royal and ecclesiastical claims; so while Gregory was scrambling in the first months after his consecration to establish himself at Tours, Felix was ostensibly promoting his own royal and episcopal connections.[29] He also took advantage of Gregory's disputes with kings and magistrates. Early in 576, when an army sent by King Chilperic was threatening Tours, Felix tried to claim an estate that belonged to the cathedral of Tours and he repeated the malicious rumors about the behavior of Gregory's brother Peter at Langres; in 580 he gave refuge to one of the men who had plotted with Count Leudast against Gregory. Gregory predictably thought that Felix was greedy and arrogant.[30] Although the two once had a discussion about clerical chastity,[31] Gregory never mentioned any visit to Nantes. When Felix was dying in 582, he acted like a metropolitan again by trying to convince his "neigh-

[26] Council of Tours a.567, Can.9, perhaps a reaction to the peculiar selection of Macliav as bishop of Vannes (*Hist.* 4.4): see L. Pietri (1983) 191–92. Perhaps at the same time Felix, other suffragan bishops, and some neighboring bishops joined Eufronius in sanctioning the convent founded by Radegund at Poitiers (*Hist.* 9.39): see above, chapter 1, section 2.

[27] Fortunatus, *Carm.* 3.6.19–28, 45, "hinc te pontifices circumdant."

[28] If the unnamed bishop in *GC* 77 can be identified with Victurius of Rennes: see McDermott (1975) 20, who also offers a more charitable interpretation of the relationship between Gregory and Felix and even suggests that they became friends.

[29] Above, chapter 2, section 1.

[30] *Hist.* 5.5, 49.

[31] *GC* 77.

boring bishops" to support his designated successor; but Gregory rejected both the candidate and an invitation to visit Nantes.[32]

In fact, Gregory never mentioned that he had visited any of his suffragan sees; in return, few pilgrims from those sees visited Tours. An ascetic from Brittany came to Tours in 577, but only because it was on the route of his pilgrimage to Jerusalem.[33] During the episcopacy of Felix apparently no pilgrims from Nantes came to Tours; his successor, Nonnichius, finally visited the church of St. Martin in 591, almost a decade after he had become bishop of Nantes.[34] From Le Mans, whose territory was contiguous to the Touraine, Gregory mentioned only one pilgrim, an itinerant preacher who was healed of his paralysis at the church of St. Martin in 577;[35] Le Mans in fact sent to the Touraine more hostile soldiers than respectful pilgrims. Only from Angers, also contiguous to the Touraine, did any appreciable number of pilgrims visit shrines of St. Martin, although several went only to Candes, which was near the boundary between the territories of the two cities.[36] So although Gregory insisted that St. Martin was "a special patron for the entire world,"[37] his own ecclesiastical province seems not to have fully conceded that claim. The popularity of saints' cults was not independent of contemporary politics and feuds, and Gregory's inability to exercise his metropolitan authority clearly affected the number of pilgrimages to the church of St. Martin from his suffragan sees. Even the cult of St. Martin could not transcend the weakness of the bishops of Tours in their own ecclesiastical province.

The social standing of the pilgrims to Tours also has important implications. Of the visitors whose social standing Gregory mentioned, 59 percent were ecclesiastics or distinguished laymen. Even though not all these visitors should be classified strictly as pilgrims, since some, for instance, were royal magistrates who came to Tours to revise the tax registers,[38] the proportion of elites among these pilgrims with identified social backgrounds was still high. But this observation does not necessarily imply that pilgrimages were therefore characteristically aristocratic or clerical under-

---

[32] *Hist.* 6.15. This exchange invites speculation. Since Felix's handpicked successor was his twenty-five-year-old nephew or grandson, perhaps he was making a subtle comment about Gregory's succession to his mother's cousin as bishop at Tours. Nantes nevertheless remained a family see, because another relative named Nonnichius succeeded Felix. Since Felix had once kept a noted ascetic waiting on his deathbed in 573 (*VP* 10.4), perhaps Gregory was now repaying him in kind.

[33] *Hist.* 5.21, 8.34. In the mid-sixth century a Breton named Johannis had lived as a recluse in the Touraine at Chinon (*GC* 23).

[34] *VM* 4.27.

[35] *VM* 2.40.

[36] *VM* 1.22, 2.48, 3.23.

[37] *VM* 4 praef.

[38] *VM* 4.6.

takings. Instead, the constraints on pilgrimages reflected the constraints on agrarian society in general. In traditional, preindustrial societies an enormous proportion, perhaps almost 90 percent, of the work force was involved in the direct production of food. Some of these food producers were pastoralists, hunters, or fishermen, but most were peasants effectively (and sometimes legally) tied to the land they worked. Early Merovingian society was no exception, and since pilgrimages were essentially activities that demanded much "leisure time" and mobility, the high proportion of elites becomes predictable. Because ecclesiastics and distinguished laymen were exempt from the direct production of food either because of their wealth or, as monks and clerics, because of their vocations, they had greater opportunities and resources to travel.[39]

Conversely, the proportion of pilgrims who were not elites, 41 percent of the pilgrims with known social backgrounds, 70 percent of all pilgrims if the unidentified ones are assumed not to be elites,[40] is all the more impressive in the face of these constraints. Not only did they not have the time or the opportunity to visit Tours easily, but the requirements of their agrarian livelihoods sometimes created dilemmas when they wanted, or were expected, to visit. Although Sundays and annual saints' festivals were celebrated on fixed dates, agrarian rhythms were not so predictable and might conflict with Christianity's festival days. Working during a festival was one common reason for people's becoming ill or suffering disasters. Some people decided to work then simply because they had no respect for a saint. In a town near Bourges one man explained why he had decided to brew beer during the festival of St. Marianus, a hermit who had died while gathering fruit: "Do you think that a man who slipped from a tree while satisfying his appetite has been included in the company of angels, so that he ought to be venerated as a saint? It is better to do what is necessary at home than to honor such a saint."[41] Others had to make a more agonizing choice between the expectations of liturgical time and the demands of agrarian time or, as Gregory commonly phrased it, between respect and rashness; so another man from Bourges decided to collect his newly mown hay on a Sunday because he "was afraid that it would be drenched at the arrival of an approaching storm and that he would lose [the results of] his labor."[42]

[39] Crone (1989) 15–16, on the percentage of food producers; and Holum (1990) 72, on imperial pilgrimages: "long-distance travel, the possession of the material resources and stamina to master distance, is one of the most effective claims to rank and power."

[40] As suggested by L. Pietri (1983) 560–61, who also, 557–63, computes the statistics on the social standing of pilgrims to Tours.

[41] GC 80.

[42] VM 4.45. As the antithesis to reverentia, the "respect" characteristic of obedient Christians, Brown (1981) 119–27 suggested rusticitas, which he translated as "boorishness." But rusticitas included a wider spectrum of meanings: see Van Dam (1988b) 12–13. A more precise antithesis is temeritas, "rashness," which Gregory in fact used to explain deviant behavior: see GM 73, 84–88.

Since the annual festivals of St. Martin likewise had to compete with the demands of the agrarian cycle, the "summer festival" on July 4 with the cutting of hay, the picking of fruit, and preparations for the next harvest, and the "winter festival" on November 11 with the aftermath of the vintage (not to mention the probability of rain and mud!),[43] pilgrimages presupposed that people had voluntarily chosen to ignore the normal obligations characteristic of small communities in a predominantly agrarian society. It is difficult to overestimate the dedication of these peasants who were prepared to devote themselves to such time-consuming pilgrimages that took them away from their livelihoods for so long.

Investigations into the geographical origins and social background of these pilgrims are useful for thinking about the politics and the sociology of early Merovingian Gaul and the impact of the cult of St. Martin, but they only begin to hint at the intensely personalized and emotional meanings of pilgrimage for the participants. Since most pilgrims were ill or crippled, and since an illness was often an indication of nonconformity with communities' norms, even many of the pilgrims from the Touraine were as "foreign" to Tours as those from other cities. And since pilgrimages leveled people by putting them into a liminal state of transition from alienation to wholeness, social distinctions soon became irrelevant; Romans and Franks, men and women, aristocrats and peasants, clergy and laity, all knelt and prayed together before the tomb of St. Martin. By choice, all pilgrims were "foreigners" and all were "poor."

Two pilgrims, Gregory and Fortunatus, provided firsthand accounts of their own journeys to Tours. Gregory had long been familiar with pilgrimages. As a young boy he had accompanied his family in visiting the shrine of St. Julian each year on the saint's festival in late summer. During one of these trips to Brioude his brother Peter became feverish, but was healed at the tomb of St. Julian; the next year Gregory developed a headache from the heat of the journey, but was healed at the nearby shrine of St. Ferreolus.[44] In 563 Gregory made a pilgrimage, apparently his first, to Tours.[45] Suffering from a severe fever and a painful infection, unable to eat or drink, he finally decided upon an *iter*, a journey or a pilgrimage, to the church of St. Martin at Tours. When he later recalled the journey in order to include it in his collection of miracles, he stressed two characteristics in particular, his longing and his resolve. His emotional attachment to the saint was now so "feverish" that it overwhelmed the fever resulting from

---

[43] *VM* 2.34, "summer festival," with *Hist.* 6.44, fruit picking in July, 8.40, haymaking in July; *VM* 4.41, "winter festival," with *Hist.* 9.5, *VJ* 36, vintage in October, *Hist.* 10.19, rain and mud in November. See L. Pietri (1984a), for the adoption of liturgical time as a form of Christianization, and Van Dam (1985) 285–98, for a more extensive discussion of the conflict between liturgical time and agrarian time.

[44] *VJ* 24–25.

[45] Probably from Lyon, although L. Pietri (1983) 552n.109 thinks he came from Clermont.

his illness; and his decision was now so firm that when his companions suggested that they turn back so that Gregory could recover, or die, at home, he insisted upon completing "the journey that he had vowed" to make. Both his longing and his resolve compelled him to finish "the journey that has been begun," and he even insisted that the completion of his pilgrimage had become a means of demonstrating whether he was "worthy" to see the church of St. Martin. Upon his arrival at Tours, Gregory and his companions celebrated vigils for a few days, until one morning he awoke and discovered that both he and one of his servants had been healed.[46]

A few years later another pilgrim arrived at Tours from Italy. Fortunatus was about the same age as Gregory and had grown up in northern Italy. Shrines dedicated to St. Martin were already common there, and at Padua one shrine even had frescoes depicting the deeds of St. Martin on one wall.[47] Like Gregory, Fortunatus too had learned about the power of St. Martin through his family, and at Ravenna he and a fellow student once received relief for their sore eyes from the oil in a lamp burning before a portrait of St. Martin. Although Fortunatus mentioned no explicit motivation, his subsequent journey to Gaul was perhaps an expression of his gratitude for the saint's assistance: "I will remember this as long as I am alive."[48] His journey was difficult, in part because he traveled across Germany and finally entered Gaul from the north, in part too because he was expected to recite his poems at the banquets of his barbarian hosts: "I was worn out from the road and from excessive toasts."[49] At Tours Fortunatus visited the shrine of "my lord Martin" and probably met Bishop Eufronius, whom he honored with some poems.[50] Even though he eventually settled at Poitiers, Fortunatus continued to visit Tours, where Gregory became another friend.

It is common to think of pilgrimages simply as responses to personal illnesses or other disasters, and in fact Gregory's information about the pilgrims to Tours seems to indicate that most were motivated by physical suffering and that only fewer than one-fifth of them came simply because of their faith.[51] Yet these firsthand accounts indicate that illnesses and healings were often secondary motivations. Both Peter and Gregory had become ill during (not before) the pilgrimages to Brioude; Gregory had no

---

[46] *VM* 1.32–33.

[47] *VM* 1.13–14; Fortunatus, *Vita S. Martini* 4.672–74.

[48] Fortunatus, *Vita S. Martini* 4.701, with the note to *VM* 1.15; and *VM* 1.13, for the healing of his father. Brennan (1985) 54–58 prefers to stress Fortunatus's interest in participating in the wedding of Sigibert and Brunhild at Metz in spring 566.

[49] Fortunatus, *Praefatio* 4, which also lists his itinerary from Ravenna to northern Gaul and then to Aquitaine.

[50] Fortunatus, *Carm.* 3.1–3; quotation from 3.1.3. Paul the Deacon, *HL* 2.13, later interpreted Fortunatus's journey to Tours as fulfillment of his "personal vow" to St. Martin.

[51] So L. Pietri (1983) 564–67.

guarantee that his journey to Tours would be successful; Fortunatus had already been healed before he traveled to Tours. For both the ill and the healthy the essential characteristics of pilgrimages were instead the vow, the dedication, and the commitment. Illness and healing were not necessarily the motivation and goal of pilgrimages, but rather opportunities for indicating submission and deference to the saints. "Faith" motivated even healthy people to make themselves unwell by undertaking the hardships of a pilgrimage, and it compelled people already ill or disabled to endure additional physical pain and emotional distress. Like the Israelites drifting through the wilderness before finally reaching the Promised Land,[52] these pilgrims had to worsen their circumstances before they had the opportunity to receive any assistance. The goal for these pilgrims was simply to fulfill their vows by completing their journeys. When Bishop Germanus of Paris once suggested rest to a deacon who was suffering from dysentery, the man refused: "It is the power of God that commands me to suffer as I deserve; for I am not leaving until I go to the church of the blessed bishop [Martin]." One lame boy wept because of his inability to finish "the journey that he had begun"; another woman discovered that her disabled hands were gradually being healed during (and not after) "the journey that she had begun."[53] Gregory too had stressed the importance of enduring the hardships of the journey itself. Once he had begun his pilgrimage to Tours in 563, he decided that he could not return home; instead, if he did not deserve to reach the promised land at the tomb of St. Martin, then, like the Israelites, he would "die in the wilderness."[54]

The miracles worked for the Israelites lost in the desert nevertheless provided some incentives; according to Gregory, the God who performed miracles at saints' shrines was the same God "who satisfied people's burning thirst by producing water from a dry rock in the desert," "who produced manna from heaven for starving people."[55] Yet it is essential to emphasize that healing alone was not necessarily an indication of a successful pilgrimage. One blind woman prepared to leave Tours even though she had not yet recovered her sight: "Blessed confessor, I thank you that I experienced and touched your holy shrine, even if I was not worthy to see it." Even though a mute man recovered his speech while traveling to Tours, he still went on to the church of St. Martin and "fulfilled his vow."[56] Just as men swore oaths of loyalty to one another, just as monks and nuns vowed to pursue their monastic life as an *iter*, a never-ending journey,[57] so pilgrims had taken vows to St. Martin, and pilgrimages became a means of

---

[52] Cf. *Hist.* 1.11.
[53] *VM* 2.12, deacon; 2.46, lame boy; 3.32, disabled woman.
[54] *VM* 1.32.
[55] *VM* 1 praef., *VP* 19.1.
[56] *VM* 2.54, blind woman; 4.40, mute man.
[57] Cf. *Hist.* 9.39.

demonstrating their commitment. The reward for their devotion was not necessarily the healing, but rather a glimpse of, and temporary participation in, a better life. Gregory had started his *Histories* with the story of Adam and Eve's expulsion from Paradise, the "abode of the angels." A pilgrimage was an opportunity for people to reverse this expulsion and escape, even if only temporarily, from "the labors of this world."[58] According to Gregory, the church of St. Martin was "the doorway to the garden of Paradise"; and one of the inscriptions in the church mentioned that the saint was now living with the angels.[59] In a description of one of St. Martin's miracles Fortunatus had compared the saint's kiss with the healing water of the Jordan River.[60] A doorway, a river to ford: with both sets of analogies the saint's church and his tomb offered an opportunity for pilgrims to imagine, and even temporarily to share, life in Paradise and the Promised Land.

2. "The Place Where His Body Is Now Honored"

A sixth-century preacher once reminded people why they had made their pilgrimages to Tours: "this place that is ornamented so gloriously with the tomb of his most holy body must be considered more fortunate and more exalted than all these others."[61] But pilgrims first had to decide which of the resting-places of St. Martin they wished to visit. At two villages in the Touraine shrines to St. Martin featured what we might call secondary tombs. Since saints were thought to be sleeping in their tombs, their beds could readily serve as alternatives. At Lyon, for instance, a bishop reconstructed the bed of Nicetius, one of his predecessors, covered it with an ornate shroud, and kept lamps burning around it. Because he and others treated this bed like a tomb, people were healed after kneeling before it. At Chalon-sur-Saône Bishop Agricola constructed a new cathedral; since the body of one former bishop had already been buried in another church, Agricola settled for having the bishop's bed moved into the sanctuary of the cathedral, where miracles of healing occurred.[62] In the case of St. Martin this assimilation was easier to accept, since his beds had already closely resembled graves. At Candes, where St. Martin had died, Gregory could hardly bring himself to describe the saint's bed as such, because St. Martin had slept on cinders on the pavement and used a stone as his pillow. Since

[58] *Hist.* 1.1.
[59] *VP* 19 praef.; Paulinus of Périgueux = Le Blant (1856–1865) 1, no. 176, trans. below, Appendix 3.
[60] Fortunatus, *Carm.* 10.6.35–36, 100. Note also Fortunatus, *VH* 12, on the cure of lepers at the tomb of St. Hilary: "the Jordan River came here to them."
[61] *Sermo* 4.
[62] *VP* 8.8, Lyon; *Hist.* 5.45, GC 84, Chalon-sur-Saône.

the small cell in which he had slept had had only a window as a door, it already resembled an oversize stone sarcophagus, "a tomb dug out of a cell," as Gregory described another monk's grave.[63] So a railing covered with a silk curtain surrounded the saint's bed, where people knelt and were healed. Martin's monastery at Marmoutier advertised another bed of the saint that also resembled a stone tomb. A nearby inscription described the coals, the cinders, the dust, and the stone pillow that St. Martin had used: "you were considered a bed here for his weary limbs." A railing surrounded this bed too, and pilgrims visited the site.[64] So while traveling to Tours pilgrims had to select among the various "tombs" of the saint.[65]

Most went of course to the saint's tomb in his church in the suburbs of Tours. The increasing significance of this church that was about a half-mile from the walls of the city proper is one important indication of the transformation of Roman into medieval cities in Gaul. By combining both an urban center and a sometimes extensive surrounding territory that itself included many smaller villages and settlements, Roman cities had integrated both "urban" and "rural" life. With the expansion of Christianity bishops had increasingly stressed the importance of the cathedrals in the urban centers, perhaps as one means of ensuring their control over their entire diocese. But they, and other patrons, also constructed many churches and shrines outside the urban centers. Some were in villages; many, such as the church of St. Martin or the church of St. Hilary, were near the urban centers. Tours and Poitiers were not the only Gallic cities in which a saint's church outside the city center attracted increasingly more pilgrims and residents, and the rise to prominence of these saint's churches marked the victory of the "suburbs outside the walls" over the old Roman urban centers.[66] During the later medieval period this settlement around the church of St. Martin even became known officially as "Martinopolis."[67]

As bishop Gregory of course lived within the city center of Tours in a residence that was near, perhaps even attached to, the cathedral. Other clerics shared this residence, and Gregory presumably hosted his guests at banquets there. Already in the first year of his episcopacy he had stamped his own identity on this residence by transforming a storeroom into an oratory and dedicating its altar with relics of, among other saints, both St.

[63] *VM* 2.45, 3.22, Candes; *VP* 20.4.

[64] *VM* 1.35, 2.39; and below, Appendix 3.

[65] Note that at Ligugé, Martin's monastery in the territory of Poitiers, his bed was apparently not a featured attraction; instead the shrine commemorated the spot where the saint had revived a dead man (*VM* 4.30). Perhaps the contrast was deliberate: if the Touraine had the shrines that commemorated the saint's resting places, then Ligugé would commemorate how St. Martin woke someone up!

[66] *GC* 44, with Galinié (1978), on the topography of Tours; and Février (1974), and Loseby (1992) 149–55, on the general trend.

[67] Gasnault (1961) 65–66.

Martin and St. Julian. Perhaps he also kept in this residence the sapphire-colored saucer that St. Martin had once acquired as a gift.[68] But even though Gregory imported these reminders of his own special relationships with these saints into his residence, he still conducted many of his services in a church in the suburbs; and because the city's wall literally separated the bishop's residence from the church of St. Martin,[69] even the bishops of Tours had to undertake a miniature pilgrimage each time they went from the urban center of Tours to the suburban "city of St. Martin."

In fact, as the importance of the church of St. Martin increased, the cathedral was losing its dynamic connection with the saint's memory, despite Gregory's efforts to revive it. As bishop Martin had once conducted most of his services in the cathedral, and while in Tours he had lived in a small cell connected to the cathedral. Gregory finally made this cell into a proper shrine. He requested Fortunatus to compose a short poem that commemorated how the saint had once clothed a poor man there and that was most likely engraved on a wall in the cell, and he placed relics of two Greek martyrs in the cell.[70] Gregory also rebuilt the cathedral. In 558 a fire had burned it and other intramural churches, and in the next year a fire had burned the church of St. Martin. As a telling indication of these churches' relative importance, King Chlothar and Bishop Eufronius had "immediately" financed a new roof for the church of St. Martin, and Eufronius had also repaired two of the churches inside the city.[71] The cathedral remained in ruins until Gregory finally rededicated it in 589/590.[72] Fortunatus was most impressed with the size of the new cathedral, its gleaming roof, and the bright illumination that the large windows provided for the frescoes on the walls: "you might think that these figures, although drawn in paint, were alive."[73] These paintings were apparently part of a cycle of frescoes that depicted some of St. Martin's miracles, and Fortunatus also provided a series of metrical descriptions from which Gregory could choose the appropriate captions to have inscribed on the walls of the cathedral.[74]

Since most of the miracles depicted in this cycle had been performed by St. Martin while a bishop, Gregory was presumably trying to promote the cathedral as a center of episcopal authority. But on his own showing not

[68] *GM* 33, *VP* 2.3, *GC* 20, oratory; *VM* 4.10, saucer.

[69] *VM* 1.23.

[70] *Hist.* 10.31; Fortunatus, *Carm.* 1.5, although conflating two distinct stories in Sulpicius Severus, *Dial.* 2.1–2, 3.10.

[71] *Hist.* 4.20.

[72] *Hist.* 10.31.

[73] Fortunatus, *Carm.* 10.6.92.

[74] Fortunatus, *Carm.* 10.6.25–72, 93–132, with the discussion of L. Pietri (1983) 828–31.

many people visited the cathedral. In it people sometimes observed lauds (then called matins) at daybreak, celebrated Easter mass, and kept the vigils before the festivals of Christmas, Epiphany, Easter, and Pentecost. But on the actual festival days of Christmas and Epiphany they then walked to the church of St. Martin to celebrate mass.[75] Although the citizens of Tours therefore continued to celebrate some of the great universal festivals in the cathedral, they seem not to have visited it often otherwise. In fact, the only people whom Gregory mentioned who went to the cathedral not intending to celebrate a service were King Clovis as part of his victory celebration, a man planning to start a feud, and some freed prisoners seeking refuge. Nor did Gregory mention a single pilgrim who visited the cathedral. Many of them perhaps never entered the urban center of Tours at all.[76]

Instead they went to the church of St. Martin; or rather, they went to the large cluster of buildings that by now surrounded the church. This collection of churches, monasteries, oratories, and shrines had become virtually a small village in its own right. The compound immediately surrounding the church of St. Martin included two large courtyards that contained additional buildings and some colonnades.[77] Day and night, the courtyards were filled with people, among them clerics, monks, nuns, royal magistrates, refugees, beggars, and pilgrims. And all of them were talking, or at least thinking, about St. Martin.

Like other churches in Gaul, and like the cathedral of Tours too after Gregory rebuilt it, the church of St. Martin had many murals and inscriptions on its walls. Bishop Perpetuus had apparently commissioned both the murals and the inscriptions when he enlarged the church in the later fifth century. Although a fire had burned the church in 559, Bishop Eufronius and King Chlothar had together restored its "previous elegance," and eventually Gregory ordered his workmen to repaint "as brightly as before" the walls that were still smudged from the fire.[78] But the church is unique in the Merovingian period because the inscriptions that described the murals still survive. For both the literate and the illiterate these murals and their accompanying inscriptions transmitted persuasive messages about proper

[75] *Hist.* 6.25, matins; *Hist.* 6.40, *VM* 4.16, Easter; *Hist.* 10.31, *GM* 86, vigils; *Hist.* 5.4, *VM* 2.25, procession.

[76] *Hist.* 2.38, Clovis; 7.47, feud; *VM* 2.35, 4.16, prisoners. The analysis in Kessler (1985) is therefore misleading. Although his general comments about the paintings in the cathedral as a cycle of "missionary art" are suggestive, the cathedral itself was too unimportant in this period for its frescoes to have much impact. Sauvel (1956) searches for later copies of these frescoes.

[77] *Hist.* 7.29, *VM* 1.31.

[78] *Hist.* 4.20, "in illa ut prius fuerat elegantia"; 10.31, "in illo nitore . . . ut prius fuerant." This repainting was perhaps completed by 584, when some refugees admired the "murals on the walls" (*Hist.* 7.22).

behavior and proper attitudes in a Christian community. Walking from the doors at the west end of the church to the saint's tomb at the other end was itself a miniature pilgrimage, and the closer people came to the tomb, the more attractive and the more rebuffing it became. Not everyone could take those final steps. A queen was probably not the only pilgrim to hesitate at the last moment: "she announced that she was unworthy and unable to approach because her sins prevented her."[79]

Entering the church demanded the same commitment and devotion required when people first began their pilgrimages. In both cases support was available. Just as St. Martin guided pilgrims on the road, so he was now prepared to lead them into the church: "Martin opens the door that you venerate."[80] The same inscription on the bell tower at the west end of the church mentioned the attitudes people needed, in particular a "deep faith." Over the doors at the west end of the church another inscription and an accompanying mural that represented the story about the Widow's Mites pointedly reminded people that generosity was the best way of dem-onstrating the depth of their faith.[81] In the stories that Gregory collected, many people apparently did rely upon these instructions, first by giving alms and then by trusting in their faith.

Once inside the church the emphasis shifted to contact and mediation between heaven and earth. In the nave a set of murals depicted the founda-tion of the church at Jerusalem and the miracle of Jesus Christ's walking on the water. Gregory had certainly pondered the significance of this particu-lar miracle, since he once compared it to a miracle of St. Martin.[82] This comparison might suggest that the mural, or set of murals, that represented some of St. Martin's miracles was already on the opposite side of the nave, in facing symmetry. The accompanying inscription invited visitors to re-quest the saint's patronage: "if you doubt, look at the miracles that are heaped before your eyes."[83] The temporal ambiguity inherent in these instructions is most important, because visitors could see representations of biblical events and of the miracles that Bishop Martin had once per-formed while alive, as well as watch the current miracles that were happen-ing in the church. To Gregory's mind, however, there was no difference between past and present, between biblical events, Bishop Martin's mira-cles, and St. Martin's miracles: "every day a visitor will see both new miracles and repetition of what happened long ago."[84] As pilgrims entered

[79] VM 1.12. For a more comprehensive discussion of the "cognitive landscape" of this church, see Van Dam (1985) 230–55.

[80] Le Blant (1856–1865) 1, no. 170; GC 11, St. Martin as guide.

[81] Le Blant (1856–1865) 1, no. 173, with Delaruelle (1963) 227–28, on the importance of charity for pilgrims.

[82] Le Blant (1856–1865) 1, nos. 174–75; and above, chapter 3, section 2.

[83] Le Blant (1856–1865) 1, no. 176.

[84] GC 6.

the church, they also entered an achronic realm that replaced historical sequence with analogical synchronism. And when ill people requested the saint's assistance, they sometimes cited precisely some of his earlier miracles.[85]

The cult of St. Martin differed from the cults of most other Gallic saints because it celebrated two festivals annually, one on July 4, the commemoration of the saint's consecration as bishop, the dedication of the saint's church by Bishop Perpetuus, and the transfer of the saint's body to the church, and the other on November 11, the commemoration of the saint's death. During the celebration of these festivals in the church of St. Martin the liturgy included readings from the saint's *Vita*. Even people who could not themselves read could still hear about the bishop's miracles, which they anyway could also see in the murals on the walls of the church. These readings were therefore less recitals than dramas, performances whose participants included the members of the congregation. Often people were healed during the readings: "while the miracle stories were being read from his *Vita*, a flash similar to a lightning bolt flared over the men."[86] So ill people looked at the miracles depicted in the murals, listened to the miracles being read from the *Vita*, and then reenacted those miracles in their own healings.

Unlike the cathedral that people's neglect had turned into something like a dusty art gallery or a museum dedicated to the saint's memory, the church of St. Martin was alive and vibrant. The murals on its walls were not simply records of past events that evoked critical admiration or teary nostalgia; instead, Gregory and others thought that they were representations of contemporary miracles, and even incentives for current miracles. Both the episodes in the murals and the similar episodes in the *Vita* were hortatory reminders of how people should behave in order to activate the same beneficial results. Fortunatus was so impressed with the quality of some of the paintings and mosaics in various churches that he thought the people depicted were "lifelike." In the cathedral at Nantes, for instance, the sunlight was so bright that "you will imagine that the paintings depicted in animate colors were alive; the art made the figures breathe again."[87] The artwork came alive; and in a telling reversal, since many of the ill people in the church were praying to come alive by being healed, Gregory and others hoped too that life would be "artlike" when St. Martin again performed his miracles.

Within the church temporal distinctions collapsed as past and present coalesced and as current behavior and attitudes provided a guarantee for

[85] *VM* 3.8.

[86] *VM* 2.29. For a more comprehensive discussion of the drama of these miracles, see Van Dam (1988) 18–24. Note Turner and Turner (1978) 148, on pilgrimage as a ritual process: "It has, like music and drama, ahistorical diachrony."

[87] Fortunatus, *Carm.* 3.7.35–36.

future benefits; by observing the festivals of St. Martin, people "would deserve the saint's patronage now and in the future."[88] Normal considerations of space also became irrelevant inside the church of St. Martin. As people progressed through the church, they also journeyed from the oppressive cares of this world to heaven. Already when they entered the church, an inscription on the bell tower encouraged them to follow St. Martin, who had previously "traveled on and sanctified that journey through the stars."[89] Over the saint's tomb was another tower or a dome that marked "the gateway to heaven,"[90] where St. Martin now reposed with other saints. His tomb therefore marked the intersection between the horizontal pilgrimage through the church and the vertical journey to heaven. Yet according to one of the inscriptions on his tomb, St. Martin was also still on earth in his grave. "Here is buried Bishop Martin of sacred memory, whose soul is in the hand of God. But he is present here, made manifest to everyone by the goodwill of his miracles."[91] The saint's miracles at his tomb marked not only the convergence of past and present, but also the intersection of heaven and earth. On one Christmas the healing of a lame man reassured the congregation of Tours about the presence of St. Martin: "through this timely miracle God has demonstrated that [Martin] is here with us."[92]

Although the church of St. Martin outside Tours was clearly a building charged with symbolic significances, some qualifications are worth noting. First, the layout and decoration of the church may have transmitted specific meanings, but it was certainly not unique in that regard. Other churches and shrines conveyed religious meanings too, perhaps even similar meanings; our problem is the lack of evidence about these other churches, not the absence of symbolic associations. Second, the symbolic power of the church spilled over to affect the surrounding compound. Not everyone was healed inside the church; some people who came to kneel at the feet of St. Martin did so outside in the courtyard "in front of the tomb."[93] And third, the temporal and spatial dislocation associated with the interior of the church was also characteristic of pilgrimages in general. Once pilgrims set out on their journeys, they separated themselves from the demands of ordinary life and from the security of their families and hometowns. Entrance into the church only magnified this sensation of timeless and spaceless dislocation by concentrating their experiences on a precise set of liturgical activities and artistic representations.

To modern readers the church of St. Martin seems to display characteris-

[88] *Hist.* 2.14.
[89] Le Blant (1856–1865) 1, no. 170.
[90] Le Blant (1856–1865) 1, no. 177.
[91] Le Blant (1856–1865) 1, no. 178.
[92] *VM* 2.25.
[93] *VM* 2.42, 50.

tics perhaps more commonly associated with the arcane theories of particle physics about such mind-twisters as the reversibility of time and the simultaneous occupation of two spaces. The fundamental difficulty, however, involves cognitive images. Gregory and his contemporaries were obviously trying to think their way through their circumstances, apply their Christian beliefs to their lives, and thereby redefine their communities and their personal relationships. In the process they resorted to a set of analogies and metaphors, and it is quite improper for modern historians to belittle Gregory's emphasis on the veneration of saints as a "material, palpable, strongly emotional, popular interpretation of Christian beliefs."[94] Just as the idiom of illness and healing provided one comprehensive metaphor for many dimensions of their communities, so the idiom of pilgrimage offered a similarly powerful analogy for other aspects of ordinary life. Sin as illness, reconciliation as healing, commitment as pilgrimage: the point is that Gregory and his contemporaries were thereby thinking and talking about their communities and society not only in general, but also in common. Educated Christian theologians under the Roman Empire had discussed religion and society in a sophisticated idiom that drew upon classical philosophy and rhetoric; modern historians interpret the past in a language that draws upon the most recent methodologies and theoretical viewpoints; just because beliefs about relics and saints' cults drew upon a different set of metaphors does not necessarily imply that they were less sophisticated or less satisfying.

3. Pilgrimages from Tours

After visiting the church and the tomb most pilgrims left. But some stayed. In fact, because proximity to a saint's tomb was itself a sign of special favor, some people obviously wanted to stay forever by arranging to have their own tombs placed in or near saints' shrines. Not all were successful. Because one man moved a stone on which St. Martin was thought to have sat in order to make space for his own tomb in the saint's church, he "insulted" the saint and soon died from a fever. In other churches the patron saints simply tossed the tombs of "rash people" out through the windows.[95] So although the interior of the church of St. Martin, like that of other churches, came increasingly to resemble a small graveyard, most people had to be content with being buried outside in a courtyard.[96]

The saint's influential presence gradually spread, however, and by the

---

[94] So Vollmann (1983) 906, "ergibt sich doch eine starke Akzentverschiebung hin zu einer sinnlich-handgreiflichen, stark emotionalen, 'volkstümlichen' Auffassung des christl. Glaubens"—representing no improvement over the characterization of Gregory's religiosity by Kurth (1919) 2:122: "C'est la foi du charbonnier."

[95] GC 6, "offensum antestitem"; Hist. 8.40, GM 88, "de temerariis."

[96] VP 16.2, graveyard; Hist. 6.10, courtyard; L. Pietri (1986), on tombs near saints' tombs.

later sixth century the cult of St. Martin had become fairly widely scattered throughout Gaul. Relics of St. Martin had been spread in several different ways. Martin himself had traveled throughout central Gaul, and some shrines commemorated his visits or miracles. At Amiens, for instance, an oratory commemorated the spot near the city's gate where Martin had clothed a freezing pauper by cutting his own cloak in half, and at Paris another oratory commemorated his healing of a leper.[97] Sulpicius Severus had first described these episodes in his *Vita* of the saint, and Gregory sometimes referred to Sulpicius's writings as warranties for his own accounts. But Gregory also included some apparently apocryphal stories about other activities and journeys of St. Martin for which there is no earlier evidence.[98] At Tours St. Martin was said to have buried the body of Catianus, the city's first bishop, next to the tomb of Litorius, the second bishop, in a church dedicated to Litorius; to have sat on a particular stone that was later honored in his church; and to have planted a vine.[99] In the Touraine St. Martin was given credit for having founded churches in various villages; for having prayed in two particular oratories; and for having raised a tree that blocked a road.[100] Outside the Touraine stories claimed that St. Martin had visited the tomb of a virgin at Artonne, near Clermont; had healed a lame priest and instructed him to build an oratory at Tonnerre, near Langres; had buried a priest at Blaye, near Bordeaux; had blessed the altar in an oratory at Sireuil, near Angoulême; and had made a spring flow at Nieul-lès-Saintes, near Saintes; and that the St. Martin buried at Brive-la-Gaillarde, near Limoges, had studied with St. Martin of Tours.[101]

These stories plainly carry the stamp of characteristics commonly associated with oral traditions. First, most of these stories served as etiological legends for some shrine, object, or other landmark that still existed during

---

[97] *VM* 1.17, Amiens; *Hist.* 8.33, Paris.

[98] Such apocryphal stories were not unique to the cult of St. Martin. One man buried in a village in the Poitou, for instance, was said to have been baptized by St. Hilary of Poitiers (*GC* 53). Fortunatus, *Vita Hilarii* 18–20, 46–48, mentioned that Hilary had convinced his daughter not to marry; and although Gregory knew of this *Vita* (*GC* 2), he still noted that "antiquity claims" that a couple buried at Saintes were descendants of St. Hilary (*GC* 59).

[99] *Hist.* 10.31, *GC* 4, St. Catianus and St. Litorius; 6, stone; 10, vine.

[100] *Hist.* 10.31, churches; *VP* 15.1, *GC* 8, oratories; *GC* 7, tree. Fortunatus once visited this tree while making a pilgrimage to Tours and classified it among the "pious memorials" of St. Martin: *Carm.* 5.14.1–6.

[101] *GC* 5, Artonne; 11, Tonnerre; 45, Blaye; *VM* 1.18, Sireuil; 4.31, Nieul-lès-Saintes; *Hist.* 7.10, Brive-la-Gaillarde. Gregory mentioned this otherwise unknown St. Martin only in passing in his account of Gundovald, who claimed to be a son of King Chlothar. The symbolism is intriguing: in 584 the pretender Gundovald was hailed as a Frankish king at the shrine of a pretender St. Martin. Prinz (1965) 22–27 is overly generous in listing Martin's "students."

the later sixth century. The churches and oratories were of course still in use, a balustrade marked the spot where St. Martin had stood at Artonne, and at Nieul-lès-Saintes a stone preserved a hoofprint of the saint's donkey. In addition, Gregory had seen the tree that St. Martin had raised and knew of a man who had become ill after having moved the stone in the saint's church. These stories therefore improved the allure of these sites and objects by providing them with a respectable historical context or pedigree. Second, some of these stories implied the additional function of reinterpreting (or inventing) past events as guarantees for present purposes. Since there is no other early information about the priest buried at Blaye, presumably only his association with St. Martin guaranteed his power to rescue people on the Garonne River. The St. Martin buried at Brive-la-Gaillarde is also otherwise unknown; but perhaps because of his nominal association with St. Martin of Tours the bishop of Limoges repaired his church in 584 and the locals venerated him and his miracles. The story describing how St. Martin had failed to go on from Blaye to Clermont was very significant to Gregory himself, since by neatly explaining why the saint had never visited his own hometown it would have helped to counter some of the early criticism at Tours that he was an interloper. Historical veracity aside, these stories were therefore useful in the later sixth century as etiological explanations and functional verifications.[102]

Sometimes Gregory mentioned his informants for these stories. His friend Aredius had told him about the miraculous power of the grapes from the vine that St. Martin had planted, and his hosts at a banquet at Saintes told him the story about the spring. It is legitimate to wonder therefore whether his informants were often not simply reacting to the presence of the bishop who as the guardian of the cult of St. Martin was only too pleased to hear more stories. In fact, Gregory had already primed the memories of his hosts at Saintes by first telling them about some of the saint's miracles. So a second common means for spreading the cult of St. Martin was the activity of the subsequent bishops of Tours, in particular of bishops such as Gregory who were uncommonly devoted to the saint. When Gregory traveled throughout Gaul, he took with him not only his stories but relics of St. Martin as well. He also sent relics to various cities, in particular at the request of bishops. At least one of these bishops later

---

[102] Nor did the elaboration of the mythology of St. Martin end with Gregory. In the early seventh century Bishop Magnobod of Angers claimed that St. Martin had attended the consecration of Maurilius, who had become bishop of Angers in 423: see [Fortunatus,] *Vita Maurilii* 58–63. And a Carolingian author associated Martin with all the bishops of Le Mans from the early fourth to the late fifth century: see *Actus pontificum Cenomannis in urbe degentium*, ed. Busson and Ledru, 44–48, 54. For a more comprehensive discussion of traditions about St. Martin in late antiquity, see Van Dam (1988); Farmer (1991) is a fine study of subsequent changes in the medieval mythology of St. Martin.

wrote a letter to Gregory describing the subsequent miracles at the new shrine; this letter is, by the way, an important indication that Gregory was not the only Gallic bishop collecting miracle stories about local saints and local shrines, or even about the cult of St. Martin.[103] Stories were "verbal relics," and as such they and other relics were gifts that the bishops of Tours and others exchanged in order to establish and maintain networks of friendship and influence.

Pilgrims were a third means for the spread of the cult of St. Martin. Upon leaving Tours people took away first of all their own experiences that they could retell to others. "Long after other mementos of the original journey . . . have been lost or broken, the stories endure. Over time, the familiar words assume an almost tangible quality. . . . [S]torytelling is a little like fingering a holy medal that is both a symbol and a source of power."[104] In the presence of the saint's tomb pilgrims had disregarded their status and privileges; but even after their reintegration into the stifling hierarchy of rank and status characteristic of early medieval society, pilgrims continued to express their intimate feelings in their own stories. The power of St. Martin enabled mute people to speak; miracle stories gave pilgrims a common voice with which to recall and share their experiences.[105] Pilgrims also took away actual relics of the saint's cult, and ordinary laymen or people intending to become ascetics were often responsible for the construction of some of the shrines to St. Martin outside the Touraine. One man, for instance, took some dust and oil from the saint's tomb at Tours and later built a church dedicated with his relics in northern Gaul; at Saintes a woman dedicated an oratory in her own house with relics of St. Martin.[106]

These relics, whether verbal or material, were clearly more than simply souvenirs of a memorable trip, because these "reverse pilgrimages" were important complements to the original pilgrimages to the saint's tomb. People had demonstrated their devotion and commitment to St. Martin by making their pilgrimages in the first place, and at the saint's church they had requested, and usually received, his assistance. Taking away relics of the saint ensured that his patronage would always be available, because now the saint was no longer simply waiting for them in his church but was actually sharing in their journeys and the accompanying hardships; in fact, by removing his relics these pilgrims themselves assisted St. Martin by allowing him to perform miracles in regions that he had not previously

---

[103] VM 2.36, relics; 4.8, letter.

[104] Slater (1986) 74, in an evocative discussion of pilgrims and their stories.

[105] For a telling example of a miracle story overcoming social distinctions, note the conversation between the distinguished abbess Agnes and a boatman at Trier; they even related the story "simultaneously" (note to VM 4.29).

[106] Hist. 8.15–16, northern Gaul; VM 3.51, Saintes.

visited "on foot."[107] The construction of a shrine or a church finally completed the circle, not least because it sometimes involved its own vow; and the actual process of construction was yet another *iter*, a "project" whose completion demanded the same dedication as a pilgrimage. Initially pilgrims had gone to the shrine of St. Martin at Tours; in return, they removed relics to new shrines for the saint. Because one common relic pilgrims often collected was dust from the saint's tomb, many of them dedicated their new shrines with dirt, bits of the ground of the saint's church, thereby almost literally re-creating the sacred topography of Tours elsewhere. In a comparable situation, by acquiring relics of the True Cross Radegund had once wanted to re-create the Holy Land in Gaul.[108] So the retelling of a story about St. Martin, the possession of a relic, or the construction of a new shrine implied that even after their departure pilgrims remained in the saint's presence and therefore in a sense remained too in the presence of his tomb. Even the pilgrims who left Tours stayed there.

Gregory was so impressed by the power of St. Martin that he claimed that the saint's reputation had spread "into almost the entire world."[109] But just as modern scholars are properly hesitant about the remoteness and the comprehensiveness of the geographical origins of pilgrims to Tours, so they can also be suspicious of the extent of St. Martin's reputation and the spread of his relics. Outside the Touraine there were indeed shrines dedicated to St. Martin. Gregory mentioned oratories in and outside Bourges, whose territory was contiguous to the Touraine. Farther away he mentioned an oratory in a monastery outside Limoges; a church at Bordeaux and a nearby oratory; a church and an oratory at Saintes; churches at Paris and Rouen, and a shrine at Avranches; an oratory at Amiens; and two other churches in northeastern Gaul.[110] He also knew of some stray shrines in Italy and Spain. The rather haphazard scatter of these shrines may reflect the randomness of the information that Gregory had acquired from his own travels and from visitors to Tours. Other literary sources mentioned other shrines dedicated to St. Martin before the later sixth

[107] *VM* 2.36.

[108] Baudonivia, *Vita Radegundis* 16, with Hunt (1981) and (1982) 128–35, on relics from the Holy Land. Note also Paul the Deacon, *HL* 3.34, for an apocryphal story about King Guntramn. When the king was unable to send an enormous gold ciborium to the Lord's tomb at Jerusalem, he instead placed it over the tomb of St. Marcellus at Chalon-sur-Saône.

[109] *VM* 3.21.

[110] *Hist.* 7.42, *VP* 9.2, *GC* 79, Bourges; *GC* 9, Limoges; *VM* 3.33, 50, Bordeaux; *VM* 3.51, 4.8, Saintes; *Hist.* 5.2, Rouen; *Hist.* 8.33, Paris; *VM* 2.36, Avranches; *VM* 1.17, Amiens; *Hist.* 8.15–16, 9.12, northeastern Gaul. Bishop Veranus of Cavaillon once told Gregory how he had been healed in "the church of the blessed Martin that was in that place" (*VM* 3.60). If this church was in Cavaillon, it was one of the few shrines to St. Martin in Provence; but Beaujard et al. (1986) 73 suggest that it was in Chalon-sur-Sâone.

century, including churches in the south at Arles,[111] Cahors,[112] possibly Auch,[113] and possibly Poitiers,[114] and in the north at Mainz, possibly Trier,[115] Metz, possibly Rheims,[116] possibly Chartres,[117] and Auxerre.[118]

Most of these shrines were in central and northern Gaul, the regions most influenced by the Frankish kings and the regions that contributed the most pilgrims to Tours. Yet even there it is important not to overstate the impact of St. Martin and his cult. Gregory once visited a church that a deacon named Vulfilaic had built in honor of St. Martin on a hill outside Trier. In their conversation Vulfilaic admitted that as a boy he had not known anything about the life of St. Martin or even the location of his tomb. Only after he had joined the monastery of Abbot Aredius of Limoges did he finally visit the church of St. Martin at Tours; then he moved to north Gaul, built this shrine, and dedicated it with a flask of oil from the saint's church at Tours.[119] His church therefore commemorated both his pilgrimage to Tours and his belated introduction to the cult of St. Martin.

Furthermore, as with the geographical origins of the pilgrims to Tours, the absences in this scattering of shrines to St. Martin are telling. First, there were virtually no shrines to St. Martin in cities and regions associated with Gregory's family. In the Auvergne only a balustrade marked the saint's visit to a small village, and only an apparently apocryphal story documented the visit. In eastern Gaul Gregory did not note any shrines to St. Martin in Lyon or Langres, where he and his brother had served as deacons and where their relatives had been bishops. Even his mother had no relics of St. Martin in the oratory of her house near Chalon-sur-Saône; when Gregory visited, he took his own.[120] After Gregory became bishop of Tours, he had imported relics of many of the saints associated with his family; yet his family, despite their connections with St. Martin, had apparently not expanded the saint's cult in a similar fashion, even in cities where family members had served as bishops and had introduced other cults.

[111] *Vita Caesarii* 1.57, for a church dedicated to the Virgin Mary, St. John, and St. Martin; Aurelianus of Arles, *Regula ad monachos* (PL 68.396), for a monastery with a church dedicated with relics of, among others, St. Martin.

[112] *Vita Desiderii* 16, 30.

[113] Fortunatus, *Carm.* 1.4, if the Bishop Faustus who built this church is to be identified with Bishop Faustus of Auch (*Hist.* 8.22).

[114] Fortunatus, *Carm.* 1.7, with Meyer (1901) 73–74.

[115] Gauthier (1980) 202–4, and (1986) 30.

[116] *Additamenta amplioris testamenti S. Remigii*, ed. B. Krusch, MGH, SRM 3 (1896) 343–44.

[117] [Fortunatus,] *Vita Leobini* 84.

[118] For references to these churches and others, including those in Spain and Italy, see Ewig (1976–1979) 2:371–84, and Prinz (1965) 29–38, although both are overly generous in some of their attributions.

[119] *Hist.* 8.15–16.

[120] VM 1.36, 3.60, GC 3.

Second, there were very few shrines to St. Martin in other cities in Gregory's own ecclesiastical province; in fact, although the church of St. Martin owned a villa in the territory of Le Mans, even the oratory on that property was dedicated with relics of St. Peter and St. Paul.[121] Some of these few shrines to St. Martin were private foundations. The only shrine to St. Martin that Gregory mentioned outside the Touraine but in his ecclesiastical province was a church near Le Mans that people had built privately and to which they finally invited the bishop only for the dedication.[122] Also in Le Mans was another church or oratory dedicated to St. Martin that a priest and a nun had constructed on their own property and endowed with their own estates.[123] So although suffragan bishops may sometimes have traveled to Tours, most apparently did not highlight the cult of St. Martin in their own sees. The cathedral that Bishop Felix built at Nantes contained some of the saint's relics, but only in a side chapel.[124] Only Bertramn, bishop of Le Mans from 586 until after 616, founded a monastery and hospice in honor of St. Martin in a village outside the city, perhaps as an act of homage for having earlier received his tonsure at the saint's tomb. Because Bertramn considered St. Martin a "special patron," he furthermore left a large donation of one hundred gold coins to the saint's tomb.[125] But Bertramn also constructed a monastery and a church dedicated to St. Peter and St. Paul, a church dedicated to the True Cross, an oratory dedicated to the archangel Michael, and another monastery and church dedicated to his mentor Bishop Germanus of Paris, and he considered St. Medard another "special patron."[126] With these impressive connections Bertramn became yet another suffragan bishop who eventually, presumably after the death of Gregory of Tours, overshadowed his own metropolitan: "Bertramn wore a pallium, as was customary for metropolitan bishops, and he ruled and guided all the bishops in the entire kingdom."[127] The evidence for the spread of the cult of St. Martin in sixth-century Gaul therefore combines with the evidence for the geographical origins of pilgrims to Tours to

---

[121] VM 4.12.

[122] VM 3.35.

[123] *Actus pontificum Cenomannis in urbe degentium*, ed. Busson and Ledru, 82–83, 93–95, with L. Pietri and Biarne (1987) 51.

[124] Above, section 1. For the possibility of a sixth-century church dedicated to St. Martin at Angers, see L. Pietri and Biarne (1987) 80–81.

[125] *Actus pontificum Cenomannis in urbe degentium*, ed. Busson and Ledru, 98, 137, tonsure; 101, 108, 143, monastery at Pontlieue and endowments; 119, "peculiaris patrini [*sic*] nostri Martini sancti episcopi"; 137, donation to tomb.

[126] *Actus pontificum Cenomannis in urbe degentium*, ed. Busson and Ledru, 101, 103, 105–7, 128, St. Peter and St. Paul; 100, 108, True Cross; 99, 115, archangel Michael; 98–99, 127, Germanus; 132, "peculiaris patroni nostri Medardi episcopi."

[127] *Actus pontificum Cenomannis in urbe degentium*, ed. Busson and Ledru, 101, with Ewig (1974) 54–56, on the possible relationship between Bertramn and the Merovingian dynasty, and Weidemann (1989), for the powers of later bishops of Le Mans.

indicate again the limited impact of the saint's cult, and apparently also of the metropolitan bishop's power, in the ecclesiastical province nominally subject to Tours.

4. Gregory's Vow

Gregory had once been a pilgrim to the church of St. Martin; by becoming bishop he had joined those other pilgrims who had stayed in Tours; and he sometimes transported relics of the saint to other cities. For after becoming bishop Gregory had taken another vow that he thought of in terms similar to those he used to describe pilgrims' vows. Just as pilgrims committed themselves to traveling to the tomb of St. Martin, so he committed himself to recording the saint's miracles. Several factors motivated his decision to become an author. One was the command of God, as revealed in no fewer than three visions. Another was his own concern that many of the saint's miracles that had occurred during the episcopacies of his predecessors had already been forgotten. The final push came, perhaps predictably, from his mother. As Gregory worried about his own literary inadequacies, his mother had observed that at least other people could understand his stories.[128] His lifelong devotion to his mother, who consistently provided much encouragement throughout his ecclesiastical career, was probably the only emotional attachment that matched his new loyalty to St. Martin. So the dutiful son now became the committed writer and devoted guardian of the saint's traditions.

Self-deprecating modesty already had a long history as a disingenuous literary device, and Gregory's description of himself as "an uneducated man" was accurate only because he adopted lofty standards of reference. The cult of St. Martin had been well served in the past. Sulpicius Severus had composed a *Vita* that became a prototype for subsequent hagiography; Paulinus of Périgueux had versified Sulpicius's writings; Bishop Perpetuus had compiled a collection of posthumous miracle stories that Paulinus of Périgueux had also versified; and Fortunatus had begun versifying Sulpicius's writings again perhaps already by the time Gregory became bishop.[129] Gregory was all too aware of his literary predecessors, and he mentioned that he had been "inspired by these stories to attempt to collect for memory some other stories . . . about the miracles of the most blessed St. Martin that happened after his death."[130] But Gregory was not just continuing the work of his predecessors, he was now competing with them too. The versification of a Paulinus of Périgueux or a Fortunatus was be-

---

[128] *VM* 1 praef.
[129] Koebner (1915) 86 suggests that Fortunatus initiated his poem independently of Gregory's interest.
[130] *VM* 1.3.

yond his abilities, although he did suggest that Fortunatus might like to "interpret" in verse his new collection of miracle stories, and hinted that some of his other writings might also be suitable for versification.[131] Instead the activities of Bishop Perpetuus provided a more attainable model, and like him Gregory now rebuilt some of St. Martin's shrines and collected additional miracle stories. In all these activities Gregory was also promoting a specific message about the saint's power. In the church of St. Martin he restored the murals that Perpetuus had once commissioned; he rebuilt the cathedral and perhaps commissioned a new set of murals about St. Martin; and he first summarized the miracle stories collected by Perpetuus before adding more. Murals and stories, images and words: the episodic nature of Gregory's miracle stories neatly mimicked the episodic nature of the murals in these churches. Fortunatus consistently claimed that the murals in some churches were so vivid that their subjects seemed to come alive. Gregory had a similar vividly visual sense about his collection of miracle stories, as if each miraculous vignette were as dazzling as a mosaic or a painting: "even though my plain account cannot ornament a page, the glorious bishop [Martin] will make that page shine with his sparkling miracles."[132] When he described the location of one miracle story, he imagined the vine-covered colonnade in visual terms as he mentioned the "clusters of grapes that flourished just as in a painting."[133] Even without artistic decoration his compilation of miracle stories was an "illuminated manuscript."

Gregory began collecting the miracles of St. Martin apparently soon after becoming bishop. The first book of the *VM* included miracles that happened before he became bishop, and the second book began with miracles that happened during the first year of his episcopacy. By the time Fortunatus completed his versification of Sulpicius's writings about St. Martin before the middle of 576, Gregory had already informed him of his own work "about the saint's miracles."[134] Since he did not complete *VM* 2 until 581, at this time Gregory had written to Fortunatus presumably only about *VM* 1. Given the difficulties surrounding his accession as bishop, Gregory's initial project was hence not only an attempt simply to preserve these miracle stories, it also put him and his connections with the cult of St. Martin into a longer tradition that went back to the accession of Martin

---

131 Fortunatus, *Vita S. Martini* prol. = *Ep. ad Gregorium* 2; and *Hist.* 10.31, *GC* praef.

132 *VM* 1 praef.

133 *VM* 4.7.

134 Fortunatus, *Vita S. Martini* prol. = *Ep. ad Gregorium* 2, "opus illud . . . quod de suis virtutibus explicuistis." Since *Vita S. Martini* 4.636–37 referred to Germanus as the current bishop of Paris, Fortunatus had apparently completed his poem before Germanus's death in May 576 (*Hist.* 5.8). He also mentioned that he had composed the poem in six months: see *Vita S. Martini* prol. = *Ep. ad Gregorium* 3.

himself as bishop. Upon closer inspection, however, this longer tradition turns out to be somewhat abbreviated, since many of the miracles that Gregory included in *VM* 1 happened during the episcopacy of Eufronius. And since Eufronius was his mother's cousin, Gregory was therefore, at least initially, also collecting stories about his own family and its long association with Tours.

But Gregory soon decided to extend his anthology to include the miracles that happened during his own episcopacy too. He seems to have collected and recorded most of the miracle stories in *VM* 2–4 nearly as they happened, only occasionally returning to earlier stories to update details. Sometimes he referred to miracles that happened "recently" or "very recently," or "at the present time."[135] Yet Gregory was not recording these miracle stories simply for his own private edification or for the interest of future readers, since he seems to have used some, and perhaps many, of them in public before his congregation. After recounting one story about a woman who admitted to having conceived what turned out to be a deformed son on the night before a Sunday, he pointedly addressed a warning directly to people about the appropriate times for "indulging your lust"; he told another story at the insistence of his listeners; and he included another story as a pointed reminder of the consequences of not listening to bishops' preaching. He even used a story about one of his own visions in a warning to an audience of "most beloved people."[136] Gregory therefore initially based most of these stories either on his own personal experiences and observations or on oral accounts that he or the custodians of the shrines collected from the participants; he then recycled some of them as hortatory stories that he included in sermons; and at some point stenographers recorded the stories in writing.[137] These written versions could then in turn serve as *lectiones*, readings that he perhaps included in the celebration of the liturgy.[138] Gregory perhaps also made each book of the *VM* available to private readers by publishing it upon completion. In fact, he himself provided a model of how other readers might use the books of the *VM* when he once finally remembered how to deal with his stomachache by recalling a miracle that he had recorded in an earlier book.[139]

The commitment and dedication that motivated Gregory meant that the literary techniques of the *VM* shared some characteristics of pilgrimages. One was the apparent timelessness of many of the miracle stories. Gregory

[135] *VM* 2.32, 40; 3.1, 22, 60; 4.1, 45, 47.

[136] *VM* 2.1, 24–25; 4.45.

[137] *VM* 3.45, custodians; 4.10, stenographer. The confusion of perspective in some stories (*VM* 3.8, 4.29) seems to indicate an oral origin that stenographers recorded verbatim.

[138] *VM* 1.6, 21; 2.1, 19.

[139] *VM* 4.1. Heinzelmann (1981) 241 suggests that Gregory published the *VM* section by section.

meticulously dated a few of the episodes, in particular those involving his own pilgrimage to Tours in 563 and his assumption of the episcopacy ten years later,[140] and in *VM* 2–4, the collection of miracles from his own episcopacy, he recorded the stories usually in a chronological sequence that emphasized the miracles that occurred on the annual festivals of St. Martin. But Gregory was not primarily concerned about either the exact dates or the chronological sequence, and many of the stories were discrete episodes with no overt chronological moorings. He was more interested instead in the replication of the past in the present, in particular because current miracles provided verification for past miracles: "Let no one therefore have any doubts about those miracles in the past when he sees the gifts of these present miracles being dispensed."[141] Gregory, and the other participants in these stories too, often seemed to have no sense of the chronological distance between themselves and Bishop Martin; as in the case of stories about a modern priest acknowledged as a saint in Brazil, "in spite of the tales' superficial documentary quality, their real purpose is to affirm the proximity of a priest who exists outside the normal confines of time and space."[142] Like the pilgrims who conversed with St. Martin in visions and reenacted his miracles, so Gregory too often spoke of the saint as if he were still alive at Tours. When, for instance, he mentioned how people appealed for the assistance of "the bishop," his narratives consistently included some ambiguity about whether he meant St. Martin or himself. In his opinion, St. Martin was still preaching now, in the later sixth century, through his miracles; and his friend Fortunatus reinforced the ambiguity by once insisting that St. Martin was still governing the congregation at Tours with Gregory.[143] Whether deliberately or unconsciously, many of Gregory's stories preserved the timelessness of the original miracles. Both the miracles from the past that Sulpicius and Perpetuus had recorded and the current miracles that Gregory recorded could equally serve as inspiration and guidance for others, because they were all miracles that St. Martin still performed at the present time. One man knew exactly why he could hope for a healing from St. Martin: "we have read about your many deeds, what you did while alive and what you have done after your death."[144] As on pilgrimages, so in the stories collected in the *VM*, life passed but time stood still.

The *VM* can also be considered a "literary pilgrimage" simply because Gregory had vowed to complete it. When he once justified his literary intentions, he conceded his hesitations about pursuing his unfinished *iter*,

[140] *VM* 1.32, 2.1.
[141] *VM* 1 praef.
[142] Slater (1986) 132.
[143] *VM* 2.40; Fortunatus, *Carm.* 5.9.6, "rite gubernantes ducitis ambo greges."
[144] *VM* 3.8.

which for pilgrims would have referred to the journey they intended to complete but which here referred to the "unfinished task" of recording these stories.[145] At the conclusion of one book Gregory was pleased that, like a pilgrim nearing the saint's tomb, he was about to fulfill his vow. In fact, again as with pilgrims, an illness gave him the opportunity not necessarily to initiate his journey or literary task but rather to complete it: "through the support of the glorious bishop [Martin] I was permitted to be capable of extending all the way to its conclusion what I [had] initially undertaken."[146] And Gregory also anticipated that the completion of his task would allow him to receive the same benefits that pilgrims expected: "I have hoped to receive this payment as a reward, that forgiveness might perhaps be given me on behalf of my sins when these stories are read in praise of the most holy bishop [Martin]."[147] One of his literary predecessors had provided a precedent, since Paulinus of Périgueux had once challenged the saint to heal his ill grandson: "Blessed Martin, if you approve of my composing something in your honor, let your approval appear on behalf of this ill boy."[148] Pilgrims provided another exemplary precedent. In many of the stories in the VM pilgrims took vows and traveled to the tomb of St. Martin; as Gregory collected and recorded those stories, he was honoring his own literary vow and hoping for the same results of healing and forgiveness. During his first pilgrimage to Tours in 563 Gregory had told his companions that if he were unable to travel to the tomb of St. Martin, they should still bury his body in the saint's church. He had completed that journey successfully, however, and later as bishop he also kept his vow to record the miracles of St. Martin; so after his death he was in fact buried next to the saint's tomb.[149]

Gregory apparently developed a reputation as an amiable raconteur, and collecting reports about the miracles of St. Martin provided him with an endless supply of anecdotes. At banquets he both told and listened to others' stories; he often exchanged stories during his travels; and one man whose hearing St. Martin healed was perhaps most pleased that he could now listen to Gregory's stories![150] Even some of the Frankish kings sought out Gregory's company; like one of the confidants of King Clovis, Gregory

[145] VM 2.19.
[146] VM 2.60.
[147] VM 1.40.
[148] VM 1.2.
[149] VM 1.32; [Odo of Cluny,] Vita Gregorii 26 (PL 71.128).
[150] VM 3.17.

too had become a "delightful storyteller." His writings did nothing to tarnish his reputation or his authority over the subsequent centuries, and medieval authors consistently praised both the vividness and the directness of his stories.[151]

Modern readers too can still enjoy Gregory's stories even as they are grateful that he has provided so much important circumstantial information about sixth-century Gaul. Yet modern historians must also remember that Gregory did not record these miracle stories simply for the benefit (or pleasure) of later researchers. His immediate audience included the members of his own congregation and the many pilgrims who traveled to the church of St. Martin, and his immediate concerns included the promotion and verification of the saint's miraculous power. As we have seen, this specific context influenced the nature of Gregory's miracle stories, since they often preserved the episodic and timeless experiences of those parishioners and those pilgrims. For listeners and readers then, and for the subsequent meaning of their stories, the synchronism between past and present was more important than any historically accurate summation or straightforward chronological narrative.

At the end of his *Histories* Gregory listed all his writings and begged they be left intact; even though he conceded that they could be versified, he did not want them rewritten, changed, or excerpted. Already in the seventh century his wish was disregarded when scribes produced a condensed version of the *Histories* that highlighted the activities of the Frankish kings by eliminating much material about churchmen.[152] Yet Gregory's insistence suggests that he imagined all his writings within a unified vision, and that he may have used similar literary devices throughout them. Even though Gregory's *Histories* followed a chronological progression from the Creation to his own times, they also often included techniques similar to those in his collections of miracle stories. With his comparisons between biblical and contemporary events, and in particular between the kings of the Old Testament and the Frankish kings, Gregory closely connected biblical times with his own times; he also frequently meandered backwards and sideways from a strictly chronological narrative; and he often inserted self-contained short biographies and stories, including miracle stories. Like his collections of miracle stories, Gregory's *Histories* was therefore more episodic than narrative, more interpretive than descriptive, and more concerned about the underlying moral and religious patterns than about the uniqueness of historical events. Like his collections of miracle stories

---

[151] *Hist.* 2.32, "iocundus in fabulis"; and the collection of later testimonies about Gregory in *PL* 71.129–36, and Bordier (1857–1864) 4:238–76.

[152] See Goffart (1987), condensed in (1988) 119–27.

too, "the *Histories* is a collection of short stories," and "the action of the work as a whole resides in the process of telling and listening."[153]

Among modern historians miracle stories spontaneously lower expectations by generating skepticism, even as a work entitled *Histories* inspires confidence. Yet the content, the literary techniques, and Gregory's own vision should compel modern historians to evaluate his *Histories* and his miracle stories together. One recent interpretation has attempted to explain the shapelessness of the *Histories* and its interest in moral ideas by classifying it as satire, "prescriptive satire" in which Gregory's "portrayals of folly, vice, and crime are contrasted to the explicit norm of the saints."[154] Such a reliance upon the conventions of a classical literary genre to explain the nature of Gregory's *Histories* is difficult to sustain. Not only does it raise the question of how Gregory ever learned about the canonical characteristics of satire,[155] but it also tends to make him consistently cynical, detached, irreverent, and sarcastic, so obsessed with "the mad and vicious world of satire" that the Merovingian kings become simply "a uniform pack of reprobates" driven by "the most elemental virility."[156] King Chilperic would perhaps have written this sort of satirical history about the bishops whom he ridiculed for their pettiness, arrogance, and lewdness, and the Visigothic King Sisebut did once write that the Frankish King Theuderic II was "a man distinguished by complete stupidity";[157] but a satirical perspective does not fit with the sensitive Gregory who loved his mother, his relatives, and his friends, who was devoted to St. Martin and other saints, and who, in addition to collecting stories about kings and saints, was equally enthusiastic about enormous trout and fine wine.[158] In fact, it is this interpretation of Gregory's *Histories* that is pessimistic, not Gregory himself, who was obviously an emotionally involved participant in many of the events described in the *Histories* and the miracle stories and not simply a satirical critic of them.

A better, alternative analogue for interpreting the literary characteristics of both his *Histories* and his collections of miracle stories is, again, a pilgrimage, which had a goal but no specific form, which involved both passionate commitment and intellectual insight, which consisted of a series

---

[153] Goffart (1988) 197. Even though most of her discussion is likewise focused on the *Histories*, Boesch Gajano (1977) rightly emphasizes the fundamental unity of Gregory's hagiography and historiography; Heinzelmann (1991) undermines his attempt to distinguish a "hagiographical discourse" and locate it primarily in Gregory's hagiographical writings by noting too many exceptions.

[154] Goffart (1988) 200.

[155] Conceded by Goffart (1988) 229.

[156] Goffart (1988) 202, 208, 209. Such acridness was perhaps more characteristic of Abbot Columbanus, who once called King Theuderic II a dog: Jonas of Bobbio, *Vita Columbani* 22.

[157] *Hist.* 6.46; Sisebut, *Vita Desiderii* 4, with Fontaine (1980).

[158] *GM* 75, *VJ* 36.

of episodic experiences, and which synchronized past and present events. Such an analogy has the advantage of helping us understand both the emotional involvement and the interpretive vision in Gregory's writings. It also implies that in critiquing medieval historiography modern historians ought to take into consideration "pilgrims' time," or rather the "timelessness" associated with pilgrimages. Rather than resorting to the conventions of a classical literary genre, Gregory was able in his writings to evoke both the lasting devotion of someone who had decided upon a pilgrimage and the sudden insights of someone who had benefited from a miracle. His initial commitment was therefore also his final commitment; for even after becoming a bishop and then a writer, Gregory always remained what he had been on his first journey to Tours, a pilgrim.

BELIEFS about saints and the miraculous healings associated with their cults provided late antique people with one means to think about themselves and their communities, to articulate some of their deepest emotions and concerns, and, perhaps, to come to terms both with their inner selves and with their roles in their communities. To read miracle stories is to read about the most intimate aspects of people's lives, including their attempts to deal with crushing misery and overwhelming uncertainty, as well as their reactions of uninhibited happiness and love. When crossed, St. Martin was sternly implacable; but he was also a gentle confidant who caressed and smiled at the people who requested his assistance. At the most basic level saints' cults always involved unpredictability. Modern analyses may sometimes leave the impression that early medieval people often manipulated saints' cults to their advantage, but in fact, for all their patronage and deference, they certainly did not control them. Relics were like radioactive elements, literally too hot to handle without safeguards; in northern Gaul the snow that fell on one saint's tomb simply melted away.[1] The techniques involved in activating this power were not always readily apparent. The wooden shanties with which people tried to enclose this tomb in northern Gaul collapsed in the wind; bishops elsewhere threatened to shut down the churches dedicated to saints who had failed to assist them against their opponents; even Gregory of Tours was sometimes so distraught that he simply started reading Psalms at random.[2] Modern historians can therefore use stories about saints and their miracles to investigate both people's inner lives and their relationships with others. In the process the study of saint's cults will also provide important, even if sometimes oblique, insights into the more conventional topics of politics, diplomacy, religion, and culture.[3]

Yet many modern historians remain distinctly uneasy in the presence of stories about miracles, and in the case of Gregory they have often minimized or outright ignored his "books of miracles" in favor of his "books of histories." The availability of translations is a telling indication. Although

---

[1] GC 71.
[2] GM 78, GC 70, threats; *Hist.* 5.49.
[3] Perhaps even into the nature of the medieval economy: see Geary (1986).

Gregory's *Histories* is available in good translations in several modern languages, until recently only an old French edition provided a complete translation of his books of miracle stories.[4] With the publication of the translations of his *VJ* and *VM* in this volume all of Gregory's eight books of miracle stories are now available in English, and in our research we can finally respect Gregory's malediction against those who would not leave all his writings "intact and complete, just as I have left them."[5]

The opportunities for further research in late Roman and early Merovingian Gaul are endlessly exciting. Many important topics and themes lack modern synthetic analyses; many other important texts require annotation and translations, or at least translations into English;[6] many important authors, such as Caesarius of Arles,[7] Avitus of Vienne, and, in particular, Fortunatus,[8] would benefit from comprehensive and up-to-date studies. Most of all we need more research that is prepared to use comparative studies and new methodologies, whether from anthropology, sociology, literary criticism, or the history of other periods. Just as the period of late antiquity bridges the end of the ancient world and the beginning of medieval civilization, so the study of the period ought to form links with the best interdisciplinary methodologies available.

---

[4] Bordier (1857–1864).

[5] *Hist.* 10.31.

[6] In particular the large collections of letters in *MGH*, Epp. 3, and the many important *Vitae* in *MGH*, SRM 2–7.

[7] See Klingshirn (forthcoming).

[8] Collins (1981) and Brennan (1985) are fine beginnings.

PART II

TRANSLATIONS

The Miracles of St. Hilary

FORTUNATUS dedicated both this collection of the miracles of St. Hilary and the corresponding *Vita* of St. Hilary to Bishop Pascentius of Poitiers. These were certainly some of his earliest hagiographical writings in Gaul, since he arrived in Poitiers by 567 but Maroveus had succeeded Pascentius as bishop of the city already sometime in 568.[1] His friend Gregory of Tours apparently read *The Miracles of St. Hilary* (*VH*) and perhaps used it for some details in his own account of King Clovis's campaign against the Visigoths in 507 (notes to *VH* 14, 22). Bruno Krusch included the *VH* in his complete edition of the prose works of Fortunatus in *MGH*, AA 4.2 (1885) 7–11. Even with this fine edition it is still sometimes a struggle to make sense of Fortunatus's ornate Latin.

1. I, Fortunatus, [dedicate this book] to Bishop Pascentius [of Poitiers], my holy lord and my most deservedly blessed father, and to the members of his church who flourish constantly with the love that blossoms in Christ.

The motivation of a swollen reputation persuaded the ancient writers of pagan books to display the wonderfulness of their own eloquence to everyone; and because they mixed up the tone of their speech, somehow these authors seemed to be simultaneously praising the marriages of kings and lamenting their deaths, [discussing,] that is, both fortunate and unfortunate events [in such a fashion] that even if these kings had died in vain without accomplishing anything, they nevertheless lived in these books just like [those men] who gave speeches or about whom speeches were made. Although I am stimulated by the inspiration of a better hope, why do I allow myself to be silent about the living merits and victories of a great confessor? 2. There is also, although improper, the stimulation of heavenly punishment, since I would scarcely repay what I owe even if I were to sing in an untiring voice continuously day and likewise night about the brightness of the blessed Hilary, that unfailing light. 3. But although I am both hand-

---

[1] See Krusch (1885a) v–vii, for some context; Meyer (1901) 9–17, and Brennan (1985) 61–62, for Fortunatus's itinerary; and above, chapter 1, section 2.

icapped by my ignorance and offended at this insult, am I to preserve my intention and persist with this overpowering languor, so that while those authors who are deceived in their many treatises still conjecture something flimsy about imaginary ghosts and with their false praises still animate corpses that have decayed into dust, I nevertheless relate nothing about the saints who endure and (what is more impressive) who every day flourish in the kingdom of Christ? Distinctions between the different factions seem especially to be the reason for [different] rewards: while pagans have preferred to entrust the fruit of their labor to the support of ineffective men, it is necessary to entrust ourselves to the intercession of the blessed men whose joy we share there [in heaven] if we address words to them here [on earth]. 4. Therefore let the nimble tongue of heralds again speak about that [Hilary] for whom my heart previously developed an affection; for he is clearly believed to be envied for his good deeds [even] if what I know about him seems to be concealed in silence. As a result he who healed the mute so that they might speak has in addition deservedly compelled me to speak about himself. 5. But the passage of the years was a thief, and I was unable to discover his many deeds while he was alive in his body[2] and his great accomplishments after he migrated to Christ and the angels who applaud him in eternal rest as a victor from the struggles of this world. Therefore I do not wish to cheat our impoverished memory of the miracles that [Hilary] in his mercy has displayed during the present time. Then everyone who listens to these miracles as is proper with trusting ears either may rejoice in recognizing past events or may believe that similar miracles will happen in the future through the confessor's power.

6. Once Probianus was hanging critically close to the end of his life. Jealous death was in a hurry to steal any hope of their young son's recovery from his parents, and because it neither thought about the sad funeral of this young boy nor observed the wishes of his grieving old parents, in its greed it by chance found an obstruction. For through the intercession of the blessed Hilary alone the opportunity for salvation had stood firm for this young boy who was about to die. 7. His father was Franco and his mother was Periculosa ["Threatening"], who was especially threatened by the death of a son and changed her name. As they prepared a funeral for their son who was already almost dead, they wept loudly and brought Probianus to the confessor's church. 8. On his own authority St. Hilary revealed the medicine of his secret skill and as usual transformed an expensive funeral into a profitable cure. A single word was effective, and suddenly he strengthened the dissolving structure of the boy's limbs and restored them to their healthy condition as if nothing had gone wrong. Soon he dried the

---

[2] On the basis of this disclaimer Koebner (1915) 80 suggests that Fortunatus researched and wrote his *Vita Hilarii* shortly after this work.

parents' tears with the appearance of great happiness and ended their mourning with the success of their prayer; already their cries were a consequence not of grief but of rejoicing. **9.** What punishments and what torments did not death itself then endure when it lost in this way the young boy it believed it had invaded? Since death was indeed unable to be victorious by striking down someone else, in its defeat it struck down itself. **10.** This Probianus was then worthy to obtain the high office of bishop in a city, and still today as a debtor for his life he has annually subsidized the lamps [in the church?] of his doctor.[3]

11. I must also contribute to people's memory this distinguished miracle for the glory of the one who performed it. Two lepers who were disfigured with sores came from Cahors. Since they had entrusted their hope for a cure to the intercession of the saint, they washed their heads and smeared their limbs with dust that had been wiped from his tomb. They faithfully applied this remedy to themselves for a long time until the ulcers and the discoloration caused by their illness were arrested and left the bodies that they had seized. Once this illness was ensnared by this cure, it was healed, left behind the [healthy] coloration that it had attacked, and did not maintain the ugly appearance that it had imposed. **12.** Despite countless sores, a single [healthy] skin was restored to all their limbs, and their faces that had been ruined by this lengthy disfigurement began to be reformed in their own likenesses, even if they were unrecognized. The purifying waters of the Jordan River were found in this most reliable fountain at Poitiers, and since these lepers did not go to this river, this river came here to them. The confessor's compassion appeared to be so praiseworthy because he removed the effort of a lengthy journey and fulfilled their requests for a cure. **13.** Oh, how apparent was the evidence of such amazing miracles when the purity of a tomb cleansed the blemishes of leprosy! What [other] doctor's skill could produce this cure? Who else offers the blessings of a medicine from this dust? **14.** Of these two lepers Castorius became a deacon and Crispius a subdeacon; and until the end [of their lives] they maintained their devotion to the one who had cured them. They properly decided to bear the yoke of that lord who had freed them from their punishment.[4]

15. A girl came whose right hand had become useless during her lifetime. Although natural causes had been influential, the contraction of her tendons had twisted her disabled hand into the appearance of a ball of

---

[3] This Probianus is probably to be identified with the Probianus who as a priest represented the bishop of Bourges at the Council of Orléans in 541, and who as bishop of Bourges attended the Council of Paris in 552 and another Council of Paris between 556 and 573. Bishop Probianus also promoted the cult of St. Ursinus, thought to have been the first bishop of Bourges (*GC* 79).

[4] Gregory also mentioned in passing the healing of two lepers at the tomb of St. Hilary, and cited "the book of his life" as a source for more of the saint's miracles (*GC* 2).

string, and the web of her fingers was weakened by being intertwined with themselves as cross-threads. She then came to the tomb of the most blessed [Hilary] and through his intercession was cured during the celebration of the liturgy. Energetic movement gradually slipped through her paralyzed joints and fingers. **16.** After a long time her hand was reborn then when it felt the confessor's gifts; her hand had come from her mother's womb dead, but it returned from his tomb alive. Behold how generous is the compassion of this benefactor! For he has restored the limbs that nature did not create at birth.

17. Nor is it proper to omit this miracle that happened to a fortunate blind man after he prayed. For while he was hurrying to the threshold [of the church] of the blessed Martin in order to recover his sight, he entered the church of St. Hilary as he was passing by. People were celebrating vigils there according to the usual liturgy. At daybreak his eyes were opened, and this man who [previously] always needed to hear about the coming of daylight [now] began to announce it to others. **18.** He for whom everything had been nighttime removed his darkness during that night, and he who had never seen the decorations of daytime began to appear as the rising sun for that day. Everything was then constructed in his presence when he was worthy to see their creation. If I may say so, behold how the world was reborn in turn for that man when he acquired his sight. **19.** Although this blind man was hurrying to visit [Hilary's] brother [Martin], he was worthy to receive his sight in [Hilary's] own church. How impressively does the goodwill of this benefactor shine when he anticipates the wishes of a suppliant!

20. Let me describe something appropriate about that royal marvel that he performed for a king. Clovis had collected armed troops in order to fight against a tribe of heretics. In the middle of the night he was worthy to see a light coming over himself from the church of the blessed man; this was advice that he first pray at this distinguished shrine and then quickly descend and engage the enemy. **21.** Clovis carefully observed this vision, and after contacting in his prayer someone who would fight on his side, he proceeded to battle with such success that before the third hour of the day he secured a victory that exceeded his human desires. Where [there had once been] a host of men, it seemed that piles of corpses had been erected from them. Behold how terribly these omens must be dreaded and how happily these miracles must be embraced. It would have been small consolation for the king to reveal this warning in a light if [Hilary] had not clearly advised [the king] by also adding verbal instructions. **22.** A similar sort of miracle once happened during the time of the Israelites. Then a column of fire was a guide; now the appearance of a light offered advice.[5] I would like

---

[5] Gregory also noted the fiery beacon that came from the church of St. Hilary and appeared over Clovis (*Hist.* 2.37).

to know why the secret marvel of that bright fire was presented so clearly; but with the inspiration of [Hilary] I will state what I seem to understand. **23.** [Hilary] did not cease to struggle against the forces of heretics in spirit just as in the past in the flesh; he believed that [the emperor] Constantius was returning again as the Arian [king] Alaric to oppose him. Because he still possessed his rich compassion even though [now] reposing in heaven, how strong is his eagerness always on behalf of Catholic Christianity! In the past he spoke words of faith at a council in order to dispute the enemy; now he has presented the weapons of victory on a battlefield.[6]

24. I am unable to know the sin of which a woman in the village of Tonat was accused. But while she was carrying water for her own use on a Sunday, her hand stiffened and the flow [of blood] in her veins dried up. Then she was advised in a dream to hurry to the saint's shrine if she wished to be healed. **25.** The woman trusted this advice and happily rushed off as if accompanied by the guide of her health. And while she was chanting Psalms in the church, the happiness of forgiveness, just like her punishment previously, appeared on a Sunday. Behold the customary love of this remarkable patron, who investigates the reasons in order to discover what she had done! O blessed Hilary, whom everyone must praise with their hearts, their tongues, and their voices! For his generous compassion is not only available but also effective for everyone.

26. Let me pass on to the results of another distinguished miracle. A paralyzed girl who was advancing in years was undeservedly living without the abilities of life. Alive only in spirit, she trembled within the carnage of her dead body; in her entire corpse only her eyes functioned, as if her eyes were keeping watch and guarding over her dead limbs. **27.** Her tongue was stiff in the opening of her throat and did not move fluently, and although her voice came from the depths of her heart, it could not arrange itself in connected words. Because her hands were weak and uncontrollable, they did not naturally perform their obligated duties, and because her feet were unstable, they did not support the potential collapse of her [other] limbs. The lump of her entire body was constructed badly and rigidly. **28.** During the festival she was brought into his church and propped up with all the other people who were awaiting his immense goodwill. Then [Hilary] fulfilled many miracles in the body of this one woman. He strengthened her weak feet and legs, he shaped her stiff tongue with flexibility and ease in speaking, he equipped her previously crippled hands for weaving wool, and he revived the features of her flesh through the generosity of his faithful gift. **29.** This aged infant finally began to speak, and with her first words she asked, notably, for the nourishment of milk. Because she requested this

---

[6] Constantius II had been Roman emperor from 337 to 361. Fortunatus described some of the highlights of Hilary's opposition to Constantius and Arianism in his *Vita Hilarii* 14–16, 21, 24–31; for a general overview, see Rocher (1987) 10–51. Alaric II had been king of the Visigoths from 484 until his death in battle against Clovis in 507.

sort of food before anything else, how else is this to be interpreted except that when she was healed, she then believed that she had been reborn?

30. Nor is this reliable marvel to be consigned to the threat of oblivion. Two merchants went to the church of the blessed [Hilary]. Since they together had a case of wax as if in common, one of them said to the other that they should generously offer it to the great confessor, even though it was such a small gift. But he spoke his words in vain to his friend who was unwilling in his heart. So while the first merchant knelt with his companion in prayer, he secretly placed the wax before the railing around the impressive tomb. 31. Soon the shape of that wax divided itself into equal halves; the half from this faithful donor was accepted, but the other half was rejected at God's command with complete disgust. Everyone was watching as this half rolled all the way to the opposite railing, as if the saint did not wish to accept what the other man had not offered to him in piety. Because [Hilary] has always rejected what does not proceed from faith, he is as sure in his judgment as he is merciful in [answering] prayers. 32. Oh, how this incorruptible judge shines! He was more scrupulous during this judicial examination than during the selection of the blossoms that scrupulously produced the wax. 33. Then the man who did not wish to offer [the wax] was convicted by his own testimony in admitting his crime and was overwhelmed by the guilt of his enormous shame. He realized that such a disgraceful dishonor had sprouted in the roots of his own conscience, and he saw the crimes of his secret thoughts revealed in his own face. He meditated, he moaned, and he wept [so much] that as the fountain of his tears flowed, he at least washed away the pollution caused by his delinquent heart. Then, because the judicial examination over the wax corrected him, he urgently brought greater gifts.

34. One night when a candle had as usual been lit, by chance it was burning over the tomb of [Hilary] who lives on through his intercession. The candle fell over, so that it blazed up where it fell on top of the shroud but without leaving any mark. For the candle was found lying there as far as its length; although its papyrus [wrapping? wick?] was burned up, it formed a boundary as it were between the fire and the shroud, with the result that the shroud was found to be protected by the candle by which it could have been burned. The candle offered this assistance in order to obey [Hilary's] command. The fire was frightened from the wax that it always [previously] knew how to overcome, and it seemed to reject the wax that it had [previously] seized to keep on burning. 35. In the midst of these events this rather comes to mind, as they say: through the confessor's power the wax extinguished the flames that it nourished, and in a reversal of the [natural] order the wax suffocated [the fire] that could have devoured it. Various elements seem to have transformed their natures: in order to prevent the fire from harming anything here, the shroud substituted for marble

and the wax for flowing water. **36.** But how difficult is it for someone who kindles the sight of the blind to extinguish the flame of a candle? And since he restores sight to the eyes of another's entombed corpse, how readily do we believe that he removes the flames from his own tomb?

37. Because I am still unsatisfied, I would like to describe the miracles of this most holy man as if in a unique fashion, but I fear that when I wish to show my devotion, I might seem to offend the listener's heart as his boredom grows. **38.** Blessed [Hilary], pardon the shortness of my text and forgive my practice of saying little even if I were to fill [many] volumes, lest I seem to cause offense to a confessor as I wish to avoid boredom among men. By no means do I intend to say more about you, so that my brevity might all the more invite people to read about you.

The Suffering and Miracles of
the Martyr St. Julian

ALTHOUGH as a young boy living in the Auvergne Gregory had certainly already heard many of the oral traditions about St. Julian and
his miracles, he apparently began to collect stories systematically
while he was a deacon at Lyon (cf. *VJ* 2) and about the time he became
bishop at Tours in 573. Initially his purposes in the *VJ* were to describe the
martyrdom of St. Julian and the gradual development of his cult at Brioude; to provide evidence of the saint's miraculous power at Brioude; to
indicate the saint's special assistance for members of his family; and to
demonstrate St. Julian's power at places other than Brioude. Since with this
last topic Gregory thought it "proper to end this small book" (*VJ* 32),
perhaps at first he intended to conclude the *VJ* with the stories about St.
Julian's assistance in establishing his authority as the new bishop of Tours
(*VJ* 34–40). So when he described his visit to the shrine of St. Julian and the
acquisition of relics immediately after his consecration, he noted them as
"some events that I experienced recently" (*VJ* 34).

But Gregory eventually included more stories, in particular a series that
he heard from Aredius of Limoges, and the addition of these stories both
blunted the original self-serving perspective of the *VJ* and delayed its completion for several years. When Gregory described a visit from his friend
Aredius, he noted that he had already mentioned him in the second book of
his *VM* (*VJ* 41); although this was presumably a cross-reference to Aredius's visit to Tours in 577 (*VM* 2.39), Gregory did not finish the second
book of the *VM* until 581 (*VM* 2.60). In contrast, Gregory did not mention
Aredius's visit to Tours in late 583 (*VM* 3.24) that he noted in the third
book of his *VM*, completed in 588 (*VM* 3.60). In the final chapter of the *VJ*
Gregory referred to his *Vita* of Nicetius of Lyon (*VJ* 50), in which in turn he
had mentioned a military expedition of 585 (*VP* 8.11, with *Hist.* 7.35–
38).[1] And in his book about the glory of the martyrs that he wrote largely

---

[1] *VP* 8.6 included some stories that Gregory heard from his deacon Agiulf, who can
perhaps be identified with the deacon who returned from Rome after the inauguration of Pope
Gregory I in 590 (*Hist.* 10.1). Coville (1928) 327–28 suggests that Gregory later added this
chapter to *VP* 8.

between 585 and 588 he referred to his *VJ* as a completed book (*GM* 64).[2] In combination these various cross-references suggest that Gregory completed the *VJ* during the early 580s, after he had finally established his authority at Tours more firmly.[3]

Early editions of the *VJ* include one by Thierry Ruinart first published in 1699 and reprinted in *PL* 71.801–28, and another by H. L. Bordier with a French translation published in 1857. The best edition is by Bruno Krusch, who included the *VJ* in his monumental edition of the works of Gregory in *MGH*, SRM 1 (1885) 562–84; he also later collated additional manuscripts that occasionally supply better or more sensible readings for the *VJ* in *MGH*, SRM 7 (1920) 737–41. In this translation of the *VJ* (and the following translation of the *VM*) the one major change from Krusch's edition involves the *capitula*. Gregory provided a list of "headings" for each of his books. Rather than following Gregory (and Krusch) in listing them as a table of contents, these translations have included them as introductory headings for each chapter. Readers should also note that because *VJ* 35–46b are numbered differently in *PL* 71, citations in modern books to those chapters of the *VJ* may also differ.

Here begins a book specifically about the glory of the martyr St. Julian, my own special patron. Amen.[4]

1. His suffering

Divine piety somehow ignites in us a great burning to acquire the way of its righteousness when it says: "The eyes of the Lord [are] over the just, and his ears [are open] to their prayers" [Ps. 34:15]. [This text] indicates that whoever has loved righteousness with his whole heart is heard by the Lord when he has offered a prayer. If only every one of us, upon beginning to sing these [words], would immediately reject the temptations of the world, ignore useless passions, set aside wicked ways, and attempt to seize the path of righteousness unencumbered and without the burden of this world's behavior. On this path Abel is acknowledged as a righteous man, Enoch is received as a blessed man, Noah is preserved, Abraham is chosen,

---

[2] See Monod (1872) 41–45, and Van Dam (1988a) 4–5, for the date of composition of the *GM*.

[3] See Monod (1872) 42–43; and above, chapter 2, section 2, for the context. Krusch (1885) 451–56 stresses Gregory's frequent revisions.

[4] "Incipit liber propriae in gloria sancti martyris Iuliani peculiaris patroni nostri. Amen." Although found only in a ninth-century manuscript, both this heading and the similar subscript at the end of the book are considered genuine by Krusch (1920) 737, 741, and (1951) XIIIn.4.

Isaac is commended, Jacob is enhanced, Joseph is protected, Moses is sanctified, David is predestined, Solomon is enriched, the three boys prophesy in the midst of the dewy flames, and Daniel feeds among the harmless beasts. On this path the apostles are directed and the blessed martyrs are glorified. You ask, "How so?" While they care for weaknesses, raise the dead, reject the present, long for the future, despise their torturers, and feel no torments, they are of course journeying to the kingdoms of heaven. Without any doubt they would not have achieved this result by their own power if they had not been heard by the Lord while they were traveling most directly on the path of righteousness.

So also the illustrious martyr Julian, who was born at Vienne and given to Clermont as a martyr, was ignited by this fire and wished for and desired these [goals] in all his plans. Even when he was with the most blessed Ferreolus, already then he burned with the fragrance of martyrdom. After he abandoned his wealth and his relatives, he came to Clermont simply because of so great a desire for martyrdom. But he did not undertake this without a divine command, since a persecution was then raging in Vienne. For he had read that the Lord had proclaimed: "If you are persecuted in that city, flee to another" [Matt. 10:23]. Therefore he came here to the territory of Clermont not because he feared death but so that by leaving his own possessions he might achieve his prize more easily. For he was always afraid that his parents might oppose him if he initiated this struggle in their presence, and that he, a soldier of Christ, might forfeit the crown of glory if he did not struggle correctly. While this persecution was raging he came to the village of Brioude, in which the incantations of that mad error [of paganism] were practiced. When by the will of God he learned that his enemies were pursuing [him], he prayed that he be hidden by a certain widow. She [first] concealed him; [then,] at the martyr's request she imme-diately exposed [him]. He spoke in this manner to his pursuers: "I do not wish," he said, "to remain any longer in this world, because with all the longing of my spirit I already thirst for Christ." They drew their swords, brandished them in their right hands, and cut off his head; the glorious martyr was then, if I may say so, divided into three parts. For his head was brought to Vienne, his body was buried at Brioude, but his blessed soul was received by Christ his maker. The old men who delivered his sacred body to the tomb were so rejuvenated that [even though] they were very elderly, they were thought of as young men. The martyr Ferreolus acquired his head; after he completed the struggle [of his own martyrdom], his body as well as [Julian's] head were placed in the [same] crypt in one tomb.[5] Lest

---

[5] Julian's friend Ferreolus was supposedly tribune at Vienne when he warned Julian to flee (*Passio* 2); but his historicity is dubious: see Heinzelmann (1982) 608.

perhaps this account seem unbelievable to anyone, let me carefully relate the events that I have heard.

2. The discovery of his head

Once when I was traveling to Lyon to meet the blessed bishop Nicetius, I decided to go to Vienne for no other reason than to pray, and in particular to visit the tomb of the glorious martyr Ferreolus. For it was impressed on my mind that I was his foster son as well as Julian's because of their long-standing love. After I prayed, I lifted the gaze of my eyes to the platform, and on it I noted some verses that read:

> This shrine contains two warriors of Christ:
> Julian and his head, and Ferreolus and his body.

I read these lines and then I asked the warden what they meant. He replied: "Long ago men founded the church of the martyr St. Ferreolus next to the bank of the Rhone River. But because of the strong pressure of the river the colonnade on that side [of the church] collapsed. The bishop then serving the cathedral at Vienne was named Mamertus. He was a cautious man and predicted that [the rest of the church] would also collapse. So with keen attention to its design he constructed another church of elegant workmanship to which he wished to transfer the holy body of the martyr [Ferreolus]. A large crowd of abbots and monks assembled for this task, and after keeping a vigil during the night, they [each] took a hoe and began to dig. Once they dug down deep, they found three tombs; immediately the thoughts of the onlookers were bewildered. For no one was certain which was the tomb of the blessed martyr. While everyone was standing around in confusion because of their ignorance, one of the bystanders (at the inspiration of God, I believe) shouted out and said: 'Ancient tradition has customarily claimed that the head of the confessor Julian was buried in the tomb of the martyr Ferreolus; and frequent repetition has publicized this tradition among the people. If each tomb is investigated by removing its lid, it is possible to discover immediately which are the limbs of the martyr Ferreolus.' The bishop listened to this advice and ordered everyone to kneel in prayer. After prayer he went to the tombs, uncovered two, but found in them [only the bodies of] individual men at rest. But when he opened the third tomb, he found in it the body of a man at rest that was intact and [clothed] in an unfaded garment; the man's head had been cut off, and he held another head embraced in his arm. The man looked as if he had been recently buried. His face was neither disfigured by any paleness nor deformed by the thinning of his hair nor decayed by any putrefaction; instead, he was so fresh and so untouched that you might think he was still preserved in a sleeping body. Then the bishop was overwhelmed with great joy and said: 'There is no doubt that this is the body of Ferreolus and this is the head of the martyr Julian.' Then the people applauded and loudly chanted Psalms. With the approval of the Lord [the tomb] was brought to this place where it is now venerated."

I have accurately reported these words just as I heard them from this warden at the martyr's tomb. Our [fellow Christian] Sollius [i.e., Sidonius Apollinaris] provides [additional] evidence for this account when he wrote to that Mamertus in these words: "In the regions of the Western world to you alone was granted the complete translation of the martyr Ferreolus along with the head of our Julian. As compensation we therefore request that a portion of his patronage should come from Vienne to us, because a portion of [our] patron has returned from here to you."[6]

3. The power of the spring in which the saint's head was washed

At the spot where the blessed martyr was beheaded, there is a sparkling spring that is gentle and filled with sweet water. [Julian's] head, after it had been cut off by his persecutors, was washed in this spring; and many cures are offered to ill people from its water. For often the eyes of the blind are illuminated after being touched by these waters, and people who suffer and burn from tertian and quartan fevers are calm once they have swallowed [some water]. And if anyone who is in pain from a serious misfortune wishes, at the urging of the martyr, to drink [from the spring], immediately upon drinking he recovers. The burning of fevers is quenched as quickly as if you were to see waves tossed on a huge funeral pyre and all its flames extinguished.

4. The old men and the woman whose husband was imprisoned

After the suffering of the blessed martyr and after the publication of the account of the old men who were restored to their former strength while they committed [Julian's] sacred limbs to burial, people who believed and made requests obtained many benefits there with the martyr's assistance. I ask that indulgence be granted [to me] as I narrate a few of these events, because I am aware that I am neither suitable for nor experienced at telling these stories and that I am neither trained in grammatical skills nor edu-

---

[6] Since Gregory considered himself a foster son of St. Ferreolus, it is peculiar that he said so little about the saint's martyrdom or cult. Nicetius was bishop of Lyon from 553 to 573 and Gregory's great-uncle: see above, chapter 2, section 1. Mamertus had been bishop of Vienne from ca. 451/452 until after 474 and once instituted penitential rogations to celebrate Ascension Day (*Hist.* 2.34): see Heinzelmann (1982) 644, and Mathisen (1990) 135. Although the first church dedicated to St. Ferreolus at Vienne was next to the Rhone River, the location of Mamertus's new church is uncertain: see Vieillard-Troiekouroff (1976) 339–40. Sidonius had been bishop of Clermont from ca. 470 into the 480s (*Hist.* 2.22–23); Gregory here quoted from his *Ep.* 7.1.7.

cated in the classics. But what am I to do? My love for my patron compels me, and I cannot be silent about these events.

A man was [brought] fettered from Spain, thrown into a prison, judged at the court of the emperor [Maximus] at Trier, and sentenced to death. His wife learned of his fate. While she was hurrying to bury her husband's body, she came to the village of Brioude. There she found some men, and after eagerly and earnestly asking various questions, she learned what had happened to the martyr and to the old men at that spot. She believed that this was a reliable recommendation and decided to hurry to the tomb of the blessed martyr so that she might present her case, reveal her misfortune, and expose all the suffering of her grief. For the men had in addition made this claim: "Mistress, we promise for certain that you will be made happy again by the martyr who once restored to their former vigor the limbs of old men that had stiffened from the decay of age." After praying she vowed that if she received her husband back alive, she would cover the martyr's tomb with a stone [shrine] in whatever space there might be. She was full of confidence and trusted the goodwill of the martyr when she arrived at Trier, where she found her husband and as a favor from the emperor received him back; she left in happiness. Inquiry was made about the time when her husband had been released from prison; the moment of his acquittal turned out to have been that hour when she requested the martyr's assistance. Then with lavish gifts she fulfilled the vow she had promised.[7]

5. The man who wished to kill another man in the church

Not far away from the shrine that this woman constructed over the tomb of the martyr was a huge sanctuary in which people worshiped an image of Mars and Mercury [set] on a very high column.[8] While the pagans celebrated their festivals at this sanctuary, and while these lifeless people were offering incense to their lifeless [gods], two young men were provoked to a quarrel in the middle of the crowd. One drew his sword and tried to kill the other. But the other man realized that no pardon was available because his own gods would not protect him. So he sought the protection of our

---

[7] Magnus Maximus was a general in Britain whose army crossed to Gaul and defeated the emperor Gratian in 383. He then established himself as emperor at Trier, where Bishop Martin once visited his court to intercede for some of Gratian's supporters: see Sulpicius Severus, *Dial.* 3.8. Maximus's army campaigned unsuccessfully against the Franks along the Rhine (*Hist.* 2.9). Although the emperor Theodosius eventually recognized the usurper, in 388 his army killed Maximus (*Hist.* 1.43): see Matthews (1975) 173–82, 223–25. But of all the emperors who had resided in northern Gaul during the fourth century, only Maximus was remembered as "the emperor at Trier" (cf. *Hist.* 1.45, *VP* 2.1). Gregory's story here is similar to the version in *Passio* 4–5, which he perhaps had read.

[8] Lambrechts (1954) suggests that this was in fact a statue of a Celtic version of the two-faced god Janus.

religion, the pardon of our confession, the remedy of our community, and the shrine of the glorious martyr. His pursuer was then unable to attack and assault him with his sword; and since he had barred the door behind himself, his pursuer seized both doorposts and tried to break down the door. Immediately his hands that gripped the planks twitched in fierce pain, and the wretch was tormented with such anguish that the tears that flowed profusely openly indicated how much pain he felt inside. The crowd was amazed, and the man who had been sheltered inside departed as a free man. The parents of the man who had been restrained by the saint's power learned about the martyr's tomb and with many pious gifts prayed on behalf of their son.

6. The conversion of the local inhabitants

While these events were taking place it happened that a priest was traveling on that road. When he learned what had occurred, he promised the parents that they would receive their son back in good health if they abandoned their paganism. On the following night the priest also had a dream in which he saw that the images that the pagans worshiped were being destroyed by [invocation of] the divine name and were lying on the ground after being reduced to dust. Four days later when the pagans wished again to offer sacrifices to their gods, the priest sadly knelt before the saint's tomb, wept, and prayed that the brightness of divine power would finally visit these pagans who were trapped in darkness, and that the blessed martyr would no longer allow his own foster children to be bound by their blindness, since he possessed the happiness of eternal enlightenment. While the priest was praying, immediately thunder rumbled, lightning bolts flashed, a storm that combined lightning and hail poured down, and everything was in chaos. The entire crowd of pagans rushed together to the shrine and knelt before the priest. Their wailing was mixed with their weeping, and everyone begged for the mercy of the Lord. They all promised the priest that if the storm departed, they would abandon the cults of the images, request the martyr to be their patron, and with pure hearts convert to his God. Then the priest offered a prayer and was worthy to obtain all that he requested. Once the storm departed, the young man believed along with his parents and on that very day was freed from his suffering. The pagans were baptized in the name of the Trinity; then they smashed the statues they had worshiped and threw them into a lake next to the village and the river. Thereafter both the Catholic faith and the power of the martyr were fully evident in that place.

7. How Hillidius liberated people from their enemies

After these events some Burgundians came to the village of Brioude and surrounded it with a large band of soldiers. They seized some people and plundered the holy vessels; then they crossed the river, killed some men with their swords, and prepared to divide up the remaining people by lot. Then Hillidius came from Le Velay and attacked these soldiers; some say that he had been motivated by the warning of a swift dove. He rallied his comrades and so [thoroughly] slaughtered and massacred the enemy that he released the captives, triumphed in praise of the martyr, crossed the river, and like a new Moses returned to the blessed shrine along with all the people who were singing. Among the people who had been rescued there was, I think, no less rejoicing than there had been long ago among the Israelites after the Egyptians had been drowned. Although no one may doubt that this victory was due to the blessed martyr, nevertheless the warning of the dove is believed to have been some sign of divine power. For the dove came to meet Hillidius as he was advancing, and when he delayed a bit as usual, it flew in circles over him. When Hillidius proceeded, the dove went ahead and returned to meet him again, as if begging him to travel more quickly. While this was happening a young man arrived and announced the capture [of the people]; then Hillidius traveled more quickly. In addition, while he was fighting the dove seemed always to fly around him. Let no one begrudgingly claim that this story about the dove is fiction and that it happened [only] to a man who was a Christian, because Orosius wrote that a Roman consul named Marcus Valerius had been assisted by a swift raven.[9]

8. The death of those who had stolen the vessels of the church

After Hillidius had defeated these enemies, four of them slipped away in flight and brought back to their homeland a paten and a pitcher that is known as an *anax*. They divided the paten into four pieces and brought the pitcher to King Gundobad as a token of their appreciation. But the queen wisely discovered the rest of the silver and along with many additional gifts restored it to that holy shrine. She loyally convinced the king that he should not forfeit the goodwill of the holy martyr over this small bit of silver.[10]

---

[9] This Hillidius was here acting apparently in a private capacity in defending the shrine at Brioude. Perhaps he is to be identified with the Helladius who corresponded with Avitus, bishop of Vienne from ca. 494 to ca. 518: see Avitus, *Ep.* 84, with Mathisen (1982) 375, and Heinzelmann (1982) 622. Gregory occasionally cited the survey of both Roman and ecclesiastical history that the Spanish historian Orosius had composed in the early fifth century (*Hist.* 1 praef., 1.6, 2 praef., 5 praef., *GC* 1, *De cursu* 3); here he referred to a passage from Orosius, *Historiae adversum paganos* 3.6. Orosius in turn had used Livy's history of Rome as the source for his story about a raven that helped a Roman soldier in battle.

[10] Gundobad was a king of the Burgundians from ca. 474 until 516 (*Hist.* 2.32–4, 3.5), and an uncle of Clotild, who married the Frankish king Clovis (*Hist.* 2.28): see Heinzelmann (1982) 619–20. The queen here was presumably his wife Carathena, who died in 506: see Heinzelmann (1982) 574. Bonnet (1890) 226n.5 concedes that the etymology of *anax* is obscure and suggests that it was a term associated with drinking bouts.

9. The paralytic Foedamia

Because of these and other comparably distinguished miracles the believers constructed a huge church there [in Brioude]. This church was celebrated because of the miracles of the blessed martyr, as I said; in it cures were often requested and sought for people suffering from paralysis, lameness, blindness, and other illnesses. A woman named Foedamia was restricted by swelling due to paralysis and felt pain whenever she moved any part of her body. Her relatives brought her and put her on display at the blessed church, so that she might earn her keep from almsgivers. On the night before a Sunday she was lying in the colonnade attached to the holy church. While the people were faithfully and piously celebrating the sacred vigils, and while she was peacefully dozing a bit on her couch, a man admonished and rebuked her in a dream. He asked her why she was not with the others who were offering vigils to God during the night. She replied that she was disabled in all her limbs and that she could not walk at all. Then [she felt] as if the man who was speaking to her supported her and led her all the way to the tomb. While she was praying in her sleep, it seemed to her as if a load of chains fell from her limbs to the ground. Once she was awakened by some sound, she knew that she had received complete health in all her limbs. Immediately she got up from her couch and to everyone's surprise shouted out her gratitude and entered the holy church. Some even say that this woman continuously described the appearance of the man who had addressed her. She always said that the man was tall, well dressed, and exceptionally elegant. On his face was a smile, and his blond hair was streaked with some gray. He moved gracefully, and he spoke openly and most pleasantly. The gleam of his skin surpassed the whiteness of a lily. And out of the thousands of men she often observed, she saw no one else like him. To many people it seemed quite reasonable that the blessed martyr had appeared to her. This woman was cured after eighteen years [of paralysis].

10. The man who tried to drag from the church a man
who had struck him

After a man lost an eye during a brawl that he had initiated, he tried to drag from the church the man who had struck him. While he was doing this, not only did he not recover his sight in the eye he had lost, but he also realized that his other eye that he thought was intact was going blind. So he confessed his sins and said: "Because I showed no compassion, I have deservedly and without compassion suffered this penalty." Along with the people who had arrived for [Julian's] festival this man knelt before the holy tomb; after he apologized to the man who had struck him, he received his sight back as well as the support [of Julian]. And so it happened that the man who had requested the saint's assistance received protection, and the man who did not believe was censured. Both men then departed, chastised but happy.

11. The man who was disabled because he yoked his oxen on a Sunday

As a result of his impudent audacity another man yoked his oxen on a Sunday and began to plow his field. When he picked up an ax in order to fix something on the plowshare, his fingers were immediately stiffened and the handle was stuck in his right hand. He was in agony because of the great pain. Two years later he went to the church of the blessed martyr and piously celebrated the vigils. Immediately on that very Sunday his hand was opened and he dropped the wooden handle that he had unwillingly held. He presented to the people an important lesson, because what had been done on a Sunday was also forgiven on a Sunday. The man extolled the glory of the martyr and departed in good health. Never again did he dare to do any work on the day of the Lord's resurrection.

12. Anagild, a mute, deaf, and blind man

Anagild was a mute, deaf, and blind man who was crippled in the joints of all his limbs. He was thrown in front of the sacred entrances [to the shrine], so that he who could not work for his nourishment and maintenance with his own hands might be supported by the donations of believers. After he had lain in front of the sacred shrine for an entire year, he was finally assisted by the power of the blessed martyr and cured of all his illnesses.

**13. The men who broke into the church during the reign
of King Theuderic**

It seems to me that just as illnesses are reversed and healed by the saint's power, so also the depravities of unbelievers are restrained and exposed by his prayer for the correction of other people, lest they seek similar [follies]. For the glory of the saint is apparent in both situations: he restores ill people to health so that they may suffer no longer, and he censures unbelievers so that they may avoid condemnation in a future court. And although I think that everyone knows something about the belligerence of King Theuderic and the illnesses of Sigivald that happened to him when he was in Clermont, nevertheless the power of the blessed martyr requires a careful exposition; then all the more readily may what has [already] been said be considered reliable. As the aforementioned king hurried to plunder Clermont, he entered the territory [of the city] and ravaged and destroyed everything. Some soldiers left his army and quickly threatened the village of Brioude, because a rumor had spread that the local inhabitants had gathered in the church with much of their wealth. Upon coming to the shrine the soldiers discovered that a crowd of men and women, along with their own possessions, had taken refuge in the church and locked its doors. The soldiers were unable to enter; so one of them, just like a thief, broke the glass in a window near the holy altar and entered [the church]; for this is the thief who does not enter through the door [cf. John 10:1]. Then he unlocked the doors of the shrine and let the army in. The soldiers seized everything, and outdoors not far from the village they divided up the possessions of these poor people along with the clerics who served this church and the other people who had been brought out later. When these events were reported to the king, he seized some of these soldiers and condemned them to die in various ways. But the man who had been the instigator of this theft and who had fled after the church had been violated died after being devoured by fire that fell from heaven. Even though many people heaped a pile of stones over his body, he was uncovered by thunder and lightning and lacked a grave in the ground. His companions who avoided the king returned to their homeland, but were possessed by a demon and ended their lives in various painful deaths. Once King Theuderic heard of this, he returned everything that had been stolen from the church. Then he ordered that no one use violence within seven miles of the church.[11]

14. The invader Sigivald

At the command of the king [Theuderic], Sigivald, a man who was very influential with the king, migrated with his entire family to the region of Clermont. There he unjustly confiscated the possessions of many people. In the process he became greedy, and under the pretext of an obscure exchange he seized a villa that Bishop Tetradius of Bourges (now deceased) had left to the church of St. Julian. But three months after he entered [the villa] he was struck with a fever and deprived of his senses, and he laid his head on his bed. His wife grieved and worried about his death; but then she was advised by a bishop that her husband should leave the villa if she wished to see him recover. She listened to this advice, prepared coaches, and brought up a wagon on which to take her husband away. As soon as

---

[11] After Clovis's death in 511 his son Theuderic had taken control of Clermont (*Hist.* 3.2). Years later when it was rumored that Theuderic had been killed in a battle, Arcadius, an aristocrat at Clermont who was the son of Bishop Apollinaris and the grandson of Bishop Sidonius, offered to betray the city to King Childebert (*Hist.* 3.9). Theuderic soon took his revenge by allowing his army to ravage the Auvergne and loot some of its villages (*Hist.* 3.12–13, *GM* 51); only the shrine of St. Julian at Brioude offered some refuge (*Hist.* 3.12; cf. *VJ* 23), although Bishop Quintianus was able to save Clermont (*VP* 4.2). Gregory's chronology for this invasion is confused, but it should probably be dated to 524: see Heinzelmann (1982) 559, and Wood (1988). Such invasions certainly caused disruption for local landowners: see *Formulae Arvernenses* 1. Although Wood (1986) 12–13 suggests that the "hostility of the Franks" mentioned in this formula refers to this invasion of 524, see the note to *VJ* 23 for other possibilities.

they left the estate, immediately they were both rewarded with God's good-will. For Sigivald deserved [to regain] his health, and his wife her happiness because of her husband's recovery. Some say that a monk saw the martyr St. Julian in the oratory of this estate talking with Bishop Tetradius and promising that he would recover for the bishop the villa that the bishop had left him as recompense for his own soul. This monk also always said that the blessed martyr had the same appearance as the paralyzed woman had previously described.[12]

15. The evilness of Pastor

Pastor, a free man from birth, was a "shepherd" in name but not in behavior.[13] He acted unjustly toward the church of the holy martyr and its many possessions. During an attack by the enemy his disrespect increased to such an extent that in his greed he did not hesitate to seize the fields that this church let to tenants and that were next to an estate belonging to the church. The priest of the church sent some of the clerics as envoys to this man so that he might accept their mediation and leave the fields that he had wrongly seized. Pastor seized his weapons and assaulted [these clerics] as if attacking a hostile enemy; the clerics were driven off by his arrows and Pastor kept the saint's possessions under his own control. But it happened that the festival day celebrating the suffering of the glorious martyr [on August 28] was soon approaching. Pastor ignored his seizure [of this property] and the injuries he had inflicted on the clerics, and five days before the festival he went to the village of Brioude. While he was merrily enjoying the happy entertainment at the house of his lodging, suddenly there was a flash of lightning and the rumble of thunder. When the thunder rumbled again, Pastor was struck with a bolt of fire that fell from heaven; but none of the other people died. He then burned like a flaming funeral pyre and, as a warning for everyone, was gradually consumed. The people who had gath-

---

[12] As bishop of Bourges, Tetradius had attended the Councils of Agde in 506 and Orléans in 511. Sigivald was a relative of King Theuderic who accompanied him on his invasion of the Auvergne (*VP* 5.2) and then remained as duke of Clermont (*Hist.* 3.13, 5.12, *VP* 12.2). He and his family were hence some of the few Franks who settled in the Auvergne, or even south of the Loire: see Kurth (1919) 1:227–41, and James (1977) 202–7. He also perhaps had Theuderic's permission to occupy various properties: see Classen (1977) 177, citing *Pactus Legis Salicae* 14.4, which mentions a "royal permit" for men who migrated. Vieillard-Troiekouroff (1976) 54 locates this estate that Sigivald tried to confiscate at Bongheat (*Hist.* 3.16), Rouche (1979) 492n.35, at Boudes. Years later before his own death in 533 Theuderic killed Sigivald and seized some of his possessions; but Theuderic's son Theudebert refused to kill Sigivald's son and eventually returned to him his father's possessions (*Hist.* 3.23–24). Sigivald's daughter Ranihild perhaps attempted to make amends for her father's behavior by leaving some woodlands to Abbot Brachio and his monastery at Pionsat (*VP* 12.3): see Vieillard-Troiekouroff (1976) 351–52. For the previous description of St. Julian, see *VJ* 9.

[13] Krusch punctuated the text in such a way that the shepherd's name was Ingenuus. Bonnet (1890) 734n.4 points out that he was instead a man of free birth named Pastor.

ered for the festival of the blessed [Julian] watched these events with amaze-
ment and were frightened by this miracle; for them this was sufficient
[warning] never again to seize any of the saint's possessions. Lest anyone
think that this happened by chance, let him note that in a crowd of innocent
people only this one sacrilegious man died.

16. The arrogance of Becco

I will now narrate what the blessed martyr did to confound the pride of
Count Becco. While he was conducting public trials, he became extremely
arrogant and unjustly oppressed many people. By chance it happened that
he lost his hawk that he had released some time ago and that had flown off
in various directions. At the same time a servant from the church of St.
Julian was walking along the road and found another hawk that seemed to
be lost. This young boy served as an attendant in the residence associated
with the church. When the news came to Becco that this boy was of course
keeping the hawk that he had found, Becco began to shout and accuse [the
boy]. "That hawk was mine," he said, "and this thief has stolen him." As
his greed increased, he had the boy bound, sent him to prison, and decided
to condemn him to the gallows on the following day. Then the [local] priest
was very unhappy and hurried to the saint's tomb. He wept and explained
the situation; then he took ten gold coins and sent them to Becco with his
trustworthy friends. But Becco rejected these gold coins as worthless and
insisted with an oath that he would never release the boy until he had
received thirty gold coins. The priest acquired these coins from the top of
the saint's tomb and sent them to Becco. Once Becco received the coins, his
greed for gold was satisfied, and he released the boy unharmed.

But omnipotent God, who endures longer than the sun [cf. Ps. 72:5],
humbled this perverse man in accordance with the riches of his goodness.
For after the cycle of this year was completed, Becco came to the saint's
festival with his entourage of retainers and entered the holy door [of the
church]. The lector who was to recite the account of [Julian's] blessed
suffering advanced, and as soon as he opened the book and pronounced the
name of St. Julian at the beginning of his reading, immediately Becco fell to
the ground with a most horrid and unfamiliar cry. With blood foaming
from his mouth he began to utter various shouts. Then he was lifted by the
hands of his retainers and brought from the church to his home. His
retainers had no doubt that this had happened because of his mistreatment
of this servant from the church. Becco contributed to the church all the
valuables that he then had with him, as much in gold as in garments, and he
then sent many gifts; but he survived to the day of his death without
[recovering] his speech.[14]

---

[14] Becco was count of Clermont probably while Sigivald was duke: see Selle-Hosbach
(1974) 54. Gregory's indignation here may indicate only his ignorance about the require-

17. The deacon who stole the sheep belonging to the church

There was a deacon who left the church and joined himself to the public treasury. After receiving authority from his patrons he committed such crimes that he could hardly be controlled by the people in neighboring regions. Once it happened that he was crossing the pastures in the mountains where the sheep went for the summer in order to collect the pasture tax that was owed to the [public] treasury. While he was unjustly pillaging various people, he saw at a distance flocks that were then under the protection of the martyr's name. He quickly ran over to these flocks and just like a hungry wolf seized the rams. The shepherds of these flocks were upset and frightened, and said to him: "We ask [you], do not take these rams, because they are subject to the control of the blessed martyr Julian." The man laughed at these words and is said to have replied to the shepherds: "Do you think that Julian eats mutton?" Then he struck and beat the shepherds and took away whatever he wished. This wretch did not know that the man who steals something from the houses of the saints also insults the saints themselves. So the Lord himself declares: "Whoever rejects you rejects me, and whoever receives the righteous man will receive the reward of a righteous man" [Luke 10:16, Matt. 10:41].

Many days later it happened that this man hurried to the village of Brioude not because of his religious piety but because of a fortuitous impulse. After kneeling on the ground in front of the tomb, he was soon struck with a fever and was afflicted with such an intense burning that he was unable to get up or to call his servant. But when his servants noted that he was kneeling much longer than usual, they approached and said: "Why are you kneeling for such a long time? Such long and devout prayer has not been your custom." For some said of him that whenever he entered a church, he would murmur a bit and leave without bowing his head. Since the man was incapable of responding when his servants interrupted him, they carried him from that place on their hands and put him on a bed in a room that was nearby. Then, as the fever became stronger, the wretch shouted that he was on fire because of the martyr. Although at first he had kept quiet, after the flames of judgment had been applied to his soul he confessed his crimes, and with whatever sound he was capable of he begged that water be sprinkled on him. But even though water was brought in a vessel and often sprinkled on him, smoke poured from his body as if from a furnace. Meanwhile his suffering limbs, as if on fire, turned black and produced such a stench that scarcely any of the bystanders could tolerate it. Still signaling with his hand the man indicated that he was [feeling] better.

---

ments of Frankish law for ransoming slaves: see Kurth (1919) 2:170–71, and Rouche (1977) 158–59, both citing *Pactus Legis Salicae* 35.9. Weidemann (1982) 1:71 points out that Frankish law required the payment of only three gold coins for the theft of a hawk: see *Pactus Legis Salicae* 7.1.

Soon the bystanders left, and this man exhaled his spirit. As a consequence there is no doubt about what place the man who departed from here with such a judgment occupied there [in Hell].

18. The man who stole a horse during the saint's vigil

During a vigil of [Julian's] festival another man seized and stole a horse belonging to a man who had come then by chance to the same celebration. The thief mounted the horse and swiftly rode away; hence, the man who had lost the light of truth was certainly not to be found at the light of dawn, and the dark of night concealed the secret theft of the man whose heart was filled with the darkness of greed. For in a Gospel the Lord said this about these sorts of actions: "Everyone who does evil hates the light" [John 3:20]. As the sky began to brighten the thief said: "Now I am safe, because I am thirty leagues from the saint's church. I think that I am now near my own house." While he was silent and thought to himself about his location, the darkness was cleared from the sky, and he realized that he was near that village [of Brioude] and had strayed among the people. Because he was afraid that his crime might be publicly exposed, he very carefully hitched the horse again in the place from which he had earlier left. This wretched man was, I think, so detained by the martyr's power in circling the village for the entire night and so deluded by the motivation [of greed] that had filled him, that he was unable to find the road that he wished. O impious greediness, what are you doing! You always hurl your admirers into confusion.[15]

19. The man who committed perjury for the sake of a small gold coin

A man loaned a small gold coin to another man; a few days later he received the coin back. But a year later when he met the man in the courtyard of the saint's [church], he demanded that his coin be repaid to him, as if he had not already received it. The other man insisted with an oath that he had repaid what he had borrowed. After they argued for a very long time, the man who had repaid [the loan] said to his companion: "How long will we quarrel with each other? Let us present this dispute to the judgment of omnipotent God. Let us go to the tomb of the martyr, and let the holy power of the patron [Julian] decide about what you will have said with the pledge of an oath." His companion did not hesitate to approach the tomb; but when he brashly raised his hands to swear a false oath, the wretched man became miserably rigid. His voice stuck in his throat, his

---

[15] This chapter contains a suggestive juxtaposition of cultural influences, since in it Gregory both paraphrased a favorite line from Virgil (cf. *VM* 1.31) and used what was apparently a Celtic word, *leuga*, "league": see Bonnet (1890) 226. For the survival of Celtic into sixth-century Gaul, see Bonnet (1890) 23–27, P.-F. Fournier (1955), and Harris (1989) 182–83; Schmidt (1980) 35–39 is more skeptical.

tongue was a lump in his throat, and there was no word on his trembling lips; he was furthermore completely unable to lower his arms that he had raised for the support of the unsuccessful oath. The crowd was astonished by these events; after the man's misdeed was made public, the entire crowd of people cried out in a single voice and prayed for the pity of the Lord and the assistance of the blessed martyr. After four or even more hours the man was restored to his senses. In a public confession he admitted the loan [whose repayment] he had unjustly demanded a second time; then he left with his health.

20. The man who pillaged and stole from the holy church

Although the man who brought violence to the holy church had often heard these stories, goodness was unable to control a wicked mind once it had been affected by a defect. Solomon offers this testimony: "Wisdom does not enter an evil soul" [Wisd. 1:4]. The saint's festival had arrived, and behold, one man in the crowd noted that the blessed church gleamed with its lavish decorations. In his wicked mind the man coveted what upon acquiring he could not conceal. While the people were leaving the church after the service of vespers, this man lingered in a corner of the church and hid himself. Once silence fell upon everyone in the quiet of the night and black darkness was covering the world, the man got up from the corner and, [because] he was of course prompted by an agent of Satan, with no hesitation he quickly jumped over the railing around the blessed tomb. He ripped a cross [decorated] with glittering jewels from the top [of the tomb] and tossed it to the ground; then he gathered curtains and drapes hanging on the surrounding walls. From them he made up a single bundle and put it across his shoulders. Then he picked the cross up in his hand and returned to the corner that he had left. He put the bundle under his head; then, drowsy and weighed down by his sin, he fell asleep. In the middle of the night the custodians walked through the holy church and saw in a corner one jewel from the cross, shining just like a star in heaven. They were disturbed and fearfully came closer. Once they brought a candle, they found the man lying there with the stolen objects that he could not carry away. During the night the man was kept in custody; then at daybreak he confessed everything that he had done. He claimed that he had become weary and fallen asleep because after walking around the church for a very long time, even with a torch he could not find a door through which he might exit.

21. The man who lost his horse during a festival

[Julian] has displayed many other [punishments] against transgressors, but these are sufficient for correcting their apathy. Now let me return to praising the good fortune that is apparent in his generous compassion for people. But first I think that this concern must not be overlooked. I certainly know about this concern from experience: [that is,] what a pious prayer to this patron accomplishes with regard to what is missing. From these stories I intend to relate only this one. A poor man piously attended the festival of the blessed martyr. After unsaddling his horse he entered the sacred church, stood intently during vigils, and passed the night with the other people in prayer. When the sky brightened [at dawn], he returned to his lodging but did not find the horse that he had left. He made inquiries at great length, but he did not find even any tracks [indicating] where the horse had gone. After two days he again returned to the pastures and asked the local inhabitants whether perhaps someone had captured and was keeping a horse or had seen a horse captured by someone else. Still he found no sort of evidence. He was upset and sad, and he returned to the saint's tomb where he revealed the reasons for his grief and misery. He said: "Saint, I have come to your threshold to offer nothing other than the prayers of my littleness. I have not unjustly stolen anything, and I have done nothing unworthy of your festival. Why, I ask, have I lost my horse? I ask that you restore what has been lost and that you return what is essential." [His eyes were] wet with tears as he said this. When he came out of the church, he saw at a distance a man holding his horse. He went to the man and asked where he was from or where he had come from and when he acquired this horse. He was told that this horse had been found at that very hour when he requested the assistance of the blessed martyr.

22. The blind man who received his sight
   A man from this place lost [sight in] his eyes after being assaulted by a demon. Because he had lost his sight, he remained in misery in his lodging; and because he was unable to do anything with his own hands, he had no hope of supporting himself. During the night a man appeared to him in a dream and suggested that he go to the church of the blessed [Julian]. The man also promised that assistance was available there if he made a pious request. The blind man did not hesitate. He picked up his staff and with the assistance of a servant entered the holy shrine. Once he had finished his prayer, he went to the archpriest named Publianus who was then in charge of the shrine and asked that he make [the sign of] the cross of Christ over his blind eyes. Publianus was of course a monk; and because he wished to avoid any arrogance, he ignored this request. But the blind man held on to him and would not release him until Publianus did what he requested. Publianus knelt before the tomb and for a very long time prayed for the martyr's assistance. Then he stretched out his hand over the eyes of the blind man, and as soon as he made the sign of the cross, the blind man received his sight. I beg of you, marvel at the martyr's power; although it is easy [for Julian] to perform miracles, now [miracles] happen in public even

through the hands of his disciples.[16] The goodwill of his power provides support; but the merit of the disciple who is seen to possess these virtues was not insignificant.

23. Gallus, who soon became a bishop, and his foot that was healed

At that time my uncle Gallus was bishop of Clermont. With regard to Gallus it does not seem proper to omit [the story of] how he was helped during his youth by the saint's power. I have often mentioned the extensive devastation King Theuderic brought upon the territory of Clermont, when both old and young were left with nothing of their possessions except the bare ground that the barbarians could not carry away with them. At the time [of that invasion] my uncle of glorious memory had lost his father; later, as I said, he governed the church at Clermont by holding the office of bishop. His possessions were so destroyed by this army that absolutely nothing was left standing. Accompanied by only one young servant Gallus journeyed all the way to the village of Brioude, most of the way on foot. While he was making this journey, it happened at a certain time that he removed his shoes because of the sun's heat; then, while walking barefoot he stepped on a cluster of thorns. This cluster of thorns had by chance been broken off and was lying on the ground; it was concealed in the green grass with one thorn pointed up. Once this thorn was pushed into and then penetrated Gallus's foot, it broke off and could not be extracted. Because a stream of blood was flowing [from this wound], Gallus was unable to walk; so he requested the assistance of the blessed martyr. In a short time the pain lessened; and although he limped, he completed the journey that he had undertaken. Three nights later the wound festered, and the pain became more unbearable. But Gallus relied [again] upon the assistance that he had received a few days previously and knelt before the glorious tomb. After he observed the vigils, he returned to his bed; and while he was waiting for the martyr's power, he fell into a heavy sleep. When he awoke, he felt no twinge of pain. Gallus looked at his foot, but did not see the thorn from the cluster that had penetrated [his foot]; then he knew that it had been eliminated from his foot. He carefully looked for the splinter, found it in his blanket, and wondered how it had been eliminated. After he became bishop he was accustomed to expose the spot of this wound where a large scar was still visible and claim that the power of the blessed martyr had been [effective] there.[17]

[16] In this sentence there is a mistake or a lacuna in the text: see Bonnet (1890) 749n.1, and Krusch (1920) 739.

[17] Some scholars have suggested that Theuderic invaded the Auvergne again in ca. 531/2 during Gallus's episcopacy: see Rouche (1979) 54–57, and Heinzelmann (1982) 703. Others have identified this devastation that Gregory "often" mentioned with the invasion of the Auvergne by king Theuderic and his army in 524 that Gregory did frequently mention (note

24. The fever of Peter, a nephew of Gallus

Much later it was time for the festival of the blessed martyr. Along with his entire household my father hurried to enjoy these celebrations. As we were making this journey my older brother Peter was afflicted with a burning fever and suffered so badly that he was unable either to retain his strength or to eat. He completed the entire journey with great suffering, and it was uncertain whether he would recover or die. Finally, with a great effort we came to the shrine, entered the church, and prayed before the tomb of the holy martyr. My ill brother knelt on the pavement and requested a cure from the glorious martyr. After he finished his prayer, he returned to our lodging; the fever moderated a bit. When night came we hurried to vigils. Peter asked that he also be brought [to vigils]. He lay in front of the tomb, and throughout the entire night he prayed for the martyr's assistance. At the completion of these nocturnal vigils he asked that they collect dust that was around the blessed tomb and either give it [to him] in a drink or hang it from his neck. Once this was done the burning fever completely vanished. Hence, on that day he was healthy, took food, and walked wherever fancy turned his spirit.

25. My own headache

A year later as we were again hurrying with great happiness to the holy church [to celebrate Julian's] festival, my head began to ache painfully from sunstroke. The pain increased and produced a fever inside me so that I was unable either to eat or to speak. For two days I was overwhelmed by this pain. On the third day I went to the church of St. Ferreolus, whose spring (which I mentioned above) was nearby. This church is about ten stades from the village of Brioude. When I came to this shrine, I was happy to go all the way to the spring; for because of the martyr's power I was

---

to *VJ* 13). But one detail does not fit with either suggestion. Gallus had been born in 486/487 (cf. *VP* 6.7); since at the time of the invasion in 524 he was therefore already in his late thirties, it is not clear why Gregory would have stated that this miracle happened "during his youth." In 507 King Clovis had sent his son Theuderic to liberate Clermont from the Visigoths (*Hist.* 2.37). Perhaps Gallus had fled to Brioude then; but when he eventually explained to his nephew Gregory the significance of his scar, Gregory confused the two expeditions of Theuderic. In fact, Gregory's accounts of Gallus's early life do not mesh well. Here he noted that Gallus's father Georgius had just died at the time of this invasion during Gallus's youth; elsewhere he mentioned first Gallus's service with Quintianus, who became bishop of Clermont in 516, then Georgius's death, and finally Gallus's service at the court of King Theuderic at Cologne (*VP* 6.2). The following chronological sequence is one plausible resolution of these discrepancies. As a teenager Gallus entered the monastery at Cournon. In 507 his father died and he escaped Theuderic's invasion by fleeing to Brioude. After 516 he served with Bishop Quintianus, perhaps as a deacon, which probably required him to be at least twenty-five (note to *VM* 1.35). Later, when he was certainly already a deacon, he served at Theuderic's court (*VP* 6.2). By the time of Quintianus's death in 525 Gallus was back in Clermont (*VP* 6.3).

confident that I would soon recover my health once this bubbling water flowed over me. I approached, offered a prayer, drank the water, cooled my mouth, and soaked my head. As the pure water ran off, immediately the pain departed and I left with my health. I returned in happiness to the tomb of the glorious martyr, and out of respect I thanked the martyr because he had deigned to assist me with his power before I was worthy to visit his tomb.[18]

26. The man with a fever who was cured at this spring

Because the martyr was decapitated at this spring, there is extraordinary power there. A man afflicted with a fever who was on the verge of death had the desire to drink some water from this spring; so he piously prayed that he might be carried to this spring. [Others] carried him in their hands and brought him to that spot. As soon as he received a drink of the water and soaked his face and head, he deserved to regain his health. This man who had been carried there in others' hands left by his own steps. He was an inhabitant of this village, but his name is forgotten.

27. The thunder that sounded in the church, and the lightning

One day a storm appeared together with strong gusts of wind and quickly descended over the village of Brioude. Lightning flashed from the clouds, and terrifying thunderclaps rumbled. The ground trembled with the crash, and almost everything was thought to have been scorched by the lightning. All that was left was hope in the power of the glorious martyr. Immediately there was a loud clap of thunder along with a flash of lightning; one fiery lightning bolt entered the door where the rope for the bell was hanging, knocked over two columns, and shattered them into bits. Then the bolt bounced back and left through the window that was over the holy tomb. But because of the blessed [Julian's] protection, none of the people was hurt. Oh, how remarkable was the blessed martyr's concern for his own foster children! He allowed the columns but not the people gathered [there] to be knocked over; he permitted the glass [in the window] but not the congregation to be shattered; and he allowed the flash [of lightning] to pass over his own tomb to prevent any harm to the entire crowd. Once the lightning bolt was ejected from the church by the power of the blessed martyr, a fire started in a haystack that killed sheep and destroyed horses. If anyone thinks that these events happened by chance, let him be all the more amazed and surprised at the power of the glorious martyr, because the fire passed through the midst of the people without harming anyone. For the

---

[18] This church dedicated to St. Ferreolus was at Saint-Ferréol-les-Minimes: see Vieillard-Troiekouroff (1976) 255–56. A stade was one-eighth of a Roman mile, which was a bit shorter than a modern mile; so this church was a little over a mile north of Brioude.

fire accomplished its intentions only there where it knew that it had permission.

28. The man who was unable to approach the tomb because of the crowd of people

A monk [from the monastery] of Abbot Aredius of Limoges came to the festival. Not only was this monk unable to approach the holy tomb because of the crowd of people, but he was unable even to enter the church. After he returned in sadness to his lodging, he lay down on his bed and fell asleep. Immediately a man stood before him in a dream and spoke; he said: "Why are you overwhelmed by sleep? Run quickly to the martyr's church, and you will find everything accessible." Although the monk was terrified with fear, he got up, believed what had been said, and quickly hurried to find out whether the advice given him was true. Upon coming to the entrance [of the church] he discovered that the people had everywhere withdrawn, and that when he entered, no one barred his way all the way to the holy altar and even to the tomb. And so the monk approached without any pressure [from a crowd], offered a prayer, and returned in happiness. Lest anyone doubt this incident, I call as a witness omnipotent God, because I learned of these events from the mouth of the abbot [Aredius] whose monk was involved in them.[19]

29. His festival

Because the people did not know the day on which the blessed martyr ought to be honored for the glory of his power and his suffering, they were sad and in their uncertainty disregarded the time for his festival. This uncertainty extended until [the episcopacy of] the blessed bishop Germanus of Auxerre. For it happened that when the aforementioned bishop visited Brioude, he asked the inhabitants when [Julian's] festival was celebrated. They replied that they did not know. Then Germanus said: "Let us pray, and perhaps the power of the Lord will reveal this date to us." They prayed, and at daybreak Germanus announced to the elders from this region who had gathered that the festival must be celebrated on the fifth day before the calends of the seventh month [August 28]. Thereafter the

---

[19] Gregory also wrote a separate account of the miracles and the death of Abbot Aredius, whom he greatly admired as another "special foster son" of St. Martin (*VM* 3.24) and who died in 591 (*Hist.* 10.29). With the support of his mother Pelagia (*GC* 102) Aredius had founded a monastery at Saint-Yrieix, near Limoges, in the oratory of which he kept relics of St. Martin (*Hist.* 8.15, *GC* 9): see Vieillard-Troiekouroff (1976) 277–78. Aredius often visited Tours (*VJ* 41, *VM* 2.39, 3.24, 4.6) and, as here, served as an informant for Gregory (*GM* 36, 41, *VP* 17 praef.). A *Vita* of Aredius survives, composed probably during the Carolingian period: ed. B. Krusch, *MGH, SRM* 3 (1896) 581–609.

people now piously gather, offer prayers to their champion, and leave with medicine for their soul and for their body.[20]

30. The possessed men

When some possessed men came, they spewed out many complaints against this saint of God. [They asked] why he invited to his festivals other saints whom they mentioned by name and whose powers and merits they described. They said: "Julian, let it be enough for you to torture us with your own power. Why are you summoning others? Why are you inviting outsiders? Behold, [here is] Martin of Pannonia, our perpetual foe, who has removed three dead men from our caverns. Also present is Privatus of Javols, who was unwilling to surrender his flock to the barbarians whose attack we had instigated. Your colleague Ferreolus has come from Vienne; he has sent you [here] as punishment for us and as protection for the inhabitants. Why are you summoning Symphorianus of Autun and Saturninus of Toulouse? You have convened a council with the purpose of inflicting ruinous torments on us." By making these comments and others like them these possessed men conjured up in men's minds the saints of God in such a way that no one doubted that the saints were lingering there. Then many ill people were cured by these saints and departed with their health.[21]

[20] Germanus was bishop of Auxerre during the first half of the fifth century (cf. GC 66). Although most scholars have accepted that Germanus died during the mid- or late 440s, some have proposed a major revision by suggesting that he died during the late 430s: see Thompson (1984) 55–70, and Wood (1984). The major source of information about Germanus is a Vita composed during the 480s by Constantius, who was probably from Lyon: ed. W. Levison, MGH, SRM 7 (1920) 247–83; ed. and trans. (French) R. Borius, SChr. 112 (1965); and trans. Hoare (1954) 284–320. Since this Vita stated that Germanus had died in Ravenna while Gregory thought that he had died in Rome (GC 40), Gregory had probably not read it. The Vita also did not include this story about the discovery of the correct date for St. Julian's festival. For September as the seventh month, see the note to VJ 36.

[21] Privatus was thought to have been bishop of Javols or Mende during the fourth century before being killed by the Alamans (Hist. 1.34, 10.29); a church in his honor was later built at Javols (Hist. 6.37): see Vieillard-Troiekouroff (1976) 169–72, and Weidemann (1982) 1:162. Symphorianus was thought to have been a martyr of the mid-third century, less likely of the late second century: see Griffe (1964–1966) 1:152–53, 160, and Heinzelmann (1982) 699–700. In the mid-fifth century Euphronius, a priest (and future bishop) of Autun constructed a church in the saint's honor (Hist. 2.15); the saint's Passio may also have been written, or rewritten, at the same time (GC 76): see Vieillard-Troiekouroff (1976) 44–45. The cult of St. Symphorianus was also celebrated at Tours (Hist. 10.31), at Thiers in the Auvergne (GM 51), and at Bourges (GC 79). On the basis of information in a "History of the suffering of the martyr St. Saturninus," Gregory claimed that Saturninus was one of the seven missionaries sent to Gaul in the middle of the third century and that he had been martyred at Toulouse (Hist. 1.30): see Griffe (1948) and (1959), and L. Pietri (1983) 19–22. This Passio may have been composed in the first half of the fifth century: see Griffe (1964–1966) 1:110–15, 134–

31. The tameness of the animals

This story is also most deserving of recollection; it concerns the tameness of the animals that were offered to this church. However much the calves strayed, however much the horses kicked, and however much the pigs squealed, once they entered the holy shrine, they were calm. Even though angry bulls are led on ropes after being bound by fifteen or more men, often I have seen them attack men so furiously that you might think that they would snap the ropes. But as soon as they entered the holy shrine, they became so quiet that you might think that they were as tame as lambs. Even now I see that many bulls are entering in the midst of the crowds; they lower their heads, move people aside with their snouts instead of their horns, and possess a certain sense of respect, as if they were approaching the tribunal of a judge. These bulls do not kick, attack anyone with their horns, or stare with fierce eyes. Instead they tamely hurry to the holy altar, kiss it, and then return with the same calmness with which they entered. Likewise the friskiness of other animals becomes calm, and all their fury is set aside when they have approached there; hence to your great surprise you might see them as tame as doves. No one at all is allowed to take any of these animals that have been offered [to this church]; and before coming to the church no one dares either to exchange or to buy [anything]. For those who have done so are often seriously battered by divine revenge. Either a fever threatens or some evil creeps up or a severe misfortune approaches, or an illness removes whatever [animal] he has stolen. Rarely does a theft occur without immediate vengeance.

32. His relics that were brought to the district [of Rheims]

Let it be sufficient to have mentioned these miracles that either happened or are happening in the vicinity of the holy church [at Brioude]. Now it is proper to end this small book by recounting a few [stories] about those [other] places that have [Julian's] relics. In the province of Second Belgica, or rather in the suburbs of Rheims, a man was motivated by his piety and zealously constructed a church in honor of the blessed martyr. After the building was completed, the man faithfully and piously sought his relics. He acquired relics and chanted Psalms while he returned; [then] he entered the district of Rheims. Not far from the road was a field belonging to a rich man from this district, and a large crowd of people had gathered to plow

---

36, 148–52, 395–402. Gregory also mentioned that men transporting relics of St. Saturninus once passed by Brioude, and that an oratory at Vialle commemorated their visit (*GM* 47): see Vieillard-Troiekouroff (1976) 337. Soon after becoming bishop Gregory placed relics of St. Saturninus in an oratory at Tours (*GC* 20). Note that St. Martin was the only one of the saints mentioned here who was not a martyr; it is also striking that he was identified as a Pannonian and not associated with Tours.

his field. As the traveler approached with these relics, one of the plowmen began to be terribly tormented and to speak as if he had lost his mind. He said: "Behold, the most blessed Julian is approaching! Behold his power! Behold his glory! Hurry here, you men; leave the oxen, abandon the plows, and let us all go to meet him!" The other plowmen were surprised and did not understand what he was talking about; so they were uncertain and wondered about both the man's shouts and his words. Suddenly the wretched man dropped his plow in the fields, fell to the ground, and pounded his fists. Then he swiftly ran and was attracted to the spot where the traveler [with the relics] of the blessed martyr was coming. The plowman cried out: "Saint, why do you torment me so? Glorious martyr, why do you inflame me? Why are you approaching a region that is not indebted to you? Why are you traveling among our homes?" As he said this, the man was agitated and went to the place where the priest had already constructed the shrine. He knelt before the holy relics and lay on the ground for a very long time. Then, as soon as the priest placed this holy reliquary on the man, immediately blood flowed from his mouth and he was cleansed from the onset of this diabolical falsehood. He confessed the saint's power and became a companion [for the traveler] on this journey.[22]

33. A similar story about his relics that were displayed in the East

An account by some reliable brothers indicates that something similar to this event happened in the East. While a man was being tormented by a demon in a cathedral in a city in the East, he announced that relics of the blessed martyr were on board a ship. Once the ship reached port, this man hurried to greet it. After he knelt on the ground in front of the ship, his contamination flowed from his mouth and nose, and the man was cleansed. News of this event was brought to the bishop, who aroused the people to light candles and proceed all the way to the harbor. The ship's captain heard [this procession] and wept for joy. He hurried to meet the bishop and insisted that he had brought nothing from the church of the blessed [Julian] except a bit of the dust that was lying about the holy tomb. But omnipotent God verified the [possessed] man's faith and did not allow the martyr's power to be hidden. Then the bishop took the relics and brought them with great honor to the holy cathedral. A merchant watched these impressive miracles and constructed a church in honor of the martyr. He placed the blessed relics in this church and thereafter saw many miracles happen there.

[22] Second Belgica was one of the old Roman provinces; for this church dedicated to St. Julian at Rheims, see Vieillard-Troiekouroff (1976) 235. The extension of the cult of St. Julian to Rheims was perhaps predictable, since throughout the sixth century the Auvergne was included in the Frankish subkingdom of Austrasia centered along the middle Rhine: see Rouche (1979) 51–85.

34. How his relics were brought to a church in Tours

Here are some events that I experienced recently. It happened that I returned to Clermont after my consecration [as bishop of Tours]. After a [further] journey I came to the church of the blessed [Julian at Brioude]. At the conclusion of his festival I ripped some threads from the shroud that covered the holy tomb, because I thought they would offer me protection; then I finished my prayer and left. At Tours monks had constructed in honor of this martyr such a church as their means allowed; now they wished it to be consecrated with his miracles. When they heard that I had brought these relics, they requested that this church be dedicated and enhanced with these vigils. But I secretly took my reliquary and at nightfall hurried to the church of the blessed Martin. A trustworthy man who was at the time standing at a distance told me that when I entered the church, he saw an immense flash of light fall from heaven, descend over the church, and then enter as it were inside.

35.[23]

On the next day when trustworthy men narrated these events to me, I concluded that this flash had proceeded from the power of the blessed martyr. The holy relics [of Julian] were placed on the altar and vigils were kept during the night; then to the accompaniment of the chanting of Psalms the relics were brought to the aforementioned church. And behold, one of the possessed people [began to] bruise himself with his hands and spit blood from his open mouth; he said: "Martin, why have you allied yourself with Julian? Why do you summon him to this region? Your presence was adequate torment for us; [now] you have invited someone similar to yourself who will increase our suffering. Why are you doing this? Why are you together with Julian tormenting us in this way?" While the wretched man was shouting out these words and others, the celebration of mass was completed. The man bruised himself for a very long time in front of the holy altar, but [finally] blood flowed from his mouth and he was freed from the disturbance of this raging demon.

36. The wine that he increased during the night

I do not think [it proper] to pass over what happened one night before the holy relics were placed there [in the church]. A monk from that place was celebrating the approach of the festivities and most generously invited some individuals to a small room in the church. He insisted that they all piously keep vigils in the church, and after pouring wine from a cask he began happily to propose toasts for the sake of their devotion. He said:

---

[23] According to Krusch (1885) 562–63, Gregory here included two chapters (*VJ* 34, 35) under one heading; later he used the same number for two chapters (*VJ* 46a, 46b).

"Through the blessed martyr God's goodwill is distributed to us as [a form of] powerful patronage. I therefore request your favor, so that you might together keep vigils with me. For tomorrow his holy relics are to be placed in this spot." They passed the night by [chanting] the sacred hymns and the celestial melodies and even celebrated the rites of mass. The monk was happy with this celebration and again began to invite for refreshments those whom he had previously invited; he said: "I thank you, because you have endured without moving during the vigils." But through the courtesy of his power the martyr did not long postpone rewarding this good intention. For when the monk entered the storeroom, he found that the cask that he had left almost half-full was now overflowing through a higher spigot so [quickly] that a puddle of running wine had flooded the ground all the way to the door. The monk was surprised at this. After putting the cask back down, he often picked it up [and found it to be] full. Absolutely nothing was lost from this cask, even though to satisfy themselves they drank much wine. Everyone marveled that the cask was always full, even until the next day. For it was the third day before the calends of the fifth month.[24]

O wonderful power of the martyr! For he produced a vintage from a cask without any blossoms; and although it is customary for wine to be collected and stored in casks, new wine was produced in this cask that overflowed only with [Julian's] power and not with [the juice from] a cluster of grapes. The cask was filled to the brim with wine, and the grapes were not brought to [the cask] but created [in it]. This was done to glorify the martyr by the Lord who impregnated the womb of the Virgin without seed and who was responsible for this mother's remaining in chastity. But this month of May had abundant fresh grapes, and Falernian wine was ready for drinking without the branches [of the vines]. In other vineyards the buds were still barely blossoming, but in this cask wine was flowing as a consequence of [Julian's] power. May was similar to October, since it made available new cups of wine; [in fact,] this May offered more than October, because although a vineyard was not to be seen in the storeroom, Falernian wine was produced in the house. Even without a winepress a fresh vintage was produced that was found not on new vine shoots but in the martyr's hidden [powers]. Although no batch of grapes from a tree was pressed, waves of wine flowed; although no [grapes] were seen to be pressed in a

---

[24] Although Gregory used several systems of chronology, when numbering the months of the year he usually began with March: see Weidemann (1982) 2:386. The fifth month would then be July (cf. VM 4.4), and the date here would be June 29. But this date does not fit with his later statement that this miracle happened during May. L. Pietri (1983) 440–41 argues that Gregory perhaps transposed the numbers and meant to write "the fifth day before the calends of the third month," which would be May; then the date here would be April 27. With that correction, since Gregory became bishop at Tours at the end of summer 573, he dedicated this church to St. Julian in spring 574.

winepress, Falernian wine was consumed. Behold, no vine was to be seen, but the cups were filled to the brim. But what am I saying? This celestial power was not lacking for these believers. For he who once at a wedding produced wine from water now abundantly offers the same to his believers without [the use of] any natural elements; and he who [once] satisfied five thousand men with two fishes has now provided abundant [wine] for [men] of goodwill. For at the moment of [the Lord's] birth the voice of an angel bore witness and said: "Glory to God in the highest, and on earth peace to men of goodwill" [Luke 2:14]. But now let me proceed to the following demonstrations of [Julian's] miracles.

37. The paralyzed man who was cured in the same place

A servant at this monastery had been crippled for a long time and was woefully carried about [by others]. Then he came to this church dedicated to the saint and celebrated vigils. When vigils were over, he returned at daybreak to his own bed. While others were carrying him in their hands, his tendons were loosened and he was cured.

38. The blind man who received his sight[25]

A girl was almost blinded by her inflamed eyes and an excessive flow of tears. Her father heard about the power of the glorious martyr and hurried with his daughter to the holy church. At daybreak after the celebration of vigils her father offered food and drink to the poor people who were listed on the register [of the poor]. While they were eating, suddenly the girl announced that she was suffering from a headache and begged that she be allowed a short nap. She slept while the feasters finished their meal; then she got up and asked to be led to the holy altar. [Even] before she was placed on the ground and carefully prayed for the compassion of the Lord, her tears were stopped and her eyes were cleansed of the swelling. She was happy as she got up. Then her father rejoiced, and she returned home with her health.

39. Another crippled man

There was another young boy whose parents lived not far from this church. Because in the second year after his birth all his limbs were crippled, he was nourished without hope of any good [result]. This boy was crippled in such a way that his knees could not be separated at all from his face. While his parents were keeping vigils at the holy church, they laid the

---

[25] The chapter goes on to discuss a blind girl. Since there are apparently no alternative readings for this heading in the manuscripts, Krusch only mentions the discrepancy in a footnote.

young boy in front of the sacred relics; a short time later they found him sitting up, with all his limbs straightened out. Then they offered a prayer and returned to their own home in happiness.

40. Perjurers

In [the territory of] Tours there is a village called Joué-lès-Tours. This village has some relics of the blessed martyr, who is frequently distinguished by great miracles, but who is particularly active in taking revenge on perjurers. For whenever someone under the influence of the enemy of mankind has committed perjury there, divine vengeance follows in such a way that immediately [the perjury] is clearly obvious either through a subsequent misfortune or through the loss of an acquaintance or through a wasting disease. In short, the martyr allows no occasion [of perjury] to remain unpunished, and despite their coarse rusticity and bold rashness the barbarians do not commit perjury there. These comments are adequate on this matter, because it is tedious to relate in sequence the specific events that happened to these [perjurers].[26]

41. His relics that the priest Aredius took

Aredius, a priest from Limoges, visited me. He was certainly a devout monk, and I have mentioned him in my second book about the miracles of the blessed Martin. While I was carefully questioning him about his life and behavior, I began to ask what miracles the most blessed [Julian] had demonstrated there [at his monastery]; for in honor of the blessed martyr Aredius had built a church and embellished it with his relics. As if he were a very bashful man, Aredius hesitated for a long time and then most reluctantly told these stories. He said: "When I first went to the church of the blessed Julian, I took a drop of wax from his tomb. Then I came to the spring in which the blessed [Julian's] blood had been shed, washed my face in the water, and filled a small jar with this water as a blessing. I call omnipotent God as my witness, that before I returned home [this water] had been transformed into the color, the consistency, and the fragrance of balsam. A bishop came to dedicate a [new] shrine [at Limoges]. Once I showed him these relics, he wished to place no other relics in the holy altar except this jar whose water had been transformed into balsam. The bishop said: 'These are authentic relics that the martyr has distinguished with the powers of Paradise.' "[27]

---

[26] "Barbarians" here perhaps refers to pagans, with whom Gregory often associated the notions of "coarse rusticity" and "rashness": see Van Dam (1988b) 12–13.

[27] For Aredius of Limoges, see the note to *VJ* 28; for this church at Saint-Julien, a few miles from Aredius's monastery at Saint-Yrieix, see Vieillard-Troiekouroff (1976) 259.

42. The paralyzed man who was cured

There are also many other stories, most of which I omit but some of which I include. An ill man whose limbs were all disabled was placed in a wagon and brought to his monastery. That night, while he was lying in this cart in front of the church, he suddenly saw this church shining with a bright light and he heard voices, as if many men were chanting Psalms in the church. While this was happening, and while the man offered a prayer, he seemed to lose his senses and forgot his pains. [Julian] approached, and the bright light that the man had seen passed before his eyes. After the light had left, the man returned to his senses and realized that he had been restored to his original health.[28]

43. The blind man who received his sight

A blind man was led by a servant and also approached [Julian's] sacred altar. When he touched his eyes to the shroud over the holy relics, he received his sight. Possessed men who are covered by this shroud have often also been cleansed. But as often as judges have pointlessly exercised their power in this spot, it was ineffective.

44. The cross that was stolen from the altar

A cross always hung over this altar. The cross was of delicate workman-ship and made of solid gold; it was so bright to the eye that you might think it was made of the purest gold. Then barbarians came, and one [of them] realized that the cross was gold, took it, and hid it in his pocket. But the man who took the cross was suddenly burdened with such a heavy weight that he was completely unable to carry the cross. Because he was struck by the martyr's power and motivated by remorse, immediately he sent the cross from his journey and restored it to the holy spot.[29]

45. How his relics were acquired

After these events [Aredius] sent one of his monks and said [to him]: "Go to the church of the blessed Julian, offer a prayer, and ask that the wardens deign to give you some of the [candle-]wax and dust that is lying by the tomb, so that once these relics are brought [here] I may receive them as a

---

[28] Aredius was apparently also the source for this and the following stories through *VJ* 45. But it is not clear that "his monastery" refers to a monastery dedicated to St. Julian at Brioude, as suggested by Vieillard-Troiekouroff (1976) 68. In *VJ* 32 Gregory had made the transition to discussing sites other than Brioude that had relics of St. Julian. So "his monastery" may be Aredius's monastery at Saint-Yrieix; then the shrine mentioned in *VJ* 42–44 would be the church Aredius founded at Saint-Julien (*VJ* 41), not the church of St. Julian at Brioude, as assumed by Weidemann (1982) 2:151–53.

[29] These "barbarians" were perhaps simply soldiers or thieves in general, not necessarily Franks, Burgundians, or other non-Romans: see Rouche (1977) 150–51.

blessing." The monk then went, requested what had been commanded of him, and received [the relics]. But as he wished to carry what he had received, he was burdened with such a weight that he was scarcely able to lift his neck. He was struck with a great shudder, knelt on the pavement, and again wept and offered a prayer. Then the monk stood up unharmed and realized that he had received permission to leave. So he set out on his journey; but as the sun was very bright, he suffered from thirst. When he came to a village that was near the road, he went to one cottage and requested water. A young boy came out of the cottage to give a reply; but when he saw the monk and his companions, he fell to the ground and seemed to be dead. His parents rushed out and blamed these men by claiming that their son had been killed by the men's skills in magic. They took their son who was almost dead and lifted him up. But the boy slipped from their hands, clapped his hands together, and began to dance and shout and insist that he was inflamed by the power of the martyr Julian. When the monk heard these words, he placed the reliquary that contained the holy relics on the boy's head and with complete faith began to pray passionately. The boy vomited blood and expelled the demon; then he left after being cleansed. The courier was confirmed in his faith and spent his entire journey chanting Psalms and giving thanks. With the martyr as his guide he came to the chosen spot. Thereafter as time went by, the martyr's power cured so many possessed people, so many people suffering from chills, and so many people afflicted by various illnesses, that their names cannot be remembered and their numbers cannot be counted.

46a. The young boy who was brought to soothsayers, and another who was cured by the saint's power

Among the other indications of [people's] receiving miracles I am also inserting this story, because it corrects unbelievers and strengthens the wise. Because the people's sins were excessive, during the episcopacy of Cautinus the territory of Clermont was devastated by a ruinous plague that the people call the plague of the groin. I went to the village of Brioude, so that I who could not be protected by my own merits might be shielded by the protection of the blessed martyr Julian.[30] While I was staying in this village, a young boy, one of my servants, was stricken by this plague. He laid his head on his bed and began to be very ill. He suffered from a constant fever and a stomachache, with the result that he immediately

---

[30] Although after he became a deacon in 563 (*VM* 1.35) Gregory served in Lyon (*VP* 8.3), he also occasionally visited Clermont (cf. *GC* 1). This plague devastated Clermont in 571: see Marius of Avenches, *Chronica* s.a.571. But since this "sudden death" also afflicted Lyon and other cities (*Hist.* 4.31), Gregory probably went directly to Brioude from Lyon. Bishop Cautinus also tried to avoid the plague, but eventually he returned to Clermont and died just before Easter.

coughed up whatever he swallowed; food offered no satisfaction to him, but seemed rather to be a poison. When my servants saw that the young boy was in his death throes, they summoned a soothsayer. The soothsayer came immediately, went to the ill boy, and attempted to apply his skills. He whispered chants, cast his fortune, tied amulets around his neck, and promised that the young boy whom he had delivered up to death would live. I was unaware that this was happening. Once these events were reported to me, I very bitterly denounced [them]. I sighed deeply as I recalled what the Lord said through the prophet Elijah to King Ahaziah; he said: "Because you have forsaken the Lord God of Israel and you have consulted the god of Ekron, therefore you will not rise from the bed into which you have ascended, but will die" [cf. 2 Kings 1:16]. For after the arrival of the soothsayer the young boy was inflamed by a more intense fever and exhaled his spirit.

A few days after his death another young boy began to suffer from a similar illness. Then I said to the servants: "Go to the martyr's tomb and bring back from it something for this ill boy. Then you will see the great deeds of God and you will recognize the difference between the just and the unjust and between someone who fears God and someone who does not serve him." The servants went and collected a bit of the dust that was lying about the tomb. When the ill boy drank some of the dust [mixed] with water, immediately he received a medicine, was restored to his strength, and, once the fever was extinguished, recovered.

So now, all you people who are unbelievers, listen, and after you will have investigated these [examples], know that what the devil does to seduce mankind is nothing. For this reason I warn [you], lest someone might postpone and ignore these [examples] if he has been sealed with the sign of the cross, if he has been washed by the cleansing of baptism, or if he has laid aside his old man and now lives in his new man. But let him seek the patronage of the martyrs through whom these miracles of healing are proclaimed; and let him request the assistance of the confessors who are deservedly called the friends of the Lord. Then he will receive what he has desired.

46b. The roses that were revealed by the will of God at his tomb

After the death of Proserius, the keeper of the martyr's shrine, the deacon Urbanus was ordained as warden for his church. At that time a miracle appeared at the saint's tomb. For while the deacon was lying awake in his bed, he heard a noise, as if the door of the church were being opened. Many hours later he heard the door again being closed. Then the deacon arose from his bed and in the advancing light went to the saint's tomb. [What had happened is] extraordinary to report! He saw that the pavement was covered with red roses. The roses were very large, and the fragrance of their scent was overpowering. The deacon also marveled at the roses placed on the carved figures on the railing, because it was the ninth month [i.e., November].[31] These roses were so fresh that you might think that they had been cut at that moment of the hour from living stems. The deacon collected these roses with great reverence, hid them, and thereafter distributed them as medicine to many ill people. For when a possessed man who came from Tours swallowed a drink soaked [with these roses], his demon was ejected, and he left after being cleansed.

47. The woman who received her sight

A woman who had been blind from birth asked to be brought by her parents to the tomb of the blessed Martin. When she had come there, for three days she knelt before the railings that were in front of the tomb of the holy bishop. She received a reply in a dream, when the holy man said to her: "If you wish to receive your sight, go to the church of St. Julian. When you request the protection of the martyr in that church, he is allied with Martin, and together they will restore the sight that you consider necessary by means of the support of their prayers." The woman arose, and because she did not know that there were relics of this martyr [Julian] in Tours, she went to Saintes. For Victurina, who was descended from a noble lineage and was the head of her family, had constructed a church on land belonging to her own villa and had placed relics of the blessed martyr [Julian in it]. The [blind] woman went to this church and prayed for three days. The third day was the festival celebrating the baptism of the Lord. While the people were standing [in the church] and listening to the teachings in the readings, suddenly loud whispering started up. The priest who was celebrating the festival wanted to quiet the noise and asked what had happened. One of the bystanders said to him: "This whispering cannot quiet down because the Lord's power has revealed a miracle. For behold, this woman who claims [to have been] blind received her sight after blood flowed from her eyes." Then once everyone knew what had happened, they all praised God.[32]

48. The relics that the priest Nanninus brought back.

Nanninus, who was then a priest at a shrine in Vibriacensis, sought relics of this glorious martyr. At the command of the blessed bishop Avitus he acquired some relics. While he was chanting Psalms and traveling to the church of St. Ferreolus, which was not far from his village, a possessed man

---

[31] Not all manuscripts include this sentence that Krusch printed in brackets. On the offices of *martyrarius* and *aedituus*, see the note to *VM* 4.11; for the numbering of the months, see the note to *VJ* 36.

[32] This church dedicated to St. Julian was probably at Saint-Julien-de-l'Escap: see Vieillard-Troiekouroff (1976) 259–60. Heinzelmann (1982) 713 by conjecture dates Victurina (or Victorina) and the foundation of her church to the late fifth or early sixth century.

was cleansed. Still chanting Psalms Nanninus proceeded on. When he had come to the midpoint [of his journey], a wicked and hostile [demon] was publicly repulsed by the saint's power, and another girl left after being cleansed.[33]

49. The many ill people who were healed by Nanninus's relics

Nanninus came to the place where he had built an oratory in the saint's honor and placed these relics in the altar. A man who had lost his eyesight came to this altar, as well as another man who had a disabled hand; after they prayed, the one man replaced his darkness with sight, and the other recovered the use of his hand after a long period of uselessness. A woman named Aeterna who was troubled by a wicked and hostile [demon came] with her daughter; after being cured at this altar she left in good health with her daughter. Several people suffering from chills have been healed at this spot.

50. Another blind man who received his sight in his church at Pernay

Since it is not surprising that the blessed Julian shares the gifts of healing with John and Martin, with whom as a victor over this world he dances in heaven, let me also relate [this story of] how he, along with Nicetius of Lyon, was distinguished with a similar power. Within the boundaries of the territory of Tours Litomeris built a church in honor of the holy martyr. In accordance with custom I was invited for the dedication, and in this church I placed relics of the martyr St. Julian along with those of Nicetius of Lyon. A bit later a blind man came [to this church], piously offered a prayer, and deserved to receive his sight. I have [also] recorded this blind man in my book about the life of St. Nicetius, because it is proper that a common miracle link the writings about each saint.[34]

Therefore let the reader who is interested in these miracles understand that he can be saved in no other way than by the assistance of the martyrs and the other friends of God. I, however, pray for the goodwill of the Lord through the patronage of the blessed martyr Julian. May he stand before the Lord and be successful as an advocate on behalf of [me,] his own foster son, so that I might complete the course of this life without the handicap of

---

[33] The location of this oratory at the *domus Vibriacensis*, which was not far from the church of St. Ferreolus at Saint-Ferréol-les-Minimes (*VJ* 3, 25–26, 41), cannot be identified: see Vieillard-Troiekouroff (1976) 352.

[34] According to the version of this story in *VP* 8.8, Gregory placed threads from Nicetius's handkerchief in this church, and Litomeris told him about the subsequent miracle. This church was in Pernay: see Krusch (1920) 737, note to 563, 15, for the correct heading for this chapter, and Vieillard-Troiekouroff (1976) 216–17. Perhaps this Litomeris is to be identified with the Litomeris who was healed of a quartan fever at the tomb of St. Sollemnis at Luynes (*GC* 21).

any blemish, and so that until the end of this life I might blamelessly retain, faithfully exercise, and manfully protect what I confessed at my baptism. Amen.

Here ends this book about the glory of the martyr St. Julian, my own special patron.

The Suffering of the Martyr St. Julian

IN A MANUSCRIPT dated by paleography to the seventh century Bruno Krusch found an anonymous account of the martyrdom of St. Julian. Because this *Passio* mentioned the saint's festival and church at Brioude (*Passio* 6) but not the discovery of the saint's head by Bishop Mamertus of Vienne, Krusch argued that it had been composed after Bishop Germanus of Auxerre discovered the date of St. Julian's festival in the early fifth century (*VJ* 29) but probably before the construction of Mamertus's new church in the later fifth century (*VJ* 2). Krusch also argued that because the author used the same terminology as Gregory of Tours (*VJ* praef., 50) in describing the saint as "my special patron" (*Passio* 6), he too was probably from Clermont. Since Krusch thought that Gregory had used the *Passio* as a source for some chapters of his *VJ*, he included it as an appendix in his edition of Gregory's writings in *MGH*, SRM 1 (1885) 879–81. He later became more hesitant over Gregory's use of this *Passio*.[1]

1. The passage of time has not yet forgotten the distinguished and venerable suffering of the most blessed martyr Julian at Clermont, whose people are happy that he came to them as their patron. For although he did not go to Clermont while fleeing martyrdom, nevertheless Christ assigned him as intercessor for our sins, so that both city and people are rewarded with the protection of such a martyr. Now it is proper for these events to be recorded for believers and to be transmitted to the future. And since it is quite obvious that the martyrs of God are venerated in every city, Christ deigned to present to the people [at Clermont] the martyr St. Julian as intercessor and patron.

2. During the time when Crispinus was governor a persecution arose against the Christians at Vienne. St. Ferreolus, himself [eventually] a martyr approved by God, then held the power of tribune in the aforementioned city.[2] He, however, exercised the responsibility of his office in such a way

---

[1] Krusch (1920) 771–72.

[2] The historicity of this Crispinus is dubious: see *PLRE* 1:232, and Heinzelmann (1982) 588. On Ferreolus, see the note to *VJ* 1.

that he [also] fulfilled the resolve of his holy religion [of Christianity]. Because the blessed Julian was a deeply committed Christian, Ferreolus enjoyed his company. But when St. Ferreolus learned about the persecution of Christians, he said to St. Julian: "I have heard that a persecution of Christians will be coming to this city, and I therefore beg that you leave these regions until the persecution against Christians is over."

3. After the blessed Julian listened to this request, he traveled to the territory of Clermont. He entered the cottage of an old woman and asked that she hide him. Her cottage was not far from [the place] where pagans worshiped their deceitful images. Soon the persecutors arrived at his hideout and asked the woman where Julian, who a short time before had fled to her cottage, was staying; the woman claimed not to know. But because the holy man did not wish to be deprived of his crown [of martyrdom], he presented himself to the persecutors and said: "Here is the man whom you are looking for; carry out the instructions that your emperors have given you." After he knelt and offered a short prayer, he presented his neck to the persecutors. Without any hesitation they drew their swords and cut off his head. As they returned, they took with them the head of the holy martyr as an example for the other [Christians] who lived in Vienne. But a surge of his holy blood flowed from his head.

4. In those days pagans celebrated their deceitful superstition in these regions. Two old men who were motivated by divine power brought the body of St. Julian from the place where he had been beheaded and respectfully buried it in a village called Brioude. As they returned, they felt that they had regained from God, as a reward for the burial, that fresh strength that they had had when young men. In that time a wealthy man from Spain stood accused before the emperor at Trier. After the man had been arraigned and confined in prison for his crime, the emperor ordered that he be executed after three days. His wife learned of his fate, and in her grief and sadness she quickly hurried to claim her husband's body. But as this woman passed by the aforementioned village, the aforementioned old men earnestly asked where she was going and why she was sad. Out of necessity she explained her predicament to them.

5. Then the old men said to the woman: "Not long ago persecutors beheaded a Christian whose body we buried with the greatest honor; as we returned, we felt that we had regained the strength that we had had as young men." Once this most pious woman had heard this news, immediately she offered a prayer at the tomb of the martyr St. Julian and promised herself that if she saw her husband alive and if he were returned alive to their house, she would construct a shrine in his honor over the tomb of the martyr St. Julian. After she had prayed for a long time, she completed the journey she had undertaken and came to the city [of Trier]. Upon entering, she saw her husband who had been freed by an imperial pardon; [in fact,] not only had her husband earned his freedom, he had also received the

honor of a reward. When his wife asked about the time at which he had received his freedom, she discovered that her husband had been freed at the moment when on behalf of her husband's safety she had asked the blessed martyr Julian that the emperor free her husband. They returned to the tomb of the blessed Julian, fulfilled their vows, and constructed an oratory as the woman had promised. Thereafter for the rest of their years they brought to his distinguished tomb gifts that they bestowed for such favors.

6. Afterward the reputation and the fame of the blessed martyr were publicized everywhere. Everyone had certain proof that the patronage of this great martyr did not abandon these people. Therefore over a long period of time pious Christians constructed a church in honor of this most blessed man. Once the church was built, it presented a high pediment; now having been decorated in honor of his name it glistens with his prerogatives and is filled with the miracles of my special patron, the martyr Julian. I will not be silent about the miracle that the Lord performed in praise of his name, with the result that on his festival day the Lord performed many divine blessings for people who were praying and offering intercessions to my special patron, the martyr St. Julian. Blind people receive their sight there, demons are scattered, and through faith all ill people are cured. In that spot there is praise for the Lord along with all peace and joy. There and everywhere Christ is blessed as God and Son of God, and his honor and kingdom are forever.

The Miracles of the Bishop St. Martin

A S BISHOP OF TOURS and therefore guardian of the cult of St. Martin, Gregory was obviously interested in the traditions associated with his patron saint. Although he once claimed that he possessed "enormous volumes" recording the saint's miracles (*Hist.* 2.1), when he included in the first book of the *VM* various stories about miracles that had occurred before his own episcopacy, he mentioned only the writings of Sulpicius Severus, Paulinus of Périgueux, and Bishop Perpetuus of Tours. He completed *VM* 1 apparently by 576.[1] He also began to collect stories about the miracles that happened during his episcopacy, most of which he included in *VM* 2–4, but some also in other books, in particular the *Histories*. Because many of these miracles took place on the festivals of St. Martin or other festivals, and because Gregory usually recorded them in chronological order during the two decades of his episcopacy, modern historians have been able to calculate a fairly precise chronology for the events and miracles in *VM* 2–4.[2] Yet at the same time Gregory continued to collect additional stories, perhaps based on oral traditions, about the miracles that Bishop Martin had performed during his lifetime. Rather than inserting them in *VM* 1 however, he instead included some of them in *The Glory of the Confessors* (*GC*), most of which he seems to have composed in 588 after he had finished *VM* 3 (*GC* 6). Even then Gregory insisted that he had recorded only a few of the many additional legends that he knew about Bishop Martin (*GC* 5).

Ruinart's edition of the *VM* was reprinted in *PL* 71.911–1008; Bordier published his edition and French translation in 1860. The best edition is, again, by Krusch, who included the *VM* in his unsurpassed edition of Gregory's works in *MGH*, SRM 1 (1885) 584–661; he also later collated some additional manuscripts that occasionally supply better or more sensible readings for the *VM* in *MGH*, SRM 7 (1920) 741–56.

---

[1] Above, chapter 4, section 4.

[2] In his edition Krusch provided some dates for *VM* 4; Schlick (1966) was apparently the first to note the chronological sequence of festivals also in *VM* 2–3. Although the dates inserted in this translation usually follow the chronology of Heinzelmann (1981), the notes indicate any important discrepancies with the chronologies of Schlick, Weidemann (1982), and L. Pietri (1983); the chronology in Corbett (1983) is sometimes not reliable.

❀ ❀ ❀

VM 1

[This book] about the miracles of the blessed bishop Martin [has been written] by Georgius Florentius Gregorius of Tours [i.e., Gregory of Tours]. I, Gregory, a sinner, [address it] to my blessed lord [bishops], my most beloved brothers in the love of Christ, and the sons of the church at Tours that God has entrusted to me.

In order to strengthen the faith of believers our Lord God today deigns to verify the miracles that he [once] deigned to work through his blessed bishop Martin while he was alive in his body. When he was in the world, God worked through him; now God distinguishes his tomb with miracles. Once God sent him as a champion for people who were about to perish; now God offers rewards to Christians through his [assistance]. Let no one therefore have any doubts about those miracles in the past as he observes the gifts of these present miracles being dispensed, because he sees, with [Martin] as the healer, the lame raised up, the blind receive their sight, demons chased away, and all other types of diseases cured.

In order to increase confidence in that book that earlier authors wrote about [Martin's] life, at God's command I will entrust his present miracles, so far as I [can] recall them, to the memory of posterity. I would not presume to do this if I had not been warned a second and then a third time in a dream. For I call omnipotent God as my witness, because once at noon I happened to see in a dream many disabled people and others suffering from various diseases being cured in the church of lord Martin. As I watched these cures, my mother who was also a spectator said to me: "Why do you delay to write down these cures that you see?" I replied: "Is it not obvious to you that I am untrained in literary culture and that I do not dare to publicize such marvelous miracles because I am ignorant and uneducated? If only Severus or Paulinus were still alive, or indeed if only Fortunatus were here to describe these events![3] If I attempt to record these events, I will be criticized as ignorant about these matters." My mother said to me: "Do you not know that because of people's ignorance the manner in which you can speak is considered [to be] more comprehensible to us? Therefore do not hesitate and do not stop recording these events, because you would commit a crime if you were silent about them."

Although I want to record these events, I am tormented by anxiety over

---

[3] After Fortunatus had completed his versification of Sulpicius Severus's writings about St. Martin (*VM* 1.2), Gregory apparently suggested that his book about St. Martin's miracles ought to be "interpreted" in verse; so Fortunatus asked for a copy: see Fortunatus, *Vita S. Martini* prol. = *Ep. ad Gregorium* 2.

two concerns, namely, sorrow and fear. I grieve because the great miracles that happened during the tenures of my predecessors have not been recorded in writing; and I am afraid because I approach this important task without any training. But because I am inspired by the hope of the Lord's goodwill, I will follow this advice. For [the God] who satisfied people's burning thirst by producing water from a dry rock in the desert [cf. Exod. 17:6] can, I think, publicize these events [even] through me who lacks eloquence. And it will certainly be obvious that God is again opening the mouth of the ass [cf. Num. 22:28] if he opens my lips and deigns to reveal these events through me, an uneducated man. But why am I afraid of my ignorance when the Lord, our Redeemer and our God, selected fishermen instead of orators[4] and countryfolk instead of philosophers to destroy the emptiness of this world's wisdom? I have confidence in your prayers: even though my plain account cannot ornament a page, the glorious bishop will make that page shine with his sparkling miracles.

1. Severus wrote a *Vita* of the saint

There are many who have written about the miracles of St. Martin either in immortal verses or in a prose style. Foremost among them is that Severus Sulpicius who had such an intense love for that saint of God that he wrote one book about the miracles of his life while he was still alive in this world; then after the death of that blessed man he wrote two books that he wished to call dialogues. In these dialogues he included some stories about the miracles of hermits and anchorites that Postumianus narrated; but he was unable to find our Martin in any way inferior [to those monks].[5] Because he considered him the equal of the apostles and earlier saints, he even wrote this: "Greece was fortunate in deserving to hear the apostle [Paul] as he was preaching; but Christ did not overlook Gaul, to which he gave Martin."[6]

2. The blessed Paulinus composed the same *Vita* in verse

The blessed Paulinus, bishop of Nola, wrote five books in verse about [Martin's] miracles that Severus had included. Then he described those miracles that had occurred after his death, that is, in the sixth book of his poem.[7] For Paulinus wrote: "When possessed men were being driven to

---

[4] Gregory may have taken the contrast between fishermen and orators from the dedicatory letter Sulpicius Severus attached to his *Vita*.

[5] Sulpicius included his friend Postumianus's stories about his journeys to Africa and the eastern Mediterranean in *Dial.* 1. Although modern editions divide the *Dialogues* into three books, they were originally published in two installments, *Dial.* 1–2 and *Dial.* 3: see Stancliffe (1983) 81–82. For the polemic about the superiority of St. Martin, see Stancliffe (1983) 104–6.

[6] Quoted, not quite verbatim, from Sulpicius Severus, *Dial.* 3.17.

[7] Gregory repeatedly confused Paulinus of Nola with Paulinus of Périgueux, the author of this poem about the miracles of St. Martin (cf. *GC* 108). Fortunatus knew little about Paulinus

leap in the air over the railings in the church, often they were hurled into a cistern because of the compulsion of a demon. Then they were pulled up unharmed and, while the people watched, were restored [to health]."⁸ I have seen this happen in my times too.

[Paulinus also wrote:] "Another demon led the body [of a man] it had possessed to a dangerous river, as if to submerge the prize that it had seized. But the assistance of the blessed confessor was not far away from this man who was about to die. For the man entered the [Loire] River, swam to the opposite bank without any harm, and even emerged in dry clothes. Once he had come to [Martin's] cell at the monastery of Marmoutier, he was manifestly cleansed." Paulinus claims that this man had been accustomed to utter many words, frequently to speak the language of unknown people, to prophesy future events, and to confess crimes. But as I said, after he reached the holy shrine, he departed with his health.⁹

[Paulinus also wrote:] "Aegidius was being besieged by the enemy; reinforcements were not available. While he was being threatened and attacked, he prayed to the blessed man; then the enemy fled and he was saved. At the very hour that this happened a man possessed by a demon announced in the middle of the church that this [aid] had been granted by the assistance of St. Martin.¹⁰

---

of Périgueux either: see Fortunatus, *Vita S. Martini* 1.20. The posthumous miracles of St. Martin that Gregory summarized in this chapter were first collected by Bishop Perpetuus of Tours and then versified by Paulinus of Périgueux in his *De vita S. Martini* 6.

⁸ Paulinus of Périgueux, *De vita S. Martini* 6.53–70. Paulinus mentioned that this cistern (*puteus*) that "supplied the flowing waters of salvation in its fountain" was in the *templum*; but despite Gregory's claim to have seen similar miracles, it is not clear whether Paulinus located this story in the small chapel constructed by Bishop Brictio (*Hist.* 2.14, 10.31) or in the larger church with which Bishop Perpetuus replaced it: see Vieillard-Troiekouroff (1976) 313.

⁹ Paulinus of Périgueux, *De vita S. Martini* 6.71–110. Since Paulinus added that the possessed man uttered "the sounds of the Huns," this story can perhaps be dated to the middle of the fifth century when the Huns were threatening central Gaul. Paulinus also mentioned that when this man was possessed, his "Gallic speech flowed with Greek words." The fact that Greek words could now be evaluated as demonic gibberish is a revealing indication perhaps of a decline of familiarity with Greek culture in fifth-century Gaul in general, perhaps too simply of Paulinus's exclusion from the aristocratic circles that promoted a renaissance of Greek philosophy during the later fifth century: see Châtillon (1967), for a possible connection between Paulinus and Sidonius, with Courcelle (1969) 236–62, and Riché (1962) 69–75, 83–84.

¹⁰ Paulinus of Périgueux, *De vita S. Martini* 6.111–51. In 458 Aegidius, then a Roman general commanding Frankish troops, was besieged by Visigoths in Arles: see Wolfram (1988) 180. Later as a renegade he established his own "kingdom" at Soissons with the support of some Franks: see above, chapter 1, section 1. Although Paulinus did mention the concern in a "neighboring region" (apparently Tours) and the announcement by a possessed man of Aegidius's success, Gregory located the announcement precisely in the church. Paulinus of Périgueux, *De vita S. Martini* 6.145–46, also claimed that Bishop Perpetuus of Tours had assisted in rescuing Arles, presumably through his prayers.

"A girl was afflicted by a paralyzing swelling and (even worse) was entangled in the error of a pagan cult. She sought out the tomb of the blessed [Martin], celebrated vigils, and was restored to her health. But when she returned to the vomit of her idolatry, she again experienced the weakness from which the bishop's assistance had freed her.[11]

"A Hun behaved savagely because of the compulsion of a demon and impulsively seized from the tomb the crown that declared the saint's merit. He quickly lost his sight. Once his pain forced him to restore his booty, he recovered his sight.[12]

"A man was compelled by a tempter to draw his sword. When he tried to strike someone in a courtyard of the confessor's [church], immediately his wrath was turned back on himself. God's judgment followed quickly, and the man stabbed himself with his sword.[13]

"Then the people were happy and wished to bring columns to decorate the blessed church. One spiteful man was opposed to this task and made many threats against a secluded riverbed, lest it offer petitioners an alternative to their wagons. When this arrogant man whipped his horse headlong into this small stream, he was suffocated and died even without the blows of a flood of water. Then, after this young man went first, the columns were brought to the blessed church.[14]

"Some claim to have seen oil increased as often as it was brought to the blessed tomb. The bishop St. Perpetuus must properly be called a disciple of the blessed [Martin]. He brought a flask of oil to the holy tomb so that the power of that righteous man might flow over and sanctify it. He also scratched some dust from the marble lid that covered the holy body and

[11] Paulinus of Périgueux, *De vita S. Martini* 6.165–214.

[12] Paulinus of Périgueux, *De vita S. Martini* 6.218–49. An actual crown "that indicated the merit of St. Martin" was apparently suspended over his tomb: see Paulinus of Périgueux, *De vita S. Martini* 6.227, for the quotation. Since Gregory never mentioned a crown, perhaps Perpetuus did not include it in his new church and instead only referred to the "crown of righteousness" in one of the inscriptions on the tomb: see below, Appendix 3. In his survey of the fifth century Gregory noted that Attila and his Huns had threatened or attacked Tongres, Metz, and Orléans before being defeated in 451 (*Hist.* 1.5–7, *GC* 71). Yet although Paulinus too commented strongly on the ferocity and treachery of the Huns, he also introduced this story by stating that then "Gaul admitted the Huns as auxiliaries." He, or more probably Bishop Perpetuus in his original version, was presumably thinking not of Attila's Huns, but of the Huns whom Roman commanders such as Litorius in the later 430s used as mercenaries: see Maenchen-Helfen (1973) 249, 267–68, and L. Pietri (1983) 97–99.

[13] Paulinus of Périgueux, *De vita S. Martini* 6.250–64. This swordsman was perhaps another Hun.

[14] Paulinus of Périgueux, *De vita S. Martini* 6.265–90. In Paulinus's account the man was possessed by a demon and warned his wife not to assist, before he fell from his horse into a small stream and suffocated in the sand. Since Gregory's version is both grammatically and logically baffling, either he misread this story in Paulinus or the text here is corrupt: see Petschenig's edition of Paulinus, in *CSEL* 16.1, p. 149, as well as Bonnet (1890) 250n.7, and Krusch (1920) 742.

mixed it with the oil; then the oil bubbled up so abundantly that a surge of oil poured out and soaked the bishop's garments with the scent of nectar. Many ill people received healing from this oil. Often storms are kept away from fields that have been sprinkled with this oil.[15]

"Once a believer who was filled with faith came to this holy church. In his thirst for the saint's favor he considered what he might take from the blessed church for his own protection. He went to the tomb and asked the warden that a bit of the blessed candle-wax from the tomb might be given to him. Upon receiving this wax the man was happy and left; with full confidence he placed [this wax] in the field where he had sowed his crop. An extremely severe storm approached that in preceding years had often destroyed the neighboring fields; but it was kept away by this blessing, and thereafter the storm was not as harmful in that region as it had usually been.[16]

"As the magnificent and desirable festival of Easter was approaching, the people piously went to the cell of the blessed [Martin at Marmoutier] in which he had often stayed and visited with angels. The people licked and kissed and moistened with their tears each spot where the blessed man had sat or prayed or where he had eaten food or laid his body to rest after his many tasks. Once a convoy of boats was ready, the people prepared to cross the [Loire] River in order to visit the blessed tomb and ask forgiveness while weeping and kneeling before [the tomb of] the confessor. As these people were crossing [the river], a wind blew up at the instigation of the tempter. One boat was swamped in the deep water, and both men and women were seized by the river. The people were tossed about among the tempestuous waves and all hope of escape was lost. Then they all shouted in unison and said: 'Martin, you who take pity, snatch the men and women who are your servants from this imminent death!' Once these words were said, behold, a gentle puff of wind brought the submerged people unharmed from the waves, and with the assistance of the water it restored everyone to the shore that they longed for. No one died; and once all were saved, they celebrated the festival of Easter with great rejoicing. For this was [another] indication of that power that divided the Jordon River and led the people between the billows of water on a dry edge when Joshua took from the bottom of the river the twelve stones that indicated the number of apostles and consecrated [them] on the bank to which they had crossed [cf. Josh. 4:20]; that rescued Peter as he was drowning and grasped his trusting right hand lest he die [cf. Matt. 14:29–33]; and that brought from the depths of the sea to the shore for which he hoped a sailor who, as he was about to drown, called on the Lord of Martin.[17]

15 Paulinus of Périgueux, *De vita S. Martini* 6.298–319.
16 Paulinus of Périgueux, *De vita S. Martini* 6.325–36.
17 Paulinus of Périgueux, *De vita S. Martini* 6.351–460. Gregory himself added the comparison with the rescue of Peter. This was a particularly apt analogy, because over the door of

"A man was eager to take something from the holy church as a blessing. He received some candle-wax from the holy tomb and, as if it were a treasure from heaven, placed it in the inner rooms of his house. It happened that the ill will of the tempter started a fire and the man's house was surrounded in ravenous flames. [The fire] spread through the dry beams and destroyed everything. Then a shout that requested the assistance of the blessed Martin was raised to heaven. The man remembered the piece of candle-wax that had been brought from the saint's church. Once this wax was found and thrown on the fire, immediately it extinguished the entire blaze. This was an unusual miracle: the wax that was accustomed to nourish a flame suppressed the force of this fire by the power of its holiness."[18]

After Paulinus had received a catalog of these stories from the bishop St. Perpetuus, he rewrote them in verse in the sixth book of his poem. But at the time when the document containing this catalog had come to Paulinus, his grandson was suffering from a serious illness. Paulinus trusted in the saint's power and said: "Blessed Martin, if you approve of my composing something in your honor, let your approval appear on behalf of this ill boy." Once the document was placed on the boy's chest, immediately the fever broke, and the boy who had been ill was healed.[19] The priest Fortunatus also rewrote in verse the complete account of [Martin's] life in four books.[20]

3. The ordination and death of the blessed Martin

Even though I am an unskillful [writer], I am, however, inspired by these stories to attempt to collect for memory some other stories (so far as I can find them) about the miracles of the most blessed St. Martin that happened after his death; for this will be [an indication of my] eagerness to record those events that are found not to have been included in the writings of [Sulpicius] Severus or Paulinus. While this world was in decline, the glorious lord Martin was bright and shining for the entire world. Rising as a new sun he was born at Sabaria in Pannonia, as an earlier account states,[21] and with the assistance of God he was sent for the salvation of Gaul. He illuminated Gaul with his miracles and signs and then, although un-

---

the church of St. Martin that faced the Loire River were an inscription describing and a mural depicting Jesus walking on the water and seizing Peter's hand: see below, Appendix 3.

[18] Paulinus of Périgueux, *De vita S. Martini* 6.467–99.

[19] Paulinus of Périgueux, *Versus de visitatione nepotuli sui*, ed. Petschenig, *CSEL* 16.1, pp. 161–64. Soon after receiving this document (*Versus* 32) Paulinus used it to heal both his grandson and his grandson's wife (*Versus* 21–23). He then sent a copy of his poem describing this miracle to Perpetuus: see *Prologus ad carmina minora*, ed. Petschenig, p. 161; Gregory presumably read this copy that was perhaps kept in the archives at Tours.

[20] On Fortunatus's *Vita S. Martini*, see note to *VM* 1, praef.

[21] Sulpicius Severus, *Vita Martini* 2; now Szombathely, Hungary.

willingly, received the honor of the episcopacy at Tours at the insistence of the people. In this office he lived a glorious and almost inimitable life for twenty-five years, four months, and ten days; in the eighty-first year of his life he died in peace in the middle of the night, [in the year] when Caesarius and Atticus were consuls.[22] It is therefore most obvious that his death on a Sunday was glorious and praiseworthy throughout the entire world; and we prove this with reliable evidence in the following [chapters]. These [coincidences] were thought to have been [indications] of his significant merit: [first,] that the Lord received him in Paradise on the day on which the same Lord and Redeemer rose from the underworld as a victor; and [second,] that the man who had always spotlessly celebrated the festivals of Sunday was received on a Sunday in [eternal] rest after the tribulations of this world.

4. How the chanting of Psalms at his death was revealed to St. Severinus

The blessed Severinus, bishop of Cologne, lived an honorable life and was praiseworthy in all respects. One Sunday while he and his clerics were as usual visiting the holy shrines, he heard a chorus of singers on high at the hour when the blessed man died. He summoned his archdeacon and asked whether the voices that he heard so attentively were also striking his ears. The archdeacon replied: "Certainly not." Then Severinus said: "Listen carefully." The archdeacon began to stretch his neck up, pricked up his ears, and with the assistance of a staff stood on his tiptoes. But I believe that this man who did not deserve to hear these songs was not of equal merit. Then the archdeacon and the blessed bishop together knelt on the ground and prayed to the Lord that divine mercy might allow this man to hear the chanting. They stood up, and again the old bishop asked: "What do you hear?" The archdeacon replied: "I hear the voices of men chanting Psalms, as if in heaven; but I do not know at all what it is." Severinus said to him: "I will tell you what this is. My lord bishop Martin has migrated from this world, and now the angels are escorting him on high with their chanting. And when there was a brief delay in hearing this chanting, the devil tried to detain him with his wicked angels; but once the devil discovered nothing of himself in [Martin], he was dismayed and left. What therefore will happen to us sinners, if this wicked faction wished to harm such a bishop?" As Bishop Severinus said this, the time was noted, and the archdeacon quickly sent to Tours a man who was to inquire carefully about these events. This man arrived and learned that the blessed man had most certainly died on the day and at the hour when St. Severinus had heard the chorus of singers.

---

[22] Flavius Caesarius and Nonius Atticus Maximus were consuls in 397, which is most likely the correct year for the death of Martin despite Gregory's own confusion (cf. *VM* 1.32, 2.1); but some scholars have preferred a "short chronology" according to which Martin died in his early sixties, not his early eighties: see L. Pietri (1982), and Stancliffe (1983) 111–33.

But if we return to the history by [Sulpicius] Severus, he wrote that at the hour [of Martin's death] he was revealed to him, holding the book of his life.[23]

5. How the same death was revealed to the blessed Ambrose

Today the blossoms of the eloquence of the blessed Ambrose spread their fragrance throughout the entire church; but at the time he governed Milan as bishop of the city. On Sundays when he celebrated the services it was customary for the lector not to presume to come with his book and read until the holy Ambrose had nodded his assent. But it happened on that Sunday, after the reading from the prophet was completed and while the lector who was to read from [the letters of] the blessed Paul was standing before the altar, that the very blessed bishop Ambrose fell asleep [while sitting] beside the holy altar. Many people were watching this, although no one at all dared to awaken him. After about two or three hours had passed, they awakened [him] and said: "Already the hour has passed. Let our lord order the lector to read the lesson; for the congregation that is watching is already very tired." The blessed Ambrose replied and said: "Do not be upset. It was very beneficial for me to nap, because the Lord deigned to reveal a great miracle to me. For you will learn that my brother Bishop Martin has departed from his body and that I was paying my respects at his funeral. Although this obligation was properly completed, I did not finish [reciting] the verses [of Psalms], because you awoke [me]." The people were equally amazed and impressed and noted the day and the time. After careful questioning they learned [that Martin's death had occurred] on the day and at the time when the blessed confessor Ambrose had said that he had attended [Martin's] funeral.

Oh, blessed man! At [the moment of] his death a crowd of saints was singing, a chorus of angels was dancing, an army of all the celestial powers was in attendance, the devil was disordered in his rashness, the church was strengthened by his power, and bishops were honored by his revelation. [The archangel] Michael received him among the angels, Mary welcomed him with a chorus of virgins, and Paradise holds him in happiness among the saints. But why am I attempting in his honor something that I am inadequate to complete? For this Ambrose is himself the honor of that man whose praise was never absent from his mouth. If only I can present even a simple account![24]

---

[23] Sulpicius had noted that shortly before hearing of Martin's death he had had a dream in which he saw Martin holding a copy of the *Vita* and smiling at him: see *Ep.* 2.3. For Bishop Severinus of Cologne, see Weidemann (1982) 1:162.

[24] This story is certainly apocryphal, because while Martin died in November 397 (*VM* 1.3), Ambrose had already died seven months earlier in April: see Palanque (1933) 556, and Homes Dudden (1935) 2:491. Yet although contemporary Italian sources, such as the *Vita* of

6. The transfer of the blessed body

It is worthwhile to insert in this reading this [story about] how, with the assistance of an angel, his holy body was moved to that place where it is now honored. Sixty-four years after the death of the glorious lord Martin the blessed Perpetuus became bishop of the honorable see of Tours. After he acquired this high office he decided, in agreement with many prayers, to lay the foundations for a larger church than had previously been over the blessed body. He encouraged this project with wise enthusiasm and completed it with marvelous workmanship. There is much that I might say about this building; but since it is still here, I have decided it is therefore better to be silent. When the blessed bishop Perpetuus came at the anticipated time to dedicate the church and to transfer the holy body from the spot where it had been buried, he assembled the neighboring bishops for the festival day as well as a large crowd of abbots and various clerics. Since he wished to complete [this transfer] on the calends of July [July 1], they kept vigils during the night. When morning came, they [each] took a hoe and began to dig up the dirt that was on top of the holy coffin. They uncovered the coffin and took hold to move it; but even though the entire crowd worked, it accomplished nothing at all during the entire day. They kept vigils for another night and tried again in the morning; but again they were unable to accomplish anything at all. Then they were upset and frightened and did not know what they might do. One of the monks said to them: "You know that it has been customary to observe this bishop's anniversary in three days; perhaps he is telling you that he is to be transferred on that day." Day and night they devoted themselves to fasts and prayers and constant chanting of Psalms, and they passed those three days without interruption. On the fourth day [July 4] they went, took hold of the coffin, but were unable to move it at all. Everyone was horrified with fear, and they were already on the verge of covering with dirt the body that they had uncovered. Then there appeared to them a distinguished old man with white hair that gleamed like snow who said that he was an abbot. He said to them: "How long are you to be confused and delay? Do you not see lord Martin standing [here] ready to assist you, if you take hold?" He tossed aside the cloak he was wearing and took hold of the sarcophagus with the other bishops. They prepared crosses and candles and recited the antiphon, and everyone chanted Psalms on high. Then with the old man's assistance the sarcophagus was very easily lifted and immediately moved to the place

Ambrose by Paulinus of Milan, did not mention this story, Gregory's account was influential enough at Milan that Ambrose's dream and his attendance at St. Martin's funeral became common episodes in Carolingian and later literary accounts and iconographical representations of Ambrose's life, in part as expressions of Milan's autonomy in Italy and its widespread influence: see Courcelle (1973) 140, 171, 175, 180–82, 191, 207, and Picard (1988) 625. For the archangel Michael and the Virgin Mary in Paradise, see *GM* 4.

where it is now honored with the approval of the Lord. This was accomplished in accordance with the wishes of Bishop Perpetuus. After the celebration of mass they went to a banquet, and although they looked carefully for the old man, they never found him; but there was no one who had seen him leave the church. I think that this had been [a manifestation of] the power of some angel who announced he had seen the blessed man and then was invisible to everyone.

After that day many miracles happened at that spot that have not been written down because of oversight. But I cannot be silent about the great events either that I saw happen or that I know for a fact happened during my lifetime.

7. Theodomund, a mute man

A man named Theodomund, whose ears and throat were obstructed, came and every day returned to the holy church. He knelt to pray, but moved only his lips; for since he was deprived of the ability to speak, he was unable to utter any words that were completely comprehensible. This man appeared to pray so persistently that he was observed to be weeping strongly while mouthing these silent words. If someone gave him some charity after considering his misfortune, immediately Theodomund donated it to poor people like himself; he begged for alms from others by nodding, but then gave the proceeds to the needy. After he had stayed in this holy spot and [displayed] this devotion for three years, one day he was advised by divine piety and went to the holy altar. He stood there and lifted his eyes and his hands to heaven; then a stream of blood and filth flowed from his mouth. He spit it on the ground and then began to moan loudly and to cough up some unfamiliar bloody globs; as a result it might be thought that someone was cutting his throat with a sword. The putrefaction hung from his mouth like bloody strings. Once the bindings on his ears and his throat were broken, he got up and again raised his eyes and hands to heaven. His mouth was still covered with blood, and he said this as his first words: "I am most grateful to you, most blessed lord Martin, because you have opened my mouth, and after this long time you have made me utter words in praise of you." All the people were amazed and surprised at this great miracle, and they asked whether he had likewise recovered his hearing. As the people watched, he replied that he heard everything without restriction. In this way Theodomund was restored to his health. He was then sponsored by Queen Clotild because of her respect for this miracle by St. Martin and sent to a school where he memorized the entire sequence of Psalms.[25] God transformed him into an accomplished cleric and allowed him to remain in the service of the cathedral for many years thereafter.

---

[25] After Clovis's death in 511 his widow Clotild retired to Tours, where she influenced the selection of some of its bishops (*Hist.* 2.43, 3.28, 4.1, 10.31).

8. Chainemund, a blind woman

A woman named Chainemund had lost the sight of her eyes and did not know how to travel along the road by sight unless someone else was leading her. She was a very pious woman, and full of faith she went to the venerable church of the blessed bishop Martin. She was, however, not only blind, as I said, but also covered with abrasions on her entire body. For a sickness had attacked all her limbs with sores, and her appearance was so horrible and so repulsive to look at that she was considered by the people as a leper. Every day she felt her way and went to the church of the glorious champion. After almost three years, while she was standing in front of his tomb, her eyes were opened and she saw everything clearly. All the weakness in her limbs disappeared, the moisture that seeped from her body was dried up, and a healthy skin grew back. She was restored to her earlier health so completely that there remained on her body not even a scar from her illness. She lived for many years thereafter and continuously thanked omnipotent God because he had restored her to health through the intervention of his blessed confessor.

9. The blessed bishop Baudinus

I will not omit [to tell] how the invocation of his name immediately calmed a stormy lake. The blessed Baudinus, bishop of Tours, was crossing to a villa by means of a boat. Suddenly a very dark cloud and strong winds approached, the quiet lake was disturbed by the force of the storm, and the boat was tossed about by the mass of waves. First the prow [of the boat] was lifted among the swells, then it was twisted between the intervals in the waves. Sometimes they were suspended on the side of a mountain of water; then, when the waves split, they descended to the depths; but the mast that offered the sign of the blessed cross did not collapse. The [passengers'] limbs were paralyzed with fear, and without hope for life everyone was already prepared to die. The old man Baudinus was kneeling and weeping as he prayed; he stretched both hands to the stars, requested the assistance of the blessed Martin, and cried that he might deign to be with them quickly. But one of the unbelievers said: "That Martin whom you are addressing has already left you, and he has not helped you in this emergency." I truly believe that this remark was made by the treacherous [devil] in order to disturb the blessed bishop while he was praying. But Baudinus repelled this javelin with the breastplate of faith and all the more requested the protection of the holy man. At the same time he urged everyone to pray. While this was happening, suddenly a very sweet fragrance like balsam covered the boat, and as if someone had gone around with a censer, the fragrance of incense was overpowering. At the approach of this fragrance the savagely violent winds stopped, the masses of nearby waves were crushed, and the lake became tranquil again. Everyone who had already been resigned to death marveled at the calmness of the waves, and once calm was restored, they were immediately returned to the shore. Let no one doubt that this storm was calmed by the arrival of the blessed man. Then everyone together thanked the Lord, because through the prayer of his bishop he had deigned to save them from this danger.[26]

10. The man who took the saint's relics to Cambrai

At this time a man from Cambrai requested relics of the blessed Martin. He received them when it was already evening, but set out while chanting Psalms. While he was crossing the Loire River, it became late; suddenly the sky was darkened, and behold! bright lightning bolts and loud thunder descended. While this was happening, two boys with spears [whose] flames produced a beacon offered a guiding light to the travelers. Their gleaming spears went ahead and offered no less of a miracle than assistance to the travelers; they also displayed the power of the blessed bishop.

11. The Sueves in Galicia who were converted

A barren tongue, [even though] wishing to relate such miracles, is inadequate. The son of Chararic, a king in Galicia, was seriously ill and had fallen into such weakness that he moved only with his breathing. But his father had subjected himself and the inhabitants of the region to that disgusting sect of Arianism. This region also was afflicted with more leprosy than was usual in other provinces. When the king saw that his son was pushed to his last moments, he said to his servants: "Some say that Martin is distinguished by his many miracles in Gaul. Tell me, I ask, what was that man's religion?" They said to him: "While he was alive in his body, he governed his people with pastoral care in the Catholic faith, and he declared that the Son was venerated with the Father and the Holy Spirit because of his equal substance and omnipotence. But now, although living in the heavenly abode, he does not cease to care for his own people with his constant favors." The king replied: "If these words that you say are true, let my trustworthy friends hurry and bring many gifts to his church; and if they obtain a cure for my young son, after investigating the Catholic faith I will believe what that man believed." Then the king weighed out gold and silver [equal] to the weight of his son and sent it to the venerable spot of the tomb. The men were brought to the tomb, presented the gifts, and prayed before the tomb on behalf of the ill boy. But because the sect [of Arianism] was still fixed in the father's breast, the boy did not deserve to receive a complete cure immediately.

---

[26] Baudinus was bishop of Tours from 546 to 552. L. Pietri (1983) 617 suggests that this storm blew up on the Loire and that Baudinus may have been trying to visit the villa thirty miles from Tours in which Gregory later stayed in 585 (*Hist.* 7.29).

The messengers returned and told the king that they had seen many miracles at the tomb of the blessed [Martin]; they said: "We do not know why your son has not been cured." But the king perceived that his son could not be cured until he believed that Christ was equal with the Father. He constructed a church of marvelous workmanship in honor of the blessed Martin, and upon its completion he announced: "If I am considered worthy to receive relics of this just man, I will believe whatever the bishops have proclaimed." And so he again sent his messengers with a larger gift. They came to the blessed spot [at Tours] and asked for relics. When the relics were as usual offered to them, they said: "We will not accept them under these conditions. We ask that instead permission be given us to place [on the tomb] something we might later take from it." Then they weighed a piece of a silk cloak, placed it on the blessed tomb, and said: "If we have found favor before the patron whom we have sought, the [silk cloak] that we have placed [on the tomb] will weigh more tomorrow, and what we sought in faith will be a blessing for us." Then they kept vigils during the night, and at daybreak they weighed what they had placed [on the tomb]. So much favor from the blessed man had been soaked into these relics that for a long time they raised the bronze weight in the air as far as the scale could have [leeway] to ascend. And when these relics were held up with great applause, prisoners confined in the municipal jail heard the voices of men chanting Psalms. These prisoners admired the sweetness of the singing and asked the guards what this was. The guards said: "Relics of lord Martin are being sent to Galicia, and therefore Psalms are being chanted." Then these prisoners wept and called upon St. Martin to free them with his appearance. The guards were frightened and turned to flee; the locks on the fetters were broken; and the prisoners emerged free from the prison. As the people watched, the prisoners went all the way to the holy relics. They wept and kissed the blessed relics, and they simultaneously thanked the blessed Martin for their release, because by his mercy he had deigned to free them. Then they obtained a pardon from the judge through the intercession of the bishop, and they left as free men. After seeing this the couriers of the relics were very happy and said: "Now we know that the blessed bishop has deigned to indicate that he is well-disposed to us sinners." And so they gave thanks and quickly returned to a port in Galicia. The protection of their patron accompanied them, so that their voyage was prosperous, the waves were gentle, the breezes were restrained, their sail fluttered, and the sea was calm.[27]

[27] Only Gregory mentioned this Chararic, who was king of the Sueves perhaps during the 550s. Men who have been identified as his son and successor include the Ariamir who convened the Council of Braga in 561 and the Theodemir whom later traditions considered the first Catholic king of the Sueves: see Barlow (1950) 4, and Thompson (1982) 203; Thompson (1980) 88, dismisses Chararic as a fictitious character.

Then the blessed Martin [of Braga], who is now a bishop there, was advised by God and came from a distant region. I do not think that this happened without divine providence, because he traveled from his homeland on the day when the blessed relics were brought from that spot, and so he entered the port in Galicia simultaneously with those relics. The relics that they received with great veneration strengthened their faith with miracles. For after his illness vanished entirely, the king's son hurried to meet them. Then the blessed Martin accepted the sovereignty of episcopal grace. The king confessed the unity of the Father and the Son and the Holy Spirit and was baptized along with his entire household. The people were freed from loathsome leprosy, and all ill people were cured; to the present day the disease of leprosy has never again appeared on anyone there. The Lord bestowed such favor there upon the arrival of the relics of the blessed patron that it would be very tedious to narrate the miracles that happened there on that day. For those people are now so evident in their love for Christ that they would all most willingly accept martyrdom if an era of persecution were to appear.[28]

12. Queen Ultrogotho

Queen Ultrogotho heard about the miracles that happened at the spot where the holy limbs [of Martin] were buried, and just like [the queen of Sheba who wanted] to hear the wisdom of Solomon [cf. 1 Kings 10:1], she piously sought to see those miracles. She therefore abstained from eating and sleeping and sent very generous alms in advance; then she went to the holy place. She entered the church, but because she was frightened and nervous, she did not dare to approach the tomb; she announced that she was unworthy and that she was unable to approach [the tomb] because her sins prevented her. Then she passed a night keeping vigils, praying, and weeping profusely. At daybreak she presented many gifts and sought to celebrate a mass in honor of the blessed confessor. During the celebration of mass three blind men who had sat at the feet of the blessed bishop for a long time after being deprived of their sight were suddenly surrounded by a great flash and regained the sight that they had once lost. After this miracle

[28] Although elsewhere Gregory noted that Martin of Braga had died after being bishop "for thirty years, more or less" (*Hist.* 5.37), according to the chronology of Barlow (1950) 3–6, Martin of Braga arrived in Galicia in ca. 550, became bishop of Dumium, the monastery he founded outside Braga, in 556, then became bishop of Braga between 561 and 572, and died in 579. Gregory also mentioned that this Martin had composed some verses "that are over the door on the south side of the church of St. Martin"; for an edition of this poem, see Barlow (1950) 282. Barlow (1950) 276, 280n.5, suggests that this was the church that King Chararic constructed at Braga or, more likely, at Dumium. Gregory probably learned about Martin of Braga from his friend Fortunatus, who exchanged some correspondence with him: see Fortunatus, *Carm.* 5.1–2.

occurred, the shouting of the people who were glorifying God was raised to heaven. The queen rushed to [see] this miracle, the people quickly joined her, and everyone marveled at the queen's faith and the glory of the confessor. Above all they praised our God who bestows such power on his saints that he deigns to work such miracles through them. For among the other lights [available] to this world God grants in the blessed Martin an immense star, and through him this world's darkness becomes light. Indeed, just like a fruitful olive tree [cf. Ps. 52:8] every day he produces fruit for the Lord by converting wretched people.[29]

13. The man who suffered from a blister and was in pain

I will not omit this story that I recall was told by the priest Fortunatus, my distinguished fellow servant. In Italy a man was infected by the poison of a blister and was in such peril that he gave up hope of living. He asked some men whether any of them had visited the church of the blessed Martin. One of the bystanders said that he had visited [the church]. The ill man asked what he had taken away from the church as a blessing. The other man replied that he had not taken anything. The ill man asked him again which clothes he had been wearing then when he visited the holy church. The man replied [that he had then been wearing] the clothes that he was wearing now. The ill man confidently cut off a small fragment of the other man's clothes and placed it on his blister. As soon as the fragment touched the limbs of the ill man, his blistering sore lost its poisonous effect; and through its medicine the fragment offered the saint's power and restored the ill man to his health.

[Fortunatus] claimed that this particular remedy was [so] effective in Italy that whenever someone suffered from a blistering sore, he would take flight to the oratory of the blessed Martin that was nearby; and if whatever was first seized either from the curtain over the door or from the draperies that hung on the walls was placed on the ill man and stuck to him, then it restored his health. This remedy healed his own natural father from a deadly blister, as Fortunatus claimed as a witness for his father.

14. The fortress in Italy called Tertium

The same man [Fortunatus] told [this story] in these words: "An oratory for the blessed Martin was built at the summit of a fortress in a region of Italy that is called Tertium ["The Third"]. During a barbarian attack each time the enemy made a raid during the night and treacherously approached a neighboring tower, one of the watchmen in the tower had a spear or a

---

[29] After the death of King Childebert in 558 his brother King Chlothar exiled his widow Ultrogotho from Paris (*Hist.* 4.20). After Chlothar's death in 561, King Charibert took her and her daughters under his protection, and she regained possession of Childebert's garden at Paris: see Fortunatus, *Carm.* 6.2.21–26, 6.6.

sword or he had drawn a knife or a dagger from a sheath, and for almost one hour a bright light was reflected from the entire sword, as if that iron [sword] had been transformed into a wax [candle]. Soon the guards were warned by this signal and were more alert during their watches; then with stones they routed the concealed enemy. In a correct evaluation this indicates the power of St. Martin, who offers constant and immediate protection to the people in his region who are devoted to him." I learned about this miracle from the aforementioned [Fortunatus].

15. The oil from the lamp beneath the portrait of the blessed [Martin]

Fortunatus also admitted that sight had returned to himself and to Felix, his fellow student in the school of rhetoric at Ravenna, when they touched their eyes with the oil that was burning in a lamp beneath a painting of the portrait of the blessed Martin.[30]

16. The procurator Placidus

Likewise in the aforementioned city [of Ravenna] the procurator Placidus was abandoned by his doctors and fled to another nearby oratory that belonged to a convent. While he was lying in its courtyard, the blessed Martin came to the abbess in a dream during the night and asked what she was doing; she replied that she was resting. The saint said to her: "I must return to Gaul now, but I admit that I have delayed for the sake of the man who is lying outside in the courtyard." Then the abbess woke up, recalled her dream, and gave assurances to the man that he would be freed from his danger because he certainly deserved to obtain [his health]. But as the aforementioned priest [Fortunatus] insists, it is much more desirable for Martin's glory to be venerated in regions in Italy than (if I may say so) [there] where his pious limbs lie buried. Hence many miracles are neither captured in words because they are [so] scattered, nor recorded in pages because they are so numerous.

17. The events that happened at Amiens

An oratory was built by believers at the gate to Amiens where the blessed man had once cut his cloak and clothed a freezing pauper.[31] Now nuns serve at this oratory, and in honor of the holy bishop they have few possessions, although often the devotion of the pious supports them. Once they owned a few beehives. When a malicious man saw these hives, he said to

---

[30] Both Fortunatus, *Vita S. Martini* 4.686–701, and Paul the Deacon, *HL* 2.13, located this shrine to St. Martin in a church dedicated to the apostles John and Paul. By the time the Lombards invaded Italy Felix had become bishop of Treviso: see Fortunatus, *Vita S. Martini* 4.665–7, and Paul the Deacon, *HL* 2.12.

[31] Original story in Sulpicius Severus, *Vita Martini* 3; the cathedral at Tours probably had a fresco of this miracle on one of its walls: see Fortunatus, *Carm.* 10.6.25–30, 103–6.

himself: "If only I could steal some of these beehives." On the following
night this man was motivated by a demon to steal three of the hives and
load them on a boat in order, of course, to appropriate what he had stolen
more easily after he crossed the river. But I believe that this theft was a
stumbling block, as was later clearly demonstrated. For when the sun was
rising, men hurried to the dock in order to cross the river. There they saw
the boat on the shore, the bees emerging from the hives in a swarm, and the
man lying prostrate at a distance. The people thought he was asleep, and
since they had already learned from the nuns about the theft that had taken
place, they hurried as quickly as possible to bind him. But when they
approached, they found that he was dead. Immediately the news was
brought to the nuns, and the people restored to the oratory what had been
stolen. They were impressed that the judgment of divine vengeance had
struck the man so quickly.

18. The oratory at Sireuil

Many people likewise deserve [to receive] the blessing they requested at
the oratory at Sireuil whose altar has been blessed by the gracious hand of
the holy confessor.[32] A paralyzed man came, and while keeping vigils
during the entire night he held a wax candle that matched his own height.
At daybreak when light was restored to the world, his legs were loosened,
and as the people watched, he jumped up with his health.

19. Bella, a blind woman

I will not pass over this story about how he dealt with blindness when a
pious woman sought out his blessed tomb. A woman from the territory of
Tours who was named Bella was gravely ill after losing the sight in her eyes.
And while she was suffering day and night from these incessant pains, she
said to her servants: "If I had been brought to the church of lord Martin, I
would have immediately received my health. For I believe that he who was
able to cure a poor man of his leprosy by the touch of a kiss can also restore
light to my eyes." Then, with a servant as a guide, she came to the holy
place, and after devoting herself to frequent fasting and praying there, she
deserved to receive the sight that she had lost. She was cured so completely
that she who as a blind woman had come with someone else leading her
often returned in the future as a guide for other blind people. After she
eventually married and had children, she gave thanks to her healer for her
health.[33]

---

[32] There is no other evidence for Martin's having visited Sireuil.

[33] According to Sulpicius Severus, *Vita Martini* 18.3–4, Martin had healed a leper with a
kiss at Paris. The cathedral at Tours probably had a fresco of this miracle on one of its walls:
see Fortunatus, *Carm.* 10.6.31–36, 93–100.

20. Ammonius, a man who was thrown down

Because I have already narrated two or three times the miracles that happened and the dangers that were resolved simply by the invocation of his glorious name, now I will describe how the blessed bishop was invoked at the very edge of death and offered support to a man who was perishing. Ammonius was an administrator for the holy church [of Martin].[34] Since he set out drunk with wine from his dinner, he was thrown from a high cliff that was next to the road when a hostile [demon] pushed him. This cliff was almost two hundred feet high. As Ammonius tumbled through this vast fall and soared downward without any flapping wings, he called for the assistance of St. Martin at each moment of his descent. Then, as if he had been knocked off his horse by others' hands, he was thrown on top of the trees that were in the valley. In this way he descended slowly, branch by branch, and without the threat of death he finally reached the ground. Lest his attacker's ambush might appear to be completely harmless because it was unsuccessful, Ammonius nevertheless slightly injured one of his feet. But upon coming to the church of the glorious lord [Martin] he knelt in prayer and was relieved of all the force of his pain.

21. Another man who was hanged

I do not think it irrelevant if [the story of] how the invocation of his name offered life to a man about to die is included in this reading. In some place a man was arrested for his crimes of theft and severely whipped; then he was brought to a gallows so that he might be executed by hanging. Since he had come to this end [of his life] and his death was already near, he requested a moment for prayer. Then, just as he was with his hands bound behind his back, he threw himself prostrate on the ground and began to weep and to call upon the name of the blessed Martin. [He asked] that he would forgive him of his misdeeds for the future, even if he would not assist him in these dire circumstances. Once he finished his prayer, he was hanged and the soldiers departed from that spot; but the man always struggled to beg for the assistance of St. Martin, even though his mouth was barely open and he was hardly moving his lips. As these men departed, immediately the hanged man's hands and feet were released. And so the man hung there for two days, until it was revealed to a certain nun that she should remove him. The nun came and found that the man was still alive. With the assistance of the blessed Martin she then took the man down from the gallows and brought him safely to the cathedral. When the people saw him there, they were amazed and surprised. They said: "How did he stay alive?" And they asked him how he had been freed. The man said: "The blessed Martin freed me from an immediate death and brought me here."

[34] For the *agentes sanctae basilicae*, see L. Pietri (1983) 625.

According to the understanding of my intelligence I think that this miracle is no less significant than the raising of a dead man. For the blessed
confessor, if I may say so, shattered the abyss of death and restored this
man to life after snatching him from the jaws [of death]. Still today this man
is alive in this world as evidence for the miracle performed by the blessed
man.

22. Leomeris, a crippled man

I will not omit what happened in the parish of Candes. This place is
distinguished by frequent miracles; for the blessed man threw aside the
burden of his flesh and [after his death] migrated to the Lord from Candes.
Then a slave named Leomeris who belonged to a man from Angers was
struck by apoplexy. His hand was crippled, his tongue was tied, and he
became stiff. For a long time he suffered from this weakness and did not
perform any work for his owner. After being admonished by his faith he
kept a vigil at the church of the blessed [Martin]; then his hand was
straightened, his tongue was freed from all obstructions, and he announced the miracle of the blessed Martin to the people. He said: "Behold!
With my testimony acknowledge what this saint of God did during this
night!" Then he returned to his own owner and told him everything that
had happened. But his owner did not accept this [as a] miracle of the
glorious bishop and reassigned the slave to his usual work. When this slave
began to work, he was again afflicted with this weakness. Then his owner
understood that this was God's mysterious [plan], and he again sent his
slave to the holy place where he had previously gone. The slave most
piously spent the night there, and at daybreak he was restored to the health
that he had earlier deserved.

23. Wiliachar, a bound man

I thought it appropriate not to omit from this account a story that I heard
the priest Wiliachar tell. [He said that] once when he had offended King
Chlothar on account of the treachery of Chramn, he fled to the church of St.
Martin. There he was bound in chains and kept under guard; but the
chains could not withstand the power of the blessed champion and were
broken. For because of some uncharacteristic carelessness [that became]
dangerous, he was seized outside in the courtyard. The men covered him
with iron [chains], bound his hands behind his back, and led him to King
Chlothar. But Wiliachar began to cry out in a loud voice and to pray that
the blessed Martin have pity on him and not allow a man who had piously
come to his church to leave as a captive. The blessed bishop Eufronius was
praying on a wall of the city [of Tours] opposite the church. As Wiliachar
shouted, immediately his hands were freed, and all the chains fell away as
their links were broken. But he was led to King Chlothar and there again
bound and held in fetters and chains. After he had repeatedly called upon

the name of the aforementioned patron, all the iron [chains] on him were shattered so [completely] that you might think that they had been like pottery. During this time this was the situation: he was not released from his bonds until he had called upon that most sacred name, but once he invoked it, all his bonds were released. Then King Chlothar realized through a penetrating insight that the power of St. Martin was at work here; so he released Wiliachar from the burden of his chains and restored him to his original freedom. In the presence of many witnesses I heard about these events from the mouth of that priest Wiliachar. If only the blessed confessor might deign to show such power to me, so that he might release the bonds of my sins just as he crumbled those massive heavy chains on top of Wiliachar![35]

24. Alpinus, a lame count

Alpinus was count of Tours, and for an entire year he suffered severely from pain in one foot. Day and night he had no rest; but as he moaned from the torture, he continually requested the assistance of the blessed Martin. One night the blessed confessor appeared to him in a dream with a smile on his happy face and carrying his usual weapons. He made the blessed sign of the holy cross over his lame foot. Soon all the pain disappeared, and Alpinus got up from his bed as a healthy man.[36]

25. Charigisil, a crippled man

Charigisil was a secretary of King Chlothar; because of swelling his hands and feet had stiffened. After these [other miracles] happened, he came to the holy church and lay there in prayer for two or three months. Then he was visited by the blessed bishop and deserved to receive health in his disabled limbs. Afterward he became a steward of the aforementioned king, and he provided many favors for the people of Tours and for those who served at the blessed church.

26. Aquilinus, who lost his senses

I will also tell this story about how the insane tricks of demons are exposed at his church. While a man named Aquilinus was hunting with his father in the forests of Francia, he developed a terrible trembling when a

[35] In 555 King Chlothar sent his son Chramn to reside in Clermont (*Hist.* 4.9, 13). Eventually Chramn began to plot with his uncle King Childebert against his father and his brothers; he also married a daughter of Wiliachar (*Hist.* 4.16–17). Although Chramn took refuge with the count of Brittany, Chlothar finally captured him and had him and his family killed in 560 (*Hist.* 4.20). Wiliachar meanwhile had fled to Tours, where he was responsible for a fire in the church of St. Martin in 559 (*Hist.* 10.31); after being rescued from Chlothar's anger, he apparently became a priest: see L. Pietri (1983) 227n.225. For another of his daughters, see *VM* 3.13.

[36] Alpinus was count of Tours from perhaps 556 until perhaps 561: see Kurth (1919) 1:206–7.

hostile [demon] ambushed him. He had a spasm in his heart, and then he seemed to have lost his senses. His parents realized that he was being injured by the attack of a demon; but as is the custom of nonbelievers, they brought bandages and potions for him from fortune-tellers and sooth-sayers. But when nothing worked as usual, their grief compelled them to seek the ready assistance of St. Martin. They said: "He who, as we hear, [once] exposed a ghost who had been venerated in the name of a false religion can [now] reveal the cunning in these attacks."[37] They moved their son from the region and brought him to the holy church. There he prayed, deprived himself with long fasts, and constantly requested the saint's assis-tance. After he had lived a long time in this faith, his trembling was com-pletely removed, and he recovered his senses as he had them previously. Then he abandoned his parents and, because of the favor he had received, served at that place; he is still doing so today.

27. Charivald, a lame man

Charivald fell into a similar ambush while hunting and lost [the use of] one side [of his body] when a hand and a foot were crippled. He was carried to the glorious church by the hands of his servants. After he devoted himself to fasting and praying for almost an entire year, he recovered health in all his limbs and happily returned to his own home. And therefore I urge that no one be tempted by soothsayers, because they will never benefit ill people. A bit of dust from the church [of Martin] is more powerful than those men with their foolish medicines.[38]

28. The rope that was cut

Who could ever investigate or know how many miracles either con-stantly happen or have happened by means of the dust or the wax from that place or by means of something else that someone could take from the tomb? I have, however, decided that to be silent about an obvious miracle that I heard from believers would be a crime. A man was [so] filled with faith that he attempted secretly to remove some relic from the saint's church; but although he often tried, he was never able [to do so] as long as he did not act for the common good. He wished to return, and during the night he came to the rope that rang the bell. He cut a small piece from the rope with his knife and took it with him. Once he returned to his home,

---

[37] According to Sulpicius Severus, *Vita Martini* 11, Martin had once exposed a false martyr by conjuring up the man's ghost, which admitted that he had been only a bandit. The cathedral at Tours probably had a fresco of this miracle on one of its walls: see Fortunatus, *Carm.* 10.6.55–60, 129–32.

[38] K. F. Werner (1978) 163 speculates that this Charivald may have been a member of a Frankish aristocratic clan whose descendants in one line soon became prominent as the Agilolfing dukes of Bavaria.

it bestowed health on many ill people; hence there was no doubt that whoever was worthy faithfully to kiss that relic escaped illness. Saint, behold what you offer to believers who seek your protection in particular! Those who have taken relics to fulfill a vow are saved by you, and they are freed with the support of your assistance. A determined faith leads to all these results, as the Lord says: "Your faith has made you well" [Luke 18:42].

29. King Charibert, who seized a villa

It seems best not to pass over the story about how the blessed man offers assistance to his servants in order to defend his possessions wherever he is in command. King Charibert hated clerics, neglected the churches of God, and despised bishops. As he slipped further into debauchery, it was announced to his ears that a certain estate that the church of St. Martin had possessed for a long time was [to be] returned to the control of his own treasury. Ancient tradition had given the name of Nazelles to that estate. After receiving this evil suggestion Charibert quickly sent his retainers who were to take that small property into his possession. And since he seemed to own what [in fact] he did not possess, he ordered that stable-keepers and horsemen be sent to that estate, and disregarding the constraint of moderation he commanded that horses be stabled there. His retainers then came, and in order to feed the horses they took the hay that had been stacked and started the task that had been ordered. As soon as the horsemen stationed there began to distribute the hay, the horses were afflicted with madness. They snorted at each other, snapped their reins, jumped into the open fields, and turned to flee. These horses were badly scattered; some were blinded, some were thrown from cliffs, some rushed into fences and were pierced through by the pointed stakes. The stable-keepers recognized the anger of God and sent the few horses that they could overtake outside the boundary of this estate; they brought those horses back safely. Then they announced to the king that this estate had been reclaimed most unjustly and that they had therefore suffered these misfortunes. They added: "Return that estate and you will have peace." King Charibert was filled with rage and is said to have replied in this way: "Whether justly or unjustly, let that estate be reclaimed; so long as I am king, the church will not own that estate." By divine command the king immediately passed away and died. After the most glorious king Sigibert assumed his kingdom, at the suggestion of the blessed bishop Eufronius he restored this estate to the ownership of St. Martin. Still today his church possesses this estate. Listen to this story, all you who exercise power! Clothe some people in such a way that you do not steal from others; and add to your wealth in such a way that you do no harm to the churches! For God swiftly avenges his servants. And therefore I suggest that whoever reads this story about powerful men not become angry; for if he becomes angry, he will admit that the story was told about himself.[39]

30. Eustochius of Poitiers

The blessed confessor appeared in a similar situation with regard to possessions that had been unjustly taken from him. Eustochius often unjustly harassed the bishop St. Eufronius regarding the legacy of his relative Baudulf, who had designated the church of St. Martin as his heir. The blessed bishop was disturbed by his constant insults and returned to Eustochius some of these possessions. But as Eustochius was carrying these possessions to his home, his only son immediately collapsed with a fever, and after simmering in pain for a night and a day he died. As quickly as his father became the owner of possessions that were not owed to him, so quickly did the son meet death. This man possessed gold and silver after the example of Gehazi [cf. 2 Kings 5:20–27]; but after his soul was afflicted with leprosy he lost what was more precious to him, his son. Nor did he ever deserve to have another son thereafter.

31. The man who committed perjury in the sacred colonnade

In order to suppress the recklessness of dishonest people I will not be silent about how quickly divine vengeance assaulted another man who had committed perjury in the sacred colonnade. Because every day believers bring supplies for that register [of poor people] whom the saint supports by his own goodwill from the alms of the pious, the blessed poor people have the custom of leaving a custodian there when many of them have left for other places. The custodian receives what has been offered. Then a pious man brought one small gold coin with the intention of [providing] support. The custodian of that place took [the coin and] did not fear to conceal it from his brothers. At the sixth hour the poor people assembled and asked the aforementioned custodian what the blessed shepherd who watched over them with his usual affection had brought for them. For they had heard that something had been donated there. The man replied with an oath: "In the name of this holy place and the miracles of lord Martin, nothing more than one silver coin came here." But he had not even completed his words, and his reply was still on his lips, when immediately he shuddered and fell to the ground. After being brought by others' hands to his own bed he began to gasp painfully. When asked by the bystanders

---

[39] After King Chlothar's death in 561 Charibert acquired control of Tours. When one of his counts attempted to collect taxes, Eufronius threatened the king with the power of St. Martin (*Hist.* 9.30); so perhaps Charibert's attempt to seize this estate was a belated form of retaliation. Although Eufronius prepared to meet with Charibert, he canceled the trip when he predicted, correctly, that the king was dead (*GC* 19). After Charibert died in 567 (*Hist.* 4.26) Sigibert and his brothers squabbled over control of Tours: see above, chapter 2, section 1.

what was wrong with himself, he replied: "I lied about that small gold coin that the poor inquired after, and therefore vengeance immediately scourged me. But I ask that you take that coin and return it to the register [of poor people]." Once the coin was returned, he immediately died.[40]

Oh, miserable man! He was trapped by his evil desire and died in such a way that he lost the reward of life and did not possess the misfortunes of the money that he acquired. Accursed greediness,

what do you not compel the hearts of men [to do]?[41]

Once you were jealous of the widow who purchased the kingdom of heaven with her two mites [Mark 12:42–44, Luke 21:1–4];[42] [now] you throw this man to the depths because of one small gold coin. And you who hanged Judas in a noose for the sale of his master [Matt. 27:5] [now] plunge this man into the lower regions because of a small coin. Let these words therefore be sufficient for restraining the rashness of evil people.

32. How his power restored me to health from an illness

Since I have narrated these events that happened to others, let me present something that the power of my propitious patron performed on behalf of my unworthy self. One hundred and sixty-three years after the death of that praiseworthy and blessed bishop St. Martin, in the seventh year of the episcopacy of St. Eufronius over the church at Tours, and in the second year of [the reign of] the most glorious king Sigibert,[43] I became ill with infected sores and a fever. Because I was unable to drink and eat, I was so worried that I lost all hope for my present life and I thought only about the soil required for burial. Death threatened me persistently and eagerly and wished to force my soul from my body. I was already close to dying. Then after I called upon the name of the blessed bishop Martin, I recovered a bit and began to prepare for a journey, although my efforts were still sluggish. For I had resolved in my heart that I ought to visit the place of his venerable tomb. Hence I was filled with such longing that I had no hope for myself to

[40] Until the later seventh century Merovingian mints rarely produced silver coins for general circulation. So the *argenteus* this beggar claimed to have received was perhaps one of the tiny silver coins made specifically for distribution to the poor: see Grierson and Blackburn (1986) 111–12.

[41] Gregory often quoted or paraphrased this line from Virgil, *Aeneid* 3.56 (cf. *Hist.* 4.46, 6.36, 8.22, *VJ* 18).

[42] Gregory used this comparison with the Widow's Mites elsewhere too (*GM* 96); perhaps he liked it because near the entrance on the west side of the church of St. Martin an inscription described and a fresco depicted this poor widow and her gift: see below, Appendix 3.

[43] Since Eufronius became bishop in 556 and Sigibert became king in December 561, the year of Gregory's pilgrimage to Tours is 563. But his correlation here with the date of Martin's death does not coincide with his earlier statement that Martin had died in 397: see the note to *VM* 1.3.

live if I hesitated to travel. And so I who had scarcely escaped a burning affliction began to be inflamed again by a fever of longing. Although I was still weak, immediately I began a journey with my companions. After traveling for two or three days I entered a forest and again collapsed with a fever. I began to suffer so badly that everyone thought I was dying. Then my friends approached, saw that I was very tired, and said: "Let us return to our own homes, and if God wishes to summon you, you will die in your home. But if you survive, you may easily complete the journey that you have vowed [to make]. For it is better to return home than to die in the wilderness." I listened to these suggestions and then wept loudly and bewailed my misfortune. I replied to my friends and said: "In the name of the omnipotent God and for the sake of the Judgment Day that all the guilty must fear, I beg of you that you consent to what I ask. Do not cease from the journey that has been begun. If I deserve to see the church of St. Martin, I thank my God; if not, take my lifeless body and bury it there, because it is my decision not to return home unless I will be worthy to be present at his tomb." Then we all wept together and continued the journey that we had begun. The assistance of the glorious lord [Martin] led the way, and we came to his church.

33. My cleric who lost his senses

One of my clerics was named Armentarius, who was well trained in the holy Scriptures. It was so easy for him to comprehend the melodies of the chants that you might think that he was writing them, not studying them. He was very dedicated in his service and reliable in his duties. At this time a poison infected him, and because of his infected sores he had lost all his senses and was reduced to such a condition that he could neither understand nor do anything at all. On the third night after our arrival we decided to keep vigils at the holy church; which we did. When morning came and the bell sounded for matins, we returned to our lodging, lay down on our beds, and slept until almost the second hour. When I awoke, my weakness and the pain in my heart had completely disappeared, and because I knew that I had recovered my former health, I was happy, and I summoned my personal servant who attended me. But Armentarius suddenly got up, stood before me, and said: "My lord, I will obey your command." Since I thought that he was still delirious, I said: "If you can, call my servant." He said: "I will perform whatever you have ordered." I was surprised and asked what had happened. He replied: "I know that I am completely healthy. But in my mind there is one missing memory, because I do not know from what region I have come here." Then he began to offer assistance to me just as he was accustomed before his illness. I was very happy and wept with joy. Then both on my behalf and on behalf of Armentarius I thanked omnipotent God, because at the intercession of our patron he had restored my body and his mind to health, and because a single encounter had by faith benefited another man who, because he was delirious, had not known how to request [assistance].

But I will not omit the conclusion. Forty days after this same day I was pleased to drink wine for the first time, although until then I had considered it distasteful because of my illness.

34. His power averted a storm from my estate

I returned and brought back three wax candles as a blessing from the blessed tomb. It is tedious to describe how many miracles were performed by this wax for people suffering from chills and for other ill people. But let me narrate one of these many miracles. Every year a hailstorm used to damage an estate that I owned and raged so violently that after its arrival it left nothing there. Then I selected one tree in the vineyards that was taller than the others and put some of the holy wax on it. After that day up to the present time the storm never struck there; instead, when it came, it passed that place by as if afraid.

35. The wood from the blessed railing

One of my servants was motivated by his faith and brought back [a piece of] venerable wood from the railing around the bed that is in the monastery of the holy lord [Martin] and kept it in his cottage for protection. I was unaware [of this]. But his family began to be severely ill—I think [because] this wood was not honored or respected as was appropriate to itself. And since the man was completely ignorant about what was happening, and since the situation was not improved but every day deteriorated further, in a vision during the night he saw a terrifying personage who said to him: "Why are you suffering this way?" The man replied: "I am completely ignorant about the reason for what has happened." The personage said to him: "You have suffered these misfortunes because you thoughtlessly keep with you this wood that you took from the bed of lord Martin. But go now, bring this wood to the deacon Gregory, and let him keep it in his possession."[44] Immediately the man brought [the wood] to me. With the greatest reverence I took it and put it in an appropriate place. Then the entire family in his home was cured, with the result that thereafter no one there suffered any misfortune.

---

[44] Gregory was apparently ordained as a deacon after his pilgrimage to Tours in 563. A council in southern Gaul had once insisted that deacons be at least twenty-five years old: see Council of Arles a.524, Can.1. If Gregory's ordination respected that recommendation, then he had been born at least by, and probably in, 538: see Monod (1872) 27–28, Weidemann (1982) 1:205–6, L. Pietri (1983) 254n.43, and above, chapter 2, section 1.

36. His power restrained my enemies

Once it happened that because of an urge to visit my venerable mother I was traveling in Burgundy.[45] While we were passing through those forests that are located across the Bèbre River, we met bandits. They surrounded us and wished to rob and kill us. Then I relied upon my usual source of assistance and requested the protection of St. Martin. His protection immediately and graciously defended me and so frightened the bandits that they were able to do nothing against us. Instead, the bandits who had come so that they might cause fear began to panic and to flee in a very swift escape. But because I did not forget the apostle [Paul who said that] our enemies ought to be satisfied with food and drink [cf. Rom. 12:20], I gave instructions to offer them something to drink. The bandits certainly did not expect this and fled as [quickly] as they could; you might think that they were beaten with cudgels or that against their will they were forced to ride to the detriment of their own horses. And so we arrived where we intended with the support of the Lord and with the assistance of our patron. It is very tedious even to recall, let alone to record, the many troubles and hardships from which he rescued me, the many dangers among which his generosity protected me, and the many sorrows I felt that he suppressed with his power.

37. People suffering from dysentery

What will I say about people suffering from dysentery, when a cure is discovered as quickly as it was requested in faith? For I saw a woman who suffered so severely from dysentery for five months that she was carried by [others'] hands to the appropriate places when necessity disturbed her. Because of excessive diarrhea she lost simultaneously both the energy from food and the strength from her body. I was a witness that she kept vigils at the church. When day returned after the darkness of night, she scratched some dust from the blessed tomb and swallowed a drink and her medicine together; then she who was supported by others when she came was returned to her home on her own feet.

38. Possessed people and people suffering from chills

And what will I say about possessed people and people suffering from chills? If abstinence and faith have been truly joined, soon all treacheries are removed from them with the assistance of their patron. Hence many of these people suffering from chills lie for the entire day between the altar and the holy tomb while they are shaken by the force of a virulent fever; but at vespers they drink [a potion mixed with] dust from the blessed tomb and

---

[45] See the note to *VM* 3.60 for the location of his mother's residence. Weidemann (1982) 1:210–11, suggests, improbably, that this journey be dated to 578 or 579.

immediately deserve to receive their health. For Paulus was a possessed man who was said to have a legion of demons. At the instigation of a hostile [demon] he climbed onto the rafters that were near the holy ceiling[46] and is said to have said: "I have been set on fire; [let Martin spare] the body that I inhabit." He threw himself down, but through the power of the blessed [Martin] he was set on the pavement so lightly that he bruised none of his doomed body's limbs.

39. Leomeria, a blind woman

Leomeria was blind and crippled and lived in poor health for a long time. On many occasions she made the journey that led to the church of the blessed [Martin] with the assistance of others' hands. While she was lying at the holy door, she was finally observed by his generosity and received her sight as well as her mobility. Oh, if only everything were displayed in public that individuals received in private when they made requests in faith! If only many retained in their knowledge the secret that the health that is sought in private is acquired by making a request in faith! But if, as I said, all these incidents were publicized, I think that not only books but even the world itself could not contain them, as the evangelist said about the Lord [cf. John 21:25].

40. Securus, a crippled man

And since my account seeks a conclusion, before my book reaches an end I will narrate to you one miracle that is still celebrated. A young man named Securus, upon emerging from his mother's womb, displayed a withered hand and foot and was so stiff because of the dryness in the joints of all his limbs that he resembled some monster; he was also bound by the yoke of slavery. When his owners saw that he could not be of any profit at all even after seven years, they carried him in their hands and placed him before the blessed tomb so that he who could not be fed by his own labor might be supported by those who passed by. But while he was lying in that place for many days, his foot that had been lame was straightened, and his withered hand was cured after the veins were filled with blood. He received the assistance of the blessed confessor, and his entire body was reshaped in such a way that you might think he had been born again. This young boy was ransomed by Count Justinus and released with his freedom; later he received baptism and remains healthy still today under the patronage of the holy cathedral.[47]

[46] L. Pietri (1983) 389 suggests that the *machina* onto which Paulus climbed was instead a wooden baldachin or ciborium over the altar.

[47] In 569 King Sigibert sent Count Justinus to ask Bishop Eufronius of Tours to preside over the reception of the relic of the True Cross at Radegund's convent in Poitiers: see Baudonivia, *Vita Radegundis* 16, and above, chapter 1, section 2.

Who will ever be able to investigate or to recall these [miracles] so systematically that he is capable of praising [Martin]? But I have desired, to the extent that I have been able to do research, to record [these miracles] faithfully, and I have hoped to receive this payment as a reward, that forgiveness might perhaps be given me on behalf of my sins when these stories are read in praise of the most holy bishop. As the poet said:

Perhaps it will also be a pleasure to have remembered these events.[48]

[Here] ends this first book.

VM 2

Here begins a second book about the miracles that happened after I came [to Tours as bishop].

I have already recorded the miracles of St. Martin that I observed and those that happened in earlier times and that I was able to learn about from trustworthy men. But because I still strongly burned with the intention of not allowing what the Lord deigned to perform in praise of his bishop to be forgotten, I wish to narrate even those events that I marvel to have happened during my tenure [as bishop of Tours]. Although I may leave little material for more eloquent men, I include these great miracles in my writings so that the cumulative number of miracles might multiply what [my lack of] expertise does not amplify in these pages.

1. How I was rescued from a fever and dysentery
   One hundred and seventy-two years after the death of the blessed Bishop Martin and in the twelfth year of the reign of the most glorious Sigibert, I, although unworthy, received the burden of the episcopacy [at Tours] after the death of the bishop St. Eufronius,[49] not because of my merit, for I am morally very corrupt and bound by my sins, but because of the assistance of a devoted God who summons those [qualities] that do not exist as if they did. In the second month after my consecration I suffered from dysentery and a high fever while I was at a villa, and I began to suffer so badly that I completely gave up any hope of living, because death was imminent. Frequently my digestive system vomited undigested food that it could not absorb, and I was repelled by food; and as the efficiency of my stomach weakened from fasting, the fever was all the more sustenance for my body.

---

[48] Virgil, *Aeneid* 1.203.

[49] Gregory mentioned that after Eufronius's death the see was vacant for nineteen days (*Hist.* 10.31). Although Gregory's chronology here implies an incorrect year for Martin's death (see the notes to *VM* 1.3, 32), Sigibert had become king at the end of 561: see Krusch (1920) 488. So Gregory was consecrated bishop in 573, shortly before August 28 (*VJ* 34): see Krusch (1951) XI.

Even expensive relief was unavailable. For there was a sharp pain that penetrated my entire stomach and went down to my intestines and that consumed me with its torment no less than the fever had distressed me. And when I reached the point that no hope of life was left, that all my thoughts were turned toward my funeral, and that the antidote of my doctor had no effect, I despaired about myself, because death had delivered me up for destruction. I called Armentarius, my doctor, and I said to him: "You have offered all the wisdom of your skill, and you have already tested the strength of all your salves, but the devices of this world have been of no use to me who am about to die. One option remains for me to try; let me show you a powerful antidote. Fetch dust from the most sacred tomb of lord [Martin], and then mix a drink for me. If this dust is not effective, every refuge for escaping [death] has been lost." Then a deacon was sent to the aforementioned tomb of the blessed champion. He brought back some of the sacred dust that they mixed [in water] and gave me to drink. As soon as I drank it, all the pain vanished, and I received my health from the tomb. The assistance available at that tomb was so effective that after this [cure] had occurred at the third hour, on the same day at the sixth hour I was healthy and went for a meal.

It seems proper to include in this reading also [this story about] how God reproved me lest I allow silly uninformed people to criticize the blessed ceremonies in my presence. On the day after I recovered I went to mass on Sunday; but because I did not wish to tire myself, I ordered one of the priests to celebrate the glorious ceremony. But when that priest for some reason pronounced the words of the liturgy incorrectly, many members of my congregation began to laugh at him and said: "It would have been better to be silent than to speak so incorrectly." During the following night I saw a man who said to me: "There must never be any disagreement about the mysteries of God." I summon God as my witness that I have not invented this story; instead, I have told you the very words that I heard. Therefore, most beloved people, let no one dare to disagree about this mystery, even if it seems to be recited in an uncouth fashion, because in the presence of God's majesty pure simplicity is more effective than philosophical cleverness.

2. The illness of Justinus

I have decided that it is also appropriate not to omit this event that escaped me in the previous book. For I mentioned those candles that I brought back from the tomb of the blessed bishop, and I said that they halted storms and prevented other illnesses.[50] While I was preoccupied with my own affairs, Justinus, my sister's husband, became ill and began to

---

[50] *VM* 1.34. In his *GM* and *GC* Gregory sometimes inserted later stories in his original catalog; here he refused to tamper with *VM* 1, which he apparently considered a closed book.

suffer very badly as the fever increased together with pains in all his limbs. A messenger, [at first] delayed, announced this news to me and demanded that if I could find any medicine, I send it to this man who was on the verge of death, lest he perish. Because I trusted in the power of the blessed bishop, I sent one of the candles with the servant and said: "Burn this candle in Justinus's presence, and as he considers its light, let him offer a prayer to the Lord and request the bishop's power to assist him." The servant was sent off and brought what I had given him. After they lit the candle before the bed of the ill man, with a knife they scraped a cinder from a plant that the fire had already consumed, mixed it with water, and offered it to the ill man to drink. When Justinus drank it, immediately he received his health. After he was restored to health, he later told me how the power of the blessed bishop assisted him. For he used to claim that as soon as the bright light proceeded from the candle to his eyes and dispelled the darkness of the night, immediately in consideration of the flame his fever retreated from his body, his stomach urgently required the energy of food after becoming weak from long fasting, and he who had been accustomed to drink only pure water to soothe his burning fever now desired wine. This was done by the bishop's power that has often offered assistance to the suffering from his generous compassion and that lavishes medicines upon the ill.[51]

3. Maurusa, who suffered from gout in her hand

I am concerned lest as I intend to proceed further, my uncouth speech disgraces this page. The pain from swelling due to gout in her hand distressed Maurusa so severely that her feet were twisted back to her shins and she was completely unable to stand up. This woman, who had suffered badly for a long time, had also been deprived of the sight of her eyes; although still alive she was thought of as if dead. She had no hope of support unless someone extended a hand of compassion. Every day she looked to the consideration of believers and begged for the necessities of sustenance. Then it happened that at a certain time she suffered more severely than usual; unless the inhalation of her breath was entering her chest, she was unable to control any of her limbs. Since she was already nearly lifeless, she asked that people bring her to the feet of St. Martin. The hands of believers brought her to that place. Because of the coercive pain she cried out for the assistance of the blessed man and prayed that he have pity on her. Then that compassion that was never accustomed to send poor people away empty-handed looked after her. During his festival the sinews of her dry nerves were loosened; over her face she made the sign of the

---

[51] Justinus was also once healed by a relic that his wife had taken from the church of St. Ferreolus and St. Ferrucio in Besançon (*GM* 70). Their daughters were Justina (*Hist.* 10.15, note to *VM* 4.16) and Eustenia (*VM* 4.36).

blessed cross with her right hand that she had not controlled for six years, and she was so restored to her feet that she returned to her own home without using anyone's assistance. But the sight in her eyes was not recovered. Two years later she again came to the tomb of the blessed patron and began to pray more earnestly, as was appropriate. Soon her eyes were opened, and she stood up with her sight restored. I have recorded this miracle at this point because she received her sight after I arrived [as bishop]; she had been cured of her illness earlier.[52]

4. The slave belonging to the priest Symon

A slave named Veranus belonged to Symon, my most faithful fellow priest. Veranus served Symon as inspector for the storerooms entrusted [to him]. While he was keeping the watch assigned to him, swelling due to gout attacked him, and he was deprived of mobility in his feet. After Veranus was afflicted for an entire year with such pains that even his neighbors located nearby carried him, suddenly his nerves stiffened, and he was completely crippled. His master Symon saw this, grieved for the loss of a faithful slave, and ordered that Veranus be brought to the feet of the blessed bishop. He made a vow and said: "Most compassionate lord Martin, if you restore Veranus to health, he will be freed from the bond of slavery to me on that very day, tonsured, and transferred to your service." Veranus was then placed at the feet of the most beloved lord [Martin], and after he lay there without moving for five days, on the sixth day he was overwhelmed by sleep. While he was asleep, it seemed to him as if he were a man accustomed to stretch his foot on his bed. Once he awoke, he was cured from all his lameness and stood up. Veranus was tonsured, received his freedom, and now serves the needs of the blessed lord [Martin]. How admirable was his ransom by this blessed man! Who ever spent a thousand talents for a ransom just as this powerful benefactor did on behalf of our misdeeds? With one blow, in one moment, and without any gold coins he freed Veranus's body from lameness and his legal standing from the burden [of slavery].

5. The paralyzed man from Auxerre

A man from Auxerre named Mallulf was brought by [others'] hands and placed before the tomb of the blessed Martin. He devoted himself to praying and fasting without ceasing, and he displayed his twisted feet. But suddenly his health was recovered, and he restored to their usual function his feet that had been straightened. Mallulf was transformed by the saint's

---

[52] Weidemann (1982) 1:207, and Corbett (1983) 55, suggest that this woman's blindness was healed on November 11, 573 during the first festival of St. Martin that Gregory celebrated as bishop of Tours.

power in such a way that although he had been brought by others' hands, he was [now] supported by his own feet; and in my presence he stood up as a healthy man.

6. Another paralyzed man from Orléans

Another paralyzed man was brought in a wagon from the territory of Orléans and came to the holy church. For many days he lay before the entrance that is alongside the baptistery and that offered access at noon; there he requested the assistance of the blessed bishop. Then it happened that one day as he lay there he was tormented more severely than usual, with the result that neighbors nearby gathered to his shouts. As the sinews of his nerves were loosened and he was lifted up, he felt an unbearable pain. And so, with the support of his patron he was raised to his feet. He wept with joy, and with the people as his witness he stood up. Immediately he became a cleric, and after being confirmed in his health he returned home.

7. A similar story about another paralyzed man from Bourges

But another lame man named Leuboveus, who was already a cleric, arrived after dragging himself along the ground, because due to the circumstances of his poverty he had no one to carry him. Day after day he sought the entrances [to the church] of the blessed Martin. One day while he was weeping outside at the saint's feet, his knees and his feet were straightened, and as the people watched, he received his health. It is well known that these three miracles happened on that day when the most glorious king Sigibert crossed the Seine River and without any attack by his army made peace with his brothers. Let no one dispute this fact, that even this was a victory for the blessed bishop.[53]

8. The blind man who received his sight

At this time a blind man was begging for a donation from almsgivers. He had no other support unless someone extended a hand of compassionate consideration, nor did he have any protection at home other than the pity of believers. One day while he was standing firmly upright in front of the holy tomb, a pain suddenly attacked him in his eyes; and while he was severely overwhelmed by this pain, his eyes began to discharge a fluid. And so, as blood was flowing from [beneath] his eyelids, he was reborn in his renewed sight, and he deserved to see the light that he had once lost.

---

[53] Soon after Gregory's accession as bishop King Chilperic sent his son Theudebert to occupy Tours (*Hist.* 4.47). In 574 King Sigibert attacked Chilperic, and both then negotiated for the support of King Guntramn; after they all finally made peace, Chilperic restored Tours to Sigibert (*Hist.* 4.49). Since Guntramn controlled the three cities of Auxerre, Orléans, and Bourges from which these three paralyzed men came, their healings might indicate St. Martin's acceptance of Guntramn as a mediator in this dispute.

9. Another blind woman

Gunthedrud was from the territory of Saint-Quentin and had lost the sight of her eyes. Under the motivation of her faith she left her home and her homeland and came to the holy church. After she served there for many days, she deserved to receive sight in one eye. Soon she abandoned her husband and children, adopted a habit, and at the instigation of the Lord became a nun in the church.

10. The woman freed from a flow of blood

But I will not be silent concerning this story [about] how a flow of blood was healed at the blessed tomb, just as [once before] by the garment of our Redeemer [cf. Matt. 9:20–22]. A woman who suffered from a flow of blood came with her husband from the district of Trézelle in [the territory of] Clermont. She took lodgings near a courtyard of the church. Every day she knelt and lay at the entrances to the holy confessor's [church], and requested assistance for her health. Then it happened that one day she approached the holy tomb, prayed, kissed it, and touched her ears and eyes to the shroud that was over [the tomb]. Immediately her flow of blood was healed, and she was cured so [completely] that she thought that she had touched a thread [from the garment] of the Redeemer. When her husband was struck with an illness, he was brought to a door of the church by others' hands; after he prayed piously, his fever vanished and he recovered. And so the man was healed of his illness and the woman likewise of her flow [of blood]. They praised God and returned to their own home.

11. The lame woman

The wife of the tribune Animus was named Mummola. One night she was terrified with fear, lost the use of one of her feet, and suffered from such disability that she was supported and carried by others' hands, and in this way intended to go where she wished. She was brought to the feet of the blessed Martin and, because of a vow, held a candle in her hand during an entire night. I was keeping vigils in the church. When the bell was rung for matins at daybreak, she stood up on her lame foot in such a way that all the disability disappeared, and she returned unimpeded to her lodging on her own feet, without anyone's assistance.[54]

12. The man suffering from dysentery who was healed

Once the blessed Germanus, bishop of Paris, came to the festival of the glorious bishop [on November 11, 574]. Ragnemod, who was then a

[54] Gregory was perhaps here observing the vigils before the festival of St. Martin on November 11, 574. Since he seems not to have mentioned the festival of St. Martin on July 4, Weidemann (1982) 1:207–8 suggests that he was then away from Tours, perhaps at Dijon to deal with the death of his brother Peter.

deacon in the service of Germanus but is now bishop [of Paris], also came, [even though] he was suffering severely from dysentery. But the blessed Germanus first went to a villa that belonged to his church and that was located in the territory [of Tours]. When he began to set out for Tours [to celebrate] the night of vigils before the festival, Germanus ordered his deacon Ragnemod to stay at the villa and said: "[Stay here,] lest perhaps you tire yourself by traveling and lest something worse afflict you." Ragnemod replied: "It is the power of God that commands me to suffer as I deserve; for I am not leaving until I go to the church of the blessed bishop. For I believe that I will be cured if I touch his tomb." Immediately he mounted his horse and came to the church. At daybreak after he received a drink [mixed] with dust from the tomb, immediately his illness vanished and he recovered.[55]

13. The blind man who recovered his sight

Ursulf was a blind man from Tours, from a district across the Loire River. He piously sought the assistance of the blessed Martin. For two months he constantly served at his church and persisted in fasting and praying. On the day of the Lord's resurrection [Easter 575] he was at the feet of his lord [Martin] and was watching the ceremony of mass with the rest of the congregation. But it happened that suddenly his eyes were opened, and he began to see everything so clearly that he went to the holy altar to receive communion without anyone's leading him. Let me explain what had been the reason for his blindness. On the first day of Lent Ursulf was ordered by his master to walk around a field.[56] He found an opening through which cattle were entering, but when he attempted to close it, he was blinded. Then, as I said, he went to the blessed tomb where he wept and cried and requested the sight that he had lost. But on the day when the goodwill of the body of the Lord was given to the congregation, the blessed bishop deigned to restore his sight; then the pupils of his eyes gleamed again as the sun was rising. What doctor, I ask, could ever be found [like] this one who contrib-

---

[55] Germanus had become bishop of Paris in 556: see Krusch (1920) 338, 381n.2. During his episcopacy he visited the church of St. Martin several times and stayed at this villa at Civray-sur-Cher: see Fortunatus, *Vita Germani* 80–81, 99–101, 174. Germanus died in May 576 (*Hist.* 5.8) and was succeeded by Ragnemod, who visited Tours as bishop again later that year (*Hist.* 5.14). Since Ragnemod did tell Gregory about other miracles that happened before he became bishop (*GC* 87), one possibility is that Gregory learned about this miracle a few years after it happened, but inserted it here in proper chronological sequence. A more likely possibility is that he revised his earlier account by bringing Ragnemod's career up to date.

[56] Gregory wrote that the man was blinded *primo die paschae* and healed *in una die resurrectionis dominicae*. Although L. Pietri (1983) 452n.78, 457 suggests that the first day was Easter Sunday and identifies the "day of the Lord's resurrection" as simply a later Sunday, the context of the story suggests that Ursulf was blinded on the first day of Lent and healed on Easter Sunday, and that the "two months" of praying and fasting corresponded to Lent.

uted two medicines for a single illness? Behold, two miracles were displayed for one blind man: first [Martin] opened the eyes of this man's body so that he might see the things of this world, and now he has illuminated the eyes of his heart lest he lust after the things of this world. He also deigned to dedicate for his service this man whom he caused to be reborn, so to speak, in this world.

14. The paralyzed girl

Nor will I pass over this story about what this patron did during his own festival [on July 4, 575]. A girl named Palatina[57] was afflicted with the swelling of paralysis, lost the use of her feet, and was so badly affected that the nerves in her knees stiffened and she bent her heels to her thighs. Her father brought her to Tours and piously placed her before the feet of the blessed Martin; she lay there for three months and begged alms from people who passed by. But on the day of the notable festival of the blessed man, while I was reciting the mass, it happened that she was faithfully praying in the spot that I mentioned earlier. While I was formally celebrating the holy ceremony, I recited the prefatory prayer about the miracles of our holy Lord; suddenly she began to shout and weep and indicated that she was being tormented. But when upon the completion of the prefatory prayer the entire congregation proclaimed the *Sanctus* in praise of the Lord, immediately her nerves that had been bound were loosened, and she stood on her own feet as the entire congregation was watching. And so, with the support of the Lord but without anyone's assistance, she walked on her own feet to receive communion at the holy altar. To this day she has remained healthy.

15. The blind man who recovered his sight

Merobaudis was from a district [in the territory] of Poitiers. While he was working at a task, he was afflicted with a terrible blindness at the instigation of a treacherous [demon]. For six years he endured this illness and suffered badly. Then he went to the sacred church of the blessed Martin, and there he constantly knelt in prayer. On the day after the holy festival while he was standing at the feet of St. Martin, suddenly it seemed to him as if lightning had flashed around him; immediately his eyes were opened, and he saw everything. He at once became a cleric in the same place, and then he left with his health.

16. The stories that a boatman told

There was also that notable miracle when on the day of Epiphany the

---

[57] In his index Krusch listed "Palatina" as the girl's name; L. Pietri (1983) 552n.111 takes *palatina quaedam puella* as "a girl at the royal court."

Lord made Falernian wine from water at the request of the blessed bishop, and he who once changed water into wine produced wine for a poor man from the bottom of a river. Once while I was traveling in the district of Baugy I came to the Loire River. When I carefully asked the boatman who was contracted to transport me to the opposite bank about places to which I might go to fish, he pointed out a spot and said: "May the blessed Martin assist you." But my companions were annoyed upon hearing these words and said that no [fish] was ever seen to have been caught in his name. The boatman [replied]: "There is no doubt that his power is responsible. For let me tell you what happened to me this year, and how I deserved [to receive] what I wished for by invoking his name and with the assistance of the Lord. For it was the day of Epiphany, and I found nothing to drink when I entered my storeroom. I exited, prayed, and said: 'Most blessed Martin, on this holy festival day give me some wine, so that I might not remain hungry while others are feasting.' While I was silently praying, I heard on the opposite bank a voice calling me to bring my boat for a man who was traveling. I took my oars and began to row over the pounding fury of the waves. When I reached the middle of the river, suddenly a huge fish was thrown from a whirlpool and fell into my boat. Immediately I seized it; and after transporting the men, I returned home, sold the fish for a container of wine, and was refreshed with the other people. Hence you will know how quickly [Martin] will appear on behalf of something for which he has been invoked, if the request is made piously." I call God as a witness that I heard this story from the mouth of this boatman.[58]

17. Duke Guntramn

One day Guntramn Boso was crossing the Loire River opposite the village of Amboise. Darkness was already closing in and a dreadful night was covering the world, when suddenly the wind shifted and the boatmen were thrown into the water. The boats that supported the bridge were separated and completely filled with water, and along with these boats everyone sank into the water up to their hips; nor [could] the boats be beached by [using] their sails. Although everyone was frightened, Boso calmly raised his voice, proclaimed the assistance of the blessed Martin, and prayed that he quickly appear and save them. Boso piously said to his servants: "Do not be afraid; for I know that the holy man's right hand has been readied to offer assistance especially when needed." As he said these words, the boats were aligned by God, the opposing wind was changed into a favorable wind, no one was lost, and they came to the shore. There the timely assistance of the blessed confessor was so helpful that they even

---

[58] Bishop Martin had in fact once helped a deacon catch a fish: see Sulpicius Severus, *Dial.* 3.10.

recovered the silver that they had lost in the voracious river when the current finally washed it up on the shore.[59]

18. Landulf, a madman

A man named Landulf, from the territory of Vienne, was so severely afflicted by the attack of a mad demon that he often thought he was being besieged by an enemy and fell to the ground; as he spewed bloody spittle from his mouth, he was treated as if a dead man. The authority of expert doctors called this sort of disease epilepsy; but the countryfolk said that this man had the "falling sickness," because he fell down. The aforementioned man realized that he was being tormented to the point of death; when he heard about the reputation of the blessed champion, he went to his holy church so that the assistance that was available to everyone might help him. But although he was full of faith when he came to this place, the savage demon boldly and eagerly assaulted him; nor was it possible for him to leave the courtyard because of this open attack by demons, although he harmed nothing in the courtyard. For the demons arrived conspicuously with the loud clatter of their weapons and tried to stab him with the useless points of their spears. If he knelt on the ground, a dreadful swarm of frogs seemed to hop over him, and he also heard voices that clearly criticized him and said: "The Martin whom you have petitioned will be completely unable to assist you, because you have been subjected to our power." Landulf did not move; instead he piously opposed these words with the sign of the cross and fearfully scattered these demons into thin air. After this hostile [demon had tried] these ineffective and unsuccessful threats, and when he saw that he was unable to claim the man for himself, he attempted to delude him with guile. The demon transformed himself into the appearance of a veteran soldier, came to the man, and said: "I am the Martin whom you are invoking. Rise and pray before me, if you wish to recover your health." Landulf replied to him: "If you are lord Martin, make the sign of the cross over me; then I will believe." But once the demon heard the name of the sign [of the cross] that is always opposed to him, he vanished as if smoke. Then Landulf stood at the feet of his glorious lord [Martin] and was affected by a mental daze; he saw that the blessed church was shining in a fresh light. The saint came out of the church and said to him: "Your prayer has been heard, and behold! you will be healed of the illness from which you suffer." And so he made the sign of the blessed cross over his head and departed. Once Landulf returned to his senses, all his attacks had departed, and he felt that he had recovered his original health.

[59] Guntramn Boso was one of King Sigibert's dukes who had killed Theudebert, King Chilperic's son, in battle earlier in 575 (*Hist.* 4.50); he had then taken refuge in the church of St. Martin. After the assassination of Sigibert later in 575, Chilperic tried to capture him (*VM* 2.27).

But after the recovery of his health he began to drink wine to excess; and after he had besotted his body that had long abstained from wine, his side, one foot, and a hand stiffened up. But when he again dedicated himself to abstinence and tonsured his head, again he was restored to his health by the power of the blessed [Martin].

19. Theudomer, a blind deacon

As I am recording these particular miracles of the blessed man briefly and not amplifying them in a more elaborate account, I pursue my unfinished task with great respect and trepidation, lest perhaps it be said by wiser men that an educated man could expand these stories at great length. But it seems to me, as I am concerned with the teaching of the church, that a history that is relevant to the building up of the church is [to be] written in a concise and clear account without any verbosity, so that it may both reveal the power of the blessed bishop and not generate any aversion in learned men. If this is accomplished, the reader will be challenged in the reading selection, and the saint will be revealed in the deed.

The deacon Theudomer suffered from a swelling on his head; when cataracts developed, the openings to his eyes were painfully blocked for four years. Then he went to the cell at Candes in which the blessed man had died. He knelt at his bed and spent the entire night [there] without moving; he moistened the ground with his tears and cherished the venerable wood of the railing with his sighs. When daylight came, the cataracts on his eyes were opened, and he deserved to see the daylight. What [cure] such as this one have doctors ever accomplished with their implements? Their efforts produce more pain than healing; and after stretching and piercing an eye with their needles they fashion the torments of death before they open the eye. If caution is lacking in this operation, the doctor is providing eternal blindness for the wretched patient. But the blessed confessor's implement is his affection, and his ointment is simply his power.

20. Desiderius, a possessed man

Desiderius was a possessed man who came from Clermont. After he had raved madly for an entire night in this cell [at Candes], at dawn he began to shout that the blessed Martin was burning him. As he was shouting, he coughed up an unfamiliar pus and blood; the demon was cast out, and he was cleansed. He left behind sand stained with his blood, and he departed from the cell as a healthy man.

21. The man who had a contracted hand

In this same place a man presented his disabled hand. His fingers were so bent that his nails were stabbed into his palms and caused him much pain; sometimes blood trickled out. This man threw himself before the aforementioned bed of the glorious lord [Martin]; the pain as well as his faith caused him to weep and pray. On the next day his fingers were straightened, and he recovered a hand that was healthy.

22. Remigia, a married woman

Remigia, a married woman, suffered from a similar disability and with great piety came to the blessed cell [at Candes]. She devoted herself to vigils and prayers; and while she was helping with the register [of poor people] who gathered there, she received a cure for her withered arm and stiffened fingers so that she might prepare drinks. And so for the entire day she helped these blessed poor people, before she returned to her own home as a healthy woman. Thereafter every year this woman brought adequate food for these aforementioned brothers.

It happened that one of her maidservants was once badly afflicted with a quartan fever. When Remigia came as usual and brought food for the poor people, she requested the assistance of the holy man. After the servant lay in the blessed cell for four days continuously praying and fasting, she was completely cured from her fever. Remigia praised God and went home with her servant.

23. Vinast, a blind man

While he was performing similar deeds and supplying the food necessary for these poor people, a man named Vinast recovered his sight. Although this man had suffered from total blindness for many years, it was his custom to travel from his own district to the saint's aforementioned cell and provide extravagant support for these poor people. After he had most piously celebrated vigils, he generously nourished these people whom he assisted as was necessary just like a servant. For many years, as I said, Vinast performed these tasks. Once, after he had simultaneously fulfilled both his pledge and his service, he knelt before the railing around the holy bed, prayed, paid his respects, and then wished to leave. But when he stood up after finishing his prayer, his eyes were slightly opened, and he saw the silk curtain that was hanging from the railing. He said: "I see [something] like a silk curtain hanging here." His servants said to him: "We know that you are in fact seeing [again]." Vinast then began to weep and to pray again that the blessed confessor would properly complete the task that he had begun. While he was earnestly praying, he fell asleep, and a man appeared to him in a vision and said: "Go to the church of lord Martin, and there you will obtain a complete cure." Vinast did not delay. He was led by the hands of his servants, and when he reached the threshold [of the church] of the blessed confessor, with the assistance of his faith he completely regained his eyesight.

24. The boy who was crippled in all his limbs

At Bourges there was a woman who conceived and gave birth to a son whose knees were bent up to his stomach and his heels back to his legs, whose hands hugged his chest, and whose eyes were closed. This boy resembled more closely some monster than the appearance of a man, and many laughed when they saw him. When his mother was criticized because she had produced such a son, she wept and confessed that he had been conceived on the night before a Sunday. She did not dare to kill him; instead, as is customary for mothers, she raised him as if he were a healthy child. After he was grown, she gave him to beggars who took him, put him on a wagon, hauled him about, and displayed him to the people; the beggars received much charity because of him. This went on for a long time. When he was eleven years old, the boy came to the festival of the blessed Martin. He was thrown inside [the church] and lay in misery before the tomb. At the conclusion of the festival he recovered his sight and his hearing. Then he returned to his usual occupation and requested alms. After almost a year or more he came again to the festival [on November 11, 575] and was placed in the spot where he had lain previously; when the celebrations of the festival were completed, all his limbs were straightened, and he received his complete health. Lest these events perhaps seem unbelievable, [let me say that] I saw this boy after he was cured, and I learned about these events not secondhand from someone else but as they were told by his lips. But since I have already mentioned that this had happened to his parents because of their sin when they desecrated the night before a Sunday, therefore, you men who are joined in marriage, watch out! Be content to indulge your lust on the other days, but observe this day without pollution in praise of God. For if [intercourse] takes place, then children are born who are crippled or suffer from epilepsy or leprosy. Let this be the proof, so that a sin that is committed on one night might not be endured for the space of many years.

25. The paralyzed man who was healed

At your insistence I will narrate this miracle that is more praiseworthy than the others. After excessive sorrow had accumulated, this miracle offered us much joy, because it revealed the power of the blessed [Martin], it deflected whatever was faltering, and it fortified the wavering hearts of the people with great firmness and certainty. For after we had kept the holy vigils during the blessed night [before the day] of our Lord's birth [on Christmas 575], we walked from the cathedral and intended to go to the saint's church. But one of the possessed people, who was bolder than the others, began to rave wildly and scratch and pummel himself; he cried out: "In vain do you seek the threshold [of the church] of Martin, and in vain do you enter the shrine of the one who has abandoned you because of your many misdeeds. Behold, because he recoils from you, he works miracles at Rome. There he bestows sight upon the eyes of blind people, restores the mobility of paralyzed people, and by his power also puts an end to other illnesses." The entire congregation was upset at the remarks of this demon, and not only were ordinary people dumbfounded in their hearts, but even I myself was struck with fear. Then we entered the church while weeping loudly. We all knelt on the pavement and prayed that we might be worthy of the holy man's presence. And behold, there was a man named Bonulf, whose two hands as well as one foot had been crippled three years previously because of the high fever from an illness; although his hands had been restored during a festival of the blessed man, he limped because his foot was still lame. He now knelt before the holy altar and prayed that he who had restored his withered hands might also straighten his crippled foot with a similar display of his power. During his prayer Bonulf was surrounded with an intense heat and, as if stabbed with a sharp point, tormented with pain in his tendons. Then the pain made the suppliant defiant, and the man who had come to request medicine began to make false statements. For Bonulf said: "O lord Martin, I sought my health from you, not torments. If I do not deserve my health, let me not be tormented by these pains." We were standing nearby weeping and hoping for the arrival of the blessed Martin. Meanwhile the sacred ceremonies were being performed and the holy gifts were placed on the altar. While the mystery of the body and blood of Christ was as usual covered by a shroud, the knots on Bonulf's tendons were softened, the skin of the man's lame knee was torn, a trickle of blood flowed out, and he stretched out a healthy foot. When I saw this, I gave thanks to omnipotent God, and as my eyes filled with tears, I addressed the congregation with these words: "Let all fear depart from your hearts, because the blessed confessor is dwelling among us, and certainly do not believe the demon who has never spoken the truth. 'He is a deceiver from the beginning and has not stood in the truth' [cf. John 8:44]." As I said these words, everyone's sorrow was dissipated by happiness. This lame man rose up before us and stood on his feet without any handicap. The entire congregation saw this, offered a shout to heaven, applauded, and said: "Glory to God in the highest; just as he once shone on the shepherds with the light of the angels, so he has today shone upon us with the presence of his blessed confessor, and through this timely miracle he has demonstrated that [Martin] is here with us." And in this way everyone was rescued from their fear of the hostile [demon] and strengthened with the assistance of Christ.[60]

[60] After the assassination of King Sigibert, his young son Childebert had been proclaimed king on Christmas 575 (*Hist.* 5.1, 8.4). Since Sigibert had previously included Tours in his kingdom, the insecurity and sorrow of this Christmas at Tours may have been an indication of uncertainty over the authority of the new king; and in fact King Chilperic soon again seized Tours (*VM* 2.27). Gregory, as usual, stressed the numerous miracles of St. Martin during this year (*Hist.* 5.6).

26. Piolus, a mute man

On the holy day of Epiphany [on January 6, 576] the blessed man appeared with a similar miracle when in the presence of the people he opened the obstructed throat of a mute man. Piolus was a cleric from Candes. He had lived since birth despite offering hands that were too twisted for any tool and therefore useless for any labor. I do not have the ability to determine why this happened, or whether this man or his parents had sinned so that he was born crippled in this way. But I do know this one fact, that the goodwill of the bishop was revealed in him just as in other ill people. For when he was ten years old, he suffered severe pains in his hands as his fingernails grew, and when he could not tolerate these pains, he went to the threshold [of the church] of the blessed confessor. After staying there for many days in great poverty, he received fingers that were straightened and hands that were healthy. Almost five years later he suffered a very serious illness, and while he was weakened by the intensity of a high fever, he lost the sound of his voice; although he was rescued from the fever, he was left without the ability to speak. The passageway of his throat was obstructed in such a way that he was unable to make any noise at all. Instead he tied three boards together with string and carried them in his hand; when these boards were clicked together, he produced the sound that he [could] not make in his throat. This skill was useful to vine-dressers as they tried to protect their vineyards from flocks of troublesome birds. But after the aforementioned man had come to the saint's church on [the anniversary of] the night on which the Lord Jesus Christ drew up streams of water and offered Falernian wine, he decided to keep vigils at the feet of the blessed [Martin]. When midnight passed, he fell asleep. In a vision he recognized some unknown danger and was petrified with fear; then for the first time he opened his mouth that had been closed with these words: "Lord Martin, free me!" And so he vomited blood from his mouth and throat and then recovered both his hearing and his speaking.

27. The paralyzed woman

After King Sigibert's death [late in 575, his young son Childebert] was rescued from an imminent death. [His uncle King] Chilperic infringed on his kingdom. Then Roccolen, with the assistance of men from Le Mans, besieged Tours so harshly that he destroyed everything and left no hope of support for the houses that belonged to the cathedral or for the houses of the poor. On the following day he sent envoys to the city [who demanded] that the clerics expel the men who were seeking sanctuary in the saint's church because of the misdeed that you know about; and Roccolen promised that everything would be consumed in a fire if there was any hesitation in doing this. When I heard these demands, I was very upset, and I went to the holy church and requested the assistance of the blessed [Martin]. And immediately a woman who had been crippled for twelve years was healed of her paralysis. But Roccolen himself advanced to the opposite bank [of the Loire River]. Immediately he was afflicted with the royal malady [of jaundice] and tormented with the ailments of Herod, which it seems tedious to describe; and just like a wax candle that drop by drop wastes away at the sight of a flame, fifty days later he was swollen from dropsy and died. But I will not be silent about the fact that at that time, either at the command of God or because of the power of the blessed man, the bed of the Loire River was swollen [with water] even though there were no floods from rain. Then the river prevented the enemy from crossing and harming the city.[61]

28. The blind woman

During the annual festival on that day [before Easter 576] when the Lord who would suffer for the salvation of the world exposed his treacherous disciple and shared a supper with his apostles, everyone hurried to the cathedral in order to fulfill vows that were pleasing to the Lord. One woman who had suffered from blindness for a long time began to weep because she was at her estate and to say: "Woe is me who do not deserve to see this festival with the rest of the congregation, because I have been blinded by my sins!" Then she wept loudly, knelt on the ground, and called upon the name of the blessed confessor; once she finished her prayer, she was restored to her original sight. After she received her sight, she then went with marvelous clarity in her eyes to the blessed church to return thanks to God. One of the possessed people was also cured by the saint's power on that day.

29. The two blind men

From Bourges came two blind men whose eyelids were withered and obscured by a sticky discharge; they knelt and prayed at the feet of the blessed lord [Martin]. This happened on the day of his festival [on July 4, 576]; and in the presence of the congregation, while the miracle stories were being read from his *Vita*, a flash similar to a lightning bolt flared over

---

[61] After the proclamation of King Childebert, his uncle Chilperic quickly sent Roccolen to Tours to capture Guntramn Boso (*VM* 2.17). Roccolen first dismantled a house across the Loire that belonged to the cathedral; then, even though Gregory reminded him of the power of St. Martin and even though he already suffered from jaundice, Roccolen still entered Tours for this festival of Epiphany and visited both the cathedral and the church of St. Martin. Roccolen soon left for Poitiers, where he died on February 29 (*Hist.* 5.4). For the painful death of King Herod, see *Hist.* 1.24; Gregory also once belittled Chilperic as the "Nero and Herod of our time" (*Hist.* 6.46).

the men. The bonds that blocked their eyelids were broken, blood flowed from their eyes, their sight was completely clear, and they deserved to see everything.

30. The mute woman

Excessive swelling combined with a fever had frozen a woman's mouth open so that she was unable to control her tongue; because she was unable to speak like a human, she instead only bellowed like an animal. At the motivation of her faith and with great confidence in her heart she went to the courtyards [of the church] of the blessed confessor. She remained there for many days and requested both alms and control over her mouth; then the saint's power took note of her. For on a Sunday while mass was being celebrated this woman was standing in the holy church with the rest of the congregation. Then it happened that during the recitation of the Lord's Prayer this woman too opened her mouth and began to chant the holy prayer with the other people. Since this woman had previously been bound by the yoke of slavery, she was redeemed by the assistance of the blessed confessor, and even now she is still a free woman with the ability to speak.

31. Another crippled woman

Through a miracle that was no less significant the blessed man revealed that he was present after being invoked. A nun named Apra suffered from a burning fever and lost the use of all her limbs; only her tongue was still at her service. Because her hands as well as her feet were crippled, she lay there and day and night requested the assistance of the blessed [Martin]. One night it seemed to her that an old man came to her and gently touched and stroked all her limbs. In the morning she awoke and with one hand discovered that her feet had been restored to health. She was surprised and did not know the reason for this cure. On another day she received instructions in her sleep and without hesitation went to the blessed church. It was the night for the vigil before [the festival celebrating] the confessor's death [on November 11, 576]. After midnight as she was keeping the vigil, she was startled by some unknown fear, and immediately her crippled hand was straightened. The congregation was amazed, and she recounted everything that she had previously suffered. She realized that it had been the power of him who had previously strengthened her feet and was now obviously straightening her hand.

32. The oil that increased at his tomb

Since I see every day such miracles as I have recorded, what will be said by those disgusting men who claimed that [Sulpicius] Severus included lies in his *Vita* of the holy bishop? For I have heard a man (who was, I think, certainly not filled with the Spirit) as he proclaimed that [the story about] the oil that increased because of Martin's blessing could not have happened; he also doubted that the flask that slipped loose and fell to the marble floor remained intact.[62] Therefore, by producing many stories as evidence I will demonstrate that this recently happened [again].

One of my deacons suffered painfully from a quartan fever. Because I repeatedly criticized him for being sluggish in going to the saint's church and for not praying from his heart that the power of the bishop assist him, he was finally goaded by my complaints and nervously knelt before the blessed tomb. After his blazing fever eased a bit, he asked that his flask that was half-filled with rose oil be brought out; for even though [relief for] his fever had made little progress, he had already spent much on it. The flask was brought out in the open. The deacon sprinkled his forehead and his temples with this oil and asked that the flask be placed beside the tomb of the blessed [Martin]. Four days later when the fever was again afflicting him, he went to the church, knelt, and prayed for a very long time. When he picked up the flask that he had left in the open, he found that it was full [of oil]. He was impressed by the power of the blessed bishop, and fearfully and respectfully he took the flask home. Once he was again anointed from the flask, immediately his burning affliction vanished entirely, and he was never again shattered by the same affliction.

With deep longing I also record a miracle about what happened next to this same flask. For while it was hanging from the wall in the lodging of the aforementioned deacon, it was assaulted by the treachery of a hostile [demon]. The flask was struck, fell down, and was smashed into bits, and the dirt quickly soaked up the oil that poured out. When a servant who was there saw what had happened, he took a container, squeezed the dirt, and recovered a bit of the oil. Then he collected the rose that had flowed out and the fragments of broken glass and brought them to me. I took these remains and carefully transferred them to another container. The amount of oil was about equal to half of a small cup, and in its container it reached a height of only two fingers. But on the next day I looked and the height of the oil was about four fingers. I was amazed at the power of the holy oil, and I left the container covered and secured with my seal. Seven days later I looked again and found there more than one pint. I summoned the deacon and showed this to him, and he insisted with an oath that he now saw in this container as much oil as had been lost in the broken flask. Still today this container is effective for people who seek a blessing in the name of God. For this deacon then sprinkled a man suffering from a similar illness with this ointment and healed him, as the oil again increased; thereafter he restored many people to health with this oil.

[62] For the stories about the oil that increased and the glass flask that did not shatter, see Sulpicius Severus, *Dial.* 3.3.

33. Allomer, a crippled man

The region of Angers might also produce its own miracle. Allomer came from this region and sought the church of the blessed confessor. He [suffered] from crippled feet and hands and was also unable to speak. During the whole of Lent he stayed at the church, constantly praying and asking that the power of the holy bishop assist him. Then came the [Palm] Sunday before holy Easter [in 577] on which our Lord arrived at Jerusalem and rode through the streets that were covered with tree branches, while the crowd that followed was shouting: "Hosanna, blessed is he who comes in the name of the Lord" [cf. Matt. 21:9]. Because it was already late in the day, Allomer was lying alone outside near the tomb. Suddenly he was shaken with terror and so fearfully horrified that he lay there as if dead. After he was overcome [in this way] for two or more hours (as he himself claimed), suddenly he awoke as if from a nap and was restored to his senses. He was raised up and was astonished [to discover] that he was healthy. He kept vigils there for the entire night, and in the morning he disclosed to me with his own mouth what had happened. Then he became a cleric and returned with his health to his own lodging.[63]

34. The blind monk

During that same year the day came for [observing] the festival [of Martin on July 4, 577] that is celebrated during the summer and that is welcome to the people. A cleric whose eye was obscured by a dark cloud that blocked the light so that he could not see came to the church of the blessed confessor. With the other people he kept vigils during the night; when he left the church as the sky began to brighten, he deserved to recover the sight that he had once lost. During the same festival three possessed men were often beating themselves and calling upon the blessed bishop. They confessed their misdeeds and begged that the saint pardon them. Finally they spit some unknown filth from their mouths and in this way were healed by the saint's power.

35. The men in prison who were released

Soon thereafter, that is, on the third day after this festival, four men were confined in prison. Because the judge had fettered them so brutally that it was not possible to offer any of them the necessary sustenance, with pure hearts they requested the assistance of the blessed bishop. As they piously did this, suddenly at noon the stocks that enclosed and restricted their feet were split, the chains were broken, and the men realized that they had been freed. Immediately they went to the door, opened it, and entered the holy

---

[63] Elsewhere Gregory noted that in 577 Gallic cities celebrated Easter on April 18 and Spanish cities on March 21 (*Hist.* 5.17).

cathedral without anyone's opposing them. The prison guards were so surprised that they did not dare to rebuke these men even with words; instead, they followed the men and took refuge with them in the cathedral. Then they most gratefully thanked God, because through the intercession of the bishop he had deigned to free them.

36. The relics that Bishop Leodovald brought back

Many people who are filled with faith experience many miracles as they carry relics of the blessed man. Bishop Leodovald of Avranches [sent] his priest and piously requested relics of the holy lord [Martin]. The priest took the relics; when he entered the territory of the aforementioned city, a paralyzed man who was brought by those carrying him in their hands met the priest when he was still in a deserted region. After the paralyzed man piously kissed the shroud that covered the reliquary with the holy relics, soon he stood on his own feet and returned home under his own power. Most blessed confessor, you perform these miracles, but it is still not sufficient for you to decorate your own church with wonders unless you also dignify with outstanding miracles the various regions that you did not visit on foot. Then a blind man quickly hurried with the assistance of his cane to meet these relics. He approached, and when the relics of the blessed [Martin] were placed in the altar and the ceremony was completed, he deserved to receive sight in his eyes. And another woman who had been mute for a long time similarly recovered the use of her speech.[64]

37. The possessed man who was cured

During these days one of the possessed people [came] to the church of the blessed man. When his demon shouted that he was suffering from many torments and admitted that he was being forcibly expelled by the blessed bishop from the body that he had possessed, the man was thrown to the ground and began to vomit putrid blood from his mouth. He lay there for almost two hours, and after the demon was expelled, he was cleansed and raised up.

38. The mute girl

A young girl who was a native of Tours was born mute from her mother's womb. Her mouth was so blocked up that she was unable to produce the cries that her years in her cradle required. Her mother worried about such a sad child, and because she constantly wept, she was advised in a vision to go to the tomb of the blessed champion. Without any fear she went and brought her daughter with her. She placed her daughter in front of the

---

[64] Leodovald had become bishop of Avranches in 576 or 577, shortly before he requested these relics: see Weidemann (1982) 1:141.

saint's tomb, and after she had prayed for a very long time, she again took her daughter with her. As she held her daughter over the censers of incense that were burning, she asked whether they produced a scent that she found pleasant. Her daughter replied: "The scent is pleasant." The grieving mother realized that these were her daughter's first words. Then she sprinkled water that she had received from the blessed fountains on her daughter's face and asked again what sort of flavor it offered her. Her daughter replied: "The flavor is wonderful." Then her mother rejoiced and brought home a healthy daughter whom with confidence in her faith she had sadly brought to the tomb of the blessed [Martin].

39. What the priest Aredius carried as a blessing

Aredius was a monk from Limoges. He came to Tours because of his great piety, and after he kissed the blessed tomb and prayed, he crossed the [Loire] River and went to the holy monastery [of Marmoutier]. There he visited each depression that the blessed man had made while praying, each spot that he had sanctified while chanting Psalms, and each place that had offered him sleep for his weary body or food as he grew weak from fasting. As Aredius wandered about and visited all these places, he came to the well that the saint of God had dug with his own labor. Aredius offered a prayer, drank the water, and took away a small flask that he had dipped [in the water] before he returned home. Thereafter the flask bestowed cures upon many ill people. Then his brother Renosind was struck by a high fever and lay on his bed. Eight days later his eyes were closed, and he lay in such [weakness] that he exhaled his spirit. The entire household wailed and grieved for the death of its patron, and as it prepared the requirements for his funeral, the priest [Aredius] had the idea of putting a drop of the water from the blessed well in the mouth [of Renosind] who was on the verge of dying. The water was brought out, and as soon as it touched his mouth, the ill man opened his eyes. Once his tongue was freed, Renosind asked that assistance be given him. He took a cup [filled with water], and as he drank, his fever immediately and completely left him. And so, as his household watched, he was raised up with his health from the bed in which he was lying.[65]

---

[65] For Aredius, see the note to *VJ* 28. The chronology of this story is puzzling. According to Gregory's account elsewhere, as a young boy Aredius had served at the court of Theudebert, king from 534 until 548, before becoming a cleric under Bishop Nicetius of Trier. He finally returned to his mother Pelagia at Limoges only after his father and his brother had died (*Hist.* 10.29). Krusch (1885) 623n.1 therefore argues that Aredius had traveled to Tours and collected this water from Marmoutier before he went to Trier. Yet Gregory explicitly noted in this story that Aredius was a priest when he helped to heal his brother, which would suggest that he had already served with Nicetius; and he did not indicate that Aredius had visited Marmoutier decades earlier than the date of 577 implied by the inclusion of the story in this

40. Sisulf, an ill man

What can my littleness next say about these miracles when this saint of God, even though taken from this world, is still preaching in this world? For although he is unable to reveal himself to people in person, he is constantly displaying himself through his obvious miracles whenever he restores sight to the blind, cures the paralyzed, and reinstates other ill people to their previous health. As I have often insisted, I think that I am unworthy to record the miracles of such a great man. But because I am rashly daring [to do so], I request the reader's indulgence. My love for my patron strongly compels me, and because I have noted that he is still preaching, let me record what happened recently.

Sisulf was a poor man from Le Mans. While he was napping in his little garden at noon, he suffered some unknown mishap and woke from his sleep. Because his fingers were bent into his palm, he lifted his disabled hands in great pain. The pain was overwhelming, and he slipped again into sleep and had a vision. For behold! Standing in front of him was a man dressed in black but with white hair. The man turned to him and said: "Why are you so upset and in tears?" Sisulf said: "Behold, reverend lord, while I was taking a short nap I awoke in pain and lost the use of my hands, but I do not know what misdeed I have committed." Then the man [replied] just as the Lord [once spoke] to his disciples [when he explained that] a man had been born blind not because either he or his parents had sinned but so that the power of God might be made manifest in him [cf. John 9:2]. He said: "Your disability reveals the anguish that awaits sinful people. Therefore go now through the villages and the fortresses, travel as far as the city, and proclaim that everyone is to abstain from perjury and usury and that on Sundays no one is to do any work contrary to the mystical rites [of the liturgy]. For behold, we will kneel and weep in the presence of the Lord and pray for forgiveness for the people, and if there is subsequent reform among the people, then there is still hope of obtaining [forgiveness]. For the wrath of the Lord is causing the hatreds and illnesses and other evils that the people endure. And therefore be prompt in announcing that people are to reform, lest they die a cruel death as a result of their own crimes. After you have done what I have ordered, then hurry to the church at Tours; I will visit you there, and I will beg the Lord that you might be healed." Sisulf said to him: "I ask you, my lord, tell me who you are; what is your name?" The man replied to him: "I am Martin, bishop of Tours." With these words of the saint the poor man awoke from his sleep. He took his staff, set out on the required journey, and announced to the

sequence of miracles. Note too that Aredius's will, made jointly with Pelagia in 572, named his brother as Eustadius and described him as deceased: ed. Pardessus (1843–1849) 1:139, no. 180, and *PL* 71.1146, with Nonn (1972) 27–28, on the uncertain authenticity of this will.

people what had been commanded of him. After these events happened, he came to the blessed church during the seventh month [September 577]. For three days he knelt there, and on the fourth day he was rewarded by the saint's power. For the skin in the palms [of his hands] that were fastened shut was beginning to putrefy; but when his fingers were straightened, blood flowed from his palms. Once all his fingers were healed, with his own mouth he described what I have narrated.

41. The blind man who received his sight
Most blessed confessor, you therefore act in your customary manner by forgiving people's sins, by healing everyone's illnesses, by bestowing your medicines on all who faithfully call upon you, and by not depriving unbelievers of whatever you generously bestow upon your own people. An inhabitant of the territory of Tours had been completely blind for almost twenty-five years, ever since cataracts had formed and his eyelids had been closed after he had been afflicted with an inflammation in his eyes. In addition to this affliction another was added: he had been struck with a club, his sight was interrupted, and one of his eyes snapped. He had lived with his blindness for twenty-five years already. Then, after receiving advice in a vision, he went to the blessed tomb, where he knelt and prayed; three days later he received sight in one eye. Because he was revived by this medicine, he began to pray more earnestly. Four days later the eye that had snapped was opened, and its sight restored. Although [the vision in] this eye was not as clear as [that in] the other, it nevertheless offered the gift of sight.

42. The man whose hand was paralyzed
A disabled man whose paralyzed hand was stiff was praying earnestly in the courtyard that is in front of the tomb of the blessed [Martin]. During the holy vigil for him [before his festival on November 11, 577] this man was rewarded; his fingers were straightened, and his hand was healed and restored to its original usage.[66]

43. The little boy who was revived
Oh, how often do I marvel at the renewal of those miracles of the prophets and other distinguished men that I have read happened long ago! But what am I saying? What those many men did while alive in this world, this man single-handedly renews every day even after his burial. What therefore am I to do? Why am I silent? Why do we few men conceal what many people proclaim? I will not delay any longer in this inertia. Let me

---

[66] During this vigil Gregory and his congregation also saw a star shining in the middle of the moon, other stars near the moon, and a halo around the moon that indicated rain (*Hist.* 5.23).

present the new Elisha for our times who brought back the corpse of a dead man alive from his tomb [cf. 2 Kings 13:21]; and the blessed confessor did this in my presence. I call upon the assistance of the undivided Trinity in order to explain the circumstances.

After his birth a little boy was given to a nurse for feeding, because no milk was available from his mother. The nurse also did not have milk, and because she did not nourish him with enough milk as was proper for his tender age, the boy who should have grown began to shrink with each passing day and was so starved that nothing remained of him except the thin skin that covered his small bones. After his mother's death this little boy lived almost one year in this death warrant; for his father he was the only reminder of his wife's love. A fever attacked this little boy who, as I said, was wasting away from hunger and dying from starvation. When this fever assailed him, his father ran to the cathedral, so that his son would not die without being baptized. After his baptism the boy received no physical relief in addition to this spiritual cure; instead, there was a stabbing pain in his eyes, his eyelids fluttered and drooped, and he no longer exhaled any breath. His father wept, and the young boy was placed before the blessed tomb. But that heavenly power that had once revived a young boy between the hands of the confessor was not lacking.[67] For as soon as the shroud over the tomb touched this young boy's clothing, immediately he breathed again. This was a marvelous miracle! For you might see his pale cheeks gradually become red as the divine power took effect and his senseless eyes open as sight was restored. Then the young boy was revived by the saint and received again by his father. He is still healthy today as a witness to this miracle.

44. The blind man who received his sight

A blind man from Poitiers had been deprived of his sight for six years. After he had knelt and prayed at the blessed tomb for three days, he recovered through the assistance of [Martin's] usual power the sight that he had lost. This happened during the festival of our patron saint [on July 4, 578] attended by Bishop Maroveus of Poitiers, a deservedly praiseworthy disciple of the most blessed Hilary. At the conclusion of the festival Maroveus rejoiced and returned to his own city with his fellow citizen who had received his sight.[68]

45. The two boys who were healed

On the night before a Sunday two young boys were sleeping in a single bed at Voultegon, a village [in the territory] of Poitiers. It seemed to them as

---

[67] Sulpicius Severus, *Dial.* 2.4.4–7, described how Martin had revived a boy near Chartres.

[68] On Maroveus, see above, chapter 1, section 2. Weidemann (1982) 1:207n.435, 209, and Corbett (1983) 56, prefer to date this festival to November 11, 577 (cf. *VM* 2.42).

if they had heard the ringing of the bell that was usually rung for matins. They rose from their bed and walked to the church. When they came into the courtyard of the church, they found there a chorus of women who were singing. Upon realizing that this was a gathering of demons, the boys were thoroughly terrified and fell to the ground. As is characteristic of their tender age they did not protect themselves with the sign of salvation; so one was deprived of his sight, and the other of his sight and mobility. After they suffered from their infirmities through the passage of many years, the one boy who had lost only his sight piously came to the church of the blessed Martin in order to offer a prayer; immediately he recovered his sight. The other boy also recovered his sight in the same holy place, but as he returned home, he was still crippled and lame. He came to the cell at Candes that contained the bed of the blessed man; and while vigils were being celebrated there on the night before a Sunday, he suddenly felt that divine power was present while the people were praying. As the people watched, the boy crawled along the ground and stood up next to the wall in which there was a window that had once been a doorway for [Martin's] blessed body. While praying and weeping for joy the boy was restored to complete health, and never again did he suffer any discomfort from these evil infirmities.

46. The lame man who was healed

A young boy named Leodulf was lame in his left foot. As he was traveling with other people who sought alms by begging, he came to [the territory of] Tours. He rested a short while and then tried to complete the journey that he had begun. He limped as he proceeded with his companions, but ten miles from the city he was overcome by the savage pain. After his companions abandoned him, he was alone on the bank of the river, crying and shouting to the many people who were gathering for the festival [of Martin on November 11, 578]. He said: "Woe is me, for because I was unwilling to attend the festival for this glorious man, his power has crippled me. Therefore I ask you, most pious Christians who fear God, compensate for my ignorance, assist me, a subdued and lame boy, and if there is still some fear of God, carry me all the way to the holy place." While Leodulf was imploring many passersby with these words, one man placed him on his wagon and brought him all the way to the holy church. He stayed there and prayed for three days, and after his feet were healed, he left with his health.

47. The crippled man whom an ox hauled about

There was a crippled man who owned an ox, in imitation of the hermit whose ox had once been his companion. This man was placed on a wagon and hauled among houses while begging alms from the pious. Then he came to Tours as the day for the festival of the bishop was approaching [on

July 4, 579]. He knelt before the tomb, prayed as he lay there, and most piously requested the assistance of the blessed bishop; then he was brought back by his companions and placed in front of the holy apse over the tomb. At the conclusion of mass, as the congregation began to receive the sacred body of the Redeemer, suddenly the bonds that held his knees tight were loosened, and he stood on his own feet. Everyone was surprised. The man gave thanks, walked all the way to the blessed altar on his own feet and without anyone's assistance, and thereafter remained in good health.

48. Another man who had crippled hands and feet

A man named Floridus, whose hands and feet were crippled, was brought from the district of Chênehutte-les-Tuffeaux, which is in the territory of Angers, to the holy cell at Candes from which the blessed confessor had migrated [after his death] to Christ. After he spent a few days keeping vigils and praying, his infirmity departed after being completely banished from his body. Then, once his limbs had been cured, he returned to his home with his health.

49. Another man who had a crippled arm

The joyful day of the blessed festival [of Martin on November 11, 579] had come, and many crowds of people had gathered. And behold, a disabled man with a crippled arm was in attendance. As he kissed the blessed tomb with his lips, moistened it with his tears, and requested the assistance of the blessed confessor with his mouth, he did not doubt his faith as he awaited the usual assistance. Then the clerics who had come advanced to perform mass, followed by the lector whose task it was to read. The lector took the book and began to read the *Vita* of the holy confessor, and immediately this man's arm was cured and he stood up with his health. Everyone was watching as he obtained the assistance that he had piously requested.

50. The blind man who received his sight

Likewise during the same festival a blind man was humbly praying for the return of his sight. When he touched the curtain that hangs from the wall outside at the saint's feet, soon blood flowed from his eyelids, and he received his sight as the people were watching.

51. People with dysentery

The illness of dysentery was afflicting many cities with its latent blisters. When in addition to these other places the city of Tours was suffering badly, many people were cured after scratching dust from the blessed tomb and drinking it. Many other people were freed [from this illness] after being smeared with the oil that was there; and the water with which the tomb was washed before Easter was also a remedy for some. Then, although many blessings were being distributed to many people, I saw one man with dysentery lying in despair. He was brought to the church and stayed awake during the night while other people were celebrating vigils. At dawn he went to the tomb, drank some dust [mixed] with wine, and returned from the tomb with his health.[69]

52. Another man who was cured of a serious swelling

Another man was seized by a severe fever. He vomited poison from his mouth, suffered excessive diarrhea in his lower parts, and lay on his bed. Then, as the poison spread, a tumor appeared on the ill man's groin and by some unbelievable means clearly moved to the sole of his foot. The tumor was the size of a goose egg. Then the tumor returned upward, and with great pain it moved across his chest and his arms and eventually reached his neck. From there it moved down his other side to his foot; then it moved back and returned to the spot where it had first appeared. As this tumor was wandering in this fashion through the ill man's limbs, no one knew where the wretched man was swollen and what was happening until the man screamed in his tears. For whenever these great pains attacked his one small body, the agony made him moan. Finally this affliction was reported to me, and I pointed out that the usual antidote was to be sought from the true doctor and was to be received from the tomb where a man on the verge of death might have life. The man's attendants quickly ran and collected dust from the tomb; they brought it to the ill man, mixed it with wine, and offered it as a drink. Once he drank it, all his pain was banished so [quickly] that at that very hour he was restored to his health.

53. The delirious man who was restored

Upon hearing about such miracles innumerable people [come] from remote regions to seek the assistance of the blessed confessor. This miracle must be considered more laudable than the others; [it describes] how he has restored to men their senses that were stolen by the skill of a demon.

A citizen of Bayeux was very disordered after drinking some wine. While he was traveling on the road, suddenly dust from a field was blown up by opposing gusts of wind. The dust was, as usual, mixed with straw and lifted into the air, and the entire sky became a single cloud of dust. The man was covered by this cloud, lost his senses, and fell from his horse. A short time later he was found by his servants and led home in a confused state. But he

---

[69] Elsewhere Gregory stated that this plague of dysentery first appeared in August 580 (*Hist.* 5.34); since VM 2.54–55 seem to refer to the festival of St. Martin in July, his reporting of the miracles of 580 is a bit jumbled. Among the victims of this plague were two sons of King Chilperic, the wife of King Guntramn, and the count of Angoulême (*Hist.* 5.34–36, 39, 50); note that in the *Histories* Gregory's account of these and other events in 580 is also mixed up. L. Pietri (1983) 447 suggests that the tomb of St. Martin was washed on Maundy Thursday.

became violent and tried to escape, even though no one was pursuing him. Why say more? He was restrained by fetters, secured in chains, and kept in custody. Because there was no opportunity to escape, he ground his teeth and drew blood by biting himself. While this was happening, his parents were advised to bring him to the church of the blessed [Martin]. There he prayed for a long time and then left with his health after pledging to return each year and fulfill his vows to the holy confessor. Next he was tonsured at a nearby monastery and ordained as a priest. He began to serve God actively, although he did not fulfill the vows that he had made to the blessed bishop Martin. Four years later, because power was again, I think, given to a hostile [demon], this man again slipped into a renewed madness. As previously, he was secured in chains and brought to the holy church. He lived there for six or more months, keeping vigils and praying; and after he fulfilled the vows that he had earlier ignored because of laziness, he returned home with his health. But because his sins continued and he was often again drunk with wine, he died with the same affliction.

54. The blind girl from Lisieux

If I describe separately both what is happening and what has happened, I will accumulate a huge collection of the confessor's miracles. Paula was an older woman from Lisieux who lost the sight of her eyes. She came piously to the saint's shrine and during the entire duration of the festival [of Martin on July 4, 580] knelt on the ground and prayed. Three days after the holy festival when her companions were urging her to leave, she asked to be brought to the tomb of the blessed [Martin]. There she knelt repeatedly and rubbed her eyes with the shroud that covered the holy tomb; then she said goodbye and departed. Once she had already boarded the boat, she said: "Blessed confessor, I thank you that I experienced and touched your holy shrine, even if I was not worthy to see it." Then, because she was weeping as she said these words, she wiped her eyes, and while doing so she received her sight. She turned and said: "Is this perhaps the church of the blessed [Martin]?" Her neighbors said that it was. Then she said: "I will return only to offer thanks to my patron for the health that I have received." Many watched as she returned and loudly praised the bishop. She finished her prayer and left rejoicing.

55. The boy who had a crippled hand

During this same festival another boy who had a withered hand came from Sens. On the fourth day after the blessed celebration while he was standing at the feet [of Martin] and praying, the people watched as his fingers were straightened. The entire congregation of people witnessed these great deeds of God. For the boy's hand was tinged with blood that slowly rose in his dry veins, and it became so moist that you might think that a sponge that had been long dry had been immersed in water and was thirstily soaking up the liquid. Once his veins were filled and his sinews strengthened, his skin became rosy and he held out his hand that was once bloodless but was now healthy.

56. The woman whose fingers were bent into her palm and who came [to Tours]

In a similar fashion a woman from Poitiers next deserved to receive a remedy. Her fingers were bent into her palm, her fingernails were, if I may say so, piercing her bones, and her entire hand was already decayed. This pious woman came to the saint's festival [on November 11, 580] and requested the medicine she hoped for. When the ceremonies were completed as usual, she said to her companions: "I came with a pure heart to request the assistance of the blessed [Martin], but because my sins were an obstacle, I did not deserve to receive what I sought. Now that my prayer is finished, let me return to my homeland still believing, through the goodness of my champion, that a prayer that is faithful to the heart might benefit a feeble body." After repeating these and similar words as if saying goodbye to the saint, she left. As the daylight was turning into evening, she took lodging along a bank of the Cher River. About midnight she was awakened and gave thanks to God because she still survived, because she was alive, because she was flourishing, and because she had touched the tomb of the blessed bishop. She offered her gratitude while weeping loudly, and then fell asleep again. And behold, a man stood before her who had hair that was white as a swan, who was dressed in purple, and who was carrying a cross in his hand. The man said: "In the name of Christ our Redeemer now you will be healed." Then he took her hand, placed his own finger among her fingers that were closed in her palm, moved them a bit, and straightened them. As she was seeing this in her dream, the woman awoke and, in praise of God, held up her hand that was healthy even though blood was still flowing from it. She returned to the church, gave thanks, and left rejoicing.

57. Another woman who was crippled while working during the festival of St. John

While the people gathered for the celebration of mass on the festival of the blessed John [the Baptist], a woman took a hoe and went to her field; she of course [hoped] that by pulling the weeds and tares she alone might clear her crops. But she could not be protected by the assurance that is a consequence of respect for the Lord's forerunner. When she began to work, immediately her hands were attacked by divine fire, and her face, as if it were discharging flames, was completely swollen with boils and blisters. This wretched woman burned no less from the anguish of embarrassment than from the pain in her body, because she had unwillingly exposed what she had done in secret. Then she quickly went shouting and screaming to the church of the blessed Martin. After she knelt before his tomb in this agony for four months, the burning was completely smothered, her body was made whole, and she was healed. For she was the slave of a man from Tours who, upon payment of half of her value, sought another slave woman.[70]

58. Another boy who was blind and crippled

A boy from Paris had the skill of sewing clothes. Because he was attacked by melancholy, that is, by a sediment of boiled blood, he suffered from a quartan fever; and as his swelling increased, his entire body was so afflicted with tiny blisters that he was thought by some to be a leper. He also suffered terrible pains in all his limbs, and he was deprived of sight in both eyes. After he heard about the reputation of the blessed bishop and his miracles that were publicized everywhere, this boy went to Tours. He came to the saint's church, and after fasting and praying for many days he recovered his sight and was restored to his earlier health. He was by birth free. But when Leudast, who was at the time count of Tours, heard that he was a talented tailor, he began to spread lies and said: "You have run away from your masters, and it will no longer be possible for you to wander about." Then he ordered that the boy must be bound and imprisoned at his own house. But the power of the angelic confessor was not lacking there. For when the boy was seized, immediately he was afflicted with the illness that he had just eliminated. Once the count saw that he could have no power over the boy who was suffering so badly, he ordered him to be released from his chains and to depart with his freedom. The boy returned to the church and was again healed.[71]

59. Another woman who was sold after being freed

Similar to the previous story is this one about a woman who was again

---

[70] L. Pietri (1983) 464 suggests that this was the festival of John the Baptist on June 24, and that the woman was then healed about "four months" later on the festival of St Martin on November 11, presumably still in 580 (cf. *VM* 2.56).

[71] King Chilperic finally replaced Leudast as count of Tours with Eunomius. Because Ansovald, Chilperic's envoy who engineered the switch, arrived in Tours for one of the festivals of St. Martin (*Hist.* 5.47), Krusch (1951) xv, and Weidemann (1983) 1:211, suggest that Leudast lost his office in July 580. But since after losing his office Leudast threatened Gregory during the following Easter and made various accusations against him that were finally heard at a council convened by Chilperic in late summer or early autumn of 580 (*Hist.* 5.49), he must have lost his countship already by the festival of St. Martin in November 579. This story about him is therefore chronologically misplaced. But perhaps Gregory was only too pleased to end *VM* 2 with a story demonstrating the power of St. Martin over a count whom he strongly disliked; he had similarly scrambled the chronological narrative in order to end *Hist.* 5 with the downfall of Leudast.

sold to the barbarians by her patron's sons after she had earned her freedom. But through the saint's power that easily protected her she became
weak and her limbs were completely crippled. For the tendons of her knees
were so twisted that the calves of her legs were touching her shins. Because
she was abandoned by the masters to whom she had been unjustly sold, she
then sought the patronage of the blessed confessor. After she stayed at his
church for a short time, she was restored both to her freedom and to her
health.

60. The pain in my eyes and my headache

Because the previous book [= *VM* 1] was begun at the point where
Paulinus [of Périgueux] had stopped and was completed in forty chapters, I
have decided to complete this book in sixty chapters. In this way the
blessed Martin might be glorified in these one hundred miracle stories,
even though after being separated from this world, preserving intact the
splendor of virginity and triumphantly completing his martyrdom even in
the midst of secret onslaughts and public insults, he already possessed the
crown of the thirtyfold, sixtyfold, and hundredfold fruit [cf. Matt. 13:23].
For I always hoped not to leave unfinished the vow that at the Lord's
command I have [now] completed in eight years. I began this book with a
miracle performed on my behalf, and I have now returned again to [a
miracle concerning] myself. I think that this miracle happened in accordance with divine providence, so that this book might be concluded [with a
story] about the man whom the beginning of the book mentioned.

For after I had described fifty-nine miracles in this book, and while I was
still eagerly waiting for a sixtieth miracle, suddenly the temple on the left
side of my head was contracted with pains. My veins twitched, tears flowed
down, and such a great agony afflicted me that I pressed hard on my eye to
prevent it from bursting. I suffered from this pain for an entire day and
night, and in the morning I went to the saint's church and knelt for prayer.
At the conclusion of my prayer I touched the painful spot to the curtain that
was hanging in front of the blessed tomb. As soon as this spot was touched,
my veins stopped twitching and my tears stopped flowing. Three days later
a similar pain attacked the right side of my head. My veins twitched and
tears gushed down. Again I got up in the morning, touched my head to the
curtain in the same manner as before, and left with my health. Ten days
later it seemed best to let my blood; but three days after letting my blood I
thought that my sufferings were due to my blood and that they would
immediately cease if a vein was at once cut; I think that this idea was
inspired by a deceiving [demon]. While I was considering and debating this
idea, the veins in both temples twitched, and the pain that had existed
previously was repeated and now attacked my entire head, not just one
part. Because I was disturbed by these pains, I hurried to the church,

requested forgiveness for my wicked idea, and touched my head with the shroud that covered the blessed tomb. Soon the pain was stopped, and I left the tomb with my health.

There are also many other miracles that the blessed man performed every day, but that it is tedious to list. If nevertheless I am still worthy to witness [more] miracles, it is appropriate to include them in another book. For as I said, these [first] two books are to be concluded with this total. I also offer great thanks to the piety of the Lord because through the support of the glorious bishop I was permitted to be capable of extending all the way to its conclusion what I [had] initially undertaken. I pray that the confessor generously grant to me, a sinner, what he has often bestowed upon the people, and that he cleanse me from the illnesses that he often notes and contemplates, that he restore to me the light of truth, that he snatch me from mistaken unbelief, that he purify my heart and my mind from the ghastly leprosy of extravagance, that he cleanse my thoughts from wicked desires, and that he dissolve and overturn my entire mass of misdeeds. Then, when I am to be placed on the left side at the [Final] Judgment, he will deign to separate me from the middle of the goats with his sacred right hand, protect me behind his back, and await the judge's verdict. And when in accordance with the judge's decision I am to be condemned to the infernal flames, he will protect me with the sacred shroud that shields him from boasting and reprieve me from this punishment. The angels will say to the King [of heaven] what they previously said about the monk who was restored to life: "This is the man for whom Martin petitions."[72] Because I am not worthy to be clothed with this splendor, let it rather be the case that I am worthy to be freed from the threatening agents of the underworld. And may I not suffer from such a punishment that I am separated from the kingdom of the God whom I have piously relied upon in this world.

Here ends this second book.

VM 3

Here auspiciously begins a third book.

As I begin, under the direction of Christ, to write this third book about the miracles of the blessed Martin, I thank omnipotent God who deigned to provide me with the sort of doctor who cleanses my infirmities, washes away my wounds, and bestows effective remedies. For before his blessed

---

[72] Gregory's memory was slightly mistaken; Sulpicius Severus, *Vita Martini* 7, had described how the monk Martin had revived a catechumen.

tomb passion is to be humbled and prayer is to be raised. If tears flow and genuine remorse follows, if sighs rise up from the bottom of the heart and guilty breasts are beaten, then weeping will find happiness, guilt will find pardon, and the grief in our breasts will end with a remedy. For often simply touching the blessed tomb compels people suffering from diarrhea to control themselves, the blind to see, the paralyzed to stand up, and even the bitterness in our hearts to withdraw completely. Although I have often experienced this [miraculous power], I consider myself unworthy to include here along with this collection of great miracles even what he deigned to perform on my behalf. But again I fear to appear guilty, if like a charlatan I conceal these miracles. Indeed, I call God as my witness that I am not deprived of [Martin's] compassion, and I trust in that hope that I have placed in his power. For however often a headache has attacked, or a pounding has struck my temples, or my hearing has oppressed my ears, or a darkness has obscured the sight in my eyes, or a pain has appeared in other limbs, as soon as I touched the painful part [of my body] either to the tomb or to the curtain hanging [there], I immediately recovered my health. I silently marveled that the pain quickly departed at the moment of contact.

1. The pain in my throat

As the first miracle in this book I will include something that I recently experienced. While I was sitting at dinner intending to eat after a fast, a fish was brought out in a dish. After I made the sign of the Lord's cross over the fish, I ate; but one of the fish bones was most painfully caught in my throat. This bone caused severe pains by stabbing my throat with its point and by obstructing my swallowing with its length; it also hindered the sound of my voice and did not permit passage to the liquid saliva that often flowed from my mouth. Since I was unable to expel the bone either by coughing or by spitting, after three days I hurried to my proven protection. I approached the tomb, knelt on the pavement, wept and cried at length, and requested the confessor's assistance. Then I stood up and touched my neck, throat, and the rest of my face with the curtain that was hanging [there]. Immediately I recovered my health, and even before I exited through the sacred doorway, I no longer felt any weakness. But I do not know what had become of the troublesome sharp bone. I did not expel it by vomiting, nor did I feel it drop into my stomach. I know only this one fact, that I felt that I had been cured so quickly that I thought someone had used his hand to pull away the obstruction that had lacerated my throat.[73]

---

[73] Since the only hobby Gregory mentioned for himself was fishing (*VM* 2.16), perhaps he had himself caught this fish. Note that he once also avidly repeated a "fish story" about the enormous trout in Lake Leman (*GM* 75).

2. The disabled girl who was cured

A girl who was twelve years old had been disabled in all her limbs for six years. As if dead she lay on a bed in her parents' house; she was unable to walk, to complete any work with her hands, to see the light, to speak any words, or to hear any conversation. At the tomb of the blessed [Martin] her parents prayed for their daughter, offered gifts, and made promises. The people met for the ceremonies, and the holy festival [of Martin on November 11, 581] was celebrated in happiness. On the third day after the festival the girl called her father and said: "I am thirsty." Her father was happy because he had been worthy to hear his daughter's voice that he had never heard before. He quickly ran, fetched a little water, and offered it for the girl to drink. After she drank the water, he said: "Give me your hand." Her father took her right hand and lifted her up. The girl stood on her own feet, raised her hands and her eyes to heaven, and said: "Omnipotent God, I thank you who looked upon my littleness and deigned to heal me through the agency of your holy bishop." And so, once her limbs were healed, she recovered her vision and her hearing and she happily returned home.

3. The man whose hand was stuck to a lever

Two years before these events occurred, a reckless man who did not respect the holy day of the Lord's resurrection took his harvest and went to a millstone. He inserted grain and began to turn the millstone by hand. When the task was completed, he was unable to open his hand; instead, against his will and with great pain he held the lever that he had picked up. Then, once he saw that he was not released, he sawed the lever on both ends and went to the saint's church. After he prayed and celebrated vigils, his fingers were relaxed and his hand was restored to its previous use. Then in another year on this holy day he performed the task for which he had earlier been rebuked by God, and again that wooden lever stuck to his hand. Crying in pain he again went to the saint's church, although he did not deserve to be heard immediately. But two years later this man too was freed from the burden of this wooden lever during the same festival that I mentioned when the girl was healed.[74]

4. The crippled man who was cured

From Limoges came a crippled man who was unable to walk and had no sight in his eyes; believers carried him on their hands and placed him before the holy tomb. After this man prayed for the compassion of the blessed

[74] Gregory sometimes described Sunday as the "day of the Lord's resurrection" (*VJ* 11, *VM* 3.56). But since in this case he clearly stated that the man had ignored the same day a year later, he was probably referring to the annual Gallic festival on March 27 that commemorated the Lord's resurrection (cf. *Hist.* 10.31): see L. Pietri (1983) 453.

bishop, his disabled limbs were straightened and he was restored to his health.

5. The blind man who received his sight

A blind man who had lacked sight in his eyes for a long time attended the same festival. After he offered a prayer and while he was standing before the holy tomb, his eyes were suddenly opened, his sight was restored, and he rejoiced.

6. The disabled boy who was cured

A boy who was a resident of Tours was weakened by a severe and prolonged illness; all his limbs were disabled, and because the bones in his legs were twisted like ropes and could not be disentangled, the fever left him without any hope of walking. After the departure of the fever the boy asked his parents to carry him to the holy church. They agreed with his request, brought him to the saint's feet, and offered a prayer that his familiar power might help their son. The boy and his parents continued to pray and fast. On the third day the light of compassion appeared; the boy's bones were disentangled, and his parents welcomed him with his health.

7. The man who made a key on a Sunday

Another man named Senator was from Craon, a village [in the territory] of Angers. When he made a key on a Sunday, the fingers on both of his hands stiffened and his fingernails pierced his palms, so that the man who wished to open a door could not open his hands. For four months his fingernails pierced his flesh and his palms festered; then he sought the confessor's assistance. After he prayed and fasted for four days, he lifted his hands that were healed and departed with his health. He praised the bishop's power and warned that no one else attempt what he had dared [to do].

8. The dead boy who was revived

At the time when these events were happening at Tours envoys named Florentius and Exsuperius came from Spain to King Chilperic. I welcomed them to a banquet at the cathedral. During our meal they claimed to be Catholic [Christians]; as a result, Florentius, the older [of the two envoys], repeatedly demanded to hear some stories about the power of the blessed man. I gave thanks to God and asked whether his name was heard in those regions [of Spain] and whether anyone read his *Vita*. After I posed these questions, Florentius said that his name was honored with splendor in those regions. He also described himself as a special foster son of the bishop and said that his great power had once been revealed on his behalf.

He said:[75] "My grandfather built a church in honor of the blessed Bishop Martin before many years passed by. When the church was completed and decorated with elegant craftsmanship, he sent pious clerics to Tours and requested relics of the bishop so that he might consecrate the shrine that he had constructed in [Martin's] name with his relics. After doing this he came every day, knelt on the ground with his wife, and requested the holy bishop's assistance. Much later I was born. When I was three months old, I was afflicted with a fever and became so weak that I was unable to suck a breast or swallow any food. Then, as the illness intensified, I rejected food, and my breathing so fluttered that only death was expected. Soon my breathing too was exhausted. Then my mother, who was grieving over the [imminent] death of her firstborn and only child, and my grandmother took my already lifeless little body into their arms and with an undeniable hope placed it before the altar of the blessed Martin. My grandfather addressed the saint as if they were seeing him visible to their eyes and said: 'Most blessed confessor, it was our great hope to transport here your relics that have expelled illnesses, extinguished fevers, scattered darkness, and cleansed other infirmities, because we have read about your many deeds, what you did while alive and what you have done after your death. For we have heard that you had revived dead men with your prayer, removed leprosy with your kiss, cured the possessed with your word, obstructed poison with your finger, and performed many other deeds. Your power will be evident here if in accordance with our faith you also now revive this little boy. If you do not do this, we will no longer bow our necks here, nor will we burn lights or show the gratitude of other honors.' After my grandfather said this, they left me, an infant, in front of the altar and departed. At daybreak they returned and were surprised to find me turned toward the altar. My mother took me in her arms, and when she realized that I was breathing again, she fed me at her breast. I drank her milk and at once regained strength. Then my mother, my father, and the entire household raised their voices to heaven, blessed God, and said: 'Now we know that you are a great God and that you alone perform miracles [cf. Ps. 72:18], you who have restored this small infant to us through the prayer of your confessor.' Thereafter they showed greater respect than previously for that shrine." I learned from the mouth of Florentius himself that these events happened this way.[76]

---

[75] Gregory introduced this story as if he intended to quote Florentius's first-person account. Yet much of the story was narrated, rather confusingly, in the third person (e.g. "his grandfather," etc.). Like some later manuscripts, for the sake of clarity this translation has transposed third-person references to first-person.

[76] Florentius was probably one of the Visigothic envoys who visited Chilperic in 582 (*Hist.* 6.18).

9. The man who had a disabled foot

A cleric from Poitiers, from an estate in that region that belonged to the holy church, was lame in one foot. He claimed that he had lost the use of the foot because of an assault by a midday demon. He cut a staff to the height of his knee, put a piece of leather on top of it, bent his foot back, and [attached] the staff to his knee; with the assistance of this peg leg he regained his mobility when he tried to move on foot. Nine years later he went to the aforementioned church. After he prayed for three days, his knee was straightened three days before the festival, and he stood up. As people arrived for the saint's festival [on July 4, 582], he informed them about how he had been healed through his power.

10. My mother's shinbone

The saint's power assisted my mother in this manner. After the pains of childbirth had passed and she gave birth, my mother developed a pain in a muscle of her lower leg. This was a sharp pain, and like a piercing nail it produced such an excruciatingly stinging sensation that often it made her faint. She was unable to alleviate this pain unless after being exposed for a long time in front of a fire it was numbed by the warmth from a fireplace; the pain also was relieved if a little ointment was rubbed on it. Why say more? After my consecration [as bishop] she came to Tours, both to visit the holy bishop and because she loved me. While she was staying at Tours for two or three months, she frequently prayed for the assistance of the blessed bishop. His usual compassion was encouraging, and the pain finally left the shinbone that had tormented this woman for thirty-four years.[77]

11. The woman whose hand was healed

The fingers of another woman from the territory of Angers were affixed to her palm. After she prayed at the holy shrine, her fingers were straightened, her hand was healed, and she departed.

---

[77] "Two or three months" after Gregory's consecration in late August 573 would place his mother's cure at about the time of the festival of St. Martin on November 11; Gregory himself had been born on November 30, the festival of St. Andrew (*MA* 38). The year of his birth is disputed. Krusch (1885) 635n.3 calculated that Gregory was born in 540. Bonnet (1890) 22n.1 both questioned this arithmetic and stressed that Gregory did not state explicitly that his mother suffered this pain after his birth. But Krusch (1920) 715n.3, and (1951) XIII.2, later collated and supported manuscripts that inserted *me* before *edidit*, "she gave birth to me." Other evidence suggests that Gregory was probably born in 538 (see note to *VM* 1.35). It is not clear why Gregory inserted this story about a miracle that had happened in 573 here in a series of stories about miracles that happened in 582; perhaps his mother visited him again then and reminded him of the earlier miracle.

12. The boy who was cured of an illness

A boy who was my servant was ill with a fever and suffered severely. His limbs burned on the outside, although he was very thirsty on the inside. But whenever he drank something, he soon vomited it from his stomach; nor could he eat any food. On the fourth or fifth day while he was being tormented by this misfortune, he asked that they bring him a bit of dust from [Martin's] tomb to drink. The dust was brought and mixed with wine; when the boy faithfully drank it, his health was restored and he recovered.

13. Theoda, whose foot was healed

Theoda was a daughter of Wiliachar, who had once been a priest. Often she suffered from swelling in her feet, and eventually she lost the use of one foot that became lame. Then she went to the blessed church. While she was offering numerous prayers in the church, her lameness was eliminated and she was restored to her health.[78]

14. The crippled man

At that time a man was walking in a villa that belonged to the register [of poor people] who were under the saint's protection. He was stooped over, as if his hips were broken. Similar to the woman [mentioned] in the verse of a Gospel [cf. Luke 13:11], he was bent forward and could not stand upright; but although stooped, he walked with the addition of two crutches under his shoulders. He came for the festival [of Martin on November 11, 582], and three days after its celebration he stood up straight, cleansed from every assault by a demon. He left with his health.

15. Gundulf, a disabled man

Gundulf was a citizen of Tours who from his infancy had lived with and served Gunthar, a son of King Chlothar. At the king's command he once climbed a tree to pick the ripe fruit. But when a branch broke, he fell, struck his foot on a rock, and was disabled. Many years later, while he continued [to suffer from] this [first] disability, he mounted a horse and quickly spurred it on to the same place. But the horse stumbled, and Gundulf was thrown and seriously wounded when the other foot that was still healthy was shattered. Then he asked to be brought to the blessed church, where he was dropped on the pavement and faithfully offered a prayer. The compassion that is always accustomed to assist afflicted people did not delay, because all his pain was immediately removed, and Gundulf stood up from the pavement with his health. For almost thirty years he

[78] For Wiliachar, see *VM* 1.23.

always limped because of his other foot, as I mentioned previously. Finally, after he had examined the misdeeds of his own conscience, he decided to convert, that is, to be tonsured and serve the holy bishop. But first he received a permit from the king that he might transfer all his possessions to the church during his lifetime. When this was done, he was tonsured and fulfilled the vow of his generous decision. Then his foot that had atrophied after the bones were broken was lengthened. And a man who previously moved about with the support of two young boys now walked wherever he wished without anyone's assistance and without any restricting lameness.[79]

16. The blind boy who received his sight

Next a young boy who was blind came from Limoges and recovered the sight in his eyes in this manner. Three years after his birth this boy was beginning to walk, his voice was becoming louder, and he was forming words with his lips. He lovingly teased his mother, offered kisses, and embraced her neck. While he was being carried in her arms, the turbulence of a demon provoked a blast of wind. Dust and chaff were lifted from the ground and blown over the boy and his mother in a huge whirlwind. Because his mother was an ignorant unbeliever and did not think of protecting herself and her son with the sign of salvation, this treachery was successful, and the young boy's eyes were filled and blocked with dust. He cried for a long time until finally comforted by his mother; but he remained blind. When he was older, he was given to beggars, so that he might wander about with them and receive some alms; for his parents were very poor. Then, twelve years after he became blind, he came to Tours on the day before the festival [of Christmas in 582 that celebrated how] the Father had joined the Word to flesh and bestowed salvation upon the world. After the celebration of the vigil before the festival and after the others left, this boy lay motionless before the saint's feet. Then he felt as if someone had pricked his eyes with a thorn, and immediately blood surged from his eyes and began to flow over his cheeks. He turned his face upward, saw a candle burning over him, cried out in a loud voice, and said: "Holy confessor of God, I thank you because I have deserved to recover my sight through your power." Behold this marvelous compassion! Behold this formidable power! For because of your extensive devotion you scatter your gifts on people. A boy who had requested charity received his sight, and eyes that for a long time had been deprived of light are [now] honored with the sight of your power. If the blackness of our many misdeeds did not obscure you from our sight, you would certainly appear in person and cry out to the ill people with the words of Peter: "Gold and silver have I none, but what I

[79] King Chlothar died in 561; his son Gunthar had died during his lifetime (*Hist.* 4.3).

have, I give to you. In the name of Jesus Christ go in good health" [Acts 3:6].

17. The ear of the secretary Siggo

For some reason I went to Rheims, where I was graciously welcomed by Bishop Egidius, who then governed the cathedral [there]. The next day was Sunday, and at dawn I went to the cathedral, sat in the sanctuary, and awaited the arrival of the bishop. At that time I was carrying with me relics of St. Martin, even though it was uncommonly bold [to do so]. Then Siggo, who had once been a secretary for [King] Sigibert, came to meet me, and I kissed him and asked him to sit next to me. [Siggo had one ear that was obstructed, and with the other he could scarcely hear what I was saying.][80] But after we talked sufficiently, he was called to the cathedral residence. In order for him to leave me immediately, the obstruction in his deaf ear was shattered; and as if sensing a strong gust of air departing from his ear, he heard the summons. Immediately he turned back, began to thank me, and said: "This is the third day since I lost hearing in this ear, but when I spoke with you, I felt that it was immediately opened." I was embarrassed lest these events be attributed to me, and I said: "Dearest son, do not show any gratitude to me, but rather to him whose power has restored your hearing. For you should know that I am carrying relics of the blessed Martin, whose power has eliminated the difficulty in your hearing."[81]

18. The disease in the herds

Once a devastating plague was ravaging the herds so severely that someone might think that no means was left for reviving the animals. One of my [servants] went to the holy church and poured into a container oil from the lamps that were hanging from the ceiling and some water. He brought the container home, dipped his finger into the liquid, and made the sign of the Lord's cross on the foreheads and backs of the animals that this disease had not yet infected. Since he was confident in his faith, this man also sprinkled this ointment in the mouths of the animals that had collapsed and were lying on the ground. Soon, more swiftly than words can say, this mysterious plague was eliminated, and the herds were saved.[82]

---

[80] Not all manuscripts include this sentence that Krusch printed in brackets.

[81] Gregory may have gone to Rheims in 583 to consult with Bishop Egidius, who later, probably after Easter (*Hist.* 6.27), led an embassy representing King Childebert to King Chilperic (*Hist.* 6.31). After serving as referendary, or secretary, for King Sigibert, Siggo had held the same position under King Chilperic, until in 576 he defected to become a supporter of King Childebert, son of Sigibert (*Hist.* 5.3). Given his connections with Sigibert and Egidius, he may once have helped them promote Gregory as bishop of Tours in 573.

[82] After Kings Chilperic and Childebert made an alliance (cf. *VM* 3.17), Chilperic tried to seize some of King Guntramn's cities. The devastation caused by the armies of Desiderius and

19. The blind man who received his sight

Six years after a citizen of Avranches lost his ability to see, he sought to be healed by the protection of the blessed confessor. He went to his church, spent much time fasting and praying, and requested the assistance of the blessed bishop. The holy festival [of Martin on July 4, 583] came, and sight was restored to this man while the people were watching the celebration of mass. So a man who had come to the holy church with someone else leading him returned to his homeland with his sight. Because of his happiness and his gratitude this man vowed that he would be tonsured in that same place; later he returned and piously fulfilled his vow.

20. A similar story about another blind man who received his sight

A man came from the regions across the sea. While he was working in a field, a sudden gust of wind and [a cloud of] dust had smothered him and he lost the sight in his eyes; and a man who had been for a long time a guide for blind people was [now] himself led home with someone else guiding him. He remained blind for three years. Then he went to the church of the blessed confessor. He remained at this church praying for four years; then he was assisted by divine power, his eyes were opened, and he deserved to see the light.

21. Julianus, a crippled man

As I have often said, his reputation was publicized and spread not only in his own city but also in other cities and into almost the entire world. Julianus came from Spain. He piously brought his disabled hands and feet to this doctor [Martin] and said: "Most holy champion, I believe that you will be able to offer me the assistance of a remedy that you have usually not refused to others who have trusted in you." Because of this confidence he persisted with his frequent prayers and did not doubt the Lord's compassion. After his feet and his hands were straightened, he was restored to his health.

22. The woman who received her sight at the saint's bed

Because in previous books I have often noted that many miracles were celebrated in the place from which he migrated to heaven, let me describe what happened recently. A woman who lived in Tours was deprived of the clearness of her sight. She went to the cell at Candes that contains the bed of the blessed bishop, because she thought that she would receive protection if she touched the railings around the bed. This bed would not be termed such except that, after spreading out cinders and putting a stone beneath his head, the Israel of our times [had] bent his neck and slept on the

---

Bladast, two of Chilperic's dukes, led to this plague among the herds in the Touraine (*Hist.* 6.31).

pavement. So this woman, with the assistance of her husband, was brought to this shrine, and for many days she prayed and performed penance there. Finally the compassion that is always shown to the grieving looked upon her and restored to the woman the sight that she had lost. Then such an intense faith burned in the woman that until the day of her death she never left that place.

23. The mute man whose brothers stole his possessions

An inhabitant of Angers placed his head on a bed after his limbs were afflicted with an ailment; then, as the fever daily increased, he lost control over all his limbs and was deprived of his hearing and his speech. After a few days he recovered from the fever, although he remained without his speech. But his brothers seized a portion of his possessions, evicted him from their family home, and said: "He has become a madman. God should not allow him either to inherit our possessions or to acquire a portion of our inheritance." For these brothers were free men and cultivated their own fields; but because they knew nothing about the affairs of God, they evicted their mute and deaf brother whom they ought rather to have loved. Although this brother lacked his [physical] senses, he maintained an awareness in his heart. Then he took some boards in his hand, clicked them together, and imitated the sound of a beggar. He came with this contraption to the aforementioned village [of Candes] and there joined the others who were requesting charity. Six years passed, during which this poor man was supported by the wealth of [the register of the poor at] the holy cell.[83] One night before a Sunday, while this man was lying in the house of his host [Martin], it happened that suddenly the place was filled with a bright light. And behold, this man was terrified with fear and knelt on the ground. Immediately there appeared to him a man who was clothed in a bishop's robe. This man touched him, made the sign of the cross of Christ on his forehead, and said: "The Lord has made you healthy. Rise, hurry to the church, and thank your God." The ill man then raised his voice in a speech of gratitude and filled the region with his shouts. Immediately everyone gathered at the spectacle and was surprised that a man whom the day before they had seen to be a mute was now speaking. Then the bell was rung for matins. The people assembled, and after they celebrated vigils, the saint's power was obviously apparent. During those days a demon was expelled from two possessed men who were cleansed in this place.

24. The oil that increased

But let me return to my friend Aredius, who was even, if I may say so, a

---

[83] L. Pietri (1983) 685, 719 suggests that this wealth belonged to the *matricula* at Candes (*VM* 2.22–23) and was distributed by the community of clerics responsible for maintaining and serving the shrine.

special foster son of the blessed confessor. Often he was privileged to see miracles [performed] by his relics. Aredius came to the saint's festival [on November 11, 583] with his usual kindness, humility, and love. Upon his departure he took with him a small jar filled with oil from the holy tomb and said: "Perhaps on my journey there is some ill person who is anguished in his heart and desires to receive a blessing from the shrine of the blessed Martin." Then in another place a pious woman approached him, held out another container [filled] with oil, and said: "Servant of Christ, I ask you to sanctify this oil with your blessing." But Aredius, lest he appear to be overcome by arrogance, said: "My power is slight; but if it pleases you, I have oil from the tomb of the blessed Martin who poured out this oil. If you believe in his great power, you will drink salvation from this oil." The woman rejoiced and sought to do what the priest recommended. Aredius's container was half-full. After he poured out some of the liquid that had been taken from the saint's church, immediately the oil bubbled up and filled the container to the top. Once the woman saw this, she marveled at the power of the blessed confessor and returned home rejoicing.[84]

25. The woman's fingers that were straightened

Another woman whose fingers were bent and fastened to her palm visited the church of the blessed bishop Martin. After a few days passed, her fingers were straightened while she was offering a prayer and requesting the saint's assistance, and she received health for her hand.

26. Another crippled woman

Years earlier a girl suffered from a serious illness and was crippled with weakness in all her limbs. After she heard about the miracles that the glorious bishop performed for particular people, she piously called upon his name. A few days later she asked to be brought to his church, in whose courtyard she lay for many days. After she offered frequent prayers and wept, she was visited by the power of the bishop. And so, with the assistance of divine mercy she left with her health.

27. The crippled boy

While a boy from the territory of Angers was staying in his parents' house, he lost the use of his hands and feet because of an attack by a clever demon, as he himself always claimed. Because his fingers were bent inward, his fingernails were hence fastened into his palm; and because the tendons of his knees withered, they twisted his feet toward his legs. For six years he was carried about with difficulty by his parents; then he was brought to the church of the holy bishop. While he was persisting in prayer, his limbs were

---

[84] On Aredius, see the note to *VJ* 28.

restored; and in accordance with the signification of his name, Floridus "flourished like a fresh flower."

28. The blind man who received his sight

A cleric had [previously] been a slave of this holy church from birth. After being attacked by a treacherous [demon] he was deprived of his sight; and since he was unable to work there, this ill man stayed in his own home. He endured this blindness for almost three years; then he went to the church of the blessed bishop. There he prayed for the customary mercy. After receiving his sight he returned to his own home.

29. The man whose hand was fastened to his mallet

When someone's slave from the territory of Tours was repairing a fence on a Sunday, his hand began to stick to the wooden [mallet]. He quickly lifted up his right hand. While he was surprised and amazed at what had happened, his hand was crippled with a great pain, his fingernails were also fastened into his palm, and all the fingers on his right hand were bent. He returned in grief to his lodging. Four years later he went to the saint's church, and after he offered a prayer, he was healed. Then he declared to the people that they not [even] consider what he had done, lest a greedy farmer pollute the celebrations of this great day and lest human weakness, by performing the work of this world, nullify the celestial mystery of the holy resurrection and of our redemption.

30. The boy with an ill stomach

A boy from Albi vomited up his food and drink because his stomach was weakened by various illnesses. After he suffered from this affliction for many days and rejected with severe bitterness whatever he seemed to eat, he was filled with faith and wished to go to the church of the blessed confessor. He fasted and prayed in this church for three days. On the fourth day, after he wished to eat some food and tasted wine on his lips, he recovered his strength. Then he gave thanks and left with his health.

31. A woman's withered right hand

There was a woman who came, as some say, from Angers. All her limbs were withered, but she displayed the fingers on her right hand that was in particular more withered than her other limbs. She knelt before the saint's tomb. Then she left and lingered for a short time in a courtyard. But the mediation of the glorious bishop assisted her. Her veins filled with blood, her skin regained its firmness, and the rest of her body recovered its strength and was cured. She had been [afflicted] with this illness because, as she admitted, she wished to bake bread on a Saturday night after the setting of the sun, which is a part of the night of Sunday.

32. The woman whose hands were fastened together

There was another woman, similar to this one, whose hands were bent inward, contracted, and fastened together. Although she suffered from severe pains, she traveled on the road and said: "If I go to the church of St. Martin, this illness will immediately disappear. For I am confident that he who often pitied people suffering from such afflictions will also assist me." After she said this and continued, as she was able, the journey that she had begun, her hands were separated but her fingers were not straightened. But when she came to the holy place and offered a prayer, immediately all her pain was removed and her fingers were healed. She moved her hands without restriction while she gave thanks.

33. The death of horses

In this year a serious disease appeared among the horses in the region of Bordeaux. A villa at Marsas, which is in this territory [of Bordeaux], was subject to the control of the blessed Martin; it had an oratory that was consecrated both in his name and with his miracles. Then when the afore-mentioned disaster appeared, people went to the oratory and on behalf of their horses vowed that if their horses escaped, they would certainly pre-sent one-tenth [of their horses] to this shrine. And since this misfortune afflicted these horses annually, the people added that they would mark their horses with a brand from the iron key that unlocked the door of the oratory. Once this was done, the saint's power was so effective that the ill horses were healed and the unaffected horses suffered no more.[85]

34. The plague that was accompanied by blisters

In the previous year the people of Tours were most seriously afflicted by a virulent plague. It included extreme weakness, so that a man who was seized by a high fever broke out completely with blisters and small pimples. The blisters were white and firm without any softness, although they did produce a sharp pain. Once these blisters became ripe, if they popped and began to discharge, then [people's] clothes stuck to their bodies and the pain increased more severely. The skill of doctors could be of no value for this illness unless the Lord's assistance was present. For many people who sought a blessing from the holy church earned a reward. But why is it necessary to mention many people when others earned this [reward] that I saw one woman earn? When the wife of Count Eborinus was afflicted by this plague, she was so [completely] covered with these blisters that neither her hands nor her feet nor any other part of her body remained without

---

[85] It is not clear whether this oratory was under the control of the church of St. Martin at Tours or his church at Bordeaux (*VM* 3.50): see Vieillard-Troiekouroff (1976) 157–58. For offerings and tithes to churches, see L. Pietri (1983) 608–10.

blemish; even her eyes were obstructed and covered with these blisters. Although she was already at the moment of death, she sought a blessing at the holy tomb. Some of the water with which the blessed tomb was washed during Easter [and the celebration of the resurrection] of the Lord was brought to her. After her sores were washed with this water, she drank some of it. Soon her fever vanished, the blisters painlessly disappeared, and she was cured.[86]

35. The two paralyzed men and the one blind man who was healed

But although there are many miracles that the entire world has experienced, I think that quite a few of them come to my attention, and I am mentioning those that [people in] the vicinity have experienced. Bishop Badegysil of Le Mans was invited to a spot in his own diocese in order to consecrate a church in the name of and with the relics of the blessed man. At the conclusion of the ceremonies while people were invoking the name of St. Martin, two paralytics recovered their mobility and a blind man recovered his sight.[87]

36. Agustus, a crippled man

Agustus was a citizen of Tours. While he was suffering from a sharp pain in his kidneys, his feet were crippled and bent nearly back to his kidneys, and he was severely disabled. He suffered from this handicap for two years. Then, after being advised by his servants, he went to the saint's church, where he fasted and prayed for seven days. His pain was removed, his feet were straightened, and he departed with his health.

37. The mute girl

At this time also a girl remained alone at her loom after her companions left. As she was sitting there, a terrifying demon appeared who seized and began to drag the girl away. But she shouted and screamed, and although she saw no assistance, she still tried to resist manfully. Two or three hours later the other women returned and found this girl half-dead, lying on the ground and unable to say anything at all. The girl signaled with her hand; but they understood nothing, and the girl remained mute. The demon that

---

[86] The plague had appeared in various cities in Gaul during 582 (*Hist.* 6.14–15) and again early in 584 (*Hist.* 6.33). For the washing of the tomb of St Martin, see the note to *VM* 2.51.

[87] Before becoming bishop of Le Mans in 581 Badegysil had been *maior domus* under King Chilperic (*Hist.* 6.9); his brother Nectarius was also influential at Chilperic's court, although after the king's assassination Badegysil had to shield him from Fredegund's animosity (*Hist.* 7.15). After Badegysil's death in 586 Gregory strongly criticized him and his wife for their harsh treatment of the people of Le Mans (*Hist.* 8.39). L. Pietri and Biarne (1987) 54 suggest that this church is to be associated with the monastery and hospice endowed by Bishop Bertramn of Le Mans at Pontlieue: see above, chapter 4, section 3.

had appeared to her was then so treacherous to the people in her household that they abandoned this place and migrated elsewhere. After the days of two or three months had passed, the girl came to the church and deserved to recover her speech. Then she narrated with her own mouth everything that she had suffered.[88]

38. The blind deacon from Châlons-sur-Marne

When a deacon from Châlons-sur-Marne, as is the custom for those people, took a drink while the others were celebrating their gratitude at matins, he was punished with the loss of [sight in] his eyes. The deacon acknowledged his guilt [and admitted] that he had done something that was not worthy of his vows; so he was excluded from food and drink, spent his nights in vigils, and was attentive in praying. While he was doing this, the news that had widely embraced the entire world finally reached his ears, [that is,] that Bishop Martin was at Tours and that before his tomb the calamities of ill people were often eliminated and soothed. This deacon did not delay and immediately ordered a journey to be prepared. Without any misgivings about the power of the blessed man he went to his holy church and there knelt on the ground and relied on prayer. After three days his eyes were opened and he recovered his sight. When I carefully attempted to extract the truth about why these misfortunes had happened to him, I learned the following story from him. He said: "Seven months ago, while I was going to the cathedral after the bell was rung for matins, I met one of my friends. I rushed to embrace and kiss him, and I began to ask whether everything remained prosperous at his home. Then I was called aside from my journey and began to share a drink with him. After it seemed proper to have expressed our affection with drinks, we said goodbye and he left. As he was leaving, my eyes closed, and my eyelids were stuck together with such stickiness that I was unable to open them at all. Then, since I was leaving in sadness with this disability, I wished to visit the tomb of the blessed bishop. Three days after I came, while I was standing near his tomb, a great burning sensation suddenly seized my eyes. I began to groan loudly and to request bravely the saint's assistance. Then blood suddenly burst from my eyes, removed the [darkness of] night, and restored the [light of] day." The deacon told this story to me and then returned to his own home with his health.

39. The woman who was crippled and blind

A blind woman whose hands and feet were bent backward sought to

---

[88] Wemple (1981) 41 suggests that this girl was attempting to conceal the shame of having been raped by attributing the deed to a demon. Reactions to similar accusations of adultery against married woman indicate both the stigma of being shamed and the involvement of the family: see above, chapter 3, section 2.

celebrate the blessed festival of the glorious bishop [on July 4, 584] with the aid of her parents. When she wished to return home on the third day after the conclusion of the festival, she knelt in the holy church and began to pray that the Lord might deign to show her the usual reward of his compassion. While she was weeping and making this request, instantly her hands were straightened and her feet were strengthened. She was led to the holy tomb and gave thanks for the health that she had received. Then she asked to be brought to the door, where she again knelt and said to her servants: "I will not rise from this spot until he who has restored the use of my feet and hands also restores sight to my eyes." As she was saying this, suddenly possessed men announced that they were being tormented and acknowledged that the presence of Martin was imminent. But although the devil, because he is a liar from the beginning [cf. John 8:44], is not to be allowed any credibility, the saint's presence was confirmed by these events. For this woman who shortly before had been guided [by others] now received her sight and testified that the blessed bishop was present.

40. The paralyzed man who was cured

A short time later a paralyzed man lying on a couch was carried on a wagon and came from Bourges. In a similar fashion he was visited by the power of the blessed bishop and stood up after being cured. He was restored to his mobility, and as a crowd of relatives watched, he was welcomed back with his health.

41. The chains around a girl that were broken

During these days a girl who had been born to parents who were already freed [from slavery] had her freedom violated and was sentenced to the bond of slavery by her patron's sons. But because she did not agree to do any work for her unjust masters, it happened that she was bound with chains and shackles. While others anticipated the blessed festival [of Martin on November 11, 584], she sat in this captivity weeping and crying because she was not present at the blessed festival. Suddenly the stocks that held her feet were split. As if already a free woman, she escaped, and although still bound in chains she went to the blessed church. But as soon as her feet touched the sacred threshold, immediately these chains were broken and fell from her neck. So she was simultaneously restored to safety and to her freedom.

42. The book containing his *Vita* that survived in flames

What if I return to the written version of his blessed *Vita*? Would it not be amazing if the sacred book of his life, when surrounded by flames, was neither destroyed nor burned? A monk from the monastery at Marmoutier went at the command of his abbot to another small community, as if to do some work. For the salvation of his soul and for the correction of his life he took with him a book containing the *Vita* of the blessed bishop. When night fell, he lay down on a bed filled with old straw and placed the book beneath his head. As he slept, a man appeared in a dream and said: "Do not sleep on this straw, because it is tainted with blood." I believe that, as is characteristic of mankind, some crime was committed on this straw and that the blessed man would therefore not allow the words [in the *Vita*] praising himself to be buried in it. The monk dismissed this first vision, and a second warning was also ineffective; but the third upset him deeply. He got up, proceeded to his work at daybreak, and ordered a servant boy to take the straw from his bed and destroy it in a fire; but he forgot about the book. In ignorance the servant boy threw the book that was concealed in the straw outside and lit a fire. After the straw was reduced to ashes and nothing remained except cinders, the book appeared undamaged; to tell the truth, neither its covers nor a single page had been destroyed. Divine power thus deigned to safeguard this commendation of its own foster son [Martin] in such a way that a fire did not burn a book about a man whom the sting of lust did not inflame in this world. But lest this story seem unbelievable to anyone, I still have this book today.

43. The two boys who were healed

Next while I was traveling, two boys who served among the stewards for the horses became ill. One of them suffered from ill health, the other from dysentery. Both were in the grip of a high fever and were so weary that after being helped up, they could not be kept on the backs of horses. I took out the dust that I had taken in a container from the saint's tomb, mixed it with water, and ordered them to drink it. Soon their fever was diminished, their agony was extinguished, and both recovered.

44. Mallulf, a crippled man

The miracles that the Lord deigns to perform every day in praise of his bishop are renowned and cannot, as I have often admitted, be described by an awkward [writer such as] myself. But to the extent that that very awkwardness is capable, these miracles will be revealed lest they seem to be concealed. Mallulf, a citizen of Tours, was afflicted with a severe illness and lay panting on his bed. He wasted away from this affliction, and his hands and feet were crippled. For five years he endured this illness. In the sixth year he asked to be brought to the saint's church. As he lay praying in this church, his illness vanished and he deserved to receive his health.

45. The hands of another man that were straightened

And lest these miracles that are described seem unbelievable to anyone because the names of the individual people are not recorded in these pages, there is a reason for this: when these people have been restored to health by this saint of God, immediately they depart and sometimes leave so quietly that, if it is proper to say so, no one sees them. Whenever a rumor arises that the power of the blessed bishop has appeared, I summon the custodians of the shrine and learn what has happened; but I do not always learn the [individual] names from these custodians.[89] But often I do record by name those people whom I was able to see or with whom I talked. A man from Bourges came to the festival [of Martin on July 4, 585]. His hands were disabled, and his fingers were fastened so [deeply] in one palm that it was thought to swarm with worms. But after the celebration of the festival the fingers on both hands were straightened, and he was restored to health. All the people saw him return with his health. The reason for his disability was that he had wished to repair a fence around his crop on a Sunday.

46. The woman whose arm was crippled

A woman from the territory of Poitiers, whose arm had withered after her ligaments stiffened, came to the tomb of the blessed man. After she spent the night praying and keeping vigils, she returned with a healthy arm; but as soon as she was subjected to slavery by her masters, she suffered the same disability. She returned again [to Tours] and was cured. Her masters came and tried to abduct her; but after they accepted a payment from the saint's wealth, they ceased. And so this woman was presented with her freedom.

47. The man who was imprisoned for a debt

In these days when a man was requested to pay back a debt that he had contracted because of his hardships and there was neither the capacity nor the means to compensate what he had borrowed, he was confined in prison. Once the creditor then saw that he could squeeze nothing [more] from the man because he had nothing [left] and that there was no one to extend him a compassionate hand, he fettered the man more tightly in chains, denied him food and drink, and said: "I will make you waste away from hunger as an example for everyone, until you pay back everything." While this was happening, the relics of the holy bishop that were being brought to a district in [the territory of] Soissons passed by on the street. The imprisoned man heard the voices of the people chanting Psalms and prayed that the power of the holy bishop might assist him. Immediately his

---

[89] L. Pietri (1983) 634–36 suggests that these *custodes*, "custodians," are to be identified with *ostiarii*, "doorkeepers," who were low-ranking clerics. Since Gregory was in Orléans on July 4, 585 (*Hist.* 8.1), he certainly did not witness this particular miracle.

bonds were loosened, and no one prevented him from entering the holy church. Then he was ransomed by pious believers and freed from the obligation of his debt.[90]

48. The blind woman who received her sight

During one festival [of Martin on November 11, 585] it happened that a woman who had lost her sight and remained blind heard about the miracles of the holy man and with an eager piety went to his church. She knelt on the dry ground in front of the tomb, and as soon as she offered a prayer, she deserved to receive her sight.

49. The paralyzed boy whose entire body was disabled

During this festival a boy came [who suffered from numerous disabilities]: the sight in his eyes was obstructed, the openings to his ears were blocked, his mouth was hampered in speaking, his hands had lost their usefulness, and his feet were deprived of their mobility. Why say more? Because of the uselessness of all his limbs he was so close to death that he barely moved except for his breathing. But when he touched the holy place, all his disabilities were completely removed. He gave thanks and departed with his health.

50. The priest who was cured of a fever

Lupus was a priest at Bordeaux. He was once so severely afflicted with a quartan fever that when the fever was present, he was unable to swallow either food or drink. Then it was time for a festival of the bishop St. Martin [on July 4, 586]. After Lupus celebrated vigils with the other clergy, at daybreak he preceded everyone else and rushed to the saint's church. As he was hurrying, he met a Jew who asked where he was going. Lupus replied: "I am suffering from a quartan fever, and now I am rushing to the saint's church so that his power might save me from this illness." The Jew said: "Martin will be of no use to you, because the dirt pressing down [on him in his tomb] has made him into dirt. In vain do you go to his shrine; a dead man will not be able to provide medicine for the living." But Lupus ignored these words of the old serpent and went where he intended. He knelt before the holy relics, offered a prayer, and discovered there two small candles made of wax and papyrus that he took and brought home. He lit the candles, drank the ashes of the papyrus [that he mixed] with clear water, and soon recovered his health. But the Jew was afflicted with this illness and

[90] During October 585 (*Hist.* 8.24) Gregory visited King Childebert at Coblenz and the deacon Vulfilaic near Trier (*Hist.* 8.13–17); so perhaps he himself delivered these relics of St. Martin to Soissons during this trip.

disturbed for a year; yet his wicked mind was never able to be converted through these torments.[91]

51. The baby who was cured

Chardegysil, whose family name was Gyso, was a citizen of Saintes. After I was welcomed to his home, he invited me to an oratory that his mother had built and consecrated with relics of the blessed Martin. After we prayed, I asked whether the bishop's power had been revealed there. Chardegysil replied: "Three years ago when my young son, whom you personally met, was still sucking at his mother's breast, he began to suffer badly. For thirty days or more he was with difficulty carried about in [others'] hands, until he was so exhausted that he was unable to suck a breast or to swallow other food. He was becoming weak, and on the sixth day after he began to suffer more severely we placed him in front of the altar. We wept and expected him to die. Because I could not endure this grief, I left home after instructing my wife to bury the boy as soon as he died. His mother was weeping as the little boy lay [before the tomb] until evening. But as the sun was setting, he raised his voice and said: 'Dearest sister, where are you?' For he was accustomed to address his mother in this way when she teased the little boy. His mother hurried forward and said: 'I am here, dearest son.' She took him in her arms and soon extended her breast; after he drank her milk, he recovered."

52. The cleric with dysentery

During the days when this [previous] story was told to me, one of my clerics suffered from a discharge from his bowels as well as a fever and a sharp pain in his stomach. Most of what he discharged from his lower parts was blood. This misfortune drastically affected him, because when his nausea increased, he immediately vomited whatever food he ate. But as soon as he drank some dust from the tomb [of Martin], his illness was completely eliminated, and he was healed.

53. The man who was released after being hanged

I have decided that this story must not be passed over in silence, because often [Martin] has extended his compassionate right hand and assisted people condemned to death. A slave belonging to Genitor, a citizen of

---

[91] The church of St. Martin at Bordeaux had been constructed by Leontius, bishop in the mid-sixth century: see Fortunatus, *Carm.* 1.6, with Weidemann (1982) 1:143. It was located on a hill outside the city, near a Jewish cemetery: see Vieillard-Troiekouroff (1976) 54–55. Gregory traveled to Bordeaux now perhaps in order to visit Gundegisil Dodo, who had become bishop in late 585 (*Hist.* 8.22); Weidemann (1982) 1:216 suggests that on this trip he also visited Blaye, Bouliac, and Rions (*GC* 45–47).

Tours, was arrested by a judge for the crime of theft and sentenced to the gallows. As he was being led away, he called upon the name of the blessed bishop and said: "Holy confessor Martin, free me from this impending danger." Then he was hanged and left alone. Suddenly a wind blew up, and he heard a voice that said: "Let us free him." And behold, the beam that supported the man was struck [by wind] from the four corners of the sky, and like a tree uprooted from the ground it was split and [pulled up] a huge pile of sod. In this way the man condemned to death was raised up and brought back to life.

Another man who had committed many crimes was contrite before God and performed penance for the evils that he had done. When he was seized without proper judicial process and condemned to a similar execution, he always called upon the assistance of the blessed confessor. After he was hanged, his bonds were broken and he fell unhurt to the ground. But men with wicked minds again seized this man whom God had delivered. When the abbot from a nearby monastery heard about this, he hurried to the count in order to petition on behalf of this man. The count was about three miles away. Once the abbot obtained the life of this accused man from the count, he returned and found him still alive. The abbot took him down from the gallows and brought him to the monastery. The man made a public statement and said: "I felt the power of St. Martin, who delivered me."

54. The mute man who was healed

A man who was from Montlouis, a village in the territory of Tours, was modest by nature and bound by the bond of marriage. In the middle of the night he was frightened as he was sleeping with his wife. In his terror he jumped up from bed, and as he fearfully wandered about his house, he lost control over his voice. Immediately he indicated with a nod to his wife that she should take him to the saint's church. He went there, and for six months he frequently lay praying before the blessed tomb. Then his tongue was loosened, and through the power of the blessed [Martin] he deserved to recover his speech, just as he had had it previously.

55. The woman whose hand was crippled

Because a woman who lived on the other side of the Loire River was doing a task on a Sunday that ancestral authority prohibits from being done on that day, her hand was bent and stiffened, and her fingers were fastened in her palm. The woman was racked with pains and went to the sacred shrine of the confessor. She promised that if she were healed of this disability, she would thereafter never do on this day of the Lord's resurrection anything that was inappropriate to the day. Immediately her fingers were loosened from her palm, her hand was straightened, and she departed.

56. The woman who received her sight

Because the compassion of the confessor is immense, it censures the unwise in such a way that it places their misdeeds before their eyes, corrects them, and restores them for the future. Another woman became ill for this reason. While she was placing a loaf of bread in an oven on a Saturday after the setting of the sun, which time is a part of the night of [each Sunday celebrating] the Lord's resurrection, her arm was afflicted with a pain. After she inserted a second and a third loaf, her hand began to tighten involuntarily on the wooden utensil she was holding. The woman realized that she had been condemned [by the judgment] of divine power and quickly discarded the utensil she was holding; but she was nevertheless unable to avoid punishment. For her hands were crippled with such severe pain that her fingernails were attached to her palms. Because she believed that she could not be healed by the potion of any doctor, she went to the church of the blessed [Martin] and there prayed piously. Her hands were straightened, she left with her health, and she promised that during each month she ought to serve one week at the holy church. It is very well known that she kept this promise for one year. But after a year she missed a week during one month and did not go to the holy church. While she was sitting in her house, one of her eyes was pierced with a pain that closed this eye; then the other eye immediately began to ache. In the space of one hour she became blind in both eyes. Immediately she confessed and fled to her proven protection [in the church of Martin]. There she humbly offered a prayer and remorsefully performed penance for her negligence. Eight days later blood flowed from her eyes and she received her sight.

57. The blind man who received his sight

One man's eyes had been covered by a thick cloud of darkness and obstructed by his eyelids that were fastened together by some stickiness; all other parts of his body were racked by terrible pains. Why say more? He piously attended the saint's festival [in 587][92] with the other people and carefully prayed that he might deserve to be assisted by the power of the blessed bishop on the day of his festival. But the confessor's power appeared before the holy ceremonies and demonstrated that it was present for the people by dispelling darkness and restoring light. Three days before the

---

[92] Corbett (1983) 59 dates the festival of St. Martin in *VM* 3.57–58 to July 4, 586; Weidemann (1982) 1:216 dates it to November 11, 586 or July 4, 587; Heinzelmann (1981) 240, prefers 587 but is undecided between July 4 and November 11; Schlick (1966) 286 prefers November 11, 587.

festival while this man was praying in the courtyard that surrounds the apse containing [Martin's] body, his eyes were suddenly opened, and he looked about and deserved to see the light. While he was giving thanks and describing what had happened to the others who were there, it was said to him that he should rather be silent and offer a prayer that the blessed bishop might quickly complete that miracle that he had begun. Then the man knelt on the ground. When he burst out in tears, his eyes were healed, and he stood up from the ground with his health.

58. The paralyzed man and the two blind men

Three days after this festival a paralyzed man was praying in this place; as he himself explained, his disability had appeared for this reason. He said that when he was a young boy and with the others was keeping watch over the flocks in a field, he fell asleep next to a spring. When the others departed at noon, he remained alone. He finally awoke from his nap; but when he tried to stand up, he was stiff with pain. Soon all his limbs were crippled; his arms were twisted outward, the tendons in his knees were stiffened, and his feet were bent toward his shins. Since he had no power to move, he produced many tears and loud shouts. His companions returned to check on the flocks and found him crying. Then he was carried in his parents' arms and returned to his home. A few days later when he experienced a bit of relief from his pains, he was entrusted to some beggars, with whom he traveled to districts and cities for ten or more years. After he came for this festival, he was healed in all his limbs. Two blind men received their sight on the same day, and two possessed men were cleansed at the bishop's tomb.

59. The boy with a fever

One of my young servants was so afflicted with nocturnal fevers that from the eighth hour of one day until the second hour of the next he was unable to find any relief from this burning. All food was repulsive to him, and he received nothing that was of any comfort. A severe pain shook all his limbs, and a pallor settled on his cheeks. While he was being carried about in this condition like an ill person by the hands of his parents, I was able with difficulty to provide for him to be brought to the tomb of the blessed bishop. After he was brought there, he drank [some of] the holy dust from the tomb that had been mixed with water. Soon all his pain vanished and his fever was extinguished by this blessing. Immediately the boy requested a private place [to relieve] his digestive system, and he was led to a corner to empty his bowels. When he answered the urge of his stomach with a powerful blast of air, two worms at once proceeded from him in the manner of serpents that appeared to men's eyes to be moved in such a way that they were thought to be alive. Once these worms had been expelled from him, the boy was at once completely healed. He took food and drink as usual; the pallor vanished and a red flush was restored to his cheeks; and he was healthy in all his limbs.

60. The miracles that happened during [my] journey

Because of circumstances it recently happened that I went to visit my mother in the territory of Chalon-sur-Saône.[93] But because I was afraid of the misfortunes that would happen to us, I dared to take some of this dust, that is, from the tomb of the blessed bishop, and to carry it with me, so that if some illness afflicted any of my companions, the saint's power would assist with his usual strength. After I came to my mother, suddenly a fever and dysentery attacked one of my servants and so exhausted and weakened him that the benefit of food was denied him and he was nourished by his fevers alone. Three days after I heard about this, I mixed the dust [with water] and brought it to the servant on the verge of death to drink. Immediately his fever vanished, his pain lessened, and he recovered.

During these days I heard [this story] from Bishop Veranus. Once while he was burning from the heat of a quartan fever, he went to the church of the blessed Martin that was in that place and was healed after celebrating vigils.[94] As I was returning from this journey to Clermont, I found that Bishop Avitus was shaking so severely from a tertian fever that even if he ate some food, he immediately vomited. But after he took a drink [mixed] with this relic [of dust], his fever lessened and he regained his strength.

[93] After her husband died, Armentaria eventually left Clermont and moved back to her own family's native region of Burgundy (cf. *GM* 83, *VM* 1.36). But because of Gregory's erratic spelling it is uncertain where Armentaria had her house and an oratory dedicated to St. Eusebius (cf. *GC* 3). Krusch's text here has Gregory visiting his mother *in terretorium Cavellonensis urbis*. Some have identified the city as Cabellio, i.e., Cavaillon, and then located the oratory at Cabrières: see Krusch (1885) 647n.1, Vieillard-Troiekouroff (1976) 73, 76, and Weidemann (1982) 1:206, 217. Others have identified this city as Cabillonum, i.e., Chalon-sur-Saône: see L. Pietri (1983) 253n.40. Chalon-sur-Saône seems the most plausible identification. Armentaria's family had a long-standing association with the city, since her uncle Nicetius, later bishop of Lyon, had been ordained as a priest in 543 by Bishop Agricola of Chalon-sur-Saône: see *Vita Nicetii* 3. And Armentaria once seems to have accompanied Gregory to visit a shrine in Chalon-sur-Saône (*GC* 84). Early in 588 Gregory visited King Childebert at Metz, which was suffering from a plague of dysentery (*Hist.* 9.13). Childebert then sent Gregory as an envoy to King Guntramn at Chalon-sur-Saône (*Hist.* 9.20). So Gregory may have visited his mother and his servant may have become ill from dysentery during this same journey.

[94] Veranus was bishop of Cavaillon. He had served as an envoy from King Guntramn to the court of Fredegund in 585 (*Hist.* 8.31); had presided at the baptism of Theuderic, the second son of King Childebert, in autumn 587 (*Hist.* 9.4); and would be one of the bishops assembled by King Guntramn in 589 to consider the riots at Poitiers (*Hist.* 9.41). Given his close association with Guntramn he may have been in attendance during Gregory's visit to the king and then told Gregory about his fever. Since Gregory's language here was imprecise, this church dedicated to St. Martin was not necessarily at Cavaillon: see above, chapter 4, section 3.

An unhealthy fever affected two of my servants and, as is often common with this affliction, a fierce pain attacked the joints of all their limbs. But after they drank of this blessing, they were healed.

During this journey I myself suffered from a painful toothache. When not just my teeth but my entire head was pierced by the pounding of my veins and by my stinging pains, and when my temples were twitching madly, I sought assistance [from this dust]. Soon my pain lessened and I recovered. O indescribable antidote! O unspeakable balm! O praiseworthy remedy! O heavenly purgative, if I may say so! This dust overwhelms the subtleties of doctors, surpasses sweet scents, and is more powerful than all strong ointments. Like scammony it purges the stomach, and like hyssop, the lungs; and like pyrethrum it cleanses even the head. Not only does it strengthen disabled limbs, but—something that is more important than all these [previously mentioned benefits]—it removes and lightens those very blemishes of conscience.

Let these stories that have been included be enough for this book. But if I am still worthy to see [more] miracles, it is proper for them to be included in another book, so that the miracles that are revealed ought rather to be publicized, not concealed. As for the rest, I request [Martin's] power so that he who reveals such [miracles] at his tomb might deign to revive me, already dead to God because of my sins, from the grave of this death. Then, when he is presented for his crown, he might obtain forgiveness for me at the moment of the resurrection of all flesh.

Here ends this third book.

VM 4

Here begins a fourth book.

The prophet warns us with very sound advice when he says: "God, your friends must be honored."[95] Likewise in another Psalm: "He who praises those who fear the Lord is united to the blessing of an eternal home" [cf. Ps. 15:4–5]. It is therefore clearly apparent to the human mind that not only those who are immune from crime but also those who are bound by the evil of injurious crime are advised to show respectful veneration for the friends of God. Not only is this something that is beneficial in this present world, but it also offers consolation in the future. For often whenever we witness the evidence of the miracles that appear at the tombs of the blessed [saints],

[95] Gregory here quoted Ps. 138:17 from the Vulgate, which followed the Septuagint; in this version the verse became one of the biblical citations commonly used to justify veneration for saints: see Van Uytfanghe (1989) 160–61, 165, 200. In modern translations of the Hebrew text the verse is Ps. 139:17, and it praises God's thoughts.

we are deservedly motivated to show the honorable respect that is owed to these [saints] from whom we do not cease to request remedies for our afflictions. We do not doubt not only that we are worthy to acquire this remission for our sins through their prayers, but also that we are saved from the infernal torments through their intervention. For we believe that just as they restrain [all] kinds of illnesses here, so they deflect the ruthless penalties of torments there; that just as they alleviate bodily fevers here, so they quench the eternal flames there; that just as they cleanse the horrible ulcers of ghastly leprosy here, so through their intervention they obtain relief for the blemishes of sins there; and that just as they restore to life the bodies of the dead here, so there they extend their hand, dig up from the waters of the Acheron those buried in sin, and restore them to eternal life. As a result, each person then cheerfully rejoices under the protection of his own patron [saint] and more eagerly repays the honor that is owed, when he realizes that he has been cleansed by his patron's power from the illness that he suffered; likewise now both I myself and countless others have experienced [the power of] the blessed bishop Martin, who is a special patron for the entire world. If only the worthlessness of my mind will allow him to be honored as is proper for a friend of God! For whenever different kinds of serious illnesses afflicted me, he often restored me to health.

1. My stomachache

Very recently I suffered from a stomachache. Although it did not always cause diarrhea, this painful ache nevertheless wandered about in the twisting corners of my intestines. I confess, often I took baths and bound hot pads over these pains in my stomach, but nothing could relieve this ailment. The sixth day dawned. As this pain was increasing more and more, I remembered that a few years previously I had been healed from this sort of stomachache by the saint's power; the written account [of that miracle] is found in the second book of this work.[96] I boldly went to the tomb, knelt on the ground, and offered a prayer. I also secretly put beneath my garment [a thread] from the curtains hanging there and with it made the sign of the cross on my stomach. Immediately the pain vanished, and I left with my health.

2. My tongue and lips

Once my tongue was so painfully swollen that often it made me stammer when I wished to speak. I found this embarrassing. So I went to the saint's tomb and licked the wood of the railing with my afflicted tongue; immediately the swelling was reduced, and I recovered. For my tongue had been very enlarged and had filled the entire opening to my throat. Three days

---

[96] Cf. *VM* 2.1.

later my lip began to throb painfully. Again I went to seek my health at the tomb; and after I touched my lip to the curtains hanging there, immediately the throbbing in my vein stopped. I believe that my pain was due to an abundance of blood; but because of the saint's power I did not wish to reduce my blood. Thereafter this disorder did not bother me.

3. The boy cured of a fever

Then a young boy was afflicted with a fever. His limbs were consumed, and because he ate no food, he reached the point of exhaling his spirit. His father wept and rushed to me; I told him to bring the boy to the church and spend the entire night in vigils. After he did this, immediately he received his son who had been healed through the power of the holy bishop.

4. The crippled man and the blind woman

A man whose fingers were bent into his palm came to the festival [of Martin] that is celebrated during the fifth month [on July 4, 588]; after he offered a prayer, his fingers were straightened and he left. A woman who had been blind for eight years knelt on the ground in front of the saint's tomb; after sight was restored to her eyes, she returned to her own region. Then three possessed men were cleansed by the saint's power.

5. The slave of Theodulf

[This miracle happened] during this same year, that is, in the thirteenth year [of the reign] of King Childebert, during the festival that celebrates [Martin's] blessed death [on November 11, 588]. Theodulf was a citizen of Tours. One night one of his slaves who was a swineherd was keeping watch over the pigs entrusted [to him] lest a wild beast seize one of them or a thief covertly steal one. Suddenly his eyes were covered with darkness, and he lost his sight. After he endured this blindness for six years, he came to this festival. Three days later he received his sight through the saint's power; then he was released by his master as a free man.

6. The many ailments that were cured

When it was time for the saint's festival [on July 4, 589] during the fourteenth year [of the reign] of the aforementioned king [Childebert], twelve paralytics were healed, three blind men received their sight, and five possessed men were cleansed.

In attendance at this festival was Abbot Aredius of Limoges, whom I have mentioned in previous books and through whom the Lord healed a paralyzed woman. For eight years this woman had been placed on a wagon; after she lay in the courtyard [of the church] of the blessed confessor, her feet were straightened and she recovered. For Aredius, a man of God, himself claimed that he had felt as it were the hand of the blessed

Martin when he made the sign of the cross and stroked the limbs of the crippled woman with the touch of salvation.

Also in attendance at this festival were Florentianus, the mayor [of the royal household], and Romulf, count of the palace. They showed great admiration for the glory of the confessor through whom the Lord then deigned to perform such miracles.[97]

7. The cluster of grapes in Galicia

Since I have mentioned the mayor Florentianus, I think it would be improper to omit what I learned from him. Once he went to Galicia as an envoy, and upon entering the presence of King Miro, he revealed the issues entrusted to him. At that time King Miro was in the city where [one of] his predecessors had constructed a church in honor of St. Martin, as I have already mentioned in the first book of this work. In front of this church's colonnade was a long arch [formed] from the branches of vines [and covered] with hanging clusters of grapes that flourished just as in a painting. Beneath this arch there was a path that led people on foot to the doors of the holy church. As the king was passing beneath this arch and entering the church in order to pray, he said to his companions: "Take care lest you touch one of these grapes and thereby by chance cause offense to the holy bishop. For everything in this courtyard is dedicated to him." One of his servants heard these words and said to himself: "I do not know whether or not these grapes are dedicated to this saint. I know only this, that it is the intention of my heart to eat some of them." As soon as he extended his hand and began to cut off the stem of a grape, immediately his right hand was stuck to the arch, his arm withered, and his hand stiffened. This servant was the king's mime, who was accustomed to excite merriment because of his jokes; but neither any laughter nor skillful sleight of hand assisted him now. Instead he began to shout because of the throbbing pain, and he said: "Gentlemen, help me in my misery, assist me in my aggravation, and relieve me of my burden. Pray for the power of the bishop St. Martin on my behalf; for I am threatened with death, tormented with a great affliction, and deprived [of my arm] by this wound." The king left [the

[97] For Aredius, see the note to *VJ* 28. King Childebert had assigned Florentianus and Romulf as tax assessors for Poitiers and Tours. Already at a banquet on Easter in early April Fortunatus had represented Gregory and the interests of Tours: see Fortunatus, *Carm.* 10.11. Upon their arrival at Tours in July, when they produced a book that listed the assessments under previous kings, Gregory reminded them that Kings Chlothar I, Charibert, Sigibert, and now Childebert had either canceled taxes "because of their fear of St. Martin" or not collected them. Gregory also immediately sent envoys to Childebert, who again canceled taxes at Tours "because of his respect for St. Martin" (*Hist.* 9.30). Presumably also at this time Fortunatus petitioned Gregory, Count Galienus, Florentianus, and Romulf on behalf of a captive girl: see Fortunatus, *Carm.* 10.12.

church], and upon learning what had happened he raged with such anger against the servant that he wished to cut off his hand, if he had not been restrained by his companions who said: "O king, laugh at the mime, but then do not add your vengeance to the judgment of God on your servant, lest perhaps you turn upon yourself the punishment with which you threaten your servant." Then the king was regretful in his heart, and he entered the church, knelt before the holy altar, wept, and offered a prayer to the Lord. He did not stand up from the pavement until the tears from his eyes had blotted out the record of this servant's transgression. After the servant was released from the chain with which he had been bound and entered the church, the king stood up from the ground, received his servant in good health, and returned to his palace. The aforementioned mayor Florentianus said that he had learned of these events, just as I have narrated them, from an account by King Miro himself. For the glorious bishop distinguishes his own city [of Tours] with miracles in the same way as he is known to be of assistance in other cities.[98]

8. The saint's church in Saintes

In this same year Bishop Palladius of Saintes requested relics of this holy confessor. In his honor he had built a church that he dedicated with these relics, and he [then] was worthy to receive there the miracles that [Martin's] own city [of Tours] had experienced. For after two or three months had passed, I received a letter from him in which he noted that three paralytics whose feet were crippled had come, and that as soon as they offered a prayer upon entering the church, their feet were straightened and they left with their health. In the same place two blind men were worthy to receive their sight after they prayed, and more than twelve people who shivered from fevers recovered after their tremors were eliminated.[99]

---

[98] Miro was king of the Sueves from 570 to 583 (*Hist.* 5.41, 6.43). For the church, see *VM* 1.11.

[99] Bishop Palladius was a descendant of a distinguished Gallic family (*GC* 59) whose members had become prominent already during the fifth century as bishops and teachers: see *PLRE* 2:821, and Weidemann (1982) 1:193–94. At Saintes he promoted the cults of Eutropis, thought to have been the first bishop of the city (*GM* 55), and of Abbot Martinus, thought to have studied with Martin of Tours (*GC* 56). But as a politician Palladius was not very adept. In 585 he consecrated a bishop nominated by the pretender Gundovald (*Hist.* 7.31); later that year at Orléans King Guntramn harshly criticized him for his disloyalty and refused to celebrate mass with him (*Hist.* 8.2, 7). Since Gregory was also then visiting Guntramn at Orléans, he and Palladius probably met. Still later in 585 Palladius lost the support of his metropolitan bishop, Bertramn of Bordeaux, and of his own clergy at Saintes (*Hist.* 8.22); and early in 587 he was accused before King Guntramn of having received envoys from Queen Fredegund (*Hist.* 8.43). In his precarious circumstances he could certainly have benefited from the support of St. Martin.

9. The two men suffering from dysentery

Two of my servants, a cleric named Dagobald and a layman named Theodorus, suffered from dysentery and a fever. They were so weakened by this illness that when it was necessary to move their bowels, they [could] not be lifted from their beds except by others' hands. But after they drank [a potion mixed with] dust from the tomb, they immediately recovered.

10. The saucers that the saint acquired

In my possession there is a sapphire-colored saucer that the saint is said to have received from the treasury of the emperor Maximus. His power often proceeds from this saucer on behalf of people suffering from chills. For [whenever] someone suffering from a violent fever that is usually accompanied by shivering comes and drinks water from this saucer, he is soon healed. At the village of Candes there is another saucer of metal and crystal likewise acquired by the saint that offers a similar blessing to ill people, if they are pious in their requests. Bodilo, who was one of my stenographers, was so mentally befuddled because of a weak stomach that he was hardly able to write and listen as usual or to record what was dictated to him. Then, after he was often verbally rebuked, he poured water into this saucer of the blessed man that I mentioned was in my possession and drained it into his mouth. Soon he was restored to his senses and performed the duties of his office more quickly than usual.[100]

11. Blederic, who had no sons

But what is the surprise if [Martin], who has often changed barrenness into fertility, restores to men their senses that have been confused by a misfortune? Blederic was a citizen in the territory of Chartres. After he took a wife, he prayed that he might be enriched by a gift of God, [that is,] by a child of his own begetting; but he was not worthy to receive any offspring from his wife. After thirty years passed by and his wife remained barren, her husband thought most carefully about the welfare of their souls and said to his wife: "Behold, the life we have lived in this world is over, and we have produced no child who ought to possess the rewards of our labor after we have died." Blederic continued: "I will go to the church of St. Martin and make it my heir, so that, since I have been denied children, in the future I and this church might possess whatever I could acquire." His sensible wife agreed with the shrewd advice of her husband. Immediately

[100] On Maximus, see the note to *VJ* 4. According to Sulpicius Severus, *Vita Martini* 20.4–7, during a banquet Maximus had had a drinking saucer presented to Martin, who then offered it to one of his priests. But Sulpicius did not indicate that anyone kept the saucer as a souvenir, and in *Dial.* 2.5.10, 3.14.5–6, he noted that Martin did not accept gifts from the emperor Valentinian or an imperial magistrate.

he went to the saint's church, offered a prayer, and invited the abbot to return home with him.[101] When the abbot arrived, Blederic gave him all his possessions and said: "Let everything that I am seen to possess belong to the control of St. Martin; and hereafter may I use only enough to be supported from my possessions as long as I am alive." After his possessions were signed over, he insisted that the abbot remain at his home. [What happened next is] amazing to report! After the passage of thirty years, as I mentioned, and during the very night when he gave all his possessions to the church, he slept with his wife, who then conceived and gave birth to a son. The fact that thereafter Blederic also had other sons clearly proves that the saint's power had been shown to this man. Blederic did not, however, break his promise after he received these sons, but left them other lands; what he had already bestowed upon the saint, he confirmed.

12. The blind woman at the villa of Ternay

In the territory of Le Mans is the villa of Ternay, which is now controlled by the authority of this holy church. A woman who had been restricted for a long time by blindness and was burdened by old age remained at the oratory of this villa, where she begged for alms and frequently called upon the name of St. Martin. During the night before a Sunday her eyes began to sting with pain. Then she knelt before the holy altar, and when blood flowed [from her eyes], she recovered her sight. But the relics in that place are of the most blessed apostles, that is, of Peter and Paul; nevertheless this woman insisted that she had been healed by the power of the holy bishop. For our faith believes that a single Lord works through the powers of many saints and that these saints are not differentiated by their powers, because the Lord makes them equal in heaven and similar on earth with his miracles.

13. The withered hand that was restored

A man with a withered and paralyzed hand came to this festival [of Martin on November 11, 589] that Bishop Aunacharius of Auxerre attended. Three days after the festival this man returned home with a restored hand.[102]

---

[101] The secular abbot governed the clerics and others associated with a shrine or church and is to be distinguished from the abbot of a monastic community: see L. Pietri (1983a). This secular abbot was often a priest, and at some churches he might also be the *martyrarius* responsible for the relics: see L. Pietri (1983) 689–90. The *aedituus* responsible for the buildings was a deacon, who might also serve as the *martyrarius* (*VJ* 46b): see Weidemann (1982) 1:230–33, 240–44.

[102] Aunacharius had become bishop of Auxerre by the time he attended the council at Paris in September 573: see Weidemann (1982) 1:141. Earlier in 589 he and other bishops had assembled with King Guntramn, who intended to convene a council on November 1 (*Hist.*

14. Baudegisil, a disabled man

Baudegisil, the son of Baudulf, was an inhabitant of the village of Gennes in the territory of Angers. He fell down disabled after he was wounded by the attack of a painful swelling. He was supported by his father, who was a poor man lacking the rewards of any work. With tears welling up Baudegisil begged his father that he might kiss the threshold of the church of St. Martin. His father immediately put his son on a boat, because he could not be transported by any other conveyance, and piously brought him to the saint's feet, that is, [to the courtyard] outside the tomb. For several days Baudegisil prayed and requested the saint's assistance; then his affliction was removed, and he was restored to his health. Once healed, he returned home with his father.

15. The man who brought wax

A man named Caelestis lived in the territory of Auch and owned many beehives. A swarm of bees left his hives, flew up high, and gathered far away. Caelestis followed but was completely unsuccessful at capturing [the bees]. He knelt on the ground, called upon the name of St. Martin, and said: "Most blessed confessor, if your power wishes to guide this swarm and restore it to my possession, then, with regard to what these bees produce in the future, I will take the honey for my use but I will send all the wax for the lights in your church." After he said this and while he was still lying on the ground, the swarm of bees at once came down and landed on a small tree that was near Caelestis. He collected the bees, put them in a hive, and brought them home. Within two or three years he gathered much [honey and wax] from this hive. After he had accumulated more than two hundred pounds of wax, the report of an enemy attack was spread. Because Caelestis did not want to see his vow unfulfilled, he buried his beeswax in a ditch in the ground. Once peace was restored, he summoned my deacon to collect the wax. One of his servants suffered very severe pains in his kidneys. When he came to Caelestis and learned from his mouth what had happened, he ordered the wax hidden in the ground to be uncovered. Although this servant suffered from pain, as I said, he took a hoe, dug up the ground, and said: "St. Martin, if you are gracious in looking upon this gift of Caelestis, and if you are my deliverance, may your power touch my kidneys when I uncover this wax." As he struck the ground with his hoe, the small openings of his kidneys made a noise and immediately his pain vanished entirely. Once healed, he was presented to the blessed church along with this beeswax.

9.41). Aunacharius may have been one of those who had already set out for this council before it was canceled (*Hist.* 9.32); so perhaps he went to Tours instead.

16. The release of a prisoner

A man from Tours was considered guilty by a judge who ordered him to be bound in chains and guarded. When the holy days arrived for [the celebration of] the Lord's resurrection [on Easter 590],[103] the judge ordered this man to be brought to another prison on the far bank of the Loire River. As the man was being escorted, not only was his neck bound with chains but his hands were also tied behind his back. When they came to the bank of the aforementioned river and waited for the boat on which they intended to cross, the man was constantly requesting the assistance of St. Martin. Suddenly it seemed to the guards as if they had been struck on the head by someone. Immediately they fell to the ground. The chains that held the man captive were broken, and the ropes were loosened and fell from his hands. The man realized that he was free, and since his guards were still lying on the ground, he left them and entered the threshold of the holy cathedral. Then he was released by the judge.

Some said that during these days prisoners in Poitiers had been released from confinement in a prison. This can leave no doubt about which confessor's power was able to distinguish both cities with these holy miracles.[104]

17. The blind boy

A small boy named Leodoald was the slave of Baudeleif, who was from a village [in the territory] of Angers whose name of old was Crû. Leodoald had been born again [through baptism] in the water and the Holy Spirit. While he was playing a game with the other boys in the street, he was running here and there as children of that age are permitted. Suddenly a current of wind gusted, blew up some dust, and filled the young boy's eyes. While he was afflicted with blindness and suffered from pains, a man appeared to his grandmother in a dream and said: "Go to the church of St. Martin, and this boy will receive his sight." The woman was filled with faith and immediately went to the festival [of Martin on July 4, 590], and

---

[103] Although the congregation at Tours also celebrated the festival of the Lord's resurrection on March 27 (cf. *VM* 3.3), L. Pietri (1983) 452n.79 argues that Gregory's reference here to "holy days" must indicate the Lenten festivities leading up to Easter. Typically, in this year the date of Easter was again in dispute (*Hist.* 10.23). This celebration of Easter also provides an appropriate context for the debate between Gregory and one of his priests over the possibility of bodily resurrection (*Hist.* 10.13): see above, chapter 3, section 3.

[104] The revolt in Radegund's convent at Poitiers that had broken out in 589 (*Hist.* 9.39–43) turned violent in 590. Chrodechild, a leader of the rebellious nuns, hired thugs to invade the convent and seize Abbess Leubovera. By mistake these men first seized the prioress Justina, who was Gregory's niece; then they took Leubovera captive. Since this outrage occurred during the week before Easter, Bishop Maroveus threatened not to celebrate Easter or baptize catechumens until the abbess was released; eventually Leubovera took refuge in the church of St. Hilary (*Hist.* 10.15): see above, chapter 1, section 2. So perhaps Gregory had this episode in mind here.

through the bishop's power she brought back her grandson after he had received his sight.

18. The blind girl

Within the territory of Angers was a little girl named Viliogund, who was blinded in similar circumstances. For while she was running about and playing a game with the other girls in the streets of the village, dust was blown up by a gust of wind and filled her eyes. She immediately suffered from pains and asked her parents that they lead her to the church of St. Martin. They did so, and as soon as they offered a prayer for their daughter, she received her sight. The aforementioned boy [Leodoald] and this girl met me as I was leaving after the celebration of holy mass, and they said that they had received their sight through the power of the blessed bishop at that very hour. This made me very happy, for I believed that the power of the blessed confessor had deigned to favor me.

19. The crippled man and the blind man

Litoveus had been disabled in his limbs from his infancy; after a fever developed, he was blinded. When he came to a previous festival, his limbs were straightened and he departed; but he was still deprived of his sight. When he returned again for this [current] festival, his darkness was removed, and he stood up after being restored to his sight.

20. Another blind man

Leudard was a slave of Eumerius, a deacon at Nantes, and had been bound by the chain of blindness for six years. During this festival he went to [Martin's] church and received his sight through the power of the blessed confessor. For he had been advised in a vision during a dream to request the assistance of this holy bishop.

21. The consecrated bread taken away by Mothar, a citizen of Tours

When a citizen of Tours was preparing to meet a king, he placed a container of wine and a loaf of bread before [Martin's] tomb, intending to leave them for one night so that what had been placed there might offer a guarantee of safety on his journey. After he collected this wine and bread, he began to travel. Then it happened that while seeking lodging he entered a man's inn. When he set down his bags, [his host's] wife, who had an unclean spirit, began to announce with loud cries the arrival of the blessed Martin and said: "Saint, why are you pursuing me? Servant of God, why are you torturing me?" Then the guest who had [just] arrived took a chalice, poured out a bit of the wine from his container, and put in it a crumb broken off from the consecrated bread. Once the raving woman drank this [potion], soon the demon was expelled in some blood and she was saved. In this place there was another woman who had been ill for a long time with chills. She accepted a piece of this consecrated bread and was healed when she swallowed it.

22. The crippled man who was healed

When Silluvius, an inhabitant of Bayeux, was in the field doing some work, he was struck with fear when the wind gusted. He began to tremble, was robbed [of the use] of all his limbs, shouted, and claimed that his death was imminent. Then his neighbors gathered for such a spectacle. While Silluvius was shouting and screaming, his nerves stiffened and he was completely disabled. Not only was the use of his limbs denied to him, but he also lacked sight in his eyes. He suffered from this misfortune for fifteen years, until he went to the festival of St. Martin [on November 11, 590]. After his limbs were strengthened and his eyesight restored, he departed.[105]

23. The blind woman and the disabled man who were healed

A crippled and blind woman named Ermegund was a citizen of Angers and an inhabitant of the village of Crû. Through a similar [display of] power during this festival she was healed and received her sight; then she departed. Charimund, a disabled man, came from Brulon and was healed by the power of the blessed bishop.

24. The many blind and possessed people who were healed

During [Martin's] festival some people, with the assistance of the favor of Christ, plainly felt his power. Leodomund, who had been blind for seven years, Domnitta, who had been blind for three years, and three other blind men in addition received their sight during this festival through the power of the blessed bishop. Many possessed people were also cleansed.

25. The girl healed of a fever

A slave girl who belonged to my priest Leo was carried in her parents' arms and went to a small villa near the city [of Tours]. For she suffered from a high fever, and day and night she was thought to be almost at the point of death. When the priest saw that she was exhausted by this severe illness, he mounted his horse during the night and rode to the church of the holy confessor. He knocked on the door of the cell in which the warden was sleeping, but he could not awaken the man. Because he was unable to enter the holy church, he offered a prayer before the apse [that contained] the tomb; and because he was filled with faith, he collected a bit of dust from

[105] Apparently immediately after this festival King Childebert summoned the bishops of his kingdom to Verdun and then Metz to hear accusations against Bishop Egidius of Rheims (*Hist.* 10.19–20); Krusch (1951) XVI, and Weidemann (1982) 1:218, 366, suggest that Gregory attended.

the ground that he took with him. He mixed the dust with water, and as soon as he brought it to the little girl to drink, her fever immediately vanished.

26. The men in prison who were freed

I had occasion to visit the presence of King Childebert. During my journey I approached on a road through a district [in the territory] of Rheims and [there] met a man. In his own account he [told] me that the prison in Rheims in which this man's slave was being held with other captives had been opened by Martin's power, and that the captives had been released from prison and departed as free men. For the prison had been constructed in this way: thick logs had been positioned on top of a foundation of beams and covered with planks, and huge stones were then placed on top to press down on the logs. The door to this prison was furthermore locked, its bar strengthened by iron and its bolt shut with a key. But the bishop's power moved these stones, as the man claimed in his account. He demolished the platform, broke the chains, and opened the stocks that held the captives' feet; since the door had not been opened, he then lifted the men in the air and brought them outside through the open roof. He said: "I am Martin, a soldier of Christ and your liberator. Depart in peace and leave with your freedom!" After I had come to King Childebert and told him the miracle worked by this power, the king confirmed that some of the men who had been released had come to him, and that he had forgiven the fee these accused men owed the [royal] treasury; those [Franks] call this fee a *fredus*. This miracle happened four days before the festival [of Martin on July 4, 591] in the sixteenth year [of the reign] of the aforementioned king.[106]

27. The servant of Bishop Nonnichius who was healed of an illness

During this festival of the blessed [Martin] Bishop Nonnichius of Nantes went to the saint's church and brought with him a servant named Baudegisill whose limbs were disabled. After the celebration of the saint's ceremony Baudegisill's limbs were restored and Nonnichius received him back with his health.[107]

---

[106] Krusch (1951) XVI–XVII suggests that Gregory went on to Rheims after attending the baptism of Chlothar II; if so, then perhaps Gregory was sent to reassure Childebert about Guntramn's intentions in recognizing Chlothar as a king (cf. *Hist.* 10.28). The *fredus* was a fine imposed for infringements on royal authority or a fee paid to a king or his representative for his arbitration in judicial disputes or for his release of prisoners (cf. *Hist.* 6.23); it is to be distinguished from the composition fee required to end feuds between families (cf. *Hist.* 7.47, 9.19).

[107] Nonnichius had succeeded his relative Felix as bishop of Nantes in 582 (*Hist.* 6.15), and can perhaps be identified with the "illustrious Nunnichius" whom Bishop Germanus of Paris had once visited when returning from Nantes: see Fortunatus, *Vita Germani* 158. Gregory

28. The disappearance of the fever of Claudius, a royal clerk

While I was staying with King [Childebert], Claudius, one of his royal clerks, was afflicted with a fever. When he was so ill from this fever that he rejected food and drink, he asked me what he was suffering. When he drank the dust that I had taken from the holy tomb of the blessed [Martin] for my safety and that I mixed [in water], soon his fever vanished and he was healed.

29. What Abbess Agnes of Poitiers said about a boatman

Agnes, the venerable abbess of the nuns at Poitiers, described this account of a miracle that happened as told to her by a merchant from Trier whom she met. She said: "While I was approaching Metz, a merchant asked me where I was from. I said: 'From Poitiers.' He asked me if I had ever gone to the church of the blessed Martin at Tours. I said that I visited there whenever I was traveling in Austria. He told me about the great blessing he had experienced from lord Martin. While he was trading salt at Metz and was docked at the bridge at Metz, he said: 'Lord Martin, I commend to you myself, the young servants that I have, and my small boat.' Then I and my servants lay down in the boat and all fell asleep. In the morning when I and my servants awoke, we found ourselves in front of the gate of Trier. Since we thought that we were still tied up at Metz, we did not know how we had traveled or how we had either sailed or flown. Simply because of the goodwill of the blessed Martin we did not feel the river, and we avoided the swelling waves of the Moselle River that cause wrecks; it is truly [amazing] that we safely passed by the rocks during the night even though no boatman was on watch, no wind was blowing, and no oar was steering [the boat]."[108]

---

had not much liked Felix, one of his suffragan bishops, and when Felix had become ill, Gregory had not supported his first choice as successor (*Hist.* 6.15): see above, chapter 4, section 1. Nonnichius's visit to the festival of St. Martin presumably indicates that Tours and Nantes were again reconciled, even if belatedly, although Gregory himself was apparently out of town visiting King Charibert. Upon his return, Abbot Aredius of Limoges visited him at Tours; this visit took place "after the festival of St. Martin" and shortly before Aredius's death in late August 591 (*Hist.* 10.29).

[108] Note that in Gregory's account Agnes starts out telling the boatman's story and the boatman himself finishes it. Agnes had died after Radegund's death in August 587 but before the revolt of the nuns at Poitiers in early 589: see above, chapter 1, section 2. It is not obvious why Gregory included this story about her visit to Metz here among miracles that happened in 591. Weidemann (1982) 1:219 suggests that King Childebert's court had perhaps been at Metz when Gregory visited (*VM* 4.26, 28); another possibility is that Gregory's subsequent visit to Poitiers for the consecration of Plato (*VM* 4.30–32) reminded him of the story. Gregory was the first author to describe the northeastern Merovingian subkingdom, with its early capital at Rheims, as "Austria" (cf. *Hist.* 5.14, 18): see Ewig (1976–1979) 1:151–52, 166–71. This kingdom of Rheims was also sometimes known simply as "Francia" (*Hist.*

30. The miracles at the monastery of Ligugé

Some time later when I had traveled to Poitiers, I was pleased to go simply to pray at the monastery at Ligugé, where the blessed man had gathered and situated a community of monks. For it is read that he revived his first dead man there, and it is written that he was led to his episcopacy from that monastery. So I looked for that attractive place, and I knelt before the railings in the corner in which he is said to have restored life to the dead man. After I poured out my tears and prayed and solemnly celebrated mass, I asked the abbot whether the Lord had displayed any miracles there. In front of the brothers who were in attendance the abbot insisted that often the blind received their sight and the disabled were healed there. He said: "My lord, because you diligently ask, I will narrate to you what recently happened. A woman who was an inhabitant of this region was afflicted with the swelling of paralysis and completely lost the use of all her limbs. She was carried about by the oxen hauling the wagon on which she had been placed, and she went to the homes of the wealthy to acquire what her poverty required. When she was then brought to this place, she knelt on the pavement, gradually struggled to approach, and piously kissed the curtain that covered the holy railing. She said: 'Blessed confessor, I believe that you are present here, and I testify that you revived a dead man here. For I believe that, if you wish, you can save me and restore me to my health, just as once you broke the jaws of the underworld and restored life to a dead man.' She flooded her cheeks with tears after she said this, and as soon as her prayer was completed, whatever was withered, whatever was crippled, and whatever was weakened on the woman's body was healed by the power of the blessed bishop." In a similar fashion when another paralytic who had come to this monastery touched the curtain over this railing, his disability completely vanished and he departed with his health. This monastery was about forty stades from Poitiers.[109]

31. The spring that the saint while alive made to flow

I left Poitiers and entered the territory of Saintes. While I was talking about the miracles of the blessed Martin during a banquet, one of the citizens piously told me this story, and the others agreed that it was true. In this territory [of Saintes] there is the village of Nieul-lès-Saintes. St. Martin, while still alive in body, came to this village and met a man who was

---

4.14, 16; 9.20, *GC* 40); modern historians now usually call it Austrasia. Fortunatus, *Carm.* 10.9.1–20, also described the rapids on this stretch of the Moselle during his own boat trip from Metz to Trier in 588.

[109] Sulpicius Severus, *Vita Martini* 7, 9.1–2, had described Martin's revival of a dead man and his reluctance to leave this monastery to become bishop of Tours. For stades, see the note to *VJ* 25; forty stades would be about 4 1/2 modern miles.

carrying water in a jar. The well from which the man was bringing this water was located in a valley about a thousand paces from the village; its inhabitants [also] carried the water they drank from this well. Then the man of God said to the man who was carrying the water: "Most beloved, I ask you, extend your hand and offer a little water for this donkey that I am sitting on to drink." The man replied: "If you think it necessary to fetch water for your donkey, go to the well and give it the water you draw. For I will not offer the water that I have laboriously carried away." After saying this, the man continued on. As he left, a woman came who was carrying water in her arms. The man of God made a similar request of her. Like Rebecca in the past [cf. Gen. 24:12–20] this woman listened to the messenger of God and said: "I will offer you and your donkey a drink, and it is no problem for me to draw water again. Only let your will be done, because you are a traveler suffering from thirst." She put down her jar and offered a drink to his donkey. Then she drew water again, filled her jar, and returned to the village. The saint followed her and said: "Let me repay you with a blessing, because you have fetched water for my donkey." He bent his knees to the ground and prayed to the Lord that he expose a flowing spring in that spot. And as soon as he finished his prayer, the ground was split and revealed a large spring to the people who were watching. Still today this spring offers a blessing to the people who live in that region. At the mouth of this spring as confirmation there is a stone that preserves the hoofprint of the donkey upon which the holy bishop sat.

32. The fire at Poitiers

I think that I should not be silent about the saint's power that was revealed at the time when Plato assumed the episcopacy of Poitiers. A house connected to the cathedral residence was burning in a huge blaze, and because a wind was blowing, sparks and coals were falling on the cathedral residence. But Plato had with him some dust from [Martin's] blessed tomb, and when he held his reliquary up in front of the fire, a wind contrary to the other wind suddenly gusted, protected the roof of the cathedral from the flames, and pushed them in the opposite direction. In this way the cathedral residence was saved.[110]

33. The servant healed of a fever

Plato's servant [suffered] from ill health and burned with a very high fever. Although he was lying in his bed and was considered as if already lifeless, as soon as Plato brought this ill man some of the dust that he had

---

[110] Plato had been Gregory's archdeacon at Tours (*Hist.* 5.49) before succeeding Maroveus as bishop of Poitiers in 591: see Fortunatus, *Carm.* 10.14, and above, chapter 1, section 2.

mixed [in water], immediately his fever vanished and the servant recovered from his suffering. But let me return to the saint's church.

34. Leudulf, a mad and disabled man

Some years previously when a great earthquake jolted the ground and everything was as thoroughly shaken as if it were about to collapse in an instant, Leudulf was badly jostled by this earthquake. Not only was he deprived of his senses, but he was disabled in all his limbs. He came to the saint's church at Tours, and after kneeling in prayer for a few days he recovered his voice and his senses and [the use of] all his limbs. As if brought back to life he returned with his health.

35. The prisoner

I think that this story must not be omitted. An innocent man was falsely accused by evil men, bound with a rope, and brought to the city [of Tours] to be thrown into prison. After he had been led to a public square and was in front of the church of the apostle St. Peter, his hands were freed and he said to his guards: "This indicates that I am innocent of the accusation that you make, because my hands have been freed by divine power." His guards were angry and bound him again more tightly, and by adding still another rope to his bonds they also, if I may say so, chained his chains. It happened that at that moment I was coming through the square from the church of St. Martin. When these men approached and met me, as soon as this prisoner saw the saint's church, his hands were immediately freed. He jumped off the horse on which he was sitting, seized my feet, and explained that he was being condemned unjustly. And so, after I spoke with the judge, this man departed without harassment.[111]

36. The mute woman

The wife of Serenatus, one of my servants, was returning from working in the fields. Her husband had gone on ahead. Suddenly she fell into the hands of her companions and slipped to the ground; because her tongue was tied and she was unable to pronounce any words with her mouth, she became mute. Then the soothsayers came and said that she had experienced an attack by a midday demon. They prescribed amulets of herbs and verbal incantations; but as usual they could provide no medicine for the woman on the verge of death. While her family mixed shouts with their weeping, her son ran breathlessly to my niece Eustenia. He announced that

---

111 Bishop Perpetuus had constructed this church dedicated to St. Peter and St. Paul in the later fifth century (*Hist.* 2.14): see above, chapter 1, section 1. It was located south of the church of St. Martin: see L. Pietri (1983) 405–7, and L. Pietri and Biarne (1987) 35. The judge was probably Gregory's friend, Count Galienus (*VM* 4.6).

his mother had reached the final point of her life. Eustenia went and visited
the ill woman, and after removing the amulets that the silly [soothsayers]
had attached, she poured oil from [Martin's] blessed tomb on her mouth
and rubbed it with wax. Soon the ill woman's speech was restored, and
after the evil deception [of the demon] was removed, she recovered.[112]

37. The people suffering from chills who were healed

After the death of the most glorious king Guntramn [on March 28, 592]
King Childebert went to Orléans. At that time one of the servants at his
royal court was seriously afflicted with a tertian fever; as his fevers appeared and disappeared, a tremor also appeared. When he complained
about his misfortune to me, I gave him some dust from the saint's tomb.
After he drank it, his tremor vanished and he recovered. But during the next
night, shortly before the day during which his tremor usually started, he
saw in a vision a most hideous person who said to him: "Behold, the time
for your tremor has already arrived. Why are you pretending? Do what you
usually do!" While he was saying this, another man came whose face
sparkled, whose hair was white as snow, whose appearance was grace-
ful,[113] and who said to the servant: "Do not tremble; instead make the sign
of the venerable cross on your forehead, and you will be healed immediately." The servant was awakened during this vision, but fortified with
the sign with which he had been commanded he never again endured what
he had suffered. A maidservant of the queen [Faileuba] was also weakened
by this fever, but after she drank this holy medicine, she was healed.

38. The blind, the paralyzed, and the possessed

A few days later when the annual day for the saint's festival returned [on
July 4, 592], I left the king and attended the festival during which four
blind men left after their sight was restored. Two possessed men were
cleansed, and two crippled paralytics left with their health after their
mobility was restored.

39. A similar story about the release of prisoners

A few days later a judge's sentence confined some guilty men among the
inmates in a prison at Tours. While these prisoners were weeping, the
power of the blessed confessor appeared by shattering the chains of these
fettered men and allowing them to go as free men to the church. Once these
men were also released by the judge, they left for their own homes.

---

[112] Eustenia was a daughter of Gregory's unnamed sister and her husband Justinus (*GM*
70, *VM* 2.2), and the wife of Nicetius (*Hist.* 5.14).

[113] Bonnet (1890) 746n.4 hints that Gregory's verbal repetition here (*vultu splendidus . . .
vultu decorus*) may be an indication of his failure to revise the first draft of these late chapters.

40. Mauranus, a mute man

In the region of Cantabria [along the north coast of Spain] a man named Mauranus rose from his bed in the morning. While he was leaving his house, it seemed to him as if someone had struck him in the neck. He immediately fell to the ground and became as if dead. For three days he [seemed] to be alive only because of his breathing, and he was considered to be as if dead. On the fourth day his eyes were opened, but he could say nothing, because the power of speaking had been taken from him. After hearing about the miracles of the blessed Martin he offered one small gold coin to some sailors and requested through nods that they bring it to the church of the blessed bishop. The boatmen left. When Mauranus returned to his own home, he saw in front of his feet a gold piece that looked like a small gold coin. But when he picked it up and weighed it, it balanced at the weight of a large gold coin. After Mauranus realized this, he said to himself: "The power of the blessed Martin has restored recompense to me for the loan that I sent to his church." He was excited with desire; but although he wished to board first one and then a second ship, he was restrained by his parents. But when he found a third ship, he could not be restrained any longer. He boarded this ship, and when they reached the high seas as the wind was blowing, the power of the holy bishop opened his mouth. Mauranus extended his hands to heaven and spoke. He said: "Omnipotent God, I thank you who have ordered me to set sail on this trip. For already before I see the church of your saint, I have been filled with his blessings." The men sailed on and landed at Bordeaux. Here Mauranus disembarked from the ship, went to the saint's church, and fulfilled his vow. I learned about this account that I have written down from his own mouth.

41. The crippled man and the prisoners who were released

When it was time for the other festival [of Martin on November 11, 592] that is celebrated in the winter, Maurellus, a slave of Duke Aginus, attended from his home in Ponthion. During the month of March he had lost the use of a knee because of some unknown assault; and because he could not walk, a peg leg was attached to his knee, as is customary for the lame. For three days he offered a prayer to the Lord, and on the fourth day, which was the day after the festival, his knee was straightened and he departed with his health. Then a few days later men who had been held by the chains of a prison were freed by divine power. They entered the saint's church, and after being absolved from their punishment by the judge, they were released.

42. Another crippled boy

A boy from the villa of Thomeau, which is near the village of Amboise in a district [of the territory] of Tours, had crippled hands and feet. He went to the saint's church, and while he and the other beggars were requesting charity for sustenance, he was assisted by the saint's power. He left after being healed.[114]

43. People suffering from fevers

Another young servant of my priest Euthimius suffered an illness and a high fever and was thought to have been killed by the affliction. The priest picked up some dust from the holy tomb and cut threads from the curtain hanging over [the tomb]. He took [these relics] with him, gave the dust to his servant to drink, and tied the threads around his neck. Soon the fever vanished and his servant was healed. In a similar fashion the priest Ulfaric also showed his concern for another servant who had a fever; this servant's fever immediately broke, and he recovered.

44. Principius, a madman

Principius was a good man and a citizen of Périgueux. He was thought to have suffered some unknown madness, and he was sometimes in such pain that he seemed to have lost his senses. After he endured this for many months, he went to the church of the blessed bishop. He remained there for four months, I think, and abstained from eating meat and [drinking] wine. After he was benefited by the assistance of the blessed confessor, he returned to his own home in good health.

45. The blind man and the crippled man

Because the ignorance of men does not follow the preaching of bishops, it prepares itself to offend God; therefore let me publicize what happened recently. Leodulf was a man from Bourges. After he had mowed his hay, he was afraid that it would be drenched at the arrival of an approaching storm and that he would lose [the results of] his labor. So at dawn on a Sunday he yoked his oxen, went to his meadow, and began to collect his hay on a wagon. But because one of his feet suddenly seemed to him as if on fire, he returned to his lodging and rested from his work. After the ceremony of mass was celebrated, he again yoked his oxen and proceeded to complete the task that he had begun. When his wagon was filled with hay, suddenly his eyes felt a sharp pain, as if they had been pierced by some prickles. Once they were closed, he could never thereafter open them. And so for an entire year he remained blind. Then he piously went to the festival of the holy bishop [on July 4, 593], and three days after the festival he was healed with the blessing of the sight that he had lost. At that time another crippled man also came, and after being healed by the saint's power he returned to his city on his own feet.

---

[114] L. Pietri (1983) 617–18 suggests that this villa belonged to the church of St. Martin.

46.[115]

A man named Paternianus came from Brittany. He was blind, mute, and deaf, and his hands had been crippled because of some infection; because all his limbs had been weakened by his illness, only his feet offered support for the man. After he came here to the church of the powerful patron and offered a prayer, he regained the sight he had lost once his eyes were opened, and he recovered the earlier use of his hands. He marveled that he had been healed by the power of the blessed bishop and proclaimed to the people his thanks for his good health. Because of gratitude for this miracle Paternianus received gifts from many people with which he ransomed several others from the yoke of captivity.

47.

At the present time a house in Bordeaux was seized by fire and began to burn fiercely. As the flames spread here and there, other houses were susceptible to this danger. When there was no doubt that these houses were being consumed by the heat of the burning wood, the people gathered in a circle and began earnestly to call upon the name of the blessed Martin. They wept and prayed that his power not allow these neighboring houses to be burned. And so the crackling of the flames began to recede as the cries of these weeping people were raised. When their shouts reached heaven, the bishop was helpful, and his assistance was immediately available. The fire collided with this prayer of supplication, and the people extinguished with their tears what they could not overcome with water. At this time my servant Launovald was seriously weakened by dysentery. As soon as he swallowed dust from [Martin's] tomb, immediately he was healed of his illness.

---

[115] Krusch (1885) 453, 649n.1, suggests that death prevented Gregory from inserting the headings for these final two chapters into the complete list of *capitula* for *VM* 4.

A Sermon in Praise of St. Martin

IN A LIBRARY in Rome, Cardinal Angelo Mai discovered this sermon in a manuscript that paleography dated to the eleventh or twelfth century; Mai published his edition of the sermon in 1852.[1] Because moisture had unfortunately damaged the last page of the manuscript, his edition omitted most of the end of the sermon. About a century later Professor Bernard Peebles found another, but this time complete, copy of the sermon in a manuscript from northern Italy that he dated to the tenth or eleventh century; he soon published the complete edition that is translated here.[2]

Peebles's discussion of the sermon is still the best available, although he acknowledged his debt to an article by Aimé Lambert, a monk at St. Martin's monastery of Ligugé who had worked only with Mai's edition.[3] The sermon clearly celebrated the festival of Martin's death on November 11 (*Sermo* 1), and the references to St. Martin as "our special shepherd" (*Sermo* 1) and "our own shepherd" (*Sermo* 2) are strong indications that it was delivered before the congregation at Tours. Lambert argued that the sermon should be dated to the sixth century on the basis of its vocabulary and parallels with liturgical texts,[4] and he thought that it predated the episcopacy of Gregory of Tours. Peebles suggested that the preacher's reference to "everything that has been written about him [St. Martin]" (*Sermo* 4) may have been an allusion to Gregory's writings about the saint; he also hinted that the sermon might have been delivered after the sixth century. At the least the sermon developed themes about St. Martin and his cult that were already common during the sixth century.[5]

[1] Reprinted in *PL* Suppl. 4.602–4.
[2] Peebles (1961) 245–48, with new numbering of the chapters.
[3] A. Lambert, "Le premier panégyrique de saint Martin," *Bulletin de Saint Martin et de Saint Benoît* 32 (1924): 316–20—regrettably unavailable to me.
[4] Summarized in Peebles (1961) 249.
[5] L. Pietri (1983) 785–86.

1. Most beloved brothers, let us rejoice in the Lord with all the happiness of spiritual joy, because the omnipotence of the Lord's majesty now delights us with the happiness of the annual festival [in honor] of his distinguished confessor, who is also our special shepherd. For this is the day on which the holy Catholic church, although spread far and wide throughout the world, dances in manifold joy as it celebrates the festival of someone whom it knows from his deeds and his words to be a partner among the citizens of heaven. This day on which Martin, the glorious bishop of God, migrated from this world to the flourishing garden of Paradise is to be venerated in the entire world. This, I say, is an illustrious day, a holy day, a splendid day, a day celebrated among men and praised among the angels, [because] on it the blessed Martin, like a retired soldier who after the many campaigns of his service has been recruited for the army of heaven, rejoices to be crowned in happiness with the garland of eternal life.

2. Dearest brothers, let us all of every age and every rank, men and women, celebrate the glorious ceremonies of this great patron in our praise, and with rejoicing in our souls, complete devotion, unlimited eagerness, and a single-minded heart let us praise these ceremonies in our celebration, since both the faithful of Christ in this world and all the saints in heaven are applauding these ceremonies. For although he whom omnipotent God has magnified and now forever keeps in his presence does not require our praise, nevertheless the goodness of our own shepherd is delighted with the obedience of pious devotion. Hence this day is deservedly praised, and this holy festival that is confirmed by such great powers and honored by such great miracles is piously observed by every Christian. For the book of his life that gleams with such marvelous descriptions of his deeds indicates the sort of honors that distinguished this most blessed shepherd in this world. The accomplishments of his powers are of course so remarkable and so widespread throughout the regions of the world, that because of his excellence they are thought to be familiar to every rational creature.

3. Martin, glorious bishop of God, let it therefore be sufficient for us, your servants, only to have mentioned this proclamation of your praise, so that we who gather to celebrate the happiness of your festival might stand piously before your presence. Accept therefore, sweet father, accept the praises of your servants that we offer, receive our wishes that we present to you, present them before the sight of the pious Redeemer, and bring back from him to us the forgiveness of heavenly favor. For you already rejoice with him in the heavenly Paradise, as immune to corruption as you are liberated of your flesh; and you repose in the midst of crowds of saints, as remote from disturbance as you have become closer to the contemplation of God. But we who are still traveling in this exile, who are still weighed

down by the corruption of the body, who still endure the treacheries of wicked enemies, and who are still constantly oppressed by various misfortunes—we require your assistance as much as we groan in deep distress every day at these evils. Therefore, because we can discover nothing worthy in ourselves and nothing appropriate to your praises, we humbly ask you that the petitions of our admiration that are presented not by an insistent voice but by a devoted conscience might be accepted through the gift of your affection. May your affection then assist us so that we who so often offend the Creator with our misdeeds might receive from him not a sentence but a pardon. And because you love the poor, and because during your youth you divided the cloak you wore and were worthy to clothe Christ [who had appeared] as a beggar, may we through your most generous intercession be clothed in the wedding garments and be worthy to attend the banquets of the King of Heaven. You who were protected not by a shield and a helmet but by the sign of the cross [once] promised that you would encounter the enemy troops in safety; [now] offer the assistance of your protection to us, so that we might be able to repel our enemies' attacks in safety and to overcome all their power under your leadership. After [the time of] the apostles such favor was bestowed upon you that you were worthy to be the one who revived three dead men; as soon as we have been revived from the death of our souls by your prayers, cleansed of every offensive infection, and established upon the faithful confession of the holy Trinity, may you likewise also make us partners in everlasting happiness.

4. I should indeed call Rome blessed, because to it have been conceded those two bright stars, namely, Peter and Paul, through whom that city was worthy to return from the darkness of unbelief to the light of truth. In a similar fashion it is obvious that Tours is blessed, because through God's generosity it could be instructed by the teaching of such a great father and in addition distinguished by his bodily presence. Blessed are the parents who produced such an admirable son; blessed are the inhabitants of the holy see of Tours to whom it was permitted to have such a respected patron. Fortunate is the region that gave birth to him, and more fortunate [still is the region] that has sent him on ahead as its intercessor in the palace of heaven. Fortunate therefore is Tours, which was illuminated by the teachings of such a great shepherd and which has been worthy to become the head of the entire region of Gaul through [the possession of] his cherished body. Not only are men's minds irrigated by his merit and the rainfall of his blessings, but adjacent regions too are overwhelmed by the fertility of their crops. But this place that is ornamented so gloriously with the tomb of his most holy body must be considered more fortunate and more exalted than all these others. Oh, how fortunate were those who were worthy to serve him and to attend his celebration, who were just in their righteousness, pure in their simplicity, chaste in their holiness, and both privately and

publicly perfected in all devotion. Blessed finally were those who saw him present in the flesh and believed him as he preached. But much more blessed are those who have desired with a ready heart to follow and imitate everything that has been written about him.

5. O most valuable shepherd, we direct our attentive eyes to you who have been given specially to us through God who provides for our salvation so that amid the fluctuations of this journey and this life you might deign constantly to govern [first] this holy flock of yours that is every day ready to serve you, and [in addition] the entire flock of the monastic order and this mixed crowd of both men and women that hurries to attend your sacred ceremonies, and so that you might be successful in protecting and defending against the fiery darts of the demon and after the death of the flesh in rejoicing without end in the heavenly Jerusalem with the reward of righteousness. May the omnipotent God who sent his only Son to die for us therefore support our desire for [eternal] life because of your favorable merits and because of our same Lord whose equal honor and identical power will endure with the Holy Spirit forever through the ages. Amen.

Inscriptions from the *Martinellus*

S OME of the manuscripts of Sulpicius Severus's works include as appendixes other texts relevant to the cult of St. Martin. This family of manuscripts is now known as the *Martinellus*; most of its manuscripts were written in France and Germany, and the earliest are dated to the early ninth century. The appendixes include various combinations, in various orders, of the following texts: a description of the church of St. Martin; an exhortation to celebrate the saint's two festivals in the church; a profession of faith attributed (wrongly) to St. Martin;[1] passages excerpted from the versification of the writings of Sulpicius Severus by Paulinus of Périgueux; passages excerpted from the writings of Gregory of Tours; and selections from later medieval authors about the cult and miracles of St. Martin.[2] The description of the church and the exhortation about the festivals seem to reflect very old traditions about the saint's cult. The description of the saint's church is formulaic in its listing of the distance between the city and the church, the church's length, width, and height, the number of windows and columns in its sanctuary, and its total number of windows, columns, and doors; as such, this description in the *Martinellus* closely resembles the equally formulaic description that Gregory provided of the church. Gregory's related exhortation to celebrate the two festivals of St. Martin was likewise similar to the exhortation about the festivals in the *Martinellus*. The relationship between the two sets of descriptions and exhortations is hence not clear. One possibility is that both sets relied upon a common source, which was perhaps an original description and an original exhortation composed during the episcopacy of Perpetuus. Another possibility is that the description and the exhortation in the *Martinellus* were actual inscriptions on the walls of the church of St. Martin, and that Gregory based his versions directly on those inscriptions.[3]

Most of the manuscripts in the *Martinellus* also include a collection of

---

[1] See *PL* 18.11–12, and *PL* Suppl. 3.733–34, for versions of this creed.

[2] For discussion of the manuscripts of Sulpicius's works, see Fontaine (1967–1969) 1:215–24, and Gilardi (1983) 149–70. A few manuscripts in the "Italian family" also include some of these texts.

[3] *Hist.* 2.14, Gregory's description and exhortation. Texts of the description and the exhortation in the *Martinellus* in Le Blant (1856–1865) 1:245–46, and Gilardi (1983) 216–17,

epigrams and poems about the early cult of St. Martin. Four poems in the collection concern St. Martin's monastery at Marmoutier, the next twelve or thirteen epigrams and poems concern the church of St. Martin at Tours, another poem mentions a shrine dedicated to five martyr saints, and a final poem is an exhortation to learn about the life of St. Martin. The four poems from Marmoutier were inscribed in or near St. Martin's cell in the monastery, and were probably composed soon after his death.[4] Bishop Perpetuus of Tours commissioned the epigrams and poems for the church of St. Martin as one aspect of his promotion of the saint's cult at Tours. Paulinus of Périgueux, who also versified Sulpicius's writings about St. Martin, composed a long poem for the nave, and Sidonius, who became bishop of Clermont, composed a long poem for the apse; the remaining short epigrams and poems are anonymous,[5] and some seem to have resembled prayers or incantations from the liturgy. Some of the epigrams and poems hint that they were engraved on the walls of the church, and one explicitly mentions "the very blocks and stones [that] are engraved with these inscriptions"; the discovery of a marble fragment containing a few engraved letters from one of the epigrams on the saint's tomb now implies that the other epigrams and poems were probably engraved too, and not simply painted or set in mosaics.[6] At some time a scribe who copied the inscriptions added headings that noted their placement in the church; but because some of these headings were imprecise or have become obscure through textual corruption, interpretations about the location of some of the inscriptions differ. Since Gregory of Tours later mentioned the murals in the church, and since one of the headings referred to a "painted representation," presumably some of the inscriptions accompanied and most likely described these murals.[7]

Another poem in the collection commemorated a shrine (*memoria*) dedicated to five saints, John the Baptist, Felix, Victor, Gervasius, and Protasius. The location of this shrine is quite uncertain. One possibility is that it was a small chapel located near the church of St. Martin.[8] Another possibility is that it was the altar in the church of St. Martin.[9] At any rate

---

with translations, 228–29. L. Pietri (1983) 381–86, 468–74, suggests a common source; Gilardi (1983) 55–68, 82–92, 116–17, 141–42, argues that the description and the exhortation in the *Martinellus* were actual inscriptions.

[4] See above, chapter 1, section 1.

[5] Gilardi (1983) 109–48 argues that Paulinus of Périgueux was also the author of all the other verse inscriptions and that Bishop Perpetuus composed the prose inscriptions; L. Pietri (1984) 625–27 is more reluctant.

[6] See Vieillard-Troiekouroff (1976) plate 14, no. 61, for a photograph, and L. Pietri (1974), for discussion.

[7] For discussion, see above, chapter 4, section 2.

[8] So L. Pietri (1983) 398–405.

[9] So Gilardi (1983) 293–94.

Bishop Perpetuus was most likely responsible for commissioning this poem too, because its last line included the obvious pun on his name that other authors also could not resist.

A final poem urged readers to learn about the life and career of St. Martin. This poem may have been yet another inscription in the church of St. Martin, perhaps located on a lectern on which a copy of Sulpicius's *Vita* of the saint was on display.[10] Another interpretation suggests that the poem was simply a literary preface in the manuscripts that included collections of writings about St. Martin and his cult, and was therefore not engraved anywhere in the church.[11] Needless to say, these remain only conjectures.

The translations here usually follow the texts in L. Pietri (1983) 802–12, although they have occasionally borrowed suggestions from the texts in the first volume of Le Blant (1856–1865), the texts, translations, and discussion in Gilardi (1983), and the discussion in L. Pietri (1984), all of which are very useful for assistance with grammatical and contextual problems. Since L. Pietri (1983) did not include a revised text of Le Blant (1856–1865) 1, no. 183, the translation of that poem follows the text in Gilardi (1983) 215. For those of us who are not specialists in paleography and epigraphy the lack of a definitive edition of the texts, along with the absence of a clear and comprehensive discussion of the relevant problems, is irritating. The new edition of these texts promised for the appropriate volume of *RICG*, whenever it appears, will certainly be welcome.

Marmoutier

Le Blant (1856–1865) 1, no. 166 = L. Pietri (1983) no. 1 = Gilardi (1983) no. 1:

"The verses begin at the entrance to the first cell of St. Martin."

Behold, we come here; alas, no one shouts out.
    Behold, we come here, but the weapons of the cross are silent.
Truly the warrior of the Lord is asleep; alas, would that he might shout out!
    The warrior sleeps, a man who must be missed.
But let us enter and with our weeping and our prayers beseech
    the Lord of the saints, the God of Martin.
Let us kneel at the place that the saint moistened with his weeping:
    his spirit will be our assistance.

[10] So Gilardi (1983) 53, 57–61, 300–303.
[11] So L. Pietri (1983) 798n.1, and (1984) 627–28.

The warrior sleeps; but you, Christ, protect us.
You who do not sleep, protect Israel.

Le Blant (1856–1865) 1, no. 167 = L. Pietri (1983) no. 2 = Gilardi (1983) no. 2:

"Next in another cell."

Here lived the man who kissed the feet of the Lord;
here lived the man who carried the weapons of the cross;
here lived the bishop who was holy and pure;
here lived the man who was chaste in body and in heart;
here lived the man whose holy faith was a shield,
the defender of the cross who was brilliantly distinguished for his
eloquence;
here lived the fortunate recluse in a cave;
here lived the man who [now] lives in Paradise.

Le Blant (1856–1865) 1, no. 168 = L. Pietri (1983) no. 3 = Gilardi (1983) no. 3:

"Next inside the cell."

Holy God, have pity on the place that you have always loved.
Cherish, enhance, protect, always love [it],
when at the completion of his life you have transferred our shepherd
to those bright, holy, and wonderful places.
Holy [God], in the shelter of your wings
protect, preserve, cherish, and always love us too.
We make our request as suppliants; may you give generously and grant
that the saint himself might simultaneously assist us.

Le Blant (1856–1865) 1, no. 169 = L. Pietri (1983) no. 4 = Gilardi (1983) no. 4:

"Next there over the location of his bed."

We see here what sorts of weapons the warrior often uses
[even] when it happened that the man was absent;
note the black coals, each of them horrifying,
and the clouds of dust, all most foul.
A cloak, a stone beneath his head, and a pile of cinders,
you were considered a bed here for his weary limbs.
A small stool was his resting place during the silent night;
during the day this stool [served] him in place of a chair or a throne.

The Church of St. Martin and Other Shrines at Tours

Le Blant (1856–1865) 1, no. 170 = Pietri (1983) no. 5 = Gilardi (1983) no. 5:

"The verses of the church begin; first [those] on the east side [of the bell tower]."[12]

As you enter the church, lift your eyes upward;
>   a deep faith recognizes the lofty entrances.
Be humble in your conscience, but in hope follow the one who calls you;
>   Martin opens the door that you venerate.
This tower is protection for the timid and an obstacle to the proud;
>   it excludes the arrogant and defends the meek in heart.
More lofty still is that [tower or dome] that has taken Martin to the citadel of
>   heaven
>   and that rises through the starry roads.
From there he summons the people, he who as a guide to Christ's rewards
>   has traveled on and sanctified that journey through the stars.

Le Blant (1856–1865) 1, no. 171 = L. Pietri (1983) no. 6 = Gilardi (1983) no. 6:

"On another side [of the bell tower]."

As you are about to enter the nave, as you venerate the threshold of Christ,
dispel the concerns of this world from your entire heart
and free your spirit from wicked desires.
The man who offers just prayers returns with his vows fulfilled.

Le Blant (1856–1865) 1, no. 172 = L. Pietri (1983) no. 7 = Gilardi (1983) no. 7:

You who are about to seek the temple of God with a calm mind

· · · · · · · · · · · · · · ·

[and] who are entering to request forgiveness for your recent sins,
>   in your spirit you should not falter in your faith.
You obtain what you seek if you ask with a pure heart.
>   As he said, faith will be your salvation.

---

[12] L. Pietri (1983) 388n.210, 819, suggests that this and the next two inscriptions were engraved on opposite sides of the doors at the west end of the church, and that people would have read them as they faced east; she also suggests that the inscription describing the Widow's Mites was over the west doors but inside the church. Gilardi (1983) 43, 242, 248–49, 251–52, argues more plausibly that the first three inscriptions were on the bell tower, and that the inscription about the Widow's Mites was on the exterior of the church.

Le Blant (1856–1865) 1, no. 173 = L. Pietri (1983) no. 8 = Gilardi (1983) no. 8:

"At the entrance on the west side [of the church], a painted representation of the widow mentioned in a Gospel."

Let whoever comes to renew his vows to the highest God
    learn to confess Christ according to the account in a Gospel.
Although he trembles in his heart and prays as a suppliant stooping on his knees,
    if he ceases his good works, his faith is certainly meaningless.
Rich and poor are alike liable to this law;
    he who lacks wealth will demonstrate his good works by his intentions.
Nor do meager and limited resources excuse anyone;
    the merit is determined by the intent, not by the value.
He who has bestowed whatever is necessary presents very much;
    although he will have given little, he wishes [to present] all the greatest gifts.
Among these piles of wealth and the gifts of the powerful we know
    that the faith of the poor widow was preferred.
As she purchased the kingdoms of heaven for two mites,
    The just father took her upward among the stars.
Not she who gave much, but she who left nothing for herself
    has deserved to be praised by the mouth of the judge God.

Le Blant (1856–1865) 1, no. 174 = L. Pietri (1983) no. 9 = Gilardi (1983) no. 9:

"Over the door on the side of [the church facing] the Loire River."[13]

The disciples were sailing on the lake at the command of the Lord. As the winds were blowing and the waves were being tossed up, the Lord walked on his feet on the lake. He also extended his hand to St. Peter who was sinking; and that man was saved from danger.

Le Blant (1856–1865) 1, no. 175 = L. Pietri (1983) no. 10 = Gilardi (1983) no. 10:

"Next."

[Here is] the most holy church of Christ which is the mother of all churches, which the apostles founded, and in which the Holy Spirit descended upon the apostles in the form of tongues of fire. In it are located the throne of the apostle James and the pillar on which Christ was whipped.[14]

13 Gilardi (1983) 45 suggests that this and the next inscription (and their accompanying murals) were on the exterior of the church over the north and south doors respectively.
14 Elsewhere Gregory recorded some stories about this pillar and other relics of Jesus at Jerusalem (*GM* 6).

Le Blant (1856–1865) 1, no. 176 = L. Pietri (1983) no. 11 = Gilardi (1983) no. 11, by Paulinus of Périgueux:[15]

["Next."][16]

You who have knelt on the ground, lowered your face to the dust,
and pressed your moist eyes to the compacted ground,
lift your eyes, and with a trembling gaze look at the miracles
and entrust your cause to the distinguished patron.
No page can embrace such miracles.
Even though the very blocks and stones are engraved with these inscriptions,
a terrestrial building does not enclose what the royal palace of heaven
acknowledges and what the stars inscribe in glittering jewels.
If you seek Martin's assistance, rise beyond the stars
and touch the heavens after having encountered the chorus of angels in the
      upper air.
There look for the patron who is joined to the Lord
and who always follows the footsteps of the eternal king.
If you doubt, look at the miracles that are heaped before your eyes
and by means of which the true Savior honors the merit of his servant.
You come as an eyewitness among so many thousands of others
when you carefully observe what must be narrated and repeat what you have
      seen.
Whatever a page in the holy books has recorded,
he renews through the restoration of God. [Many] rejoice in his gift:
the blind, the lame, the poor, the possessed, the distressed, the sick,
the disabled, the oppressed, the imprisoned, the grieving, the needy.
Every remedy rejoices in the marvels of the apostles.
Whoever has come in tears, leaves in happiness. All clouds vanish.
A medicine soothes whatever guilt disturbs.
Seek his protection; you do not knock at these doors in vain.
Such lavish generosity extends into the entire world.

Le Blant (1856–1865) 1, no. 177 = L. Pietri (1983) no. 12 = Gilardi (1983) no. 12:

"On the arch of the apse above the altar."

How awesome is this place! Truly it is the temple of God and the gateway to heaven.[17]

---

[15] The translation of this inscription in Hillgarth (1986) 31–32 is based on the slightly different text edited by Petschenig, *CSEL* 16.1 (1888) 165.

[16] Gilardi (1983) 258–59 proposes *item* as the heading for this inscription.

[17] Quoted from Gen. 28:17, the story of Jacob's vision of a ladder between heaven and earth. Le Blant (1856–1865) 1:CVII, and (1892) 457–58, suggests that liturgical prayers inspired these inscriptions in the apse.

Le Blant (1856–1865) 1, no. 178 = L. Pietri (1983) no. 13 = Gilardi (1983) no. 13:

"On one side of the tomb."

Here is buried Bishop Martin of sacred memory, whose soul is in the hand of God. But he is wholly present here, made manifest to everyone by the goodwill of his miracles.

Le Blant (1856–1865) 1, no. 179 = L. Pietri (1983) no. 14 = Gilardi (1983) no. 14:

"Next on the other side [of the tomb]."

He has fought the good fight, he has completed the race, he has preserved the faith. And so there is reserved for him a crown of righteousness that the Lord, the just judge, will restore to him on that day.

Le Blant (1856–1865) 1, no. 180 = L. Pietri (1983) no. 15 = Gilardi (1983) no. 15:

"Next on the top [of the tomb]."

Confessor by his merits, martyr by his suffering, apostle by his actions,
    Martin presides from heaven here at this tomb.
May he be mindful [of us], and by cleansing the sins of our wretched life
    may he conceal our crimes with his merits.

Le Blant (1856–1865) 1, no. 181 = L. Pietri (1983) no. 16 = Gilardi (1983) no. 16, by Sidonius:[18]

"Next in the apse."

The body of Martin that is venerable for the entire world
    and in which honor lives [even] after the years of his life
was at first covered here by a chapel with ordinary decoration
    that was not appropriate for its own confessor.
The citizens never ceased being burdened with shame
    from the great reputation of the man and the trivial renown of the place.
Perpetuus, who is the sixth bishop in succession,
    eliminated the long-standing disgrace[19]

[18] Also quoted by Sidonius himself in his *Ep.* 4.18.5.

[19] Gregory listed Martin as the third bishop of Tours and Perpetuus as the sixth (*Hist.* 10.31). But during the episcopacy of Perpetuus when Sidonius composed this poem, people at Tours probably still remembered the heated feuding during the episcopacy of Brictio. So in this line the phrase *ab ipso* was perhaps intentionally ambiguous enough to be understood either as "the sixth bishop after him," i.e., after Martin and therefore the eighth overall, or as "the sixth bishop who eliminated the long-standing disgrace from himself." By obscuring the episcopal sequence Sidonius also obscured the status of the two bishops who had served during Brictio's exile from Tours (*Hist.* 2.1): see Gilardi (1983) 280–82, for the verbal

by removing the inner sanctuary of the small chapel
    and constructing an impressive edifice on a larger building.
With the assistance of the powerful patron the church grew
    in size, and simultaneously the builder grew in merit.
The church is capable of rivaling the temple of Solomon,
    a building that was the seventh wonder of the world.[20]
For if that temple glittered with jewels, gold, and silver,
    this church surpasses all precious metals through faith.
Ravenous envy, be gone; let our ancestors be forgiven, and
    let our babbling descendants neither alter nor add anything.
Until the coming of Christ who revives all people,
    may the walls of Perpetuus endure perpetually.[21]

Le Blant (1856–1865) 1, no. 182 = L. Pietri (1983) no. 17 = Gilardi (1983) no. 18:

"In the shrine [of the holy relics? of the holy saints?]."

This residence contains the crowns of five blessed [saints].
If you read the inscription carefully, you will also learn their names
that remain and always will remain recorded in heaven.
Here St. John the Baptist rejoices from the womb.
Here [are] pious Felix and Victor; gracious Gervasius
and holy Protasius are here as witnesses throughout the ages
who have demonstrated the true faith by their suffering, their blood, and their
    deaths.
Joined together, these five fingers from the body of Christ
fashion with their great struggle a lofty palm
that they ornament with perpetual blossoms worthy of God.[22]

Le Blant (1856–1865) 1, no. 183 = Gilardi (1983) no. 19:

"Next, the verses there."

If your faith is holy, and if your mind is devoted to Christ

---

ambiguity, and above, chapter 1, section 1, for the context. Sidonius also credited Perpetuus, again ambiguously, with eliminating the long-standing *invidia*, the "disgrace" of the small church and/or the "dispute" between factions.

[20] Gregory classified Solomon's temple as the third wonder of the world (*De cursu* 4).

[21] The manuscripts of the *Martinellus* add a further comment in prose: "The burial of St. Martin [took place] on November 11; he rested in the peace of the Lord at midnight." Perhaps this was the original epitaph for the saint's tomb: see L. Pietri (1983) 468. Gilardi (1983) 140–41, 289–90, considers it another inscription (no. 17) added by Bishop Perpetuus to the end of Sidonius's poem.

[22] For Gregory's comments on these martyrs, see *GM* 13–15, 19, 44, 46; and above, chapter 1, section 1.

and steady under the weight of the merits of the sacred bishop,
here, diligent reader, you can learn about Martin's
birth, military service, baptism, deeds, parents,
teaching, habits, proclamations, wars, triumphs,
sufferings, homeland, dangers, sayings, labors,
distinctions, miracles, lifetime, proclamations, and commendations.

Actus pontificum Cenomannis in urbe degentium: ed. G. Busson and A. Ledru, *Actus pontificum Cenomannis in urbe degentium*. Société des archives historiques du Maine, Archives historiques du Maine 2 (1901).

Agathias, *Historiae*: ed. R. Keydell, *Agathiae Myrinaei Historiarum libri quinque* (1967)—trans. J. D. Frendo, *Agathias: The Histories* (1975).

Avitus of Vienne: ed. R. Peiper, *MGH*, AA 6.2 (1883).

Baudonivia, *Vita Radegundis*: ed. B. Krusch, *MGH*, SRM 2 (1888) 377–95.

Bede, *HE = Historia ecclesiastica*: ed. and trans. B. Colgrave and R.A.B. Mynors, *Bede's Ecclesiastical History of the English People* (1969).

Cassiodorus, *Variae*: ed. Th. Mommsen, *MGH*, AA 12 (1894); ed. Å. J. Fridh, *CChr*.lat. 96 (1973)—trans. S.J.B. Barnish, TTH (1992).

Councils of Gaul: ed. C. Munier, *Concilia Galliae a.314–a.506*, and C. de Clercq, *Concilia Galliae a.511–a.695*. *CChr*.lat. 148–148A (1963)—de Clercq's edition reprinted with French trans. in J. Gaudemet and B. Basdevant, *Les canons des conciles mérovingiens (VIe–VIIe siècles)*. SChr. 353 (1989).

Diplomata: see Pardessus (1843–1849), and Pertz (1872).

Epistolae aevi Merowingici collectae: ed. W. Gundlach, *MGH*, Epp. 3 (1892) 434–68.

Epistolae Arelatenses: ed. W. Gundlach, *MGH*, Epp. 3 (1892) 5–83.

Epistolae Austrasicae: ed. W. Gundlach, *MGH*, Epp. 3 (1892) 111–53, reprinted in *CChr*.lat. 117 (1957) 405–70.

Formulae Arvernenses: ed. K. Zeumer, *MGH*, Leges 5 = Formulae (1886) 28–31.

Fortunatus

   Carmina and *Vita S. Martini*: ed. F. Leo, *MGH*, AA 4.1 (1881).

   Vitae: ed. B. Krusch, *MGH*, AA 4.2 (1885).

      VH = Liber de virtutibus sancti Hilarii: trans. Van Dam, in this volume.

      Vita Germani episcopi Parisiaci: again ed. B. Krusch, *MGH*, SRM 7 (1920) 372–418.

      Vita Radegundis: again ed. B. Krusch, *MGH*, SRM 2 (1888) 364–377.

Fredegar, *Chronica*: ed. B. Krusch, *MGH*, SRM 2 (1888) 18–168—*Chron.* 4, ed. and trans. J. M. Wallace-Hadrill, *The Fourth Book of the Chronicle of Fredegar* (1960).

Gislemar, *Vita Droctovei abbatis Parisiensis*: ed. B. Krusch, *MGH*, SRM 3 (1896) 537–43.

(pope) Gregory I, *Registrum epistolarum*: ed. P. Ewald and L. M. Hartmann, *MGH*, Epp. 1–2 (1891–1899); ed. D. Norberg, *CChr*.lat. 140–140A (1982)—trans. J. Barmby, NPNF 2d series, 12–13 (reprinted 1983).

Gregory of Tours

   Hist. = Historiae: ed. W. Arndt, *MGH*, SRM 1 (1885) 31–450; ed. B. Krusch and W. Levison, *MGH*, SRM 1.1 (1937–1951)—trans. O. M. Dalton, *The*

History of the Franks by Gregory of Tours (1927), vol. 2; trans. L. Thorpe, *Gregory of Tours: The History of the Franks* (1974).

GM = Liber in gloria martyrum: ed. B. Krusch, *MGH*, SRM 1 (1885) 484–561—trans. Van Dam (1988a).

VJ = Liber de passione et virtutibus sancti Iuliani martyris: ed. B. Krusch, *MGH*, SRM 1 (1885) 562–84—trans. Van Dam, in this volume.

VM = Libri de virtutibus sancti Martini episcopi: ed. B. Krusch, *MGH*, SRM 1 (1885) 584–661—trans. Van Dam, in this volume; *VM* 1, trans. W. C. McDermott, in Peters (1975) 133–34, 147–78.

VP = Liber vitae patrum: ed. B. Krusch, *MGH*, SRM 1 (1885) 661–744—trans. James (1991); *VP* 6–7, trans. W. C. McDermott, in Peters (1975) 180–95.

GC = Liber in gloria confessorum: ed. B. Krusch, *MGH*, SRM 1 (1885) 744–820—trans. Van Dam (1988b).

MA = Liber de miraculis beati Andreae apostoli: ed. M. Bonnet, *MGH*, SRM 1 (1885) 826–46, reprinted with French trans. in Prieur (1989) 2:564–651.

De cursu = De cursu stellarum ratio: ed. B. Krusch, *MGH*, SRM 1.2 (1885) 857–72—*De cursu* 1–16, trans. W. C. McDermott, in Peters (1975) 209–18.

Jonas of Bobbio

Vita Columbani: ed. B. Krusch, *MGH*, SRM 4 (1902) 64–108—trans. D. C. Munro, in Peters (1975) 75–113.

Vita Iohannis abbatis Reomaensis: ed. B. Krusch, *MGH*, SRM 3 (1896) 505–17.

Lex Salica: ed. K. A. Eckhardt, *MGH*, Leges 1 = Leges nationum Germanicarum 4.2 (1969)—trans. K. F. Drew, *The Laws of the Salian Franks* (1991).

Libellus de ecclesiis Claromontanis: ed. W. Levison, *MGH*, SRM 7 (1920) 456–67.

Liber historiae Francorum: ed. B. Krusch, *MGH*, SRM 2 (1888) 238–338—*Liber* 1–4, 43–53, trans. Gerberding (1987) 173–81.

Liber Pontificalis: ed. L. Duchesne, *Le Liber Pontificalis. Texte, introduction et commentaire*, vol.1 (1886); ed. Th. Mommsen, *MGH*, Gesta pontificum Romanorum (1898)—trans. R. Davis, *The Book of Pontiffs (Liber Pontificalis) . . . to AD 715*. TTH (1989).

Marculf, *Formulae*: ed. K. Zeumer, *MGH*, Leges 5 = Formulae (1886) 36–106.

Marius of Avenches, *Chronica*: ed. Th. Mommsen, *MGH*, AA 11 (1894) 232–39.

Orosius, *Historiae adversum paganos*: ed. C. Zangemeister, *CSEL* 5 (1882)—trans. R. J. Deferrari, *FC* 50 (1964).

Pactus Legis Salicae: ed. K. A. Eckhardt, *MGH*, Leges 1 = Leges nationum Germanicarum 4.1 (1962)—trans. K. F. Drew, *The Laws of the Salian Franks* (1991).

Passio = Passio sancti Iuliani martyris: see Appendix 1.

Passio Praeiecti episcopi et martyris Arverni: ed. B. Krusch, *MGH*, SRM 5 (1910) 225–48.

Paul the Deacon, *HL = Historia Langobardorum*: ed. L. Bethmann and G. Waitz, *MGH*, Scriptores rerum Langobardicarum (1878) 45–187—trans. W. D. Foulke, *History of the Lombards* (1907; reprinted 1974).

Paulinus of Nola: ed. G. de Hartel, *CSEL* 29–30 (1894)—trans. P. G. Walsh, *ACW* 35–36, 40 (1966–1975).

Paulinus of Périgueux: ed. M. Petschenig, *CSEL* 16.1 (1888) 17–165.

Procopius: ed. and trans. B. H. Dewing, LCL, 7 vols. (1914–1940).
Sermo = Sermo in laude sancti Martini: see Appendix 2.
Sidonius Apollinaris: ed. and trans. (French) A. Loyen, Budé, 3 vols. (1960–1970); ed. and trans. W. B. Anderson, LCL, 2 vols. (1936–1965).
Sisebut, *Vita Desiderii*: ed. B. Krusch, *MGH*, SRM 3 (1896) 630–37.
Sulpicius Severus: ed. C. Halm, *CSEL* 1 (1866); *Vita* and *Epistolae*, ed. and trans. (French) J. Fontaine, *SChr.* 133 (1967)—trans. A. Roberts, NPNF 2d series, 11 (reprinted 1973) 1–122; *Vita, Epistolae* and *Dialogi*, trans. Hoare (1954) 1–144.
Victricius of Rouen, *De laude sanctorum*: ed. J. Mulders and R. Demeulenaere, *CChr.lat.* 64 (1985) 69–93—excerpts trans. Hillgarth (1986) 23–28.
Vita Caesarii episcopi Arelatensis: ed. B. Krusch, *MGH*, SRM 3 (1896) 457–501; ed. G. Morin, *Sancti Caesarii Arelatensis opera varia* 2 (1942) 296–345—excerpts trans. Hillgarth (1986) 32–43; trans. W. Klingshirn, TTH (forthcoming).
Vita Chrothildis: ed. B. Krusch, *MGH*, SRM 2 (1888) 342–48.
Vita Desiderii Cadurcae urbis episcopi: ed. B. Krusch, *MGH*, SRM 4 (1902) 563–602, reprinted in *CChr.lat.* 117 (1957) 345–401.
Vita Eligii episcopi Noviomagensis: ed. B. Krusch, *MGH*, SRM 4 (1902) 663–742.
Vita Genovefae virginis: ed. B. Krusch, *MGH*, SRM 3 (1896) 215–38.
Vita Lupicini: see *Vita Patrum Iurensium.*
Vita Nicetii episcopi Lugdunensis: ed. B. Krusch, *MGH*, SRM 3 (1896) 521–24.
Vita Patrum Iurensium: ed. B. Krusch, *MGH*, SRM 3 (1896) 131–166; ed. and trans. (French) F. Martine, *SChr.* 142 (1968).

Barlow, C. W. (1950), ed. *Martini episcopi Bracarensis opera omnia*. Papers and Monographs of the American Academy in Rome, vol. 12. New Haven.

Beaujard, B., P.-A. Février, J.-C. Picard, C. Pietri, and J.-F. Reynaud (1986). *Province ecclésiastique de Lyon (Lugdunensis Prima) = Topographie chrétienne des cités de la Gaule des origines au milieu du VIIIᵉ siècle*, ed. N. Gauthier and J.-C. Picard, vol. 4. Paris.

Beck, H.G.J. (1950). *The Pastoral Care of Souls in South-East France during the Sixth Century*. Analecta Gregoriana 51. Rome.

Boesch Gajano, S. (1977). "Il santo nella visione storiografica di Gregorio di Tours," in *Gregorio di Tours*, pp. 27–91. Convegni del Centro di studi sulla spiritualità medievale 12. Todi.

Bonnet, M. (1890). *Le Latin de Grégoire de Tours*. Paris.

Bordier, H. L. (1857–1864), ed. and trans. *Les livres des miracles et autres opuscules de Georges Florent Grégoire évêque de Tours*. 4 vols. Paris.

van den Bosch, J. (1959). *Capa, basilica, monasterium et le culte de saint Martin de Tours. Etude lexicologique et sémasiologique*. Nijmegen.

Boswell, J. (1988). *The Kindness of Strangers: The Abandonment of Children in Western Europe from Late Antiquity to the Renaissance*. New York.

Braudel, F. (1989). *The Identity of France, I: History and Environment*, trans. S. Reynolds. New York.

Brennan, B. (1985). "The Career of Venantius Fortunatus." *Traditio* 41:49–78.

———. (1985a). "The Conversion of the Jews of Clermont in AD 576." *Journal of Theological Studies* n.s. 36:321–37.

———. (1985b). "Senators and Social Mobility in Sixth-Century Gaul." *Journal of Medieval History* 11:145–61.

Brown, P. (1978). *The Making of Late Antiquity*. Cambridge, Mass.

———. (1981). *The Cult of the Saints: Its Rise and Function in Latin Christianity*. Chicago.

———. (1982). *Society and the Holy in Late Antiquity*. Berkeley and Los Angeles.

———. (1983). "The Saint as Exemplar in Late Antiquity." *Representations* 1.2:1–25.

———. (1988). *The Body and Society: Men, Women and Sexual Renunciation in Early Christianity*. New York.

Buchner, R. (1933). *Die Provence in merowingischer Zeit. Verfassung—Wirtschaft—Kultur*. Stuttgart.

———. (1955). "Einleitung," in *Gregor von Tours, Zehn Bücher Geschichten*, ed. and trans. R. Buchner, 1:VII–LI. 4th ed. Darmstadt.

Bynum, C. W. (1991). *Fragmentation and Redemption: Essays on Gender and the Human Body in Medieval Religion*. New York.

Cameron, A. (1968). "Agathias on the Early Merovingians." *Annali della Scuola normale superiore di Pisa*, 2d ser., 37:95–140.

———. (1976). "The Early Religious Policies of Justin II," in *The Orthodox Churches and the West*, ed. D. Baker, pp. 51–67. *Studies in Church History* 13. Oxford. Reprinted in her *Continuity and Change in Sixth-Century Byzantium* (London, 1981), chapter 10.

Carrias, M. (1972). "Etude sur la formation de deux légendes hagiographiques à l'époque mérovingienne. Deux translations de saint Martin d'après Grégoire de Tours." *Revue d'histoire de l'église de France* 58:5–18.

Chadwick, H. (1981). "Pachomios and the Idea of Sanctity," in *The Byzantine Saint: University of Birmingham Fourteenth Spring Symposium of Byzantine Studies*, ed. S. Hackel, pp. 11–24. London.

Chadwick, N. (1965). "The Colonization of Brittany from Celtic Britain." *Proceedings of the British Academy* 51:235–99.

Chadwick, O. (1948). "Gregory of Tours and Gregory the Great." *Journal of Theological Studies* 49:38–49.

Châtillon, F. (1967). "Paulin de Périgueux, auteur de la *Vita Martini*, et Sidoine Apollinaire panégyriste des empereurs." *Revue du moyen âge latin* 23:5–12.

Classen, P. (1977). *Kaiserreskript und Königsurkunde. Diplomatische Studien zum Problem der Kontinuität zwischen Altertum und Mittelalter*. Byzantina Keimena kai Meletai 15. Thessaloníki.

Claude, D. (1963). "Der Bestellung der Bischöfe im merowingischen Reiche." *Zeitschrift der Savigny-Stiftung für Rechtsgeschichte* 80, Kanonistische Abteilung 49, pp. 1–75.

———. (1964). "Untersuchungen zum frühfränkischen Comitat." *Zeitschrift der Savigny-Stiftung für Rechtsgeschichte* 81, Germanistische Abteilung, pp. 1–79.

Collins, R. (1981). "Observations on the Form, Language and Public of the Prose Biographies of Venantius Fortunatus in the Hagiography of Merovingian Gaul," in *Columbanus and Merovingian Mentality*, ed. H. B. Clarke and M. Brennan, pp. 105–31. British Archaeological Reports, International Series 113. Oxford.

Corbett, J. H. (1983). "*Praesentium signorum munera*: The Cult of the Saints in the World of Gregory of Tours." *Florilegium* 5:44–61.

Courcelle, P. (1964). *Histoire littéraire des grandes invasions germaniques*. 3d ed. Paris.

———. (1969). *Late Latin Writers and Their Greek Sources*, trans. H. E. Wedeck. Cambridge, Mass.

———. (1973). *Recherches sur saint Ambroise. "Vies" anciennes, culture, iconographie*. Paris.

Coville, A. (1928). *Recherches sur l'histoire de Lyon du Vme siècle au IXme siècle (450–800)*. Paris.

Crone, P. (1989). *Pre-industrial Societies*. Oxford.

Dalton, O. M. (1927). *The History of the Franks by Gregory of Tours, I: Introduction*. Oxford.

Danforth, L. M. (1989). *Firewalking and Religious Healing: The Anastenaria of Greece and the American Firewalking Movement*. Princeton.

Delaruelle, E. (1963). "La spiritualité des pèlerinages à Saint-Martin de Tours du Ve au Xe siècle," in *Pellegrinaggi e culto dei santi in Europa fino alla 1^a crociata*, pp. 199–243. Convegni del Centro di studi sulla spiritualità medievale 4. Todi.

Descombes, F. (1985), ed. *Viennoise du Nord = RICG* 15. Paris.

Desideri, P., M. Forlin Patrucco, S. Boesch Gajano, and A. Prosperi (1984). "Il culto dei santi." *Quaderni storici* n.s. 57:941–69.

Dill, S. (1926). *Roman Society in Gaul in the Merovingian Age.* London.

van Esbroek, M. (1981). "Les textes littéraires sur l'Assomption avant le Xᵉ siècle," in *Les Actes apocryphes des apôtres. Christianisme et monde païen,* ed. F. Bovon et al., pp. 265–85. Geneva.

Ewig, E. (1974). "Studien zur merowingischen Dynastie." *Frühmittelalterliche Studien* 8:15–59.

———. (1976–1979). *Spätantikes und fränkisches Gallien. Gesammelte Schriften (1952–1973),* ed. H. Atsma. 2 vols. Munich.

Fabre, P. (1948). *Essai sur la chronologie de l'oeuvre de saint Paulin de Nole.* Paris.

Farmer, S. (1991). *Communities of Saint Martin: Legend and Ritual in Medieval Tours.* Ithaca and London.

Février, P.-A. (1974). "Permanence et héritages de l'antiquité dans la topographie des villes de l'Occident durant le haut moyen âge," in *Topografia urbana e vita cittadina nell'alto medioevo in Occidente,* pp. 41–138. Settimane de studio del Centro italiano di studi sull'alto medioevo 21. Spoleto.

Fontaine, J. (1963). "Sulpice Sévère a-t-il travesti saint Martin de Tours en martyr militaire?" *Analecta Bollandiana* 81:31–58.

———. (1967–1969), ed. and trans. *Sulpice Sévère, Vie de saint Martin.* 3 vols. = *SChr.* 133–35. Paris.

———. (1972). "Valeurs antiques et valeurs chrétiennes dans la spiritualité des grands propriétaires terriens à la fin du IVᵉ siècle occidental," in *Epektasis. Mélanges patristiques offerts au Cardinal Jean Daniélou,* ed. J. Fontaine and C. Kannengiesser, pp. 571–95. Paris.

———. (1979). "L'aristocratie occidentale devant le monachisme au IVème et Vème siècles." *Rivista di storia e letteratura religiosa* 15:28–53.

———. (1980). "King Sisebut's *Vita Desiderii* and the Political Function of Visigothic Hagiography," in *Visigothic Spain: New Approaches,* ed. E. James, pp. 93–129. Oxford.

———. (1982). "Le culte des saints et ses implications sociologiques. Réflexions sur un récent essai de Peter Brown." *Analecta Bollandiana* 100:17–41.

Fournier, G. (1962). *Le peuplement rural en Basse Auvergne durant le haut moyen âge.* Paris.

Fournier, P.-F. (1955). "La persistance du Gaulois au VIᵉ siècle d'après Grégoire de Tours," in *Recueil de travaux offert à M. Clovis Brunel,* 1:448–53. Paris.

Gäbe, S. (1989). "Radegundis: sancta, regina, ancilla. Zum Heiligkeitsideal der Radegundisviten von Fortunat und Baudonivia." *Francia* 16.1:1–30.

Gager, J. G. (1982). "Body-Symbols and Social Reality: Resurrection, Incarnation and Asceticism in Early Christianity." *Religion* 12:345–63.

Galinié, H. (1978). "Archéologie et topographie historique de Tours—IVème–XIème siècle." *Zeitschrift für Archäologie des Mittelalters* 6:33–56.

Ganshof, F. L. (1964). *Feudalism,* trans. P. Grierson. 3d ed. London.

Gasnault, P. (1961). "La 'Narratio in reversione beati Martini a Burgundia' du pseudo-Eudes de Cluny (sources et influence)," in *Saint Martin et son temps = Studia Anselmiana* 46:159–74.

Gauthier, N. (1980). *L'évangélisation des pays de la Moselle. La province romaine de Première Belgique entre antiquité et moyen-âge (IIIe–VIIIe siècles)*. Paris.

——. (1986). *Province ecclésiastique de Trèves (Belgica Prima) = Topographie chrétienne des cités de la Gaule des origines au milieu du VIIIe siècle*, ed. N. Gauthier and J.-C. Picard, vol.1. Paris.

Geary, P. J. (1986). "Sacred Commodities: The Circulation of Medieval Relics," in *The Social Life of Things: Commodities in Cultural Perspective*, ed. A. Appadurai, pp.169–91. Cambridge.

——. (1988). *Before France and Germany: The Creation and Transformation of the Merovingian World*. Oxford.

George, J. (1989). "Poet as Politician: Venantius Fortunatus' Panegyric to King Chilperic." *Journal of Medieval History* 15:5–18.

Gerberding, R. A. (1987). *The Rise of the Carolingians and the* Liber Historiae Francorum. Oxford.

Gilardi, F. J. (1983). "The Sylloge epigraphica Turonensis de S. Martino." Ph.D. diss., Catholic University of America, Washington, D.C.

Goffart, W. (1985). "The Conversions of Avitus of Clermont, and Similar Passages in Gregory of Tours," in *"To See Ourselves as Others See Us": Christians, Jews, "Others" in Late Antiquity*, ed. J. Neusner and E. S. Frerichs, pp. 473–97. Chico.

——. (1987). "From *Historiae* to *Historia Francorum* and Back Again: Aspects of the Textual History of Gregory of Tours," in *Religion, Culture, and Society in the Early Middle Ages: Studies in Honor of Richard E. Sullivan*, ed. T.F.X. Noble and J. J. Contreni, pp. 55–76. Kalamazoo.

——. (1988). *The Narrators of Barbarian History (A.D. 550–800): Jordanes, Gregory of Tours, Bede, and Paul the Deacon*. Princeton.

Graus, F. (1965). *Volk, Herrscher und Heiliger im Reich der Merowinger. Studien zur Hagiographie der Merowingerzeit*. Prague.

——. (1989). "Hagiographie und Dämonenglauben—zu ihren Funktionen in der Merowingerzeit," in *Santi e demoni nell'alto medioevo occidentale (secoli V–XI)*, pp. 93–120. Settimane de studio del Centro italiano di studi sull'alto medioevo 36. Spoleto.

Grierson, P., and M. Blackburn. (1986). *Medieval European Coinage. With a Catalogue of the Coins in the Fitzwilliam Museum, Cambridge, I: The Early Middle Ages (5th–10th Centuries)*. Cambridge.

Griffe, E. (1948). "Le véritable emplacement du Capitole romain de Toulouse." *Bulletin de littérature ecclésiastique* 49:32–41.

——. (1959). "Toulouse romaine et chrétienne. Controverses et incertitudes." *Bulletin de littérature ecclésiastique* 60:117–34.

——. (1964–1966). *La Gaule chrétienne à l'époque romaine*. 3 vols. Rev. ed., Paris.

Gurevich, A. (1988). *Medieval Popular Culture: Problems of Belief and Perception*, trans. J. M. Bak and P. A. Hollingsworth. Cambridge Studies in Oral and Literate Culture 14. Cambridge.

Harries, J. (1978). "Church and State in the *Notitia Galliarum*." *Journal of Roman Studies* 68:26–43.

Harris, W. V. (1989). *Ancient Literacy*. Cambridge, Mass., and London.

Head, T. (1990). *Hagiography and the Cult of Saints: The Diocese of Orléans, 800–1200.* Cambridge.

Heather, P. (1992). "The Emergence of the Visigothic Kingdom," in *Fifth-Century Gaul: A Crisis of Identity?,* ed. J. Drinkwater and H. Elton, pp. 84–94. Cambridge.

Heinzelmann, M. (1976). *Bischofsherrschaft in Gallien. Zur Kontinuität römischer Führungsschichten vom 4. bis zum 7. Jahrhundert. Soziale, prosopographische und bildungsgeschichtliche Aspekte.* Munich.

———. (1981). "Une source de base de la littérature hagiographique latine: le recueil de miracles," in *Hagiographie, cultures et sociétés IVe–XIIe siècles. Actes du Colloque organisé à Nanterre et à Paris (2–5 mai 1979),* pp. 235–57. Paris.

———. (1982). "Gallische Prosopographie 260–527." *Francia* 10:531–718.

———. (1991). "Hagiographischer und historischer Diskurs bei Gregor von Tours?" in *Aevum inter utrumque. Mélanges offerts à Gabriel Sanders, professeur émérite à l'Université de Gand,* ed. M. Van Uytfanghe and R. Demeulenaere, pp. 237–58. Steenbrugge and The Hague.

Heinzelmann, M., and J.-C. Poulin. (1986). *Les vies anciennes de sainte Geneviève de Paris. Etudes critiques.* Bibliothèque de l'Ecole des Hautes Etudes, IVe section, sciences historiques et philologiques 329. Paris.

Herzfeld, M. (1986). "Closure as Cure: Tropes in the Exploration of Bodily and Social Disorder." *Current Anthropology* 27.2:107–20.

Herzlich, C., and J. Pierret (1987). *Illness and Self in Society,* trans. E. Forster. Baltimore and London.

Higounet, C. (1953). "Les saints mérovingiens d'Aquitaine dans la toponymie," in *Etudes mérovingiennes. Actes des journées de Poitiers 1er–3 mai 1952,* pp. 157–67. Paris.

Hillgarth, J. N. (1986), ed. *Christianity and Paganism, 350–750: The Conversion of Western Europe.* Philadelphia.

Hoare, F. R. (1954), trans. *The Western Fathers: Being the Lives of SS. Martin of Tours, Ambrose, Augustine of Hippo, Honoratus of Arles and Germanus of Auxerre.* New York.

Holum, K. G. (1990). "Hadrian and St. Helena: Imperial Travel and the Origins of Christian Holy Land Pilgrimage," in *The Blessings of Pilgrimage,* ed. R. Ousterhout, pp. 66–81. Illinois Byzantine Studies 1. Urbana and Chicago.

Homes Dudden, F. (1935). *The Life and Times of St. Ambrose.* Oxford.

Hunt, E. D. (1981). "The Traffic in Relics: Some Late Roman Evidence," in *The Byzantine Saint: University of Birmingham Fourteenth Spring Symposium of Byzantine Studies,* ed. S. Hackel, pp. 171–80. London.

———. (1982). *Holy Land Pilgrimage in the Later Roman Empire AD 312–460.* Oxford.

James, E. (1977). *The Merovingian Archaeology of South-West Gaul.* British Archaeological Reports, Supplementary Series 25(i) and 25(ii). Oxford.

———. (1979). "Cemeteries and the Problem of Frankish Settlement in Gaul," in *Names, Words, and Graves: Early Medieval Settlement,* ed. P. H. Sawyer, pp. 55–89. Leeds.

———. (1982). *The Origins of France: From Clovis to the Capetians, 500–1000.* New York.

James, E. (1988). *The Franks*. Oxford.

———. (1991), trans. *Gregory of Tours: Life of the Fathers*. Rev. ed., Liverpool.

Kessler, H. L. (1985). "Pictorial Narrative and Church Mission in Sixth-Century Gaul," in *Pictorial Narrative in Antiquity and the Middle Ages*, ed. H. L. Kessler and M. S. Simpson, pp. 75–91. *Studies in the History of Art 16*.

Kleinman, A. (1980). *Patients and Healers in the Context of Culture: An Exploration of the Borderland between Anthropology, Medicine, and Psychiatry*. Berkeley and Los Angeles.

Klingshirn, W. (1985). "Charity and Power: Caesarius of Arles and the Ransoming of Captives in Sub-Roman Gaul." *Journal of Roman Studies* 75:183–203.

———. (1990). "Caesarius' Monastery for Women in Arles and the Composition and Function of the 'Vita Caesarii.' " *Revue Bénédictine* 100:441–81.

———. (forthcoming). *Caesarius of Arles: The Making of a Christian Community in Late Antique Gaul*.

Koebner, R. (1915). *Venantius Fortunatus. Seine Persönlichkeit und seine Stellung in der geistigen Kultur des Merowingerreiches*. Beiträge der Kulturgeschichte des Mittelalters und der Renaissance, vol. 22. Leipzig and Berlin.

Krüger, K. H. (1971). *Königsgrabkirchen. Der Franken, Angelsachsen und Langobarden bis zur Mitte des 8. Jahrhunderts. Ein historischer Katalog*. Munich.

Krusch, B. (1885). "Georgii Florentii Gregorii episcopi Turonensis libri octo miraculorum," in *MGH, SRM* 1, pp. 451–820 [introduction, text, notes].

———. (1885a). "Prooemium," in *MGH, AA* 4.2, pp. v–xxxiii [introduction to Fortunatus's *Vitae*].

———. (1920), ed. "Passiones vitaeque sanctorum aevi Merovingici cum supplemento et appendice," in *MGH, SRM* 7 [introductions, texts, notes].

———. (1951). "Gregorii episcopi Turonensis decem libri historiarum. Praefatio," in *MGH, SRM* 1.1, editio altera, pp. ix–xxii.

Krusch, B., and W. Levison (1937–1951), ed. "Gregorii episcopi Turonensis libri historiarum X," in *MGH, SRM* 1.1, editio altera [text, notes].

Kurth, G. (1919). *Etudes franques*, 2 vols. Paris and Brussels.

Lambrechts, P. (1954). "Note sur un passage de Grégoire de Tours relatif à la religion gauloise." *Latomus* 13:207–17.

Le Blant, E. (1856–1865), ed. *Inscriptions chrétiennes de la Gaule antérieures au VIIIᵉ siècle*. 2 vols. Paris.

———. (1892), ed. *Nouveau recueil des inscriptions chrétiennes de la Gaule antérieures au VIIIᵉ siècle*. Paris.

Leclercq, H. (1948). "Chape de saint Martin," in *Dictionnaire d'archéologie chrétienne et de liturgie*, ed. F. Cabrol and H. Leclercq, vol. 3.1, cols. 381–90. Reprinted. Paris.

Le Goff, J. (1984). *The Birth of Purgatory*, trans. A. Goldhammer. Chicago.

Lelong, C. (1960). "De l'importance du pélerinage de Tours au VIe siècle." *Bulletin trimestriel de la Société archéologique de Touraine* 32:232–37.

Loseby, S. T. (1992). "Bishops and Cathedrals: Order and Diversity in the Fifth-Century Urban Landscape of Southern Gaul," in *Fifth-Century Gaul: A Crisis of Identity?*, ed. J. Drinkwater and H. Elton, pp. 144–55. Cambridge.

Lotter, F. (1979). "Methodisches zur Gewinnung historischer Erkenntnisse aus hagiographischen Quellen" *Historische Zeitschrift* 229:298–356.

Loyen, A. (1960–1970), ed. and trans. *Sidoine Apollinaire, I: Poémes; II-III: Lettres.* 3 vols. Paris.

McCormick, M. (1989). "Clovis at Tours, Byzantine Public Ritual and the Origins of Medieval Ruler Symbolism," in *Das Reich und die Barbaren*, ed. E. K. Chrysos and A. Schwarcz, pp. 155–180. Veröffentlichungen des Instituts für österreichische Geschichtsforschung 29. Vienna and Cologne.

McDermott, W. C. (1975). "Felix of Nantes: A Merovingian Bishop." *Traditio* 31:1–24.

McNamara, J. A., and S. F. Wemple (1976). "Marriage and Divorce in the Frankish Kingdom," in *Women in Medieval Society*, ed. S. M. Stuard, pp. 95–124. Philadelphia.

McNeill, J. T., and H. M. Gamer (1938). *Medieval Handbooks of Penance: A Translation of the Principal* Libri Poenitentiales *and Selections from Related Documents.* New York.

Maenchen-Helfen, O. J. (1973). *The World of the Huns: Studies in Their History and Culture*, ed. M. Knight. Berkeley, Los Angeles, and London.

Marignan, A. (1899). *Etudes sur la civilisation française.* 2 vols. Paris.

Mathisen, R. W. (1982). "PLRE II: Suggested *addenda* and *corrigenda*." *Historia* 31:364–86.

———. (1984). "The Family of Georgius Florentius Gregorius and the Bishops of Tours," in *Medievalia et Humanistica = Studies in Medieval and Renaissance Culture*, n.s. 12:83–95.

———. (1989). *Ecclesiastical Factionalism and Religious Controversy in Fifth-Century Gaul.* Washington, D.C.

———. (1990). "Episcopal Hierarchy and Tenure in Office in Late Roman Gaul: A Method for Establishing Dates of Ordination." *Francia* 17.1:125–40.

Matthews, J. (1975). *Western Aristocracies and Imperial Court A.D. 364–425.* Oxford.

Meyer, W. (1901). *Der Gelegenheitsdichter Venantius Fortunatus.* Abhandlungen der königlichen Gesellschaft der Wissenschaften zu Göttingen, philologisch-historische Klasse, neue Folge, Band 4, Nro. 5. Berlin.

Monod, G. (1872). *Etudes critiques sur les sources de l'histoire mérovingienne*, vol. 1. Paris.

Munitiz, J. A. (1981). "Self-Canonisation: The 'Partial Account' of Nikephoros Blemmydes," in *The Byzantine Saint: University of Birmingham Fourteenth Spring Symposium of Byzantine Studies*, ed. S. Hackel, pp. 164–68. London.

Murray, A. (1983). "Peter Brown and the Shadow of Constantine." *Journal of Roman Studies* 73:191–203.

von der Nahmer, D. (1987). "Martin von Tours: sein Mönchtum—seine Wirkung." *Francia* 15:1–41.

Nelson, J. L. (1978). "Queens as Jezebels: The Careers of Brunhild and Balthild in Merovingian History," in *Medieval Women*, ed. D. Baker, pp. 31–77. *Studies in Church History*, Subsidia 1. Oxford. Reprinted in her *Politics and Ritual in Early Medieval Europe* (London and Ronceverte, 1986), pp. 1–48.

de Nie, G. (1987). *Views from a Many-Windowed Tower: Studies of Imagination in the Works of Gregory of Tours.* Amsterdam.

———. (1991). "Le corps, la fluidité et l'identité personnelle dans la vision du monde de Grégoire de Tours," in *Aevum inter utrumque. Mélanges offerts à Gabriel Sanders, professeur émérite à l'Université de Gand*, ed. M. Van Uyt-fanghe and R. Demeulenaere, pp. 75–87. Steenbrugge and The Hague.

Nonn, U. (1972). "Merowingische Testamente. Studien zum Fortleben einer rö-mischen Urkundenform im Frankenreich." *Archiv für Diplomatik* 18:1–129.

Palanque, J. R. (1933). *Saint Ambroise et l'empire romain*. Paris.

Pardessus, J. M. (1843–1849), ed. *Diplomata, chartae, epistolae, leges aliaque instrumenta ad res Gallo-Francicas spectantia*. 2 vols. Paris.

Peebles, B. M. (1961). "An Early 'Laudatio Sancti Martini': A Text Completed," in *Saint Martin et son temps = Studia Anselmiana* 46:237–49.

Pertz, K.A.F. (1872), ed. "Diplomata regum Francorum e stirpe Merowingica," in *MGH*, Diplomata imperii 1, pp. 1–88.

Peters, E. (1975), ed. *Monks, Bishops and Pagans: Christian Culture in Gaul and Italy, 500–700*. Philadelphia.

Picard, J.-C. (1988). *Le souvenir des évêques. Sépultures, listes épiscopales et culte des évêques en Italie du Nord des origines au Xe siècle*. Rome.

Pietri, C. (1984). "Les origines du culte des martyrs (d'après un ouvrage récent)." *Rivista di archeologia cristiana* 60:293–319.

Pietri, L. (1974). "Les tituli de la basilique Saint-Martin édifiée à Tours par l'évêque Perpetuus (3e quart du Ve siècle)," in *Mélanges d'histoire ancienne offerts à William Seston*, pp. 419–31. Paris.

———. (1982). "La succession des premiers évêques tourangeaux: essai sur la chronologie de Grégoire de Tours." *Mélanges de l'Ecole française de Rome, Moyen Age–Temps modernes* 94:551–619.

———. (1983). *La ville de Tours du IVe au VIe siècle: naissance d'une cité chré-tienne*. Collection de l'Ecole française de Rome 69. Rome.

———. (1983a). "Les abbés de basilique dans la Gaule du VIe siècle." *Revue d'histoire de l'église de France* 69:5–28.

———. (1984). "Une nouvelle édition de la sylloge martinienne de Tours." *Francia* 12:621–31.

———. (1984a). "Calendrier liturgique et temps vécu: l'exemple de Tours au VIe siècle," in *Le temps chrétien de la fin de l'antiquité au moyen âge IIIe–XIIIe siècles, Paris, 9–12 mars 1981*, ed. J.-M. Leroux, pp. 129–41. Colloques inter-nationaux du Centre national de la recherche scientifique, no. 604. Paris.

———. (1986). "Les sepultures privilégiées en Gaule d'après les sources lit-téraires," in *L'inhumation privilégiée du IVe au VIIIe siècle en Occident. Actes du colloque tenu à Creteil les 16–18 mars 1984*, ed. Y. Duval and J.-Ch. Picard, pp. 133–42. Paris.

Pietri, L., and J. Biarne (1987). *Province ecclésiastique de Tours (Lugdunensis Tertia) = Topographie chrétienne des cités de la Gaule des origines au milieu du VIIIe siècle*, ed. N. Gauthier and J.-C. Picard, vol. 5. Paris.

Prieur, J.-M. (1989), ed. *Acta Andreae*, 2 vols. = CChr., Series Apocryphorum, vols. 5–6. Brepols.

Prinz, F. (1965). *Frühes Mönchtum im Frankenreich. Kultur und Gesellschaft im Gallien, den Rheinlanden und Bayern am Beispiel der monastischen Ent-wicklung (4. bis 8. Jahrhundert)*. Munich and Vienna.

Rawson, B. (1986). "Children in the Roman Familia," in *The Family in Ancient Rome: New Perspectives*, ed. B. Rawson, pp. 170–200. Ithaca.

Reydellet, M. (1977). "Pensée et pratique politiques chez Grégoire de Tours," in *Gregorio di Tours*, pp. 171–205. Convegni del Centro di studi sulla spiritualità medievale 12. Todi.

Riché, P. (1962). *Education et culture dans l'occident barbare VIᵉ–VIIIᵉ siècles*. Paris. English trans.: *Education and Culture in the Barbarian West, Sixth through Eighth Centuries*, trans. J. J. Contreni (Columbia, 1976).

———. (1981). "Columbanus, His Followers and the Merovingian Church," in *Columbanus and Merovingian Mentality*, ed. H. B. Clarke and M. Brennan, pp. 59–72. British Archaeological Reports, International Series 113. Oxford.

Rocher, A. (1987), ed. and trans. *Hilaire de Poitiers, Contre Constance. SChr.* 334. Paris.

Rollason, D. (1989). *Saints and Relics in Anglo-Saxon England*. Oxford.

Rouche, M. (1977). "Francs et Gallo-Romains chez Grégoire de Tours," in *Gregorio di Tours*, pp. 141–69. Convegni del Centro di studi sulla spiritualità medievale 12. Todi.

———. (1979). *L'Aquitaine des Wisigoths aux Arabes. Naissance d'une région*. Paris.

Rousselle, A. (1976). "Du sanctuaire au thaumaturge: la guérison en Gaule au IVᵉ siècle." *Annales, économies, sociétés, civilisations* 31:1085–1107. English trans.: "From Sanctuary to Miracle-Worker: Healing in Fourth-Century Gaul," in *Ritual, Religion, and the Sacred: Selections from the Annales, économies, sociétés, civilisations*, vol. 7, ed. R. Forster and O. Ranum, trans. E. Forster and P. M. Ranum (Baltimore and London, 1982), pp. 95–127.

———. (1990). *Croire et guérir. La foi en Gaule dans l'antiquité tardive*. Paris.

Saller, R. P. (1987). "Men's Age at Marriage and Its Consequences in the Roman Family." *Classical Philology* 82:21–34.

Sauvel, T. (1956). "Les miracles de saint Martin. Recherches sur les peintures murales de Tours au Vᵉ et au VIᵉ siècle." *Bulletin monumental* 114:153–79.

Scheibelreiter, G. (1979). "Königstöchter im Kloster. Radegund († 587) und der Nonnenaufstand von Poitiers (589)." *Mitteilungen des Instituts für österreichische Geschichtsforschung* 87:1–37.

Schlick, J. (1966). "Composition et chronologie des *De virtutibus sancti Martini* de Grégoire de Tours," *Studia Patristica* 7 = *Texte und Untersuchungen* 92:278–86.

Schmidt, K. H. (1980). "Gallien und Britannien," in *Die Sprachen im römischen Reich der Kaiserzeit*, ed. G. Neumann and J. Untermann, pp. 19–44. *Bonner Jahrbücher*, Beiheft 40. Cologne.

Selle-Hosbach, K. (1974). *Prosopographie merowingischer Amtsträger in der Zeit von 511 bis 613*. Bonn.

Semmler, J. (1989). "Saint-Denis: von der bischöflichen Coemeterialbasilika zur königlichen Benediktinerabtei," in *La Neustrie. Les pays au nord de la Loire de 650 à 850. Colloque historique international*, ed. H. Atsma, vol. 2 = Beihefte der *Francia*, Band 16/2, pp. 75–123. Sigmaringen.

Shaw, B. D. (1987). "The Age of Roman Girls at Marriage: Some Reconsiderations." *Journal of Roman Studies* 77:30–46.

Sitwell, G. (1958), ed. and trans. *St. Odo of Cluny: Being the Life of St. Odo of Cluny by John of Salerno and the Life of St. Gerald of Aurillac by St. Odo*. London and New York.

Slater, C. (1986). *Trail of Miracles: Stories from a Pilgrimage in Northeast Brazil.* Berkeley and Los Angeles.

Stafford, P. (1983). *Queens, Concubines, and Dowagers: The King's Wife in the Early Middle Ages.* Athens, Ga.

Stancliffe, C. (1983). *St. Martin and His Hagiographer: History and Miracle in Sulpicius Severus.* Oxford.

Stroheker, K. F. (1948). *Der senatorische Adel im spätantiken Gallien.* Tubingen.

Tchernia, A. (1983). "Italian Wine in Gaul at the End of the Republic," in *Trade in the Ancient Economy*, ed. P. Garnsey, K. Hopkins, and C. R. Whittaker, pp. 87–104, 196–99. London.

———. (1986). *Le vin de l'Italie romaine. Essai d'histoire économique d'après les amphores.* Bibliothèque des Ecoles françaises d'Athènes et de Rome, fasc. 261. Paris and Rome.

Thompson, E. A. (1980). "The Conversion of the Spanish Suevi to Catholicism," in *Visigothic Spain: New Approaches*, ed. E. James, pp. 77–92. Oxford.

———. (1982). *Romans and Barbarians: The Decline of the Western Empire.* Madison.

———. (1984). *Saint Germanus of Auxerre and the End of Roman Britain.* Woodbridge.

Turner, V., and E. Turner (1978). *Image and Pilgrimage in Christian Culture: Anthropological Perspectives.* New York.

Van Dam, R. (1985). *Leadership and Community in Late Antique Gaul.* Berkeley and Los Angeles.

———. (1986). "Paulinus of Périgueux and Perpetuus of Tours." *Francia* 14:567–73.

———. (1988). "Images of Saint Martin in Late Roman and Early Merovingian Gaul." *Viator* 19:1–27.

———. (1988a), trans. *Gregory of Tours, Glory of the Martyrs.* Liverpool.

———. (1988b), trans. *Gregory of Tours, Glory of the Confessors.* Liverpool.

———. (1992). "The Pirenne Thesis and Fifth-Century Gaul," in *Fifth-Century Gaul: A Crisis of Identity?*, ed. J. Drinkwater and H. Elton, pp. 321–33. Cambridge.

Van Uytfanghe, M. (1981). "La controverse biblique et patristique autour du miracle, et ses répercussions sur l'hagiographie dans l'antiquité tardive et le haut moyen âge latin," in *Hagiographie, cultures et sociétés IVᵉ–XIIᵉ siècles. Actes du Colloque organisé à Nanterre et à Paris (2–5 mai 1979)*, pp. 205–31. Paris.

———. (1989). "Le culte des saints et l'hagiographie face à l'écriture: les avatars d'une relation ambiguë," in *Santi e demoni nell'alto medioevo occidentale (secoli V–XI)*, pp. 155–202. Settimane de studio del Centro italiano di studi sull'alto medioevo 36. Spoleto.

Vieillard-Troiekouroff, M. (1976). *Les monuments religieux de la Gaule d'après les oeuvres de Grégoire de Tours.* Paris.

Vinay, G. (1940). *San Gregorio di Tours.* Turin.

Vollmann, B. K. (1983). "Gregor IV (Gregor von Tours)," in *Reallexikon für Antike und Christentum*, ed. T. Klauser et al., vol. 12, cols. 895–930. Stuttgart.

Wallace-Hadrill, J. M. (1962). *The Long-Haired Kings.* London.

———. (1983). *The Frankish Church*. Oxford.

———. (1988). *Bede's Ecclesiastical History of the English People: A Historical Commentary*. Oxford.

Ward, B. (1982). *Miracles and the Medieval Mind: Theory, Record and Event 1000–1215*. Philadelphia.

Weidemann, M. (1982). *Kulturgeschichte der Merowingerzeit nach den Werken Gregors von Tours*. 2 vols. Römisch-Germanisches Zentralmuseum, Forschungsinstitut für Vor- und Frühgeschichte, Monographien Band 3.1 and 3.2. Mainz.

———. (1989). "Bischofsherrschaft und Königtum in Neustrien vom 7. bis zum 9. Jahrhundert am Beispiel des Bistums Le Mans," in *La Neustrie. Les pays au nord de la Loire de 650 à 850. Colloque historique international*, ed. H. Atsma, vol. 1 = Beihefte der *Francia*, Band 16/1, pp. 161–93. Sigmaringen.

Wemple, S. F. (1981). *Women in Frankish Society: Marriage and the Cloister 500 to 900*. Philadelphia.

Werner, J. (1961). "Fernhandel und Naturalwirtschaft im östlichen Merowingerreich nach archäologischen und numismatischen Zeugnissen." *Bericht der römisch-germanischen Kommission* 42:307–46; also published in *Moneta e scambi nell'alto Medioevo*, pp. 557–618. Settimane de studio del Centro italiano di studi sull'alto medioevo 8. Spoleto.

Werner, K. F. (1978). "Important Noble Families in the Kingdom of Charlemagne—a Prosopographical Study of the Relationship between King and Nobility in the Early Middle Ages," in *The Medieval Nobility: Studies on the Ruling Classes of France and Germany from the Sixth to the Twelfth Century*, ed. and trans. T. Reuter, pp. 137–202. Amsterdam.

Whittaker, C. R. (1987). "Circe's Pigs: From Slavery to Serfdom in the Later Roman World," in *Classical Slavery*, ed. M. I. Finley = *Slavery and Abolition* 8.1:88–122. London.

Wightman, E. M. (1985). *Gallia Belgica*. Berkeley and Los Angeles.

Williams, G. H. (1951). "Christology and Church-State Relations in the Fourth Century." *Church History* 20.3:3–33, and 20.4:3–26.

Wolfram, H. (1988). *History of the Goths*, trans. T. J. Dunlap. Berkeley and Los Angeles.

Wood, I. (1983). "The Ecclesiastical Politics of Merovingian Clermont," in *Ideal and Reality in Frankish and Anglo-Saxon Society: Studies Presented to J. M. Wallace-Hadrill*, ed. P. Wormald, D. Bullough, and R. Collins, pp. 34–57. Oxford.

———. (1984). "The End of Roman Britain: Continental Evidence and Parallels," in *Gildas: New Approaches*, ed. M. Lapidge and D. Dumville, pp. 1–25. Studies in Celtic History 5. Woodbridge.

———. (1985). "Gregory of Tours and Clovis." *Revue belge de philologie et d'histoire* 63:249–72.

———. (1986). "Disputes in Late Fifth- and Sixth-Century Gaul: Some Problems," in *The Settlement of Disputes in Early Medieval Europe*, ed. W. Davies and P. Fouracre, pp. 7–22. Cambridge.

———. (1988). "Clermont and Burgundy: 511–34." *Nottingham Medieval Studies* 32:119–25.

Woolf, G. (1990). "World-Systems Analysis and the Roman Empire." *Journal of Roman Archaeology* 3:44–58.

Young, B. K. (1986). "Quelques réflexions sur les sépultures privilégiées, leur contexte et leur évolution surtout dans la Gaule de l'Est," in *L'inhumation privilégiée du IVe au VIIIe siècle en Occident. Actes du colloque tenu à Creteil les 16–18 mars 1984*, ed. Y. Duval and J.-Ch. Picard, pp. 69–88. Paris.

Zelzer, K. (1977). "Zur Frage des Autors der Miracula B. Andreae apostoli und zur Sprache des Gregor von Tours." *Grazer Beiträge* 6:217–41.

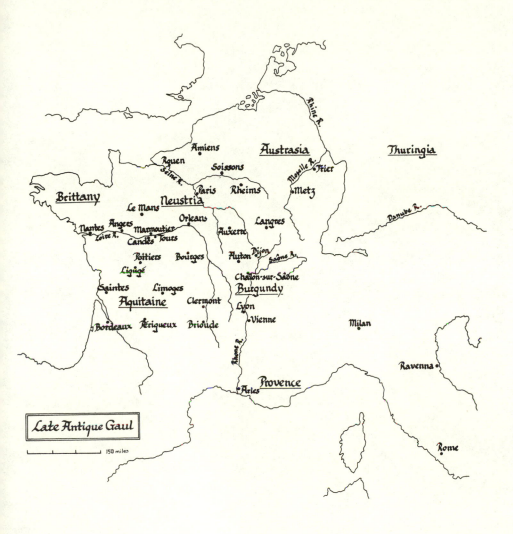

Late Antique Gaul

150 miles